THE SUNDAY SERVICE OF THE METHODISTS

THE SUNDAY SERVICE OF THE METHODISTS

Twentieth-Century Worship in Worldwide Methodism

Studies in Honor of James F. White

Edited by

Karen B. Westerfield Tucker

KINGSWOOD BOOKS

An Imprint of Abingdon Press
Nashville, Tennessee

Library of Congress Cataloging-in-Publication Data

The Sunday service of the Methodists: twentieth-century worship in
   worldwide Methodism: studies in honor of James F. White / edited
   by Karen B. Westerfield Tucker.
         p.   cm.
   Includes bibliographical references.
   ISBN 0-687-01134-5 (alk. paper)
   1. Methodist Church—Liturgy—History—20th century. 2. Public
worship–Methodist Church.   I. White, James F.   II. Tucker, Karen
B. Westerfield.
BX8337.S86   1995
264'.07—dc20   95-36924
                                                                      CIP

Unless otherwise noted, all Scripture quotations are from the New Revised Standard Version Bible, copyright © 1989 by the Division of Christian Education of the National Council of the Churches of Christ in the USA. Used by permission.

The music reproduced on pages 223–26 is copyright © 1988–1993 by Swee Hong Lim. Used by permission.

The music reproduced on pages 248–49 and 252–53 is copyright © 1995 by The United Methodist Church, Zimbabwe Annual Conference. Used by permission.

The music reproduced on pages 250–51 is copyright © 1990–1995 by Patrick Matsikenyiri. Used by permission.

The music reproduced on pages 279–82 is copyright © 1991–1993 by Simei Ferreira de Barros Monteiro. Used by permission.

This book is printed on acid-free, recycled paper.

96 97 98 99 00 01 02 03 04 05 — 10 9 8 7 6 5 4 3 2 1

MANUFACTURED IN THE UNITED STATES OF AMERICA

Contents

Preface

So far as I am aware, no other Christian communion has elicited, at world level, a descriptive and analytical study of its Sunday worship such as is offered for Methodism in this volume. Among Roman Catholics, Eastern Orthodox, Lutherans, Reformed, and Anglicans, it is the last-named who have published the most complete collections of liturgies within their particular communion and thus displayed, albeit rather incidentally, the inculturation of the established *ordo*. Most notable have been the compilations made by J. H. Arnold, Bernard Wigan, and Colin Buchanan that chronicle worldwide revisions of the Anglican eucharistic liturgy throughout the twentieth century.[1] These collections, however, have concentrated upon the precise reproduction of service book materials; only minimal commentary is provided concerning the theological implications of the language and performance of the rite, and the practice and reception of the service within the local context are not discussed.

Representative eucharistic services of liturgical "families" have been published or are expected to appear in ecumenical anthologies of liturgical texts, but again these generally lack the components of analysis and description.[2] Indeed, for many Protestants, including Methodists, the liturgy of the eucharist is only an occasional service of the congregation; hence collections of eucharistic texts are not sufficient to give an accurate picture of what typically happens in Sunday worship.

Worldwide Methodism presents an interesting case study for an examination of Sunday morning worship and its development over the course of the twentieth century. First, the Methodist family comprises various branches: the British, the North American, the mature offspring of each of these two traditions, and the united Churches that have included Methodism as a founding constituency. As will be seen, these Churches are related as kin and thus share certain characteristics, but they also have their own distinct identities. Second, the practice of Methodist worship often reflects the geographical and cultural diversity of the contexts into which the denomination has been introduced. The flexible approach of Methodism has allowed for some degree of inculturation: use of particular liturgical texts and forms of worship is generally not mandated, and Methodists are encouraged to hold in tension liturgical order and freedom of expression.

Third and finally, throughout the twentieth century, members of the worldwide Methodist family have been involved in ecumenical interaction through both the ecumenical movement and the liturgical movement. An ecumenical commitment is demonstrated by the willingness of Methodists to engage in bilateral and multilateral dialogues at the national and international levels and, after intensive study and prayerful reflection, to form united Churches with Christians of other denominations. The influence of both the ecumenical and liturgical movements is evident in many of the Methodist worship resources produced in the second half of the twentieth century. These imitate or adapt—and perhaps provide a model for—the liturgical revision of other Christian groups. In addition, Methodism's association with other social and theological movements, such as the Social Gospel movement and liberation movements, has impacted the way Methodists in some regions conceptualize and celebrate worship.

These three features clearly are not unique to the Methodist family; other Protestant communions may find parallels here. A Methodist particularity is the connection to a common eighteenth-century ancestor, John Wesley, who claimed the world as his parish. Although there are variations in the degree to which the Wesleyan heritage is embraced (directly or indirectly) by different members of the Methodist family, appeals to the denominational progenitor and his interpretation of the Christian faith (in prose and poetry) remain important for all Methodists. Commonalities and differences in the connection with John Wesley and in worship praxis will be evident in the essays that follow.

A word of thanks is owed to the persons who participated in the writing and preparation of this book. I am particularly indebted to the authors of the essays, many of whom I have never met face to face, but with whom I share an interest in the theology, history, practice—and future—of Methodist or united Church worship. They have given generously of their valuable time to contribute to this volume, and have been enthusiastic supporters of the project.

Geoffrey Wainwright offered his linguistic skills by translating Simei Monteiro's essay from the Portuguese into English. The electronic wizardry of Roberta A. Schaafsma and Roger L. Loyd, librarians at the Duke University Divinity School, enabled me to have access to information not usually available to the uninitiated. Sean C. Turner kindly spent hours on the tedious task of proofreading. I am grateful to Rex Matthews of Abingdon Press, who was an able and patient midwife, assisting this editor/author in the labors of bringing forth her first-born volume.

But the most profound thanks must go to James F. White, who shortly will celebrate his sixty-fifth birthday. Professor White's literary output has provided information, inspiration, and insight for forty years in the areas of architecture, the history and theology of the liturgy, the sacraments, the practice of worship, and liturgy and justice. United Methodist congregations (and others) have prayed using liturgical texts crafted by his hand. Protestants, Catholics, Anglicans, and Orthodox around the world know his work, which—in some cases—has been translated into languages other than English. This son of Wesley has truly manifested a catholic spirit. And so in this volume we honor the life and achievements of James F. White and anticipate, *Deo volente*, much more in the future.

Karen B. Westerfield Tucker
Duke University
Pentecost 1995

Contributors

Vinton R. Anderson has been a bishop of the African Methodist Episcopal Church since 1972, and before that date pastored congregations in Kansas and Missouri. A native of Bermuda who was educated and then remained in the United States, he has been an advocate of civil rights and ecumenical work, and in 1991 was elected to the Presidium of the World Council of Churches. As chairperson of the Commission on Worship and Liturgy for the A.M.E. Church, he was instrumental in the development and production of the most recent hymnal and worship book.

Paul W. Chilcote is currently Associate Professor of Church History and Wesleyan Studies in the Rev. Louis Nippert Chair of Church History at the Methodist Theological School in Ohio. Previously he taught in the Africa University Faculty of Theology (Mutare, Zimbabwe), at St. Paul's United Theological College (Limuru, Kenya), and at Wesley College (Bristol, England). A recipient of the Ph.D. from Duke University, his most recent book is *She Offered Them Christ* (1993), a study of women preachers in Wesley's day. He has also pastored United Methodist congregations in North Carolina and Indiana.

Douglas R. Cullum, a minister in the Free Methodist Church, is Assistant Professor of Religion and the College Chaplain at Roberts Wesleyan College, Rochester, New York. His pastoral experience includes service with Free Methodist and United Methodist congregations in Florida, North Carolina, and New York. A doctoral candidate at Drew University, his dissertation seeks to locate the founding era of the Free Methodist Church in relation to the larger currents of nineteenth-century religious history and American Methodism.

A. Raymond George was educated at the Universities of Oxford, Cambridge, and Marburg. An ordained minister in the British Methodist Church, he has devoted most of his life to theological education,

11

having been Principal of Wesley College, Headingley, and of Richmond College, London. He was, for many years, convener of the Faith and Order Committee of the British Church, and served as a member of the Faith and Order Commission of the World Council of Churches. In the course of the 1970s he served both as President of the British Methodist Conference and as the Moderator of the Free Church Federal Council. Upon retiring from his last teaching post at Wesley College, Bristol, he became Warden of the New Room, Bristol. He is the author of the classic work *Communion with God in the New Testament* (1951).

Katheru Gichaara is a former secretary of the Africa Association for Liturgy, Music, and the Arts (AFALMA). A pastor of the Methodist Church in Kenya who has served churches in Nairobi, he is currently pursuing doctoral studies in theology and culture at Emory University in Atlanta, Georgia. His essay entitled "Christological Image of Christ as an African Medicine-Man" has been published in *Church Divinity 1989–90*.

Robert W. Gribben is minister of Wesley Church, Melbourne, a congregation of the Uniting Church in Australia. Ordained in 1970, he holds degrees from Melbourne and Cambridge Universities. He has served on his Church's national liturgical commission since its inception, and is the author of the official commentary on its worship book. He has taught liturgical studies in Australia, the United Kingdom, and Switzerland, and has twice been elected President of the Australian Academy of Liturgy.

Thomas Harding is an ordained minister in the United Church of Canada. After fifteen years in pastoral ministry, he completed his doctoral studies at Trinity College, Toronto, serving as tutor in liturgics and homiletics at Trinity and as sessional lecturer in Christian worship at Emmanuel College. The author of *Presbyterian, Methodist and Congregational Worship in Canada Prior to 1925* (1994) and *Patterns of Worship in The United Church of Canada 1925–1960* (1995), he is currently Executive Director of The Churches' Council on Theological Education in Canada: An Ecumenical Foundation.

Hoyt L. Hickman served as a United Methodist (former Methodist) pastor in Western Pennsylvania from 1954 to 1972, and from 1972 was on the staff of the General Board of Discipleship in the

Section on Worship where he had major responsibilities for revising and producing United Methodist liturgical resources. He has taught worship studies, on occasion, at both Vanderbilt Divinity School and The Theological School, Drew University. Retired since 1993, he continues to write and consult in the field of liturgy.

Walter F. Klaiber, a pastor of the former Evangelical United Brethren Church in Germany and now the United Methodist Church, Central Conference, Germany Area, was elected to the episcopacy of the Evangelisch-methodistische Kirche in 1989. He has taught New Testament and Greek at both the University of Tübingen (where he received his doctorate under Ernst Käsemann) and the Methodist theological seminary at Reutlingen, and from 1977 to 1989 was the Dean at Reutlingen. *Ruf und Antwort* (1991) and *Gelebte Gnade* (1993) are his most recent publications.

Swee Hong Lim, since 1989, has been the lay ministry staff member (worship and music) at the Wesley Methodist Church, Singapore. He received his undergraduate training at the Asian Institute for Liturgy and Music, Philippines, and most recently completed the degree of Master of Sacred Music at the Perkins School of Theology, Southern Methodist University. His music has been used at events such as the 16th World Methodist Conference in 1991. One of his hymns, "Lord, Have Mercy," has been published in the Asian hymnal *Sound the Bamboo* (1990).

Eric J. Lott received theological training at Richmond College (London University) and completed graduate study and doctoral research in Indian Religions at Lancaster University. A missionary in South India from 1959 to 1988, he taught Indian Religions and Worship at Andhra Christian Theological College from 1964 to 1976. From 1976 to 1988 he was Professor of Indian Religions at United Theological College, Bangalore, where he also served as Director of the Inter-cultural Worship Program and as Editor of *Bangalore Theological Forum*. He has published widely in both English and Telugu, and though now residing in England, is currently a part-time Visiting Professor at U.T.C. Bangalore.

Patrick Matsikenyiri is a layman of the United Methodist Church in Zimbabwe who, as a composer and choral conductor, has been instrumental in the growth and introduction of African Church

13

music. He was the first chairperson of the Africa Association for Liturgy, Music, and the Arts (AFALMA), and is a member and coordinator of the Ecumenical Arts Association (EAA) of Zimbabwe. Educated at the Shenandoah Conservatory of Shenandoah University, he is now on the faculty of Africa University at Mutare, Zimbabwe, where he is Lecturer in African Music and Culture.

Simei Ferreira de Barros Monteiro serves as Professor of Liturgy and Hymnology at the Methodist School of Theology (Faculdade de Teologia da Igreja Metodista) in São Bernardo do Campo, São Paulo, Brazil. She is a worship consultant for the Methodist Church in Brazil, and is active in ecumenical liturgical work, particularly for CLAI (Latin American Liturgy Network) and the World Council of Churches. A Methodist laywoman, poet, composer, and author, many of her songs appear in music collections throughout Latin America, and her book *O Cântico da Vida* (The Song of Life, 1991) explores the relationship between liturgical song and theology. Soon to be published is *Mulher e Liturgia: Texturas da Vida* (Women and Liturgy: Textures of Life).

Edward W. Poitras is Professor of World Christianity at Perkins School of Theology, Southern Methodist University. From 1953 to 1989 he served as a United Methodist missionary in Korea, most of the time on the faculty of the Methodist Theological Seminary in Seoul. In addition to theological writings (mostly in the journal *Sinhak Gwa Saige* [Theology and the World]), he has translated several volumes of theological literature into Korean and modern Korean literature into English. Under the Korean name Pak Tae In he has published books of essays in Korean and contributed several hundred columns and articles to Korean newspapers and periodicals.

Don E. Saliers, a musician, composer, and teacher in liturgical studies, was educated at Yale and Cambridge Universities. He is currently Professor of Theology and Liturgics and Director of the Master in Sacred Music Program at Emory University in Atlanta, Georgia. For the past twenty-five years he has been engaged in worship renewal both ecumenically and within the United Methodist Church, and was a consultant and contributor in the development of *The United Methodist Hymnal* (1989). Among his most recent books are *Worship as Theology: Foretaste of Glory Divine* (1994) and *Worship Come to Its Senses* (forthcoming in early 1996).

Grant S. Sperry-White, currently Assistant Professor of Church History at Saint Paul School of Theology, Kansas City, Missouri, received the Ph.D. in theology from the University of Notre Dame. A graduate of Harvard College, he has also studied at Oxford University. His research interests include the history of early Christian worship, the relations between Jews and Christians in antiquity, ancient Christian asceticism, Syriac-speaking Christianity, biblical interpretation in early Christianity, and the dynamics of Christian self-definition in antiquity.

Geoffrey Wainwright has taught theology in Europe, Africa, Australia, and North America. An ordained minister of the British Methodist Church, he is now Robert E. Cushman Professor of Christian Theology at Duke University. As a long-time member of the Faith and Order Commission of the World Council of Churches, he chaired the final edition of *Baptism, Eucharist and Ministry* at Lima in 1982. Since 1986 he has been co-chairman of the Joint Commission between the World Methodist Council and the Roman Catholic Church. His books include *Eucharist and Eschatology* (1971), *Doxology* (1980), and *Methodists in Dialogue* (1995).

William W. Watty, a native of Dominica, serves as the President of the Conference of the Methodist Church in the Caribbean and the Americas. He has pastored churches in the British Virgin Islands, and in the South Trinidad and North Trinidad circuits, and was Chairman of the South-Caribbean District. Educated at Union Theological Seminary (Kingston, Jamaica) and the Universities of Birmingham and London, he has been Staff Secretary of the Student Christian Movement in Britain, a Tutor at Kingsmead College, Selly Oak, and President of the United Theological College of the West Indies, Jamaica.

Karen B. Westerfield Tucker, who received a Ph.D. in theology (liturgical history) from the University of Notre Dame, is Assistant Professor of Liturgical Studies at The Divinity School, Duke University. She is currently an assistant editor for *Studia Liturgica*, and is the editor for the *Proceedings of the North American Academy of Liturgy*. A minister of the United Methodist Church, she was a local church pastor and campus minister in Illinois, and now serves the denomination as a liturgical consultant to the World Methodist Council.

H. D'Arcy Wood was born in Tonga; he is the son of Methodist missionaries, and is a minister of the Uniting Church in Australia, currently serving at Canberra City Parish. Educated at Melbourne University and at Princeton Theological Seminary, he later taught theology at Parkin-Wesley College, Adelaide. He chaired the Commission on Liturgy of the Uniting Church from 1977 to 1988, and more recently was President of the National Assembly (1991–1994). He is also a former President of the Australian Council of Churches and of the Australian Academy of Liturgy.

Chapter 1

Form and Freedom:
John Wesley's Legacy for Methodist Worship

Karen B. Westerfield Tucker

In the year 1784 John Wesley sent to the Methodists in the newly emancipated American colonies a revision of the 1662 *Book of Common Prayer* for the purpose of "feeding and guiding those poor sheep in the wilderness":

> I have prepared a liturgy little differing from that of the church of England (I think, the best constituted national church in the world) which I advise all the travelling-preachers to use, on the Lord's day, in all their congregations, reading the litany only on Wednesdays and Fridays, and praying extempore on all other days. I also advise the elders to administer the supper of the Lord on every Lord's day.[1]

Wesley's *Sunday Service of the Methodists in North America*, which was adopted at the 1784 Christmas Conference as the "prayer book" for the Methodist Episcopal Church, would go through later textual revisions not only for the Methodists in the United States, but also for Methodists in "His Majesty's Dominions" (e.g., Canada) and in Ireland and Great Britain.[2] Designed as a service book for Methodist corporate worship, the *Sunday Service* included for Lord's Day usage a lectionary, proper collects, services for morning and evening prayer, an edited and abbreviated Psalter, an order for holy communion, and orders for baptism (for infants and those of "riper years"). Minimal provision was made for daily prayer: a thirty-day cycle of psalms for morning and evening devotion, and the Litany stipulated for Wednesday and Friday recitation; as Wesley indicated in his "cover letter," all other prayer was to be extempore. The service book concluded with occasional services for communion of the sick, marriage, burial, and ordination. John and Charles Wesley's *A Collection*

17

of Psalms and Hymns for the Lord's Day was frequently bound with the text of the *Sunday Service.*

Wesley's liturgical text would stand as the basis for subsequent worldwide Methodist liturgical development until the ferment wrought by the ecumenical and liturgical movements of the twentieth century. Even though some Methodists have abandoned Wesley's textual foundations in favor of other formulations, Wesley's fundamental intentions for Methodist worship, it may be argued, still remain operative for the Methodist people around the world.

That Wesley wanted the Methodist people to have an established form for their worship is clear by his selection of the *Book of Common Prayer* as the model, a choice undoubtedly also dictated by his desire to keep the Methodists within the Anglican fold. Wesley's concern for freedom and flexibility in worship is evident in the numerous provisions for extempore prayer that dot the text of the *Sunday Service.* Indeed, the absence of any rubrical reference to hymn singing in itself may be an indicator of the freedom expected alongside of the form, the placement of the hymns being left to the preacher's discretion; for it is hard to imagine, either in the late eighteenth century or in the late twentieth, Methodist worship without sung praise and prayer. Freedom within the structure of the established services was preferred, an option that Wesley himself utilized, as is evident from a 1786 letter from Wesley to the American Methodist Freeborn Garrettson: "I do not confine myself: I constantly add Extemporary Prayer, both to the Morning and Evening Service."[3]

In Wesley's comments about worship and the liturgy the synthesis between freedom and form becomes clear. Throughout his life, several concerns appear to have been central for him in the shaping and practice of worship which, in turn, may have determined, at least in part, the theological criteria by which Wesley made his 1784 revision. Minimally, these criteria provide keys by which Wesley's thinking may be interpreted.

Theological Criteria for Wesley's Liturgical Revision

"Farther Thoughts on Separation from the Church," written by Wesley in December 1789 and published in *The Arminian Magazine* in 1790, summarizes his life and makes reference to his basic theological and liturgical values, showing both consistency and development over his long and variegated career. While the primary intention of the document is to convey Wesley's rationale for the Methodist movement, it provides a summary of what may be judged to be his general liturgical criteria.

> From a child I was taught to love and reverence the Scripture, the oracles of God, and next to these to esteem the primitive Fathers, the writers of the three first centuries. Next after the primitive Church I esteemed our own, the Church of England, as the most scriptural national church in the world. I therefore not only assented to all the doctrines, but observed all the rubric[s] in the Liturgy, and that with all possible exactness, even at the peril of my life.
>
> In this judgment and with this spirit I went to America, strongly attached to the Bible, the primitive Church, and the Church of England, from which I would not vary in one jot or tittle on any account whatever. In this spirit I returned, as regular a clergyman as any in the three kingdoms; till, after not being permitted to preach in the churches, I was constrained to *preach in the open air.*
>
> Here was my first *irregularity.* And it was not voluntary, but constrained. The second was *extemporary* prayer. This likewise I believed to be my bounden duty, for the sake of those who desired me to watch over their souls. I could not in conscience refrain from it; neither from accepting those who desired to serve me as *sons in the gospel.*[4]

Herein can be located five fundamental criteria: the primacy of Scripture; the normativity of Christian antiquity, especially the first three centuries of the Church's life; the example of the Church of England and its liturgy; the use of human reason ("I therefore not only assented to all the doctrines"); and the necessity of evangelical experience or "experimental" religion (implied in the two "irregularities" he describes).[5] Clearly these criteria embrace the basic influences upon Wesley throughout his life: classic Anglicanism with its emphasis on the authority and interrelationship of Scripture, reason, and tradition; the Non-Jurors' stress on Scripture, the early Church, and the "pristine" Church of England (especially as manifest in the 1549 Prayer Book); the centrality of Scripture, evangelical piety, and freedom in the expression of worship emphasized by the Moravians and the Puritans; and the normativity of Scripture and reason embraced by Latitudinarian movements (but with a reaction against their heterodoxy).

19

Scripture

Throughout the expanse of his writings, Wesley, who identified himself as *homo unius libri* from an early age,[6] affirmed Scripture as the definitive revelation and supreme authority in all matters, including worship. Creedal and conciliar decisions of the Church, Wesley believed, had no authority unless they conformed to the witness of Scripture.[7]

While Wesley affirmed that Scripture was the primary standard and norm, clearly he did not mandate that it be the blueprint for Christian worship; valid forms could indeed "flow" from Scripture:

> "But is not the Bible the only rule of Christian worship?" Yes, the only *supreme* rule. But there may be a thousand rules *subordinate* to this, without any violation of it at all. For instance the supreme rule says, "Let all things be done decently and in order." Not repugnant to, but plainly flowing from this, are the subordinate rules concerning the time and place of divine service. And so are many others observed in Scotland, Geneva, and in all other Protestant churches.[8]

In this respect he stood counter to the radical Puritans who insisted upon explicit precedents in Scripture for worship practices (*sola Scriptura*), considering postcanonical practices in worship as superstitious corruptions.

Christian Antiquity

England of the seventeenth and eighteenth centuries experienced a renaissance in the study of Christian antiquity which was spurred on by the reprinting of a wide spectrum of early Christian works. Christian antiquity historically had been used apologetically and polemically for matters related to ecclesiastical polity, doctrine, and practice, and in Wesley's day it continued to be so employed (even by Wesley himself). In addition, theological movements such as those represented by the Pietists, the Latitudinarians, and the Non-Jurors mined the ancient writings in an attempt to renovate Christianity of their time by restoring and implementing early Christian ideals and practice. Ancient liturgical texts were used to justify or refute the practices delineated in the *Book of Common Prayer* and provided resources and examples for substitutes during and after the Commonwealth.[9]

Wesley valued Christian antiquity of the first three centuries, for he believed it represented the doctrine and practice of true, uncorrupted, scriptural Christianity and therefore could serve as a suitable model for the renewal of the Church:

> The primitive church may thus far at least be reverenced, as faithfully delivering down for two or three hundred years the discipline which they received from the apostles, and [the apostles] from Christ.[10]

He read with great interest primary and secondary accounts of early Christianity and recommended such reading to others;[11] through his *Christian Library* some early Christian literature was made readily available. Under the influence of the Non-Jurors, he was persuaded that the *Apostolic Constitutions* and *Canons* (today regarded as dating from the fourth or fifth century) were exemplary of genuine apostolic practice. Although Wesley later dismissed these documents as not authentically apostolic, he was inspired by some of the practices described therein, such as the possibility of women serving in ministry, the celebration of the eucharist on every Lord's day (and daily eucharist following certain Christian festivals[12]), and the use of late-night vigils—which became the Methodist watchnight services.

Although Wesley's imitation of early Christian practice was the root of much of his problem while in mission in Georgia, he adhered throughout his life to the standard of primitive practice and employed it to inspire, justify, and defend Methodist practices which he maintained were "truly primitive and apostolical."[13] Wesley was convinced his 1784 revision of the liturgy conformed to primitive practice, a sentiment hinted in his statement that the American Methodists were "now at full liberty, simply to follow the scriptures and the primitive church."[14] The "primitive" quality of Wesley's service was recognized by the early American Methodists who, until 1792, kept unchanged their "venerable Father's Abridgement."[15]

The Church of England and Its Liturgy

Although he did not regard the Church of England as without fault, Wesley considered it (and its liturgy) to be scripturally sound and the best extant representative of apostolic practice by a national Church, a refrain that is echoed throughout the scope of his writings. Accordingly, Wesley believed that the Methodists generally admired and approved of the *Book of Common Prayer* as he did, even though he like others found portions of it to be contrary to Scripture—particularly in the so-called damnatory clauses of the Athanasian

21

Creed and in the absence of a provision for extemporary prayer.[16] His devotion to the integrity of the liturgical services in the *Book of Common Prayer* is made eminently clear by the fact that they formed the basis for the 1784 revision. Wesley did not jettison the *Book of Common Prayer* but revised it, and in doing so kept the Methodists from heterodoxy and the position of Dissent.[17] Wesley's *Sunday Service* is basically a conservative revision, characterized more by omission than by addition to the text.

In one of the few places where Wesley provided a rationale for his revision of the Prayer Book, a notice dated at Bristol, September 9, 1784, which was appended to the *Sunday Service,* he records both his sentiment for the Church of England's liturgy and his desire to avoid changes simply for alteration's sake:[18]

> I believe there is no Liturgy in the World, either in ancient or modern language, which breathes more of a solid, scriptural, rational Piety, than the Common Prayer of the Church of England. And though the main of it was compiled considerably more than two hundred years ago, yet is the language of it, not only pure, but strong and elegant in the highest degree.
>
> Little alteration is made in the following edition of it, (which I recommend to our Societies in America) except in the following instances:
>
> 1. Most of the holy-days (so called) are omitted, as at present answering no valuable end.
>
> 2. The service of the Lord's Day, the length of which has been often complained of, is considerably shortened.
>
> 3. Some sentences in the offices of Baptism, and for the Burial of the Dead, are omitted.—And,
>
> 4. Many Psalms left out, and many parts of the others, as being highly improper for the mouths of a Christian Congregation.

Reason

Reason, for Wesley, served as a critical and necessary corollary to Scripture and the life of the Church (ancient and modern) as a determinant for orthodoxy, since religion and reason were fundamentally intertwined.[19] Not simply the exercising of the God-given gift of the human intellect, reason more importantly was the perceiving of divine revelation through the agency of the Holy Spirit:

> He [Wesley] defined reason as a faculty of the soul which includes the simple apprehension of concepts, the power of judgment by which we discern the agreement and disharmony of the concepts which we apprehend, and discourse, which is the motion of the

22

mind from one judgement to another. By reason we are able not only to master a trade or craft or skill, but also to understand God's revelation, the nature of His dispensations, and the meaning of repentance, faith and salvation; we need it, too, for the proper exercise of conscience. But it has definite limitations. It cannot produce faith.[20]

Repeatedly Wesley acknowledged that Christian worship and Christian practice were to be judged by conformity to both Scripture and reason. These criteria justified experiments in worship that varied from the liturgy of the Church of England, particularly in those matters judged to be nonessentials or to have scriptural and apostolic precedent (e.g., extempore prayer).[21] Wesley, however, did not advocate indiscriminate alteration of the Prayer Book, nor did he approve of the more radical proposals for Prayer Book revision that had been offered (including the "rational" revisions that would later lead into Unitarianism).

Wesley also recognized the judicious use of reason coupled with Scripture when he admitted the possibility of various styles of worship, as long as the basic faith was maintained.[22] Modes of worship were a matter of conscience informed by godly considerations; worship was not to be dictated or prescribed by others, for rational human beings had a God-given right to worship as they were persuaded.[23] Wesley's declarations were in part leveled against Rome, for he believed the right of private judgment to be the hallmark of the Protestant Reformation. But he also addressed the Church of England, which, since its establishment, had required subscription to "human compositions." The treatment of his Puritan forebears, in particular, was abhorrent to him, as he acknowledged in his "Thoughts upon Liberty":

> So, by this glorious Act, thousands of men, guilty of no crime, nothing contrary either to justice, mercy, or truth, were stripped of all they had, of their houses, lands, revenues, and driven to seek where they could, or beg, their bread. For what? Because they did not dare to worship God according to other men's consciences! So they and their families were, at one stroke, turned out of house and home, and reduced to little less than beggary, for no other fault, real or pretended, but because they could not assent and consent to that manner of worship which their worthy governors prescribed![24]

Since modes of worship were accountable to Scripture and conscience, Wesley affirmed that variations from or omission of established liturgical forms, such as those of the *Book of Common Prayer*, were permissible; an individual did not necessarily need to conform to the worship patterns of the Church (even the Church of England) in which membership was held.[25] Indifferent matters, those not necessary for salvation or true worship, did not have intrinsic worth and therefore did not require allegiance. Accordingly, many of the Church's rites and ceremonies fell into the category of adiaphora, for they were merely outward circumstantials of inner religion which, in their stringent use, had caused the suffering of many.[26]

Wesley was not a radical iconoclast; he himself did not abandon externals,[27] but differentiated between whether they were simply used or relied upon as essentials. Neither was he a liturgical anti-nomian; clearly the practice of the Church of England functioned as a guideline and model for him (and the Methodist movement) as did ancient practice, Scripture, and godly reflection. In the sermon "Catholic Spirit," Wesley wrote:

> I do not mean, "Embrace my modes of worship," or, "I will embrace yours." This also is a thing which does not depend either on your choice or mine. We must both act as each is fully persuaded in his own mind. Hold you fast that which you believe is most acceptable to God, and I will do the same. I believe the episcopal form of church government to be scriptural and apostolical. If you think the presbyterian or independent is better, think so still, and act accordingly. I believe infants ought to be baptized, and that this may be done either by dipping or sprinkling. If you are otherwise persuaded, be so still, and follow your own persuasion. It appears to me that forms of prayer are of excellent use, particularly in the great congregation. If you judge extemporary prayer to be of more use, act suitably to your own judgment. My sentiment is that I ought not to forbid water wherein persons may be baptized, and that I ought to eat bread and drink wine as a memorial of my dying Master. However, if you are not convinced of this, act according to the light you have. I have no desire to dispute with you one moment upon any of the preceding heads. Let all these smaller points stand aside. Let them never come into sight. "If thine heart is as my heart," if thou lovest God and all mankind, I ask no more: "Give me thine hand."[28]

Evangelical Experience

To the classic Anglican triad of Scripture, the tradition of the Church, and reason, Wesley added another factor: the spiritual experience of an individual and of the community.[29] Experience was not equal in authority to the other three criteria, given the variability in experiences that could be present, a reality which Wesley found problematic with the Quaker movement. The Holy Spirit's presence and work in worship was important, but was not to be seen as providing the normative "pattern" for worship. Wesley stressed, "For though the Spirit is our principal leader, yet He is not our rule at all; the Scriptures are the rule whereby He leads us into all truth."[30] Nevertheless, Wesley the pragmatist often judged the efficacy of worship (and the general life of the church) by the resultant spiritual good: it proclaimed the gospel of salvation; it could lead to the conversion of the soul; it was truly edifying; and it issued forth in practical charity. Innovative practices, such as those drawn from primitive Christianity, were justified not only by their antiquity, but additionally by the witness of the Spirit in concrete human experience.

Although it is unfortunate that Wesley did not present an explicit rationale for the theological criteria by which Methodist worship was to be formulated, it still is possible, as has been shown, to glean relatively consistent patterns in his thought spelled out during the course of his life. Appeals to Scripture, Christian antiquity, the Church of England, reason, and evangelical experience are found scattered in the various methods he employed to disseminate his perspectives on Christian worship. These theological criteria were then operative in the determination of Methodist worship praxis.

Matters of Liturgical Praxis

Worship in Spirit and in Truth

Wesley's often-repeated claim that Methodist worship should be "in spirit and in truth" was not a denial of ordered forms as, in fact, Wesley urged Methodist attendance at Church of England worship, encouraged organized worship within the Methodist Societies, and in 1784 presented the Methodist people with a liturgical book. Rather, the preference for spiritual worship stood over and against what was deemed spiritual idolatry and the mere "form of godliness."[31] At least three concerns centered on the matter of outward forms. First, as has been seen, Wesley insisted that liturgical forms ought neither to be imposed nor mandated, for such regulation had led to persecution and the disunity of the Church. Second, externals, if used, were not to offend, hinder, or inhibit true worship. Careful introduction of the *Sunday Service* to the North American Methodists was suggested to Freeborn Garrettson by Thomas Coke lest a "precious soul" be greatly injured.[32] Finally, rites and ceremonies were never to be a substitute for the inner religion, the religion of the heart:

> I have never read or heard of, either in ancient or modern history, any other Church which builds on so broad a foundation as the Methodists do; which requires of its members no conformity either in opinions or modes of worship, but barely this one thing, to fear God, and work righteousness.[33]

Hence Wesley affirmed that there could be latitude in the shape or forms of worship as long as truly Christian experience found rational expression.

Just as external forms were to be judged accordingly, so too worship in "spirit and truth" was to be scrutinized so as not to take too strong a contemplative form devoid of corporate and social manifestations. For Wesley, as for Methodists since, Christianity is a "social religion":

> "What is it to worship God, a Spirit, in spirit and in truth?" Why, it is to worship him with our spirit; to worship him in that manner which none but spirits are capable of. It is to believe in him as a wise, just, holy being, of purer eyes than to behold iniquity; and yet merciful, gracious, and longsuffering; forgiving iniquity and transgression and sin; casting all our sins behind his back, and accepting us in the beloved. It is to love him, to delight in him, to desire him, with all our heart and mind and soul and strength; to imitate him we love by purifying ourselves, even as he is pure; and to obey him whom we love, and in whom we believe, both in thought and word and work. Consequently one branch of the worshipping God in spirit and in truth is the keeping his outward commandments. To glorify him therefore with our bodies as well as with our spirits, to go through outward work with hearts lifted up to him, to make our daily employment a sacrifice to God, to buy and sell, to eat and drink to his glory: this is worshipping God in spirit and in truth as much as the praying to him in a wilderness.[34]

In this description of the content and purpose of Christian worship it is clear that worship (*leitourgia*) has an ethical dimension that issues forth in service (*diakonia*): liturgy is the work of prayer and praise to God, in "thought and word and work," and at the same time service with, by, and to God's people. Worship in "spirit and truth" moves beyond personal piety to care for the neighbor. Wesley noted that "it is the best worship or service of God, to imitate him you worship," and to that end, Methodist worship included the collection of alms for the poor, prayer for the sick and needy, and sermonic admonitions to care actively for those in distress.[35] A rubric in the 1784 "Order for the Administration of the Lord's Supper" provides for the reception of money for the poor during the reading of the scripture sentences following the sermon, a practice that continues (though perhaps in a different location within the order of service) among many members of the Methodist family today.

Decency and Simplicity

Worship in "spirit and in truth" was to be simple, unpretentious, sincere, and heart-felt. On this matter Wesley believed Methodist worship to stand in striking contrast to the current practice of Anglican worship which he criticized as stale and spiritless. In a letter dated September 20, 1757, Wesley gives a lengthy defense of Methodist worship:

> The longer I am absent from London, and the more I attend the service of the Church in other places, the more I am convinced of the unspeakable advantage which the people called Methodists enjoy: I mean even with regard to public worship, particularly on the Lord's Day. The church where they assemble is not gay or splendid, which might be an hindrance on the one hand; nor sordid or dirty, which might give distaste on the other; but plain as well as clean. The persons who assemble there are not a gay, giddy crowd, who come chiefly to see and be seen; nor a company of goodly, formal, outside Christians, whose religion lies in a dull round of duties; but a people most of whom do, and the rest earnestly seek to, worship God in spirit and in truth. Accordingly they do not spend their time there bowing and courtesying, or in staring about them, but in looking upward and looking inward, in hearkening to the voice of God, and pouring out their hearts before Him.
>
> It is also no small advantage that the person who reads prayers, though not always the same, yet is always one who may be supposed to speak from his heart, one whose life is no reproach to his profession, and one who performs that solemn part of divine service, not in a careless, hurrying, slovenly manner, but seriously and slowly, as becomes him who is transacting so high an affair between God and man.
>
> Nor are their solemn addresses to God interrupted either by the formal drawl of a parish clerk, the screaming of boys who bawl out what they neither feel nor understand, or the unseasonable and

unmeaning impertinence of a voluntary on the organ. When it is seasonable to sing praise to God, they do it with the spirit and with the understanding also; not in the miserable, scandalous doggerel of Hopkins and Sternhold, but in psalms and hymns which are both sense and poetry, such as would sooner provoke a critic to turn Christian than a Christian to turn critic. What they sing is therefore a proper continuation of the spiritual and reasonable service. . . .[36]

Decorum for Methodist worship was defined by Wesley as a well-ordered and sensible pattern of worship, the postures of kneeling for prayer and standing for singing, and the avoidance of congregational chatter during and immediately at the conclusion of the service.[37] The decency sought was also ideally reflected by the plain dress of the Methodist people and by their modest, largely undecorated, worship spaces. Although Wesley encouraged the physical separation of men and women during worship, this practice often proved difficult to enforce.[38]

Simple but dignified language for prayer, preaching, and exhortation was desired for Methodist worship. To achieve the stated goals of preaching—to invite, to convince, to offer Christ, and to build up[39]—it was necessary to speak the language of the hearers. In this vein Wesley wrote in the Preface to his *Sermons on Several Occasions*:

> I design plain truth for plain people. Therefore of set purpose I abstain from all nice and philosophical speculations, from all perplexed and intricate reasonings, and as far as possible from even the show of learning, unless in sometimes citing the original Scriptures. I labour to avoid all words which are not easy to be understood, all which are not used in common life; and in particular those kinds of technical terms that so frequently occur in bodies of divinity, those modes of speaking which men of reading are intimately acquainted with, but which to common people are an unknown tongue. Yet I am not assured that I do not sometimes slide into them unawares: it is so extremely natural to imagine that a word which is familiar to ourselves is so to all the world.[40]

The desire to speak the language of the people was linked, undoubtedly, to the Methodist inclination toward proclaiming the Gospel in the "highways and hedges." At first Wesley found the notion of field preaching "vile," but later he regarded the practice as vital on account of the pressing need to seek and save the lost, and the unwillingness of local Anglican parish churches to open their doors to the urgency of his message.[41]

One of Wesley's most adamant concerns was that singing in

worship should be simple. Choral song was to be kept in the mouths of the congregation rather than be rendered by a select few. It may be for this reason that Wesley deleted existing rubrics (and did not add any substitutes) in reference to sung service music or anthems in the *Sunday Service*. In addition, by avoiding the anthems of choirs, Wesley also avoided polyphonic music of harmony and counterpoint, which he thought destroyed the power of the melody to affect the passions. Congregational singing of the melody not only imitated what Wesley believed to be early Christian practice, but also invited fuller congregational participation and the opportunity to sing "with the spirit and the understanding also."[42]

Freedom of Expression

Congregational hymn singing, in its simplicity, was an exercise of liturgical freedom; the singing of hymns in the Sunday liturgy did not receive judicial sanction in the Church of England until 1792, after which hymns readily supplanted the use of metrical psalmody.[43] Charles (the principal poet and hymnwriter) and John Wesley (who functioned primarily as editor) nourished the desire for singing by the publication of hymn books and hymn booklets for a variety of occasions, drawing upon Charles's original material as well as other sources. Each compilation was, in many respects, a "little body of experimental and practical divinity,"[44] for the theology of the Methodist movement was essentially encapsulated in hymnic form, with the hymns functioning as agents of evangelism and catechesis as well as vehicles for the praise of God in divine worship.

The option for extemporary prayer in Lord's Day worship, as already noted, gave Methodists freedom to exercise vocally the movement of the Holy Spirit. But clearly Wesley never intended that free prayer should entirely replace previously formulated prayer which, like extemporary prayer, echoed and reflected spiritual promptings. He also recognized that free prayer had the potential for rigidity, formality, and overstylization, accusations that had been frequently levied against the use of Prayer Book prayers.[45] Allowing for extemporary prayer granted the choice to worship leaders to determine the most appropriate style of prayer for the congregation and the occasion.

Freedom in worship, therefore, did not mean *absolute* freedom, but flexibility within certain parameters: theological, liturgical, and cultural. Outward forms or structured patterns of worship were desirable, and were to be used to enable faithful, active, and full worship of God; the forms, as vehicles of spiritual worship, were never to be ends in themselves.

A Guide for Wesley's Spiritual Descendants

Wesley's liturgical guidance for the people called Methodists encompassed much more than the text of the *Sunday Service*. Side by side with the publication of the service book, Wesley conveyed the expectation that there would be a certain "ethos" characteristic of Methodist worship: an organized, coherent, simple—and variable—form; freedom of expression as warranted by the movement of the Spirit, the particular occasion or event, and the context of the worshipers; the articulation of concern for the needy which leads to intercessory prayer, discipleship, and service; and active participation of the congregation in song and prayer. Even Wesley's own Prayer Book revision, wittingly or unwittingly, provided a model for later imitation by demonstrating that no liturgical text is sacrosanct or above revision or alteration. These assumptions have been retained by Methodists of later generations in North America, the United Kingdom, and beyond. Although at particular times certain factors have held greater sway or influence than others, study of the history of liturgical development in worldwide Methodism shows that all of Wesley's criteria, as have been identified and defined, have remained present and operative. Wesley bequeathed to the Methodists a vital liturgical legacy that has served as a foundation for the building of the Church as a house of prayer.

Chapter 2

From *The Sunday Service* to
"The Sunday Service":
Sunday Morning Worship in British
Methodism

A. Raymond George

From Wesley to 1932

The form of Methodist Sunday morning worship in any country presumably owes something to the inheritance from John Wesley, but it is perhaps especially fitting that some account of this Wesleyan inheritance should be given in this chapter devoted to Great Britain. John Wesley was a clergyman of the Church of England, and the Sunday morning service of that Church was contained in the *Book of Common Prayer* of 1662. The principal Sunday morning service of most of Christendom has been a liturgy of word and sacrament; even in some Churches of the Reformation, where the communion has not been a weekly event, the service of the word has been based on the ante-communion or first part of the eucharistic liturgy. Thus in the Anglican Prayer Book the place for the sermon falls in the first part of the Communion service. It is a peculiarity of Anglicanism and, as we shall see, to some extent of Methodism, to lay an equal or sometimes an even greater stress on Morning Prayer, which in origin is simply part of the divine office, to be said morning and evening daily throughout the year. The Church of England morning service thus consisted of Morning Prayer, popularly called Mattins or Matins, the Litany, and the Holy Communion, which in eighteenth-century parish churches was very often reduced to the ante-communion, stopping short of the sacramental part of the order. In addition to this, Wesley instituted preaching-services in his preaching-houses and chapels at 5:00 a.m. and 5:00 p.m. His followers were sometimes reluctant to attend the Church Service in addition to these, and he preached on the need to attend the Church Service.[1] The Conference of 1766, in the course of an argument that the Methodists were not dissenters, said:

> But some may say "Our own service is public worship." Yes, *in a sense*: but not such as supersedes the Church Service. We never designed it should. . . . It presupposes public prayer, like the sermons at the university. Therefore I have over and over advised, use no *long prayer*, either before or after sermon. Therefore I myself frequently use only a collect, and never enlarge in prayer, unless at intercession, or on a Watch night, or on some extraordinary occasion.
>
> If it were designed to be instead of Church Service, it would be essentially defective. For it seldom has the four grand parts of public prayer: deprecation, petition, intercession and thanksgiving. Neither is it, even on the Lord's day, concluded with the Lord's Supper.[2]

In 1784 Wesley published *The Sunday Service of the Methodists in North America, With other Occasional Services*, sometimes described as his abridgement of the *Book of Common Prayer*.[3] Thomas Coke took it to America, and with it a letter from Wesley, dated from Bristol September 10, 1784, in which the following passage occurs:

> And I have prepared a Liturgy little differing from that of the Church of England (I think, the best constituted national Church in the world), which I advise all the travelling preachers to use every Lord's Day in all the congregations, reading the Litany only on Wednesdays and Fridays and praying extempore on all other days. I also advise the elders to administer the supper of the Lord on every Lord's Day.[4]

Subsequent editions, not identical, some of them containing no reference to North America, do not substantially affect the matter of the Sunday morning service. We conclude that Wesley's ideal was, at 5:00 a.m., a simple preaching service and, later on Sunday, Morning Prayer and the Lord's Supper, but without the Litany. The rubrics of the Lord's Supper provide for a sermon. The services would have a distinctive tone, partly through the use of hymns, especially those of his brother Charles, though hymns are not indicated in the rubrics for Wesley's services of Morning Prayer and the Lord's Supper.[5]

The disputes after John Wesley's death about the relation of Methodism to the Church of England resulted in 1795 in "Articles of

Agreement for General Pacification." It was agreed that in certain chapels the Lord's Supper should be administered by persons appointed by the Conference "on Sunday evenings only" with certain exceptions. "Nevertheless, it shall never be administered on those Sundays, on which it is administered in the Parochial Church."[6] It was always to be administered in England according to the form of the Established Church, but with liberty to give out hymns and to use exhortation and extemporary prayer.

> Whenever Divine Service is performed in England, on the Lord's Day in Church-hours, the officiating Preacher shall read either the Service of the Established Church, our venerable father's Abridgement, or at least, the lessons appointed by the Calendar. But we recommend either the full Service, or the Abridgement.[7]

Strictly speaking, this recommends Mattins and Litany, for the advice to use the Litany on Wednesdays and Fridays only was sent to America and not given to England. It is likely, however, that no great use was made of the Litany, though in a few places it survived on occasional Sundays even into the present century. The Lord's Supper was not a regular part of the Sunday morning service because it would often be held rather in the evening, a practice virtually unknown in the Church of England at that time. In any case, the disputes about whether the traveling preachers might administer the sacraments had diminished sacramental observance in Methodism and it was probably in many places not administered every Sunday.

The recommended Sunday morning service then was Morning Prayer, presumably with hymns and sermon, though a sermon is not integral to its structure. But the somewhat plaintive "at least" of the Methodist resolutions in 1795 shows that the use of Morning Prayer was far from being universal; indeed we have evidence that it was not. What replaced it as the main morning service was even less traditional. The 5:00 a.m. preaching service did not continue at that hour, but what eventually emerged in most Methodist chapels as the main morning service was a kind of expanded version of the 5:00 a.m. service. It came to have two lessons, four or five hymns, extemporary prayer, and a sermon.[8] Its form was never prescribed. Despite the resolutions of 1795, Methodists have always felt free to choose their own forms, subject to local custom. The forms "authorized" by the Conference, even for the sacraments, are not prescribed as compulsory by the law of the Church, let alone of the state.

Methodism was not a dissenting body, in other words a Church that arose from dissent from the Prayer Book of 1662; but as the dissenting Churches came to be known as Nonconformist or Free Churches, Methodism came increasingly to be reckoned among them, and in some respects to adopt their style, though often with strong traces of its Anglican origin, especially in regard to the sacraments.

The Church of Scotland and the English Free Churches indeed developed a similar type of preaching-service from a very different starting point. It might therefore be argued that this is a natural form for worship to take without the need for any further explanation. It is also possible that a certain enrichment that developed in the nineteenth century both in these Churches and in Methodism, e.g., the use of a lesson from each Testament, was in part due to the subconscious feeling that the Anglican usage was in some way "correct."

Methodism then, from just after Wesley's death till well into the twentieth century, had two types of Sunday morning service. Morning Prayer was used in a small minority of chapels, though they were among the leading chapels, and, partly through the colleges where ministers were trained, this spread to the overseas missions. But most chapels had the Free Church type of preaching-service. In either case this would be followed from time to time by the Lord's Supper, probably much abbreviated, and not all would stay for it.

From 1797 onwards there were many splits from Wesleyan Methodism; these non-Wesleyan bodies did not use Morning Prayer, but only the simple preaching-service. Some of them produced various books of their own with forms for the sacraments, but probably these were not much used, and the Lord's Supper would be informal and extempore.

The Wesleyans continued for a long time to use at the Lord's Supper either the Prayer Book or later editions of the *Sunday Service*. In 1882 they authorized a new book, *Public Prayers and Services*, which included Morning Prayer, the Litany, and the Lord's Supper or the Holy Communion.[9] This was based on the Prayer Book of 1662 rather than on the *Sunday Service* of 1784. But the Declaration as to the Forgiveness of Sins, which Wesley had replaced by a collect, is restored in a slightly altered form, and the collect is kept as an alternative. The rubric about the collect, epistle, and gospel was reduced to "Then may be read the Collect, Epistle and Gospel for the

Day," and there was no mention at all of a sermon. This reveals that the Lord's Supper, when it was observed, was usually "tacked on" after a morning or evening service which had had its own lessons and sermon. The omission of the epistle, gospel, and sermon, however, made nonsense of the "word" part of the Lord's Supper, and many probably simply omitted it and started at the offertory sentences.

From 1932 to 1975

In 1932 the various branches of British Methodism, with very small exceptions, united to form the Methodist Church. At first, of course, the churches went on as before, using their existing hymn books and, in some cases, service books, but it was clearly necessary for new books to be produced. In 1933 the *Methodist Hymn-Book* was published.[10] In Methodism the hymn book, unlike the service book, is in the hands of every worshiper on Sunday, and this work was therefore a powerful unifying influence. It included well over two hundred of Charles Wesley's hymns.

In 1936, after the discussion of a preliminary draft, there was published *The Book of Offices, being the Orders of Service authorized for Use in the Methodist Church, together with The Order for Morning Prayer.*[11] It was explained that "the Order for Morning Prayer is included for the convenience of the Methodist Churches where it is in use." The Litany disappeared without trace, though it continued to be occasionally used in a very few places. Some forty or so churches continued to use Morning Prayer, often called "the liturgical service." It is virtually identical with the 1882 service.

The vast majority of Methodist churches, however, continued to have what we have described as a Free Church type of preaching-service. It might go as follows:

Possibly an introit sung by the choir

Possibly a sentence of scripture as a call to worship

Hymn

Prayer and the Lord's Prayer

Hymn or possibly a psalm sung

Old Testament lesson

Hymn

35

New Testament lesson

Children's address

Possibly an anthem sung by the choir

Prayer, sometimes called the "long" prayer

Notices

Collection, during which there is an organ voluntary, after which the collection is received by the preacher, placed on the communion table and dedicated with a short prayer

Hymn

Sermon

Hymn

Benediction

The prayers would probably be extemporized, said freely by the preacher in his or her own words, presumably after some thought during the preparation of the service. The officiant, usually a minister or local preacher, was normally and significantly described as the "preacher." In a very few churches the hymn between the lessons was sometimes replaced by a canticle, and this, together with the occasional use of a psalm to replace the second hymn, reveals a kind of attempt to recapture a little of Morning Prayer. There had been a campaign on the theme "Preacher, remember the children," and it had become normal to give a short address to the children, which sometimes regrettably replaced one of the lessons. One of the hymns also might be chosen as specially suitable for children. They had perhaps already attended morning Sunday school, and might leave at some point during the service; they would probably return for afternoon Sunday school. The Conference from time to time produced a lectionary, but this was often disregarded.[12] A disadvantage of this order, as indeed of Morning Prayer and sermon, is that the sermon is placed so far from the lessons. This difficulty was sometimes surmounted in the free service by moving the New Testament lesson to a place just before the hymn before the sermon, but the placing of the long prayer and other items between the lessons is hard to justify.

As in the previous century, holy communion would occasionally follow the morning service for those who wished to stay. The 1936 book, however, provided two forms of it. The first was substantially the service of 1662 and 1882, but it began with three Methodist rubrics: the first is "This Office may be used with Hymns and Sermon as the Order of Worship in our Churches at such times as the Communion Service is held." This sensible and traditional suggestion was rarely taken seriously, and indeed no indication was given as to where the sermon should be placed.

Then came this rubric, repeated from 1882, except that "may" has replaced "shall": "When the earlier part of the Communion Service, commonly called the Pre-Communion, has been read in Public Worship on the same day, the Minister may commence with the Offertory Sentences." Its meaning is not entirely clear. It possibly means that the pre-communion may be said before the "break" or exodus of many of the people. Then the minister resumes at the offertory sentences. But in a very few churches, when there was an evening communion, the pre-communion was said as part of the morning service. However, many ministers omitted the pre-communion altogether and began at the offertory sentences or indeed later. After the "break" they would have a communion hymn, then the offertory for the poor, and then perhaps start with the second paragraph of the exhortation which precedes the confession ("Ye therefore that do truly and earnestly repent of your sins. . . ."). The service would rarely be used in full, except perhaps at 8:00 a.m. on Easter day, and then it would lack a sermon.

The third of the preliminary rubrics in 1936, also substantially repeated from 1882, was: "The Minister, in conducting the Service according to the following Form, shall have full liberty to use Hymns, and extempore Prayer." A custom arose in some places of praying extempore almost at the end, just after "Glory be to God on high."

The service that follows these rubrics does not differ greatly from 1662. The chief changes, in addition to those already mentioned, were the provision of Commandments of the Lord Jesus as an alternative to the Ten Commandments, the omission in the confession of "The burden of them is intolerable," the alteration of "you" to "us" in what 1662 calls the absolution, the addition of a proper preface for All Saints' Day, the omission of the last three words from "a full, perfect and sufficient sacrifice, oblation, and satisfaction," thus destroying what some regard as a triple chiasmus, the alteration of "faith in his blood" to "faith in Him" in the first post-communion prayer, and the insertion of Hebrews 13:20-21 before the traditional blessing.

"An Alternative Order of Service for the Administration of the

Lord's Supper or the Holy Communion" was intended to appeal to those who came from the smaller Methodist Churches rather than from the Wesleyan Methodist Church. Whereas in the former Wesleyan Methodist churches the service books would normally be distributed to the congregation, often during the pause between the "normal" service and the communion service, in many of the other churches the congregation would not normally have service books and the minister would largely extemporize the service, though he might read the narrative of the institution from a Bible. It was therefore intended to produce a simple and less traditional order of service, with the possibility of some extemporization, which might appeal to those churches. The result is a Lord's Supper without any word service, which in the circumstances was intelligible and sensible, for the normal preaching-service would precede it. There was some traditional material and the eucharistic thanksgiving began traditionally with the passage from "Lift up your hearts" to the end of the Sanctus. Then followed:

> Then either the Minister shall pray extempore, giving thanks for the redemption of the world through the sacrifice of Christ, for the forgiveness of sins thereby procured for us, and for our fellowship with the blessed company of all faithful people, in heaven and earth.
> Or, the following thanksgivings may be used.

There follows the prayer of oblation, which in 1552 was deliberately placed after the administration as the first post-communion prayer; and then a prayer about "the blessed company of thy faithful people," which incorporates the end of the prayer for Christ's Church militant in the first order. Next comes a liberalized version of the prayer of humble access, not so described. Then without any introduction the minister reads "the words of institution," actually the narrative. It will readily be seen that the heart of the service lacks the customary structure and many of the historic elements of the eucharistic thanksgiving. This service gradually made its way among the churches for which it was intended, but unfortunately, as many would think, some of the former Wesleyan Methodist churches also took to using it, probably because it was complete in itself and did not involve starting in the middle, as the first order did in practice when it followed a normal word service.

Other services might follow the word service or be contained within it, e.g., Baptism, Public Reception of New Members, or the Covenant Service. In that period infants were often baptized in the afternoon in the presence of the Sunday school, but it was not uncommon for baptism to come, without a break, at the end of the morning service.

In 1960 the Conference adopted a report on Christian worship.[13] After a survey of general principles, this proposed a new order of service; the main innovation was that it placed just before the last hymn a "Prayer of dedication of both the offering and ourselves, thanksgiving, petition, and intercession, followed by the Lord's Prayer to gather all into one. (Some prefer that thanksgiving should precede dedication.)" This form and position of the "long" prayer helpfully reduced the gap between the lessons and the sermon, and the prayer could be considered as *response* to the word. The report also proposed a simpler alternative as an amendment to the order in general use; it was in fact almost identical with that described earlier; the long prayer was still in the middle. Then came "An Order of Service when there is Holy Communion (when the full order in the *Book of Offices* is not used)." This, following the Roman Mass, removes the penitential material and "Glory be to God on high" to a point early in the word service, which has the intercession near its end. Those who leave do so during a hymn, and then comes the offertory for the poor, followed by the uncovering of the elements, and "Lift up your hearts." The avowed intention was to relate the ante-communion to the usual order of service. It was not at first widely followed, but it was a foretaste of things to come.

In 1960 there was published *Hymns and Songs, a Supplement to the Methodist Hymn Book.*[14] The book contains many hymns of the twentieth century and indeed of the 1950s, but also some traditional hymns not found in the 1933 book.

The next big change occurred in 1975, but the services intended for the book of that year were first circulated as "separates" in experimental forms. It was in this period that there was a widespread shift from "thou" to "you" as the form of address to God. One of the experimental services had parallel "thou" and "you" columns, but a little before 1975 it was decided to go over to "you" and gradually this became common in extemporary prayer also. Many hymns, of course, retained "thou"; Methodism wisely did not experiment with altering them.

From 1975 to the Present

In 1975 the Conference authorized the *Methodist Service Book*, which is still the official book today.[15] It made, at least theoretically, a striking change in the Sunday morning service. Morning Prayer totally disappeared from the book, and indeed it has gradually died out, probably completely. It was said at the Conference service for the last time in 1975.

The book contains "The Sunday Service," a deliberate use of the title of Wesley's book of 1784, but in a somewhat different sense. The first general direction of the service is: "The worship of the Church is the offering of praise and prayer in which God's Word is read and preached, and in its fullness it includes the Lord's Supper, or Holy Communion." Another general direction says that "The Sunday Service may be used on other special days and occasions." What follows is a service of Holy Communion, which is thus established as a kind of norm for Sunday worship, though we shall come later to what follows that, namely, "The Sunday Service without the Lord's Supper."

The order for the Sunday Service is now given. The basic elements are marked in the book by an obelus, and the other sections may be omitted. In this outline the latter are indicated by the number being in brackets. We use the technical names for the various parts, which are often not so named in the book.

The Preparation

[1] Hymn

[2] Collect for purity

[3] The Commandments when they are to be read. The Commandments of the Lord Jesus and the Ten Commandments are printed in appendices and a general direction indicates that they are appropriately used on the first or another Sunday in Advent or Lent respectively.

[4] Confession of sins

[5] Assurance of forgiveness

6 The Collect of the day, or some other prayer

[7] Hymn, or *Gloria in Excelsis Deo* (Glory to God in the highest)

The Ministry of the Word

8 The Old Testament lesson, or the Epistle, or both

[9] Hymn

10 The Gospel

11 The Sermon

12 The Intercessions: other possible forms are in an appendix

13 The Lord's Prayer

[14] Blessing for those who leave

The Lord's Supper

15 The Peace

[16] The Peace may be given throughout the congregation

[17] The Nicene Creed

THE SETTING OF THE TABLE[16]

[18] Hymn

19 The elements are brought or uncovered

20 The minister takes them

THE THANKSGIVING

21 The minister says the great prayer of thanksgiving. This anaphora is on traditional lines, with the customary responses. It is Eastern in style in that it proclaims the mighty acts of God fairly fully, without proper prefaces, though a general direction does indicate a point where special thanksgivings may be inserted. The absence of proper prefaces, like the provision of only one anaphora, was a deliberate attempt to keep the page simple. The anaphora deliberately has no part of the epiklesis, or invocation of the Spirit, before the narrative of the institution.

THE BREAKING OF THE BREAD

22 The minister breaks the bread, in silence or with an appropriate sentence and response.

23 Silence

THE SHARING OF THE BREAD AND WINE

[24] A version of the prayer of humble access

25 The minister and assistants receive communion. The minister may say an invitation.

26 The words of administration.

27 The covering of the elements.

THE FINAL PRAYERS[17]

28 Silence

29 Post-communion prayer

[30] Hymn

[31] Blessing

32 Dismissal

The versions of the main ecumenical texts were those composed by the International Consultation on English Texts (ICET), except for the Lord's Prayer. This appeared simply as "Our Father . . . ," but at the end of the book there was printed both a "thou" version and a "you" version. The former was what the British body called the Joint Liturgical Group described as the modified traditional version, and the latter was a version, briefly popular in ecumenical circles, with "Do not bring us to the time of trial."

Another section of the book contains "Collects, Lessons and Psalms," which are based on the proposals of the Joint Liturgical Group in its *Calendar and Lectionary*,[18] slightly adapted for Methodist use. The section includes a two-year lectionary providing a collect for each Sunday, an Old Testament lesson, an epistle, and a gospel for each Sunday morning, and an Old Testament lesson and a New Testament lesson for each Sunday evening. There are also morning and evening psalms for each Sunday, mostly, but not exclusively, drawn from those to be found in the *Methodist Hymn-Book*; this list is purely Methodist. Each Sunday has a theme; on some Sundays there are separate themes for each of the two years. It has been somewhat criticized in non-Methodist circles as "didactic" and "thematic," but as the *Calendar and Lectionary* states, in the post-Pentecost period, the lessons were chosen first and gathered into groups before the themes were settled.[19] That there are thus links between the lessons on any one Sunday is surely a great advantage, especially to the preacher. There is an innovation in the calendar, namely that the liturgical year begins on the ninth Sunday before Christmas, so that there is a nine-week preparation for Christmas just as there is for Easter. In each set one of the morning lessons is the controlling lesson, which is an Old Testament lesson till just before Christmas, a gospel from Christmas till the Sunday after Ascension, and an epistle, including Acts and Revelation, from Pentecost to the end of the year. The whole year thus goes from creation to the heavenly city. Many of the collects, especially those for what someone has called the "active" part of the Christian year, are the traditional Anglican ones, modified into the "you" style.

One of the advantages of this lectionary was its wide ecumenical acceptance. It was not used in Roman Catholic churches, but most other Churches in Great Britain adopted it; the Church of England, for example, adopted it, with some modifications, for the eucharistic lectionary in *The Alternative Service Book 1980*.

Thus at a stroke the problems about the lessons were solved. There were no longer four possible lessons on a Sunday morning, namely, Old Testament and New Testament lessons ultimately derived from Morning Prayer and the epistle and gospel of the Holy Communion. There were only three, which were meant for use whether the service was Holy Communion or not. Indeed the nature of the service was fundamentally changed; it was no longer a Free Church preaching-service, with some links to Morning Prayer and some to a 5:00 a.m. service followed occasionally by the Holy Communion, or in practice by the latter part of the Holy Communion. The service was henceforth to be simply Holy Communion or, when there is no communion, a service of similar shape.

"The Sunday Service without the Lord's Supper" is such a service. Following dissenting precedents, it begins in the style of a directory, though that word is not used, rather than an actual order of service. It begins:

> In many Churches of the Reformation tradition it has been the custom, once on a Sunday, for the shape of the service to reflect that of the complete order of Word and Sacrament even when there is no celebration of the Lord's Supper, and the outline that follows is offered as a guide for this purpose.

Its main points are as follows. The preparation includes a prayer of adoration unless that theme has been sufficiently expressed in a hymn; then comes confession of sin with an assurance of God's forgiveness. The Ministry of the Word includes usually not less than two readings of scripture; the use of the lectionary is strongly recommended. There is, of course, a sermon. The Response includes thanksgiving and intercession in whatever order is thought fitting, and the dedication of ourselves and the Lord's Prayer. Hymns are inserted, and any of the prayers may be extemporized; the opening prayers may include the collect of the day.

Clearly all of these items correspond to items in the full service with the Lord's Supper, except the thanksgiving. In the full service with the Lord's Supper there is a eucharistic thanksgiving or anaphora. Here there are thanksgivings and dedication without reference to the Lord's Supper. By analogy with the Roman Catholic use of the term *missa sicca* (dry mass), this type of service is occasionally known as a "dry" service, and similarly this type of thanksgiving might be termed a "dry anaphora." A list of principal subjects for such a prayer is given:

> God's work in creation; the revelation of himself to men; the salvation of the world through Jesus Christ; the gift of the Holy Spirit; anything for which at the particular time it is especially appropriate to give thanks.

All this material is followed by this scheme:

The Preparation

1 Hymn

2 Prayers of adoration and confession, with an assurance of God's forgiveness

The Ministry of the Word

3 Hymn

4 The Old Testament lesson, or the Epistle, or both

5 Hymn

6 The Gospel

7 The Sermon

8 The Apostles' Creed

9 Hymn

The Response

10 Prayer of Thanksgiving and Dedication

11 Intercessions (with a reference to the form in the full service and the forms in an appendix)

12 The Lord's Prayer

13 Hymn

14 Dismissal

The content of these items is not at this point further indicated, except that a prayer of thanksgiving and dedication is given in full, and four other such dry anaphoras are given in an appendix. In most of these one can trace these elements from a eucharistic anaphora: preface, oblation of ourselves, epiklesis on the people, and very brief intercession.

Other appendices contain two prayers for possible use during communion, namely the ICET version of the Agnus Dei (Lamb of God) and the "Lord, I am not worthy," and also the traditional and ICET versions of the Apostles' Creed.

The book then contains "The Lord's Supper or Holy Communion (1936 Service)," i.e., the first service from that book, retaining the "thou" version. The text is virtually unchanged, but the rubrics are described as "simplified." In fact the notorious "Here may be read the Collect, Epistle and Gospel for the Day" is replaced by "Here are read the Collect, Epistle and Gospel of the Day," and this is followed by "The Sermon may be preached before or after the Nicene Creed."

"The Sunday Service without the Lord's Supper" is, of course, a new norm for the preaching-service or dry service. Indeed, apart from Morning Prayer, the hints in 1795 and the suggestions of 1960, there had never previously been a norm; it was a matter of custom. This new form differs from the previously customary form in that it has nothing at all to do with Morning Prayer or with a 5:00 a.m. preaching-service, but is based on the eucharist. The chief difference in practice is the possibility of using three lessons instead of simply Old Testament and New Testament and, more importantly, the transference of the main prayers to a point after the sermon, though that had been foreshadowed in the 1960 report. This remedies the main defect which we observed in the old type of Free Church service, namely, that the sermon was so remote from the lessons; it also has a clear pattern of proclamation followed by response.

When we ask how these services came to be used in practice, we must consider certain general tendencies which to some extent shaped the 1975 book but increased after it. Some of these are part of that so-called liturgical movement which has influenced all the Churches in this century. Its main emphasis has been that the liturgy is "the work of the people," as the Greek word *leitourgia* more or less implies. The service should not be dominated by priest or preacher, but the people should actively participate. The absence of this insight seemed to do no harm in Methodism in the days of the great pulpit giants of the past, perhaps because the singing of five hymns is a greater measure of active participation than is often realized. However, it is now a common, though by no means universal, practice for members of the congregation to read the lessons and sometimes the main prayers in the word service. A General Direction of the Sunday Service indicates items in which "laymen" may be invited to share, including the distribution of the bread and wine. This was very rare in former Wesleyan Methodist churches, perhaps because the minister was at one time described as "administering the sacrament," whereas now we should say "presiding" at it. There has indeed been some controversy as to what precisely presidency involves.

Another feature of the liturgical movement generally has been a better balance of word and sacrament, and on the Protestant side this has meant more frequent eucharists. A town church in Methodism may very likely now have two eucharistic services a month, one in the morning and one in the evening; it may indeed have a third one each month at 8:00 a.m. A few churches have one every Sunday an hour or so before the main morning service, except perhaps when it is the main morning service anyway. Moreover, the people are more willing to stay for communion, and the fact that the Sunday service is one piece has contributed to this. Now people do not often leave before communion, and the provision of a short blessing for those who leave, followed by a short break or pause, has largely fallen out of use. Communion is now no longer seen as a privilege of members. This change is sometimes supported by the argument that Methodism is committed in principle to the "open table," and reference is made to Wesley's phrase, a "converting ordinance." This is quite unhistorical; in the early days of Methodism some ticket of admission was required, usually a class ticket, as an indication of a genuine desire to flee from the wrath to come. The point of the remark about the converting ordinance was that it was a means of grace to those who were seeking salvation but had not yet felt they had received an assurance of it, as well as to those who had. The Wesleyan Methodist Church at any rate, at least officially, always thought it wrong for the Lord's table to be open to all comers. In the twentieth century this feeling has largely disappeared, though many ministers, if they find people who are not members coming to communion, would afterwards privately suggest to them that they should consider seeking membership.[20]

More recently it has been asserted in many denominations that it is baptism, not confirmation, which entitles people to receive communion; this is part of the widespread debate about the meaning of confirmation, now often described as a "rite looking for a theology." This leads to debate about children receiving communion. At first any children who had not departed before communion simply stayed in their seats when the communicants went forward. Then the custom arose that they should go forward and receive a blessing, but now it is widely, though not universally, felt that in appropriate cases they should be able to receive communion. The Conference of 1987 encouraged this by laying down certain guidelines, but it is doubtful whether their exact observance is easily practicable.[21]

A minor consequence of eliminating the break concerns the collection. It seems unreasonable to take two collections during one continuous service, especially as eucharists are more frequent. The General Directions indeed discourage it, but in accordance with the long tradition of giving alms for the poor at the communion service, which goes back to Justin, a General Direction, after speaking favorably of having only one collection, says "Provision should be made from it for those in need. If for good reason there are to be two collections, one of them should be taken as the congregation enters or leaves." Often such collections are for the local benevolent fund, as the old poor fund is now called, or for some other named charitable cause. Some place has to be found for the taking of the main collection, which is usually for the general church funds, preferably at the setting of the table, when it can be somewhat related to the bread and wine, or at the dry service before the prayer of thanksgiving and dedication.

A more important change has taken place in the pattern of Sunday. Earlier in this century it was popularly said that one should preach to the saints in the morning and to the sinners in the evening. Often the evening services were somewhat livelier and better attended than those in the morning. Now for various reasons the evening congregations have greatly declined, and are mostly elderly. The afternoon Sunday school has largely disappeared, and the morning Sunday school, originally the smaller session, has been replaced by what is often called junior church. The children attend at the same time and for the same length of time as the adults, usually being for part of the time with the adult congregation, and part of the time in their own adult-led groups, but on some Sundays being with the adults for the whole time.

The part-time arrangement usually takes the form that the children go out after the second hymn, often with a blessing. Before this there is usually a brief acknowledgement of their presence rather than a full children's address. But in some churches they start off in their own groups, and come in toward the end of the service. The preacher asks them what they have been doing; they show the

47

preacher their expression work, usually in the form of drawings or paintings which they hold up for the congregation to see; and the preacher often expresses delighted surprise that they have had the same subject as that on which he has preached to the adults.[22] Then come the collection, the final hymn, and the blessing. On the communion Sunday they may come in before the Lord's Supper and receive the communion.

This arrangement in any of its forms used to be called family worship but is now called all-age worship. A report to the 1994 Conference emphasized its desirability and outlined its requirements.[23] It tends toward a less traditional and more innovative style of worship. It is in some danger of trivializing worship, though its advocates of course do not intend that.

Morning communions, as we have seen, are more frequent than they once were; so a typical month might be: first Sunday, full service with the Lord's Supper, with the children "in," i.e., present with the adults, for a while, either at the beginning or for the Lord's Supper; second and fourth Sundays (and fifth, if there is one), a dry service with the children "in" for part of the time; third Sunday, dry service with the children "in" throughout.

The result of these changes is that the morning service is the better attended and the livelier of the two, but they to some extent work against an exact observance of the orders of service. For example, the service, whether or not including the Lord's Supper, has among its opening prayers a confession of sin, and when the children are usually there at the beginning, they ought not to be given the impression that this is the chief element of prayer; and when they are there at the end, their presence tends to produce an undue simplification and shortening of the main prayer of the dry service, unless indeed part of this, e.g., the intercessions, is taken before they come in. The services indeed can often be found in a "purer" form in the evening.

How then does the morning service go in practice? The lectionary is followed very patchily. The general order of the word service is loosely followed. The order of the Lord's Supper is usually followed more exactly. One widespread variant is that the creed is almost always omitted. This is sensible at the Lord's Supper, for the creed, originally meant for baptisms, did not come into the Western liturgy for many centuries and the ground is covered by the anaphora. Some, however, use it at the great festivals, so that it may not be entirely forgotten. The Apostles' Creed is hardly ever said at the dry service, partly perhaps because this would require the distribution of the books, which are hardly ever given to the people at this service. The main change from earlier orders, namely, the removal of the main prayer to a point after the sermon, has been widely accepted; what has unfortunately not been well accepted is that it should include thanksgiving and dedication, though the latter can be sketchily covered by the prayer at the reception of the collection. Often the "long" prayer is now announced as the intercessions, and the element of thanksgiving is mixed up with adoration in the first set of prayers, if indeed it is included at all. Preachers generally seem not to have grasped the concept of a "dry" anaphora. In general it may be said that the practice of praying extempore has considerably declined. Most preachers now read prayers from some printed collection or else read prayers which they have composed previously.

Other tendencies are the use of Taizé chants, Iona liturgies, and the introduction of new elements such as banners, drama, and liturgical dance. A more "charismatic" style, sometimes derided as "happy-clappy," is adopted in some places, with much greater exuberance and a different style of music. Advent candles are widely used, and sometimes palm crosses. In general, Methodist worship is more varied than it used to be, though these changes are probably more common in the larger churches. In all these matters discernment is needed to distinguish helpful innovation from ephemeral gimmicks.

In 1982 the Conference authorized a new hymn book in succession to the 1933 book; representatives of some other Churches joined in its preparation; it was published in 1983 as *Hymns and Psalms: A Methodist and Ecumenical Hymn Book*.[24] Nevertheless many churches, and not only those that might be termed "charismatic," supplement it with some other book. There is some tension between lovers of traditional hymns and those who prefer more modern songs and choruses. This subject was considered in a report on Music in the Church which was received, though not adopted, by the Conference of 1994.[25]

In 1990 the Joint Liturgical Group produced a new lectionary, *A Four Year Lectionary: JLG2*, with explanatory introductions by Raymond George and Neville Clark.[26] The Conference of 1992 adopted a Methodist version of this: *Lessons, Psalms and Collects*.[27] This is a four-year lectionary with three lessons for the principal service.

There are no lessons for a second, i.e., evening, service, though the Methodist version suggests that two of the lessons from the cycle two years distant might be used. The term "controlling lesson" is no longer used, though the lessons still go throughout the year from the creation to the heavenly city. Themes are no longer stated, but there are still links between the lessons—the great advantage of this lectionary. An innovation is that, with a few exceptions, one year is devoted to each of the four gospels. This carries further the method of the Roman three-year lectionary. The Methodist version adds, as it did to the previous lectionary, provision for such Methodist occasions as Aldersgate Sunday; it also adds psalms entirely taken from *Hymns and Psalms*, and some interim guidance about collects. There is now considerable pressure on ecumenical grounds to adopt the *Revised Common Lectionary*, related to the Roman Lectionary, though not identical with it.[28]

The use of inclusive language, which was not considered by those who prepared the book of 1975, has become an important issue; a list of optional changes to the 1975 book was published later, which could be stuck in over existing phrases. A report on the whole subject was presented to the Conference of 1992.[29] ICET has now been replaced by ELLC (English Language Liturgical Consultation) and ELLC's recommendations in *Praying Together* are for the most part being followed in the composition of new services, though some of them are being challenged in other Churches, and may in the end be modified.[30]

The Conference of 1991 authorized a new set of services *Entry into the Church*, an optional alternative to those in the 1975 book. The service for the baptism of small children is the one most likely to be used frequently in the Sunday morning service. The Faith and Order Committee has now begun to produce fresh eucharistic texts which may be used experimentally. They are, generally speaking, on traditional lines; each has a different anaphora. They are for Advent, Christmas and Epiphany, Lent and Passiontide, Easter and Ascension, Pentecost and times of renewal, and there are three for Ordinary Time together with one for Ordinary Time especially when children are present.[31] They are in preparation for a complete new book, which it is hoped will be published in the next few years. A report on worship was presented to the Conference of 1988, but it did not suggest a new order of worship.[32]

We have traced the official norm from Wesley's *Sunday Service* of

1784 to the "Sunday Service" of the *Methodist Service Book* of 1975. We have also demonstrated that British Methodists have shown considerable freedom in varying from the norms. If it is asked what theology lies behind all these forms of worship, the answer would involve a vast discussion of the relation between the *lex orandi* (law of praying) and the *lex credendi* (law of believing). A major work on this subject has been written by a Methodist minister of the British Conference now teaching in North America, Geoffrey Wainwright, and the first word of its title is a key word for any such discussion: *Doxology: The Praise of God in Worship, Doctrine and Life; A Systematic Theology.*[33] We trust that the whole story shows a sincere attempt to ascribe due glory to God.

The Prayer of Thanksgiving (1975)[34]

Lift up your hearts.
We lift them to the Lord.
Let us give thanks to the Lord our God.
It is right to give him thanks and praise.

Father, all-powerful and ever-living God,
it is indeed right, it is our joy and our salvation,
always and everywhere to give you thanks and praise
through Jesus Christ your Son our Lord.
You created all things and made us in your own image.
When we had fallen into sin, you gave your only Son to
be our Saviour.

He shared our human nature, and died on the cross.
You raised him from the dead, and exalted him to your
right hand in glory, where he lives for ever to pray for us.
Through him you have sent your holy and life-giving Spirit
and made us your people, a royal priesthood,
to stand before you to proclaim your glory and
celebrate your mighty acts.
And so with all the company of heaven we join in
the unending hymn of praise:

Holy, holy, holy Lord,
God of power and might,
heaven and earth are full of your glory.
Hosanna in the highest.
Blessed is he who comes in the name of the Lord.
Hosanna in the highest.

We praise you, Lord God, King of the universe,
through our Lord Jesus Christ,
who, on the night in which he was betrayed,
took bread, gave thanks, broke it, and gave it to his disciples, saying,
"Take this and eat it. This is my body given for you.
Do this in remembrance of me."
In the same way, after supper,
he took the cup, gave thanks, and gave it to them, saying,
"Drink from it all of you.
This is my blood of the new covenant,
poured out for you and for many, for the forgiveness of sins.
Do this, whenever you drink it, in remembrance of me."

Christ has died.
Christ is risen.
Christ will come again.

Therefore, Father, as he has commanded us,
we do this in remembrance of him,
and we ask you to accept our sacrifice of praise and thanksgiving.

Grant that by the power of the Holy Spirit
we who receive your gifts of bread and wine
may share in the body and blood of Christ.

Make us one body with him.

Accept us as we offer ourselves to be a living sacrifice,
and bring us with the whole creation to your heavenly kingdom.
We ask this through your Son, Jesus Christ our Lord.

Through him, with him, in him,
in the unity of the Holy Spirit,
all honour and glory be given to you, almighty Father,
from all who dwell on earth and in heaven
throughout all ages. Amen.

Chapter 3

Historic Tradition, Local Culture: Tensions and Fusions in the Liturgy of the Church of South India

Eric J. Lott

The eucharistic liturgy of the Church of South India (CSI) was authorized and published in its first form early in 1950, just over two years after this pioneering ecumenical body uniting Anglicans, Methodists, and Reformed had come into being.[1] Significantly CSI's emergence as a united Church had been immediately preceded (in August 1947) by India's achieving political independence. The dynamics at work in the shaping of the new liturgy interlink with the preceding political and cultural struggle in a complex way, but the connections are clear, as we shall see. Equally complex are the ways in which the histories of Methodist worship relate to this liturgy; at least some of these connections, too, will be drawn out.

In general, enthusiastic ecumenical acclaim greeted the emergence of the CSI liturgy. Louis Bouyer, for example, a leading pre-Vatican II Catholic liturgical scholar, pronounced it to be "more satisfactory than any liturgy that emanated from the Reformation," and potentially an instrument of valid eucharistic consecration.[2] An Anglican liturgist's response was unreservedly enthusiastic: "Perhaps the best liturgy in Christendom."[3]

Not all Anglicans responded with such superlatives, for criticisms came from both wings of their liturgical spectrum. It was insufficiently "catholic" for some.[4] At the "evangelical" extreme, a colleague in South India in the early 1960s, an Australian Church Missionary Society (CMS) missionary, used to refer disparagingly to this and other liturgical developments in CSI as "the great Anglican swallow!" He looked for a more charismatic style. For Indian Christians nurtured in the Methodist, largely British Methodist, tradition, in itself this liturgical "Anglicanism" was not overtly problematic. It does, however, provide a clue as to why the most vigorous criticism came from churches of the Reformed tradition.

Briefly, the Church of South India brought together the following traditions: Anglican (mainly CMS-funded, with a few Protestant Episcopal and some Society for the Propagation of the Gospel [SPG] congregations, one large section of SPG churches opting to remain Anglican); Presbyterian and Congregational churches that had already formed the South Indian United Church, and Reformed congregations of the Basel Mission; Methodist churches of British origin, with American Methodist churches joining neither the South nor the North Indian union schemes. Similarly, Churches of Lutheran tradition (from America and Europe) did not join, whereas the Baptists (American, Canadian, and British) did join the union in the North though not in the South. Nor were the older Churches of Syrian origin (or the Roman Catholic Church, of course) part of the union, except insofar as some Syrian Christians had, in the nineteenth century, become Anglican.

The union forged within CSI, therefore, is by no means inclusive of all major Christian bodies in South India. As hinted above, to some extent, this meant that one prominent concern in shaping the new liturgy was to maintain an acceptable balance between the Anglican (and Methodist) tradition on one side and the Reformed/Independent tradition on the other. That this was the case in an Indian context illustrates how strongly "colonial" concerns were still dominant, however much those responsible for the creation of the new liturgy[5] were aware of the very different issues thrown up by the twentieth-century liturgical movement.

Among other emphases the concern for a more clearly early church "shape" was undoubtedly one of the insights of the liturgical movement that the CSI liturgy incorporated very effectively. Gregory Dix's *The Shape of the Liturgy* was crucial here. In the CSI liturgy, the Preparation and the Ministry of the Word are followed by the Breaking of Bread. The third part itself makes a deliberate return to the "four-action shape" of offertory, blessing, fraction, and communion. The blessing, or eucharistic prayer, contains what had emerged as fundamental elements of this prayer probably by the second or third century: thanksgiving for creation and redemption, the Church's acclamation of "Holy, holy, holy . . ." (the Sanctus), the

Institution and Anamnesis, and the Epiklesis or invocation of the Holy Spirit.

It is of historical interest to note, however, that even by 1935 the Federation of Evangelical Lutheran Churches in India had prepared (and published in 1936) a eucharistic service already including many of these "shape"-related insights of the liturgical movement. It is difficult to believe that this service was not known to some members of the CSI Worship Committee, yet its significance apparently was never acknowledged. Neither did any Lutheran church in India seem to recognize its significance, for it never became part of any church's regular worship.

Characteristic Features of the CSI Liturgy

What, then, are the features of the CSI liturgy that initially stand out as impressive?

First, some very general comments.

(1) Compared to all the previous communion services of the participating churches, there is in this liturgy a strong element of *celebration*. It is thoroughly doxological in content and in most Indian congregations will communicate a strongly celebrative character, with as much emphasis upon resurrection faith and eschatological hope as upon the death of Christ. Also celebrated is the experience of new ecumenical togetherness. The Breaking of Bread section begins with the exclamation:

> Behold, how good and joyful a thing it is, brethren, to dwell together in unity.
> We, who are many, are one bread, one body, for we all partake of the one bread.

Lying behind the joy of such liturgical togetherness (even if only anticipatory) is also the brokenness of Indian social life into its many castes.

Ecumenical celebration was especially real in the worship of a cathedral like that of the Church of the Epiphany at Dornakal, where I worshiped, preached, and often presided over the great weekly eucharist from 1959 to 1964. The Dornakal diocese also rejoiced at that time in being congregations of Anglicans and Methodists come together in worship and ecclesial life for the first time. The cathedral had been built for Anglican worship; the bishop had been brought up a Methodist. Half the diocese was Anglican, half was Methodist, though twenty years later the diocese was unfortunately divided into two again, largely along the boundaries of those earlier traditions.

Worshiping in this cathedral was a deeply "epiphanic" experience. No doubt the presence of colorful tribal people, the vigorous singing of Telugu lyrics, the indigenous styles of architecture used in building the cathedral, and the sense of the sacred the congregation conveyed by a wide range of body-language, all contributed to the experience of epiphanic celebration. But the content of the liturgy itself was also an important factor, and that in spite of a somewhat unimaginative and literal translation into Telugu from the English.

(2) The liturgy's strongly *corporate* character is one specific reason for this sense of celebration. There are some thirty congregational sections, from full-length prayers to one-line responses, usually doxological in tone, and often biblical in wording.[6]

(3) The *flexibility* of many sections (especially in the Preparation) is another feature that Methodists will probably applaud. In some instances the option offered is that of extempore prayer, though there are apparently few instances where this is done in a formal congregational eucharist.

(4) Three brief periods of *silence*, by way of contrast to celebrative exuberance, add to the sense of epiphanic blessing. Silent meditation is, of course, prominent in Indian spirituality from ancient times. In the CSI liturgy there is silence before and after confession of sin, and then just before the Prayer of Humble Access (Cranmer's) which precedes the sharing in bread and wine.

(5) There are a number of acts featured in the liturgy—some now recognizable as typical of modern liturgical reform—that most people find add to its celebrative solemnity.

(a) The presiding presbyter, invariably dressed in a white cassock, takes what is often called the "basilican position," i.e., standing behind the table and facing the congregation. This enhances both the sense of togetherness and the celebrative intent of the liturgy.

(b) When present, the *deacon* has a distinctive role, being expected to read the gospel and lead the intercessions, as well as generally assisting. Otherwise lay people may take these parts. However, as in other Churches, the Church of South India has been trying for several years to work out a more specifically *diaconal* ministry for deacons, whether in the church or in the wider community.

(c) At the opening of the service and to begin the Breaking of

Bread, there are two *"entrances,"* highlighting key points in the movement of the liturgy. There is the "little entrance" when the opening procession from the rear of the church is headed by a lay person carrying the Bible to be placed on the table (at the time of the readings to be brought to the lectern). The "great entrance" (to use terms from the Eastern tradition) is when bread and wine are brought up along with the offerings, again by lay people.

(d) Often the mode of offering is distinctive. People place their offerings, either on arrival or at the time of the offertory, in brass pots found either just inside the doors or at other vantage points. This—and the practice of individuals or families on special celebratory occasions (such as birthdays or finding employment) bringing their offerings to the front in person and receiving a special blessing—is a typically *Indian* way of offering. In more rural areas the offering may well be some form of "first-fruits"—fruit, vegetables, the first milk, part of the first wage, etc.

(e) An action specifically approved of by Methodists at the time of introducing the liturgy (and ridiculed by certain Reformed responses) was the way of passing the peace with two hands, beginning from the presiding presbyter and working line by line (in a rather formal way) back through the whole congregation.[7] Derived in extended form from the Syrian tradition in India, this practice has occasioned some discussion because of the traditional Indian taboo on men touching even the hands of women other than wives or close relatives. Many congregations have now come to accept that in a worship situation the presbyter (or someone duly appointed) is "allowed" to convey the peace in this way, or some other culturally permissible *modus operandi* has been worked out (e.g., a woman appointed to the women's side of the church).

(f) The fraction (or ritual breaking of the bread) after the eucharistic prayer and just before sharing together is another action that adds to the general sense of meaningful liturgical movement. As one of the four key actions in the eucharist (along with taking, giving thanks, and sharing) it is moved from the "little drama" within the Institution passage back to its original place as an act of breaking-for-sharing. It is accompanied by the Pauline words, "The bread we break is a sharing in the body of Christ" (1 Corinthians 10:16). Or, as an option, there is the phrase from ancient tradition *Ta Hagia tois hagiois*, freely translated as "The things of God for the people of God." From the perspective of almost half a century later, this, or something very similar, is now commonplace in many recent liturgies introduced into western churches, along with a number of other features in the CSI liturgy.

(g) As might be expected, there was as much discussion concerning the rubrics for the conduct of communion as for its content. Reformed representatives, for example, were alarmed at the instruction to the presbyter to take the bread and then the wine at those moments when the words are read that refer to Jesus' actions of taking bread and wine. This seemed to many of them to imply a sacrificial intent.

(h) Concerning the form of giving the wine, there is freedom to do this in the "manner customary to the congregation." There is a specific option of administering "by tables" culminating in a blessing, which was recognized as the customary Methodist way. It is also said that the wine may be administered with a spoon, a method rejected by a Methodist missionary, H. W. Page, on the grounds that it was disliked by many. He admitted, however, that his Methodist bishop was "rather enamoured with it."[8] Lying behind this option is a question of considerable theological and practical significance: one chalice, or individual glasses? Only Anglicans had introduced the former practice to Indian congregations. In a culture where it is taboo to drink from the same vessel as that from which any other person has drunk, use of the common chalice calls for considerable religious conviction, even when the wine in the chalice is in some way poured so that the lips of the communicant are not touched (e.g., with a spoon or with a lipped chalice). To drink from the same cup as that used by a person of a lower caste, or a person known to be suffering from some disease, entails very great faith-commitment.

(6) To bring to a close this brief description of the main distinguishing features of the CSI liturgy, we might note a few of the prayers/psalms:

(a) The Gloria in Excelsis is usually a burst of song very early in the Preparation (where it was found in some early liturgies). In all the main South Indian languages there are exuberant indigenous forms of this ancient Christian psalm. But there are also alternatives to the Gloria. There is the Trisagion so important in the Syrian traditions of India: "Holy God" (by the leader); "Holy and Mighty, Holy and Immortal, have mercy on us" (by the congregation)—this repeated three times. Or there is a "Litany of the Lamb," derived from the Book of Revelation and reflecting the Reformed tradition.

(b) Immediately after the offering and before the eucharistic prayer proper, there is prayer said together for the Risen Christ's presence that many find deeply impressive (taken from the ancient Mozarabic tradition):

> Be present, be present, O Jesus, thou good High Priest, as thou wast in the midst of thy disciples, and make thyself known to us in the breaking of the bread. . . .

Reception and Inculturation of the Liturgy

Acceptance of this new liturgy by CSI congregations was initially quite erratic. Early on, the claim was made that non-Anglican churches adopted it far more readily, presumably because they were not quite so strongly locked into another form of liturgy. Now it is evident that there are few congregations where this is not the normal Sunday service for the eucharist. Because congregations from the Anglican tradition usually celebrate the eucharist every Sunday, with Methodists and others usually celebrating once a month, this liturgy has eventually made what is arguably a greater impact on these former Anglican congregations.

Style of celebration does, of course, vary greatly. And this relates to the question concerning indigeneity that we move on to in a moment. There is a noticeable difference of liturgical style between former Anglicans on the one hand and Methodists and others from "nonconformist" traditions on the other. The former tend to celebrate with more corporate ritual, whether distinctively Indian or from ecclesiastical tradition. There are more likely to be parts that are in sung form, again whether indigenous or imported. However, this question of indigenous form—the Indian cultural embodying of Christian faith and liturgy that is crucial for authenticity—is complicated by the extent to which congregations are exposed to the westernizing process.

Many western Christian visitors to Indian cities have been disappointed to find that church worship has seemed so similar to that of their own country, perhaps even by comparison stilted in style and archaic in language. This sense of alienation from Indian cultural life is usually even more pronounced in those Methodist, Baptist, and other Churches that are not part of the CSI. And in the case of the CSI liturgy, when the English of the earlier editions is used, it seems quaintly Elizabethan with its "thou wast"s, and even offensive in its gender bias. Liturgical conservatism in most Indian congregations is such that neither the modest revision in more simple linguistic style of the early 1970s,[9] nor the radically different Alternative Liturgy authorized by the Synod in 1985, have been widely used. It is the liturgy of 1950 (minimally revised in 1954) that now provides most CSI congregations with a sense of ecclesial identity. Liturgical conservatism ensures that little is changed by calls from time to time for greater indigeneity.

In less middle-class urbanized congregations (i.e., in vernacular-speaking and in rural congregations), however, the presence of Indian cultural elements in Christian worship is much more marked. Footwear is left outside the sacred worship place; offerings (often grain or vegetables) are given on entry; deep obeisance to the focal point of worship is commonplace; the divine Name may be repeated (perhaps *sub voce*) many times; all sit on the floor, usually women on the left, men on the right, children in front; there is frequent coming and going throughout a service that may last well over two hours. Singing with wonderful vernacular lyrics is done in a manner similar to Hindu devotional songs, with rhythm provided by tabla or mridanga drums and small cymbals, and musical accompaniment by violin, flute, and the all-pervasive hand-harmonium (late to India, but now decidedly indigenous; similarly western pop music and the guitar are sometimes effectively Indianized). Sermons are very free-flowing and make extensive use of illustrations from natural and domestic life, and of spontaneous questions and answers, but employ little of the homiletic structure expected in the west. With all this and much more to be found in countless Sunday services throughout the sub-continent, even if not in the more urbanized congregations, it cannot be claimed that there is *no* indigeneity in the way in which the CSI liturgy is celebrated.

That the liturgy lends itself to an indigenous form of celebrating is illustrated by the "Sung-Service" (*Gītā-ārādhana*) which has frequently been used in the cathedral that was previously a Methodist church (and built in very Gothic-looking style by the British Methodist missionary, C. W. Posnett). A gifted Indian presbyter of the Medak diocese, M. Vidyanandam, rewrote all the congregation's parts of the liturgy in poetic Telugu form, then composed music in classical Carnatic style, the *rāga* or tune/mood for each part being suited to the intention of the concerned response or prayer. With a singing group able to lead the congregation, and with adequate congregational practice, the result was a vigorous musical celebration in the way worship should surely be. The slightly oversophisticated style of both words and music did mean, however, that for less literate congregational members there was little genuine sense of participation. It seems probable that the indigenous musical form of the liturgy introduced (largely by Dr. Selvanayagam Israel) at Tamilnadu Theological Seminary, Madurai, is more inclusive in linguistic and musical style, and therefore even more authentic as truly corporate *celebration*, with cultural style most aptly matched to faith's intention.

We acknowledge, therefore, that there have been genuinely indigenous forms of celebrating the CSI liturgy (and no mention has been made above of the rich *diversity* of cultural style both possible and necessary for more fully inclusive expression of Christian faith in India).[10] What is to be our verdict, though, concerning the liturgy itself? Is it an authentic expression of Indian Christian faith, worship and spirituality? What is its understanding of how faith and culture interact, of how Christian liturgy is to be contextual and engage indigenous cultural consciousness and social experience?

A Truly Christian and Truly Indian Liturgy?

It is significant that the two missionaries who figure most prominently in the compiling and later interpreting of the liturgy, L. W. Brown and T. S. Garrett (both CMS Anglicans and both later to become bishops) were both fully aware, or possibly were later made aware, that the faith-culture issue is crucial in liturgical discussion. As convenor of the group responsible for drafting the liturgy, Brown's role was the most important.[11] Later he found it necessary in his writing on *Relevant Liturgy* to propose at the outset that as part of a process of indigenizing Christian worship we need a "rebirth of images," for "liturgy" means the activity of a living body.[12] However, this is followed immediately by the uncompromising assertion that "the core of Christian worship is something given, unchanging and unchangeable, relevant for all people at all times and in all places." Such a strong revelationist emphasis will inevitably entail a degree of ambivalence on the question of liturgical acculturation and indigeneity, even when it is recognized that a phrase like "the core of Christian worship" can be variously interpreted. Brown, furthermore, went on to argue for caution: whatever the compulsion to indigenous liturgy, "it cannot be hurried or forced," it must never be a self-conscious concern.[13]

In view, however, of the long theological and cultural conditioning of the Indian Church by the powerful colonial missionary presence, it could be argued that to seek very deliberately and "self-consciously" for more authentic indigenous ways of faith and worship is precisely what was and still is needed. When, therefore, T. S. Garrett very frankly posed the question whether this CSI liturgy, "though pretending to have [its] birth in South India [is] really a miscellany of foreign liturgical writings . . . rather than emerging from South India's worshipping congregations," even such a loyal apologist has to acknowledge that "there may be considerable truth in this criticism."[14]

Yet Garrett went on to argue both that the liturgy was sufficiently "Indian" and that any lack of explicitly indigenous features was entirely appropriate given the pastoral and ecumenical needs of the then newly united Church of South India. As a minority community comprising some 3 percent of the total population (even if much more than this in some parts of the south) and surrounded both by powerful Hindu classical traditions as well as by deep-rooted primal folk traditions, many Christians feel their sense of identity acutely threatened. They need a liturgy that is clearly distinct from prevailing cultural life in style and substance. This kind of argument against radical inculturation, even when motivated only by pastoral concern rather than by theological conservatism, ignores the even greater threat to an integrated sense of Indian Christian identity resulting from a culturally alien liturgical ethos.

That the CSI liturgy has sufficiently authentic "Eastern" character has often been argued, as by Garrett, on the grounds that so many features are derived either from the specifically Indian Syrian tradition or from the Byzantine tradition. Reference has already been made to the "little entrance" with the Bible, to the "great entrance" with bread, wine, and offerings, and to the Trisagion, which L. W. Brown described as "the constant hymn of praise of the Jacobite Church (in India)."[15] Garrett, too, referred to "this act of adoration" as "hallowed by ancient use in India,"[16] and in so much of his liturgical writing indicates his deep admiration for this Indian Syrian tradition.

As one who for many years lived and worked among Christians of this tradition, and was highly regarded as an historian of "the

Indian Christians of St. Thomas," L. W. Brown's liturgical consciousness was even more clearly shaped by this Syrian tradition. In fact
both Brown and Garrett, along with another Anglican (A. M. Hollis)
and a Presbyterian (J. R. McPhail) early in the drafting process argued
that their liturgical starting point should be the "Indian Liturgy"
compiled earlier by mainly Anglican missionaries in India from
largely Syrian sources.[17] In the end this was not considered pastorally
feasible.

Reference is made earlier in this essay to the Syrian influence on
the form of the peace and to the inclusion of an epiklesis. Even if both
carry some residual element of the concept of a localized and ritually
channeled sacred power usually seen as lying behind Syrian practice,
each is rigorously reworked in the transposed form used by CSI. The
epiklesis, following the "remembrance" of Christ, is intended to
ground the whole eucharistic action in the life of the Holy Spirit. It
is a prayer for the sanctifying of "us and these thine own gifts of bread
and wine, that the bread which we break may be the communion of
the body of Christ. . . ." Then, within the anamnesis just mentioned,
there are two congregational responses that are based on the Syrian
tradition. Both strongly doxological, the first is especially impressive
(and has been adopted by a number of new liturgies since):

> Amen. Thy death, O Lord, we commemorate, thy resurrection we
> confess, and thy second coming we await.
> Glory be to thee, O Christ.

And finally we might note the Syrian derivation of one of the two
litanies of intercession (coming after readings, sermon and creed) as
well as the addition of that phrase in the Benedictus qui venit—
"Blessed be he *that hath come and is to come* in the name of the Lord"—
suggesting the coming of Christ in the incarnation, in the sacrament,
and in the final parousia. In general, considerable skill was shown in
the way these various Syrian-derived sections are transposed into
the rather different liturgical intention of the CSI liturgy.

This does not, however, make for a distinctively "Indian" liturgy,
unless the term "indigenous" is taken in an unusually limited sense.
It is, though, significant that in the discussions between the members
of the drafting group, and in the written responses to the first draft
by various liturgists and theologians representative of the participating Church traditions, the question of authentic indigeneity finds

very little place.[18] Only the Reformed theologian Markus Barth referred to this issue, and he does so very caustically. "I have not," he wrote, "found anything reminiscent of India. . . . The Liturgy seems cut out for Europeans who want to be reminded of home." He felt it unfair to burden a young Church with the liturgical language and concerns of the sixteenth and seventeenth centuries.[19]

One of the few Indians to speak out along similar lines was E. L. Anantarao (a former Methodist) from the diocese of Medak: "We Indians want to be one in this act of worship more than any other. We are not in the least bit bothered about western theological differences. . . ."[20] The reference here is in particular to questions concerning the sacrificial character of the eucharist and the manner of Christ's presence. These were the concerns exercising especially those responding from the Swiss Reformed Church. And this Eurocentric view of what constitutes acceptable Christian liturgy was, inevitably, a strongly inhibiting factor in the creation of this CSI liturgy. Moreover, it was this theological conditioning that helped to create also the pastoral expectations in the Indian Church about which the drafters were understandably sensitive. Whatever our expectations, in fact the immediate post-colonial period in India was not the time to look for a creative and authentic indigenous liturgy.

Yet the Indian Methodist Anantarao and probably Methodists generally, such as the missionaries on the Liturgy Committee, J. S. M. Hooper and A. Marcus Ward, would not have forgotten that they belonged to a tradition in which it was "the heart strangely warmed" that was vitally important to worship and its expressions. The tendency to liturgical conformity in Wesleyanism had not quenched this earlier spirit entirely.

Of great significance in the Indian cultural context is the way in which so many of the hymns of the Wesleys—central to a Methodism "born in song"—parallel very closely the *bhakti* or "love-devotion" so prominent in major strands of the Indian religious heritage. Innumerable phrases in Charles Wesley's writings could well have been written by, for example, the Tamil-speaking Alvar poet-saints pouring out their ecstatic experience of God around a thousand years earlier. It is not entirely accidental that probably still the finest translation of those Hindu poems of passion for God is the pioneering work in *Hymns of the Alvars* published in 1929 by the Methodist J. S. M. Hooper. The cultural conditioning of the colonial age of which they were part and the felt need for ecumenical acceptance in this new liturgy prevented that liberated and creative inculturation for which Methodism's foundational experience, in fact, calls out.

How much, then, has changed in the period since 1950? In the Catholic Church in India, there has been outstanding liturgical innovation, particularly under the creative liturgical leadership of D. S. Amalorpavadass at the National Biblical Catechetical and Liturgical Centre, Bangalore, from the time of Vatican II up to the time of his tragic death in the late 1980s. The "Indian Mass," for which Amalorpavadass was largely responsible, appropriates with great liturgical and theological skill the classical cultural/religious traditions of India. Long before his death, however, the Vatican had come to regard some of the Centre's innovations as diverging dangerously from Catholic liturgical tradition, though the "Indian Mass" is still celebrated each Wednesday evening at the Centre in Bangalore.

In 1973 Amalorpavadass wrote that indigenization is not merely a matter of appropriating cultural and religious traditions. "Indigenization takes account of all the realities that constitute human existence today." It calls for "entry into the dynamism . . . of human history."[21] In any case, he argues, the interaction of cult and culture entails, especially in India with its diversity of cultural and social life, "pluriformity in the liturgy," even though dependent on "a basic dynamic unity."[22] It can, however, be questioned whether the "Indian Mass" adequately meets these two requirements, in spite of its undoubted excellence as a piece of liturgical inculturation. It could be said that it is overly dependent on one style of classical cultural tradition (and that the rather elitist "Brahmanic" tradition of India); and it does not immediately engage with the "historical realities" of India's socioeconomic injustices. Its spirituality gives an impression of disengagement from the painful and turbulent historical process of which Indian Christians are part.

The "Alternative Liturgy" authorized by the Synod of the Church of South India in 1985, as well as incorporating numerous features reminiscent of Indian religio-cultural tradition, also gives an immediate impression of engaging with the tragic socioeconomic realities of Indian life.[23] Yet hope of transformation shines through strongly. However much creative translating work is still needed if this "Alternative Liturgy" is to be accessible to vernacular congregations, it stands as an impressive attempt to respond liturgically to the realities of Indian Christian life and faith. Unfortunately, ecclesiastical leadership does not seem to have felt able to incorporate this liturgy into regular congregational worship. The reasons for this are complex, involving the political, ideological, and communal tensions within the Church of South India's hierarchy as much as the innate liturgical conservatism of the congregations, and the general lack of concern for dynamic liturgical reform.[24]

The Church of South India is left, therefore, with its 1950 liturgy. Indigenous ways of celebration are far from impossible; but in itself the liturgy seriously lacks that authentic indigeneity for which Christian faith and theology look today.[25]

Chapter 4

Uniting in Worship:
The Uniting Church in Australia

Robert W. Gribben

Methodists in Australia

Europeans came to live in the land of Australia—many aboriginal people would say they "invaded" it—from 1788. Although there had been earlier sightings and possible landfalls by Dutch and French mariners, the island continent was claimed for the British Crown, and it was British people (including many Irish) who settled there, voluntarily or involuntarily. Those who had no choice were convicts transported for various crimes, many of them petty, and they were accompanied by their guards and governors, and by some free settlers. It was not until gold was discovered in the early 1850s that free immigration rose to significant numbers.

Although Presbyterian, Congregational, and Methodist Christians had settled in Australia, the dominant religion of the colonies was the Church of England Anglicanism of the late eighteenth century. This was the Anglicanism of the military establishment; the Prayer Book offices were formally read in prison chapels and barracks churches. It was the Anglicanism also of the English evangelical revival in its various forms, including the enlightened social reform of William Wilberforce and the now separating and fissiparating societies of John Wesley. The latter proved remarkably adaptable to the new conditions, and moved quickly toward establishment in the burgeoning villages and towns of the colonial countryside. The Methodists had no need of ordained ministry to begin a chapel, and one was built wherever there were local citizens to support it and local preachers to conduct a service.[1]

None of these denominational imports was monochrome. Before

long, the Anglican Church felt the impact of the Oxford movement, the Presbyterian Church experienced the tension between established and free kirk polities, and for the Methodists: the full gamut of theological, political, and liturgical differences being worked out by the Wesleyan, Bible Christian, Primitive, and United Methodist Churches. All this on the other side of the world.[2]

The various Methodist Churches united in 1902 to form a single national Conference, the Methodist Church of Australasia. The idea of further Christian unity was in the air even then, inspired in part by the federation of the Australian colonies to form the Commonwealth of Australia in 1901, but it took half a century more before some of the Churches acted in a concrete way. No doubt further changes in Australia's self-understanding as a nation in the 1970s assisted the process. We no longer looked to Britain and Europe for cultural and religious leadership as we had in former times; indeed, Australians began to explore their own distinctive approach to the arts (i.e., music, literature, theater, film, the visual arts), and it was inevitable that theology, liturgy, and church life should follow. A Basis of Union for the Congregational, Methodist, and Presbyterian Churches was put forward in the 1960s, and after modification[3] and a complex series of votes in the 1970s, the Uniting Church in Australia was formed from these three Churches on June 22, 1977.

The Uniting Church

The Basis of Union went further than a mere federation of churches.[4] Certainly, the need to bring together the gifts of the three traditions for the sake of the Gospel was recognized. There was much talk of the special contributions each had made to church history and even to liturgical praxis, but some of this was sentimental, blind to the radical changes occurring in Australian (and secular, western, mid-twentieth-century) society. The Basis of Union went deeper: it acknowledged that in uniting, the three Churches sought "to bear witness to that unity which is both Christ's gift and his will for the Church"; further, that "none of them has responded to God's love with a full obedience" in the past, and so together they looked "for a continuing renewal in which God will use their common worship, witness, and service to set forth the word of salvation for all mankind."[5] A new thing, therefore, was being sought: a reaching back to common roots to be faithful to the common Gospel, a vision much deeper and broader than any of the constituent denominations. It was not realized at the time, but this vision posed a serious threat to the preservation of Congregational, Methodist, and Presbyterian ways of doing things, including worship.

Liturgical experimentation had pre-dated union, of course. The Methodist Church was officially committed to the *Book of Offices* of 1936[6] (copies were imported directly from England, and had no Australian content), but in the 1960s, a spate of liturgies (and para-liturgies) were created for such occasions as national youth conventions which proved very popular for local use. New resources from Britain and, increasingly, the United States were examined and sometimes utilized. There was freedom to borrow such material, both by official policy (and by extension of the *ex tempore* principle!) and by the fact that the Methodists in Australia were strongly Free Church—in James F. White's categorization[7]—and probably always had been. The "liturgical establishment," again to borrow from White,[8] looked kindly on more substantial sources such as the British Conference's *Methodist Service Book* of 1975.[9]

Into this liturgical ferment came the Uniting Church in 1977. The "official" books of each of the three Churches were duly authorized for use in the new Church.[10] For some congregations and ministers, this guaranteed very little change. A few, more committed to the ideals of unity, deliberately introduced the books and customs of the Churches other than their own. The need for a bolder approach occurred where congregations had actually combined and/or had sold their former buildings. It was soon obvious that some publication was needed with the Uniting Church in Australia imprint, and the paperback booklets began.[11]

Uniting Church Services for Communion, 1980

The first publication—and the only one pertinent to the purposes of this essay—was *Holy Communion*.[12] This contained three orders of service, called Holy Communion One, Two, and Three. Holy Communion One was described as "drawing upon the ancient liturgies of the church," a curious title for what was in fact the modern ecumenical (though admittedly ancient) structure of a liturgy of word and table, with a eucharistic prayer slightly adapted from a contemporary Anglican source, *An Australian Prayer Book* (1978).[13] In fact, the liturgy represented an acceptable modern form of the eucharist as received by the Anglican-Methodist tradition, with proper prefaces and the narrative of the institution included in the Great Prayer of Thanksgiving. Its language was contemporary (using "you" rather than "thou"), and one of its central theological themes, the blessing of God for the natural environment, reflected present concerns (e.g., "You have given us this earth to care for and delight in, and with its bounty you preserve our life"). While the service looked familiar to Anglicans and Methodists *au fait* with liturgical developments, the influence of Vatican II was also there: the penitential rite, for instance, came at the beginning, as did the "Glory to God in the Highest" (*Gloria in Excelsis Deo*), and there were "offertory prayers" prior to the great prayer of thanksgiving, and an epiklesis within it.

Holy Communion Two, "reflecting insights of our reformed traditions," carried forward the recognized marks for Presbyterians and (perhaps less so for) Congregationalists, notably scriptural language, a prayer for illumination prior to the readings, an invitation to communion and a "warrant" before the "Great Thanksgiving and Prayer of Consecration," and a repetition of the words of institution at the fraction.

Holy Communion Three, using internal logic, should have been the monument to the Congregationalist tradition, and parts of it attempted to be so. Some of its language was consciously less formal, such as the confession, "I confess to almighty God, and to you, my Christian friends . . . ," and the invitation, which included the following words:

> Come, not because you are strong, but because you are weak; come, not because of any goodness of your own, but because you need mercy and help; come, because you love the Lord a little and would like to love him more.

The difficulty is that only sentiment could view these examples as typical of Congregationalism, which classically was not the "soft side" of the Protestant tradition but as "high church" as Wesley or the Scottish Kirk at their highest.[14] The great prayer was in fact a truncated version of Prayer IV of the 1970 Roman Rite, chosen because it had a "narrative style." These decisions were mixed up with an intention to provide a form which, as the introductory title said, was "more suited for use in small groups and in ministering to the sick," particularly where only the minister had a book; therefore there were almost no congregational responses, no Sursum Corda, no Sanctus or Benedictus. The irony is that this liturgical mish-mash became popular for *ordinary* services, because Australian Protestants evidently liked a shorter service, with informal (not to say individualistic) language and with minimal responses.

This booklet of *Holy Communion* served the Uniting Church well, in general. Congregations were introduced to three different liturgical styles, loosely based on extant traditions. The booklet was deliberately didactic at points; for instance, sub-headings divided the Great Thanksgivings (e.g., Invocation of the Holy Spirit, The Institution of the Lord's Supper, and Memorial Prayer; curiously, the preface was not so designated). It was also easy to handle, and, as the young might say, "not heavy." Years after the production of *Uniting in Worship*, a book of much greater integrity and authority, there are still requests for reprinting the "little blue booklet."

Uniting in Worship

The national Assembly of the Church in 1982 resolved "to begin work on the publication of a comprehensive collection of services and other resources for use in worship," though the Uniting Church Worship Services series of booklets continued for three more years. Regular progress reports were made to subsequent Assemblies that officially encouraged the process: this process probably operated largely by inertia and not by conscious assent by the Church. The "liturgical establishment" (which included this writer) carried the day and the two-volume resource *Uniting in Worship* was published in 1988.[15] The provision of two volumes was the result of careful liturgical choice: one a *Leader's Book* (674 pages), the other the *People's Book* (362 pages). The *Leader's Book* contains full provision for all the services, plus a substantial collection of alternatives to the various prayers throughout the liturgies. The *People's Book* includes outlines of the various services, plus any essential congregational responses; it also has a liturgical psalter, and an anthology of prayers for private and corporate use. Thus, the people are assisted in following the structure of any service, in anticipating where they are going, and in knowing what to say together as appropriate. They are rescued from getting lost in a sea of words that are not used. The hope was that the contents and style of the *People's Book* would both help the people pray corporately and release them to look up and participate in the action. In fact, it would appear that our people perceived a significant difference between the little blue booklet which they used at holy communion (and comparable booklets used at special times) and the substantial, indeed handsome, bound volume now placed in their hands. Ancient tribal memories of imposed books of common prayer were revived, though *Uniting in Worship* is a model directory of public worship. The study of how the book has fared in congregational use I leave to my colleague D'Arcy Wood's essay, which follows. It is to the service book's provision for "word and table" that I now turn.

The Service of the Lord's Day

The most notable feature of the Sunday liturgy is that there is only one such service, called "The Service of the Lord's Day."[16] The title was intended—perhaps too subtly—to allude to Mr. Wesley's *Sunday Service*. It is, as its subtitle indicates, "a Service of Word and Sacrament." Equally clear is the fact that the sacrament is *not* celebrated every Sunday in most Uniting churches, so the structure of the rite is such that one can move from the Gathering of the People of God to the Service of the Word, omit, if desired, the Sacrament of the Lord's Supper that follows, and conclude with the Sending Forth of the People of God without more of a gap than there should be. Note that the Assembly Commission on Liturgy operates on general ecumenical liturgical principles, and intends thus to provide a good model while not, in fact, reflecting the current practice of congregations or many of their pastors. For good or ill, seeds of discontent are sown by such a decision.[17]

The Gathering section includes acts of adoration, confession, assurance of forgiveness and doxology; the latter is used in its general sense and includes the "Glory to God in the Highest" as one example. Hymns and songs of adoration and doxology may well be provided from the *Australian Hymn Book* which was produced as the result of ecumenical endeavor.[18] Certainly by the 1960s, Methodist liturgical practice understood that the "first prayer" in a service ought to include elements of praise and penitence, and that the "second prayer" (usually longer) ought to focus upon petition and intercession, so it was no surprise that confession should occur in this section, and not in its "Cranmerian" position after the Service of the Word. The older custom, following the *Book of Offices*, may well have required the devout to confess twice: once in the normal preaching service, and again after the few had remained behind for a separate service of holy communion. The standard services in both Presbyterian and Congregational books made a similar provision. No such division and duplication, either of the service or the prayers, is envisaged in *Uniting in Worship*, and this is one of its most radical provisions. Word and sacrament form a unitive whole. Almost universally, by my impression, this has been welcomed.

The Service of the Word

The most obvious innovation is the position of the sermon in the liturgy. At the time of union in 1977, many churches were following the pattern "Approach—Word (scriptures and sermon)—Response" for the non-sacramental Sunday service. The new order strengthens this tendency: the sermon no longer comes at the end, just before the final hymn and benediction, but in the center, thereby allowing for response in prayer and at the offertory. The liturgical logic of this pattern was more easily accepted by ministers than by laity, many of whom felt that the sermon had been demoted from its position as the climax of the service.

Early in the union, the Uniting Church officially adopted a form of the Common Lectionary, the three-year cycle which came out of Vatican II, and was subsequently adapted by various non-Roman Churches.[19] Lectionary usage is one of the notable and widely accepted changes in our practice. For many former Methodists (and others), the "Word" section of the service now "feels" different. There is a sense in which the lectionary means that the scripture as such is to be absorbed more intentionally week by week; before, we only heard the thematic readings in preparation for the sermon. More thought needs to be given to how focus upon the reading of the scripture lessons is achieved in modern liturgy. Perhaps this may be accomplished through the use of added silence, music, procession, change of posture, or other symbolic action. One Presbyterian custom adopted in many Uniting churches has been the bringing in of the Bible by an elder[20] or other lay person at the start of the service. Perhaps it ought to be brought in only after the Gathering and at the beginning of the Service of the Word proper.

The Sacrament of the Lord's Supper

When the sacrament is celebrated, there is the further problem of getting the length of the service of the word in proper balance with the service of the Lord's Supper. This is partly posed by the middle-class Protestant view of the length of the whole service, the "sacred hour," and hence the focus is on balance rather than length. The issue with the Supper is more the time taken for distribution than for the other parts, but this is often not perceived by the worshipers. Even more work is required to change the mood of the service, a problem acknowledged in one of James F. White's many *bon mots*: "As usually celebrated (if that is, indeed, the proper term) it is unduly long, unduly lugubrious, and unduly penitential."[21] Renewal of sacramental practice (for instance, in achieving a weekly celebration) will require adaptation and change.

When we come to the sacrament, some changes at least are more typical of denominational heritage. The passing of the peace is frequently practiced, though it seems to be understood more as a sign of human fellowship than of the unity wrought in the face of human barriers by the cross of Christ. Is that largely a Methodist interpretation? Presbyterian custom, where the sacramental action was "bracketed" by the solemn greetings of "the Grace" and "the Peace" by the minister, had a very different flavor.

The Commission on Liturgy met one of its challenges at the point of the great prayer of thanksgiving. In Holy Communion One of the 1980 booklet, the Methodist (and otherwise universal) custom had been followed of incorporating the institution narrative in the eucharistic prayer as one of the mighty acts of God for which we give thanks. Holy Communion Two had articulated the Reformed principle derived from Calvin that the scriptural warrant for the Lord's Supper needed to be read before the eucharistic action began. In preparing *Uniting in Worship*, the Liturgy Commission now determined to reconcile the issue by providing for these two ways as alternatives in a single service. Thus, a warrant is provided at the start of the service of the sacrament. It is a direct quotation of 1 Corinthians 11:23-26 from the Revised Standard Version,[22] followed by these words:

> With this bread and this cup
> we do as our Saviour commands:
> we set them apart for the holy supper

to which he calls us,
and we come to God with our prayers of thanksgiving.

To use an exact citation from scripture is part of the "warrant" tradition. When, as in the "prayer" tradition, the institution narrative is included in the great prayer of thanksgiving, the historic liturgies of both East and West harmonize the various scriptural accounts rather than provide an accurate quotation, and this custom is followed in *Uniting in Worship*. In the printing of the great thanksgiving, the narrative of the institution is indented in the prayer and there are rubrics to indicate that these words are to be omitted if the warrant has already been used (care was taken that such an omission would not disturb the flow of the prayer). In no case is the narrative used more than once; it is used *either* as a warrant *or* in the eucharistic prayer.[23] Nor is it to be repeated, as had been the custom in parts of the Reformed tradition, at the fraction or the distribution.

It has been interesting to note reactions to this careful and irenic provision. Many pastors and more congregations had never noticed the difference, partly because they had never experienced the other tradition. Some could not see that it mattered. Older ministers, better versed in church history, understood its significance, though some, including those of a Methodist background, wondered if insistence on the warrant now smacked of "legalism" and was irrelevant to the problems (including the theological) of the Church today. The dual provision however was generally appreciated for its spirit and its role at a time when the churches are still in the process of uniting. It will be interesting to see if the "warrant" survives the next liturgical revision.[24]

The Service of the Lord's Day also shows the influence of Dom Gregory Dix's "shape," the fourfold division of the sacramental action into a quasi-scriptural "taking, giving thanks, breaking and giving"; that is, setting the table, offering the great prayer of thanksgiving over the bread and wine, breaking the bread, and distributing it among the people. The chief contrast here to previous Methodist practice is that the bread is no longer broken during the words of institution (as many had continued to do following the 1662 *Book of Common Prayer*), but as a distinct act after the great prayer. This does not seem to have had many difficulties in reception, excepting where a kind of liturgical fundamentalism continues: a sense that we are "copying" what the Lord did at the last supper. The neat fourfoldedness suits our love of the didactic, and perhaps the acceptability of the methods of Christian Education (a fatal but typical confusion).

Where there are other differences between the uniting traditions, they relate chiefly to ritual action and ceremonial custom: the setting of the table, the method of distribution, the nature of the elements, and so on. The Uniting Church has been content to leave these matters to the local Council of Elders to decide. It has laid down some recommendations which touch on received Methodist practice. For example, a provision in the notes to the Service of the Lord's Day states that:

> The minister should stand behind the table, facing the people. The table furnishings should be placed in such a way that the people have an uninterrupted view of the liturgical action.[25]

Such a statement ought to encourage some Councils of Elders to replace the tiny table hidden away under the pulpit—directly imported from late Wesleyan custom in Britain—with a decent free-standing table. In many places, the liturgical movement in general has achieved a considerable re-ordering of old sanctuaries and the construction of some attractive new ones. And in this, the former Methodists have had the good example of fine Presbyterian design.

Methodist Liturgical Contributions to the Uniting Church

Some other aspects may touch on the Methodist heritage. At several points in the service book, the Methodist commitment to social justice and to mission finds expression, not that these things are confined to Methodists nor have Methodists always been faithful in their practice. Nevertheless, it would be hard to imagine a liturgy approved by Methodist tradition that did not articulate or declare them. The issues, however, are universal and contemporary.

First, in the standard Great Prayer of Thanksgiving, there is a reference to the experience of God by the aboriginal peoples of Australia, an allusion achieved by the use of a phrase familiar to them but which nevertheless has a universal (and biblical) reference: "In time beyond our dreaming you brought forth. . . ." The myths of the Aborigines speak of the "Dreamtime," but to have used that explicit word would have confined the meaning of the phrase and invited the charge of tokenism; as it is, dreaming is also a common mode of revelation in Scripture and Christian spiritual practice. The ambiguity—or the echo—has been found helpful and reconciling.

Second, there is an echo of the Methodist tradition of the "open table," or at least of a theology of grace by which the table is open to all those who have at least some degree of faith:

> By water and the Spirit
> you open the kingdom to all who believe,
> and welcome us to your table:
> for by grace we are saved, through faith.

John Wesley is frequently claimed to have welcomed everyone to the Methodist celebrations of the sacrament, but this is not quite true: he was willing to give a ticket of admission to those who convinced him (or the superintendent minister) that they at least "desired to flee from the wrath to come"; that is, to penitent baptized sinners. The note of repentance appears earlier in the liturgy, and also, properly, in the Baptism (and Covenant[26]) services. *Uniting in Worship* also provides several invitations to the Lord's Table, mostly from the words of Scripture.

The same paragraph touches on a third feature which, though it can be found in Calvin and Cranmer, is welcome to Methodists: the use of direct or indirect scriptural quotation in prayer. The reference to John 3:5 is here combined with Ephesians 2:8, and the latter for good reason. The Commission on Liturgy wished its new prayer to reflect the fact that the Uniting Church treasured its evangelical and reformed heritage. How was it to do this without raising old ghosts or sounding anti-ecumenical? One way was to draw on the characteristic Protestant practice of praying the Scriptures by which words from the heart resonate with the images and metaphors and often the exact phrases of the biblical authors. Thus the whole Christological section of the Great Thanksgiving is an extended paraphrase of Ephesians 2:4-8:

> In the fullness of your mercy
> you became one with us in Jesus Christ,
> who gave himself up for us on the cross.
> You make us alive together with him,
> that we may rejoice in his presence
> and share his peace.[27]

Fourth, eucharistic prayers usually include toward their conclusion petitions for particular fruits of communion: these may be for a closer communion with God in Christ, for the gifts of the Spirit, or that the Church may be a more faithful instrument of God's peace and justice. The Uniting Church's prayer speaks, as may be expected, of unity, but of unity in mission:

> Make us one with him [Christ],
> one with each other,
> and one in ministry in the world,
> until at last we feast with him in the kingdom.

The missiology is carefully stated: one in ministry *in* the world; that is, one in the ministry of Christ who is already and always on mission in the world. Whether Methodists have been too confidently ministering *to* the world as if the Church's mission were its own and not fundamentally Christ's is a judgment for another essay.

A further example of this missionary emphasis is the way in which the whole Service of the Lord's Day ends. The liturgy does not simply stop with a final hymn and a benediction (not to mention a sung Amen). The fourth section is called "The Sending Forth of the People of God": liturgy issues in mission; worship in evangelism and service. There are two ways of enacting the sending forth. The blessing may be prefaced by an exhortation, called (after the "Lima liturgy") a "Word of Mission." The rubric explains, "A verse of Scripture, e.g. the sentence of the day or a verse from the readings of the day, or a brief charge to the people, may be given." The pastor is thus encouraged to apply his or her homiletical theme as a practical commissioning of the faithful at this point. Alternatively (depending on whether the pastor thinks the last word of the liturgy should be mission or blessing for mission), the blessing may be followed by a dismissal. The familiar and ecumenical "Go in peace to love and serve the Lord" is printed in the text, so that the congregation may reply "In the name of Christ. Amen." There are also seven further examples in the anthology of material in the *Leader's Book*. No one should be able to leave such a service thinking that Christian faith and commitment stops at the church door. In the words of Charles Wesley: "Forth in thy name, O Lord, I go / my daily labour to pursue."

Conclusion

At several points in this essay I have revealed the benefits of hindsight. I think that *Uniting in Worship*, like the Uniting Church itself, is no mere preservation of denominational heritages. Two hundred years of church life in the antipodes had certainly meant that traditions once sharply distinguished in sixteenth-century Europe were no longer significantly divided (and did not Mr. Wesley say Methodists and Calvinists were within a hairsbreadth of each other?), and further division was not justified in the face of the evangelical needs of late twentieth-century Australia. Nor, in bringing together the insights and emphases of three families of Churches, was it sufficient to bring forth the treasures of only those three, for nothing less than the total experience of the catholic Church of all the ages is sufficient for the needs of a multicultural nation and world.

To put it simply: While we are guardians of the memory of John Calvin and John Owen and John Wesley, and they were, as the Puritan John Robinson said of the early reformers, "precious shining lights of their times," the challenge now is to be simply Christian: to be universal and ecumenical. It will be just as important for this generation to hear the faith story from Athanasius or Anthony of Egypt, Monica or Julian of Norwich, Kagawa of Japan, Martin Luther King, Jr., or Mary MacKillop,[28] as from the saints of our denominational past. It is, perhaps, more important still to listen for fresh words and deeds from around the world today.

And when we seek for authentic ways of worshiping in the next century, we will be simply Christian as well. We will not establish truth by being different from Roman Catholics or Anglicans, as our denominational history might suggest. Instead we will borrow their best ideas, adapting them to the emphases of our heritage, no doubt, but joyfully sharing the same intention to listen to God's Word, to baptize, and to break bread with Christ and our neighbor. If we are truly Protestant, we will be protesting, speaking *for* the truth, challenging our own and other Christian communities to more faithful witness and worship. That is why—under grace—the Uniting Church was formed, and it is to this discovery of unity in diversity that our liturgies must now witness.

Chapter 5

Text and Context in a Newly United Denomination: The Liturgical Experience in Australia

H. D'Arcy Wood

The Story from 1977

Many united Churches have been formed in the course of this century. In Australia the name "Uniting" was chosen as an indication of openness to further unions. Since the union of 1977 no new negotiations for a wider union have begun, although the Uniting Church has useful dialogues at the national level with Anglicans, Lutherans, Churches of Christ (Disciples), and Roman Catholics.

As Robert Gribben has outlined in his chapter, the National Commission on Liturgy was hard at work from 1977, and indeed before that date in a preliminary way. A series of booklets appeared from 1980 to 1985 which were followed in 1988 by the production of the hardback *Uniting in Worship* with two versions: a *Leader's Book* (674 pages) and the *People's Book* (362 pages).[1] In book reviews and in personal comments from members of other denominations, the commendations have been very warm; there are Anglicans and other clergy, even a few Roman Catholics, I am told, who make frequent use of it. But acceptance in the Uniting Church itself has not been unequivocal. The Commission hoped that 50 percent of the approximately 3,000 congregations would be equipped with a set of the *People's Book* within five years. This has not happened. No accurate figures of sales are available, but an estimated 20 percent of Uniting congregations have a set of the *People's Book*. Nor is there any sign that sales will increase to any great extent in the next few years.

Why this limited acceptance? The reason most often given for not purchasing the *People's Book* is the cost, which is no doubt one reason but probably not the major one. There was a strong element in each of the Churches that united (Congregational, Methodist, and Presbyterian) which resisted any use of liturgical books in the pews except, of course, a hymnal. For some reason, printed or duplicated pieces of paper handed out on entering the church building were acceptable, but a book was not. The growth of the charismatic movement, which makes much use of songs and choruses on overhead transparencies, but very little use of anything printed or duplicated on paper, has accentuated this tendency.

However one should not underestimate the influence of *Uniting in Worship*. Virtually all ordained ministers of the Word and deacons[2] own the two volumes, and so do a significant number of lay preachers (lay preachers conduct services in hundreds of local churches each Sunday). How much use these owners make of their handsome books (which won awards for book production) is almost impossible to estimate, but certainly the services for marriage, funeral, ordination, induction, commissioning of lay preachers, and commissioning of elders are very widely used. In the *People's Book* there is no outline of these six services, as the Commission assumed that a special printing of these services for each occasion would be the norm, and this generally has proven to be the case. Separate booklets containing offprints of the marriage, funeral, and initiation services have sold well. As a local pastor I make extensive use of the small marriage and initiation booklets, handing them over to engaged couples and to families about to present a candidate for baptism or confirmation.

As explained in the preceding chapter, the Service of the Lord's Day was regarded by the Commission on Liturgy as the foundation for any liturgical reforms. A minority of congregations employ the service as the Commission hoped: with the congregation following the outline and using responses and prayers from the *People's Book*, while the presiding minister uses both the *People's Book* and the extra resources, especially one of the eucharistic prayers, from the *Leader's Book*. The practice of other congregations is for the minister to use parts of the new Service of the Lord's Day and for the people to respond either from memory (especially with the Sanctus, the Lord's Prayer, and the Agnus Dei) or from a locally printed "pew sheet." In this way many congregations, probably a majority, are familiar with the Service of the Lord's Day, but many of the worshipers never have handled the *People's Book*.

A third group of congregations does not use the Service of the

Lord's Day at all. When the Lord's Supper is observed, the form of holy communion is that of the 1980 "blue booklet" of the Uniting Church or some other resource, including orders of service from pre-union days. Since the majority of ministers ordained before 1977 were Methodist, it is fair to assume that the British *Book of Offices* of 1936 is used in dozens of congregations, possibly hundreds, especially in rural areas.

The overall picture is one in which the influence of *Uniting in Worship* outstrips the sales of the books. At no point has the Commission suggested or implied that its orders of service are mandatory. They are authorized by the National Assembly but not prescribed. In the preface that is found in both volumes of *Uniting in Worship* I made this comment:

> The status and authority of published services is a matter of some debate within the Uniting Church. It is important to avoid both understatement and overstatement of the authority of *Uniting in Worship*. Its services and resources are not *required* to be used. Ministers and other worship leaders have the right to use other books, provided that these conform to the doctrine of the Uniting Church. On the other hand, *Uniting in Worship*, with the approval of the Assembly behind it, sets a standard for worship. It is normative in the sense that it is a standard against which other services may be measured.
>
> This does not mean, of course, that the services in *Uniting in Worship* are intended to be used rigidly and without imagination. All worship should be geared to the particular situation of the congregation, be it large or small, urban or rural. All the resources in *Uniting in Worship* are therefore designed to be used in a flexible way. Indeed most of the services have many options within them, and there are frequent invitations to use free prayer.[3]

Strategies for Change

Throughout its work the Commission on Liturgy has aimed to help ministers and congregations to change from the minister-dominated, wordy, and inflexible styles of former times. The Commission has been guided by writings and liturgical publications from the ecumenical Church. It has sought to present, in forms which are digestible by Australians, the fruits of biblical, historical, theological, and liturgical scholarship. The style and content of *Uniting in Worship* are consequently very different from earlier books. Some critics say it is too traditional, but this criticism is probably motivated by resistance to all ordered liturgy, in some cases, and in other cases by disappointment at the often formal language in which the prayers and responses are cast. As the quotation above indicates, the Commission always expected that the printed resources would be supplemented by freshly written or extempore prayers.

The Commission decided on four strategies for the promotion of its liturgical reforms: (1) Appearances, by representatives of the Commission, at sessions of the National Assembly, synods (there are seven, corresponding largely to state boundaries) and presbyteries (fifty-four in total); and the making of written reports to all these bodies. (2) The appointment of a full-time worship consultant to conduct education programs for a two-year or three-year period. (3) Liaison with the six theological colleges in which future ministers are given, by decision of the Assembly, some liturgical preparation. (4) The publication of a *Guide to Uniting in Worship*.[4]

Concerning the first, the Commission is responsible to the Assembly which appointed it, and all published services are referred to the Commission on Doctrine of the Assembly and then to the Standing Committee of the Assembly. But the synods have always been very influential in the life of the Church, so attempts have been made, over the years, to present progress reports.

The presbyteries, containing anything from a handful of parishes (in more remote areas) to seventy or more parishes, are directly responsible for the oversight of parish life and of the ordained ministers. The polity of the Uniting Church is basically Presbyterian, despite the fact noted above that most of the ministers and members in 1977 came from the Methodist tradition. Most presbyteries meet four or more times per year, which means there are several hundred meetings across the country annually. Personal representation from the Commission at these meetings has been infrequent, but in the late 1970s a crucial decision was made which has ensured good and frequent contact with most of the presbyteries. This decision was to urge each presbytery to appoint a "Presbytery liaison person for liturgy." These people have not only conveyed and interpreted liturgical developments to presbyteries but have been contributors to the development of new services being prepared by the Commission. Because, in nearly every case, the liaison person has added this task to numerous others, the effectiveness of the scheme has varied greatly from place to place, but in some instances at least the work done has been very impressive.

The second strategy sprang from a proposal by the publishing agency of the Uniting Church, the Joint Board of Christian Education, that a worship consultant be appointed by the Commission to travel the continent introducing *Uniting in Worship* and conducting workshops on various topics. The funding for this appointment was by way of an advance against future royalties from the sale of *Uniting in Worship*. I was the person chosen for this role, and for two years, 1989 and 1990, I traveled widely, making fifty flights in the first year and forty in the second. The presbytery liaison persons, and sometimes synod staff as well, helped me set up workshops. I visited forty-four of the fifty-four presbyteries—some of them twice—and most of the workshops were one and a half or two days in length. I concentrated in the first year on introducing the Service of the Lord's Day, its theology and structure, and the practical issues involved. These practical concerns included helping people to embrace change. To avoid over-wordiness, I introduced music along with *Uniting in Worship* material, both songs and liturgical responses. The first part of the process resembled an extended service of worship with commentary, after which people tackled particular aspects of the service in small groups. Membership of each workshop was usually between ten and thirty persons, with a mixture of ordained and lay.

In the second year I revisited some presbyteries and went to others for the first time. The range of topics was wide, and participants could work in groups, on at least two topics, from a list which included the use of music, the participation of children, the new liturgy of baptism, the use of local worship committees, the service of healing, the writing of original prayers, and the preparation and presentation of scripture readings. The Presbyterian Church (U.S.A.) publication *Reformed Liturgy and Music* was a useful resource for many of these topics.

In January 1990 there was a national workshop in Adelaide extending over five days, and most presbyteries were represented. Material from *Uniting in Worship* was used, as well as other material. Creative use of printed liturgy was emphasized and the results were encouraging. Services for various seasons of the year were prepared and presented by groups, and a group of children showed how well they can prepare and participate along with adults.

Two of the aims of the worship consultant strategy were not realized. One was the involvement of older youth. The scheduling of the workshops was not suitable to many of them, and there was a further problem: most of the youth workers in the Uniting Church, and their leaders, tend to avoid printed liturgical material. Many of the services of worship aimed at youth have a rather charismatic or ad hoc flavor. The other aim was the involvement of ministers whose liturgical education was limited; those who attended workshops were mostly those interested in liturgical creativity and liturgical change, whereas those content to "do as we have always done" were little influenced by this strategy or indeed by other strategies.

It should be added that not all ministers and lay people who would own the label "charismatic" have been untouched by *Uniting in Worship* and the associated strategies for liturgical renewal. In the town of Geraldton in Western Australia, where a presbytery was meeting, I attended Sunday morning worship with about one hundred persons of all ages. The minister, a charismatic, led the service with much participation by children, and with much hand-clapping and chorus-singing. To my surprise, he wove together extempore prayers with prayers from *Uniting in Worship* in a most skillful manner. Very few of the congregation would have recognized his sources, but the effect was remarkable; he avoided the thinness and repetitiveness of much extempore praying, but there was an intensity and enthusiasm which could not but impress the visitor. Other charismatics would use *Uniting in Worship* only on presbytery or synod occasions, with the possible exception of services mentioned earlier, namely marriage, funeral, commissioning of elders, and the commissioning of lay preachers. It is difficult to know whether charismatic ministers have been using the Service of Healing from *Uniting in Worship*, which I regard as one of the most creative inclusions in the book.

The third strategy was liaison with theological colleges. There are six colleges (equivalent to theological seminaries) which are approved institutions for the preparation of candidates for ordination. In each college there are also students preparing for work in the Church other than through the ordained ministry. This strategy did not receive very much attention in the period 1988 to 1991; however, one factor worked strongly in favor of liturgical reform. When the regulations of the Uniting Church were drawn up in the period 1973 to 1976, a list of required topics for ministerial education was approved, and this list included the formal study of liturgy. In some colleges in the 1970s none of the faculty was well prepared to teach liturgy (the full-time faculty numbers range from as few as four to around fifteen), but in other colleges the teaching of liturgy has been undertaken with skill and enthusiasm. The Commission on Liturgy has provided resources to faculty members from time to time.

The fourth and last strategy was the publication of a *Guide to Uniting in Worship*. During preparation of *Uniting in Worship* over several years, notes were made in Commission meetings identifying material to be included in the *Guide*. Robert Gribben usually took these notes and he wrote the bulk of the *Guide*. It is a model of clear, sensible and scholarly advice on the conduct of worship. Naturally most space is given to introducing aspects of worship that were not familiar to many ministers and lay preachers. The *Guide* appeared in 1990 which was too late for most of the workshops conducted by the worship consultant in that year, but in the period since 1990 it has proved to be most valuable, not least in theological colleges and in lay preacher classes.

The Blending of Traditions

When the *Basis of Union* was published in final form in 1971, it was accompanied by two appendices: "Concerning the Celebration of the Sacraments" and "Concerning the Ordering of the Ministry." Although not technically part of the document which was voted on and approved in the mid-1970s, these brief additions give a clear indication of things to come. In the first, the following words appear:

> In order that the sacraments may be administered with due regard to the ends for which they were instituted, the Uniting Church will on an early occasion set up a Committee on Public Worship (or a Liturgical Commission, or some such body) to guide the Church's life of worship. Until the work of such a Committee has been assessed and approved by the appropriate council or councils of the Church, ministers and congregations will continue to be guided by the books used for these purposes in the three Churches at the time of union, namely *The Methodist Book of Offices*, *The Book of Common Order of the Presbyterian Church of Australia*, *A Book of Public Worship* and *A Book of Services and Prayers*.[5]

This was designed to reassure Congregationalists, Methodists, and Presbyterians on two matters: the ordering of worship would have a priority in the new denomination, and second, change would not be drastic nor would it be rushed. Both of these assurances have been honored.

It should be noted that, well before union in 1977, the three Churches were already blending together. There had been cooperation in theological education for more than half a century; there was collaborative mission work in the inner city and the remote hinterland, called "the outback"; there were joint parishes. The worship of the three Churches was also similar, although differences could be discerned, not least in the actions and movements at holy communion. Presbyterians would commonly begin the worship service with a procession where the open Bible was carried in and placed on the lectern or pulpit. Since union, congregations of non-Presbyterian background have frequently taken up this practice. The bringing of the gifts of bread and wine to the table just prior to the beginning of the eucharistic liturgy proper was little known except among some Presbyterian congregations; this has now become fairly common across the continent.

The distribution of the elements is one place in the service where older habits have often persisted. This is sometimes on account of the furnishings, e.g., former Congregational and Presbyterian buildings do not usually have a communion rail, whereas Methodists would be accustomed to "come forward" to a rail for communion. Smaller Methodist churches in rural areas did not always have a rail, and in these places communion would be distributed to communicants sitting in their pews. But in larger Methodist churches, some hundreds in number, a rail was not only a prominent feature but was used every time the sacrament was celebrated.

Most of these larger churches are still in use. In a minority of cases, two neighboring congregations of different denominational backgrounds have combined for worship in a single building. In these blended communities, a monthly celebration of communion constitutes the most common pattern, often with the method of distribution varying month by month. Early in the life of the Uniting Church, the Commission on Liturgy identified nine methods of distribution which allow for variety in location (e.g., at the table, rail, or pew), posture (standing, sitting, and kneeling), and reception (e.g., with the congregation partaking as a body, or with individuals determining the moment of reception). The Commission was under some pressure to state preferences between the various methods but it has always refused to do so, preferring to encourage ministers and elders[6] to decide the issue locally.

The blending of the three traditions has been hastened by the fact that many ministers ordained in recent years have had no direct experience of any of the three traditions which entered the union. These people were brought up in the Uniting Church or else came from some other denomination, mostly Anglican, Church of Christ, or Pentecostal. In a parish such as my present one in Canberra, the national capital, worshipers come from many denominations across Asia and the Pacific. Others are from a variety of Australian churches. The Service of the Lord's Day seems to form a solid meeting ground for this variety of backgrounds. As to distribution of communion, the church has no rail, so the elements are taken to the people in their pews. In the smaller evening services, the communicants usually form a circle and receive the elements standing. The larger of the two congregations of the parish (the one which worships in English; the other is in Tongan) was originally Congregationalist; some of the older members resist the idea of coming forward for communion as for them it resembles Anglican and Roman Catholic practice.

In many other respects, the three denominations were difficult to distinguish from each other before union in, for example, the style of preaching, the place of children in worship, the range of theological views, and liturgical dress. It has therefore been easy, generally speaking, for worshipers to "migrate" from one denominational style to another.

Hymns and Readings

One of the greatest unifiers of the three denominations which formed the Uniting Church was the adoption of the *Australian Hymn Book*.[7] In 1968 an ecumenical team of Anglicans, Congregationalists, Methodists, and Presbyterians, officially appointed, began work on a new hymnal. They were joined in 1971 by Roman Catholics from the Sydney archdiocese. In 1977, only three months after the inauguration of the Uniting Church, the completed book appeared and was quickly adopted by the great majority of Uniting Church congregations. The sales far outstripped the estimates given by the Hymn Book Committee to the publisher, William Collins of London. There was, as with most new hymnals, much grieving over the loss of some cherished hymns, but the new book contained a fair representation of familiar Congregational, Methodist, and Presbyterian hymns, as well as modern material from a variety of Asian, African, American, and European as well as Australian sources.

A slightly adapted version of this hymnal has sold well in New Zealand, with some sales in the United Kingdom, especially to schools.

In 1991 an expanded committee began work on a revised edition. This time the committee included representatives from the Anglican, Church of Christ, Lutheran, Presbyterian, Roman Catholic, and Uniting Churches (part of the Presbyterian Church did not enter the union of 1977). The potential constituency of the new book is therefore about 70 percent of Australia's Christians.

The effect of the *Australian Hymn Book* in giving disparate groups in the Uniting Church a common corpus of hymns and songs has been significant. Unfortunately some congregations in the 1980s and 1990s have ceased, or almost ceased, using their copies of the *Australian Hymn Book* and have replaced hymns with scripture choruses, rock music and folk material. I am not suggesting that this sort of church music has no legitimate place, but I do believe it is short-sighted to restrict any congregation's diet to this sort of nourishment. If, as John Wesley pointed out, hymns have a significant teaching function in the church, the more memorable and long-lasting hymns and songs are an important way of transmitting the faith from one generation to the next. More ephemeral music and words will not do this adequately.

At the inception of the Uniting Church, the Commission published an adapted version of the three-year Roman Catholic lectionary. This was quickly taken up by a majority of parishes. Ordained ministers, whether of evangelical, charismatic, classical Reformed, or high-church persuasion, have stayed with this lectionary over the years. The Common Lectionary from North America was printed in the *Leader's Book* in 1988, and since that time the Revised Common Lectionary has replaced it. The promotion of this series of closely related lectionaries by the Commission has helped preachers and worship leaders to use the wide variety of resources originating in North America, in the form of biblical commentaries and liturgical material.

As with the publication of the *Australian Hymn Book*, the extensive use of the lectionary has had a unifying effect on the Uniting Church's widely differing congregations. Since the lectionary printed in the *Leader's Book* is now out of date, the Commission is about to print a booklet with the three-year cycle of readings. This will supplement and not replace the one-year list of readings which, printed on a single sheet, can be seen pinned to church office noticeboards and ministers' study walls right across the continent.

In addition to materials from overseas, the Uniting Church has its own commentary on the lectionary called *With Love to the World*. This appears as a booklet every three months. The style is devotional and pastoral, and the standard of biblical scholarship is generally good. There are several writers in each issue. In the course of a particular week the three readings from the following Sunday's lectionary are commented on, as are the appointed psalm and three other scripture selections, thereby making seven readings for the week. Many preachers use the commentaries in their preparation for Sunday, but the main purpose of *With Love to the World* is as a guide for daily Bible reading. Since the booklet is linked to the lectionary, it has a distinct advantage over other long-established publications such as *The Upper Room*, also widely used in Australia. The sales of *With Love to the World* are about 15,000 per issue which is a very satisfactory distribution for a country the size of Australia and a church the size of the Uniting Church (the denomination has the allegiance of about 8 percent of Australia's population of seventeen million).

The Uniting Church in the 1990s and Beyond

Only two members of the Commission on Liturgy which produced *Uniting in Worship* still serve on the Commission. Meetings are now held in the northern city of Brisbane.[8] This new Commission concentrates on two things: first, responding to requests for new or revised services (a Service for the Birth of a Still-Born Child is a new service, while the Ordination of Ministers of the Word and Ordination of Deacons are revisions); and second, engaging in educational projects. Because of the size of Australia and the lack of money for work by national agencies, this education takes the form of publications. It is a brave attempt, but far more is needed. As part of the 1990 edition of *Working Together Nationally* (an annual report to members of synods) I wrote this:

> The Uniting Church in Australia needs a careful plan for development of leadership in worship and preaching. This should include theological colleges, continuing education of ministers, training of musicians, continuing education of lay preachers and elders. Unless

91

the church understands and develops its worship, we cannot expect its mission, evangelism, social outreach and pastoral care will be properly directed.[9]

Progress is being made on all these fronts, but this progress is rather piecemeal.

While *Uniting in Worship* is still a basic resource—and is about to be translated into Korean, for use in Korea as well as Australia—many other resources are being utilized. The value of liturgical freedom inherited by the Uniting Church has given permission for local ministers and leaders to determine which resources will be employed. The worship book of the 1991 Canberra Assembly of the World Council of Churches, *In Spirit and in Truth*, is much used. The publications of Scotland's Iona Community are making an increasing impression. Australian publications such as those of Mediacom in Adelaide, with resources for each week of the year, are gaining acceptance steadily. In 1994 at Canberra, a newly re-formed National Council of Churches was inaugurated. The service of inauguration, replayed several times on national television, showed what can be done when music, movement, text, and environment (a large Roman Catholic church) are combined in a creative way; Uniting Church people played a major part in the preparation of this service.

This list of influences—and others might be added, such as evangelical publications from the United States—shows how eclectic the Uniting Church is. It is one of the most ecumenically-committed Churches in the southern hemisphere. Suspicion of ecumenism still exists, but is not widespread. This stance enables the Uniting Church to use liturgical material from a variety of sources. Sometimes the material is used uncritically (such is the danger in an eclectic atmosphere), but there is an ecumenical openness which permits creativity. Although worship in some places is dull or overly backward-looking, in many places it is alive, participatory, and enthusiastic. With its background in the Reformation and the Evangelical Revival of the eighteenth century, the Uniting Church naturally places great emphasis on Scripture. This biblical base is the control which prevents creativity from diverging into territory which might be hard to recognize as Christian. While New Age thinking has penetrated some parts of the Uniting Church, it is not a major influence.

Earlier in this chapter I quoted from the appendix to the *Basis of Union* which deals with worship. It is a cautious statement. The changes in worship since the writing of that appendix in 1971 have been profound. Worship is now much more participatory; the range of music has increased; ecumenical influences have become greater; and, perhaps most encouraging of all, ministers and elders give greater priority to worship than they did in the 1960s and 1970s. The 1960s was the period of so-called secular theology and this tended to put the Church and its worship into question. While, in the 1990s, the churches in Australia have not regained the confidence of the 1950s, they are seeking, and often finding, positive new ways of worship and proclamation.

Chapter 6

Ordered Liberty: Sunday Worship in the United Church of Canada

Thomas Harding

In 1925, through a union of Methodists, Congregationalists, and two-thirds of Canadian Presbyterians, the United Church of Canada was born. Committed to the evangelization of the nation and the creation of a Christian society (nineteenth-century evangelism wedded to twentieth-century social gospel), it was to be a "united and uniting church." A fourth partner, the Canada Conference of the Evangelical United Brethren, joined in 1968. Negotiations with the Anglican Church of Canada culminated in the rejection of a proposed Plan of Union by the House of Bishops in 1975, however, and two years later, discussions with the Christian Church (Disciples of Christ) were quietly set aside. But the initial vision remained—that of a *Canadian* Church which would be a *uniting* Church.

Historically, patterns of worship in the United Church of Canada fall into three periods: the "classical period" (1925 to the 1960s), the "period of transition" (the 1960s to the 1980s), and the "ecumenical convergence" (the 1980s to the present). These are marked by the publication of three sets of liturgical resources: the *Hymnary* (1930) and *Book of Common Order* (1932); the *Service Book for the use of ministers* (1969), *Service Book for the use of the people* (1969) and joint Anglican-United Church *Hymn Book* (1971); and *A Sunday Liturgy* (1984) and four other liturgical booklets "for optional use," *Songs for a Gospel People* (1987), *Voices United: A Sampler for Congregations* (1993), and other materials in preparation for new liturgical resources to be published in 1996.[1]

The undergirding principle of United Church worship is that of *ordered liberty*, as outlined in the preface to the *Book of Common Order*:

> In the Churches which united to form The United Church of Canada there was an ordered liberty in common worship. They followed lines marked out by Apostolic practice and hallowed by the general usage of Christendom, but they shrank from a uniformity that might quench the Spirit of God in the soul of man. In our worship we are rightly concerned for two things: first, that a worshipping congregation of the Lord's people shall be free to follow the leading of the Spirit of Christ in their midst; and second, that the experience of many ages of devotion shall not be lost, but preserved,— experience that has caused certain forms of prayer to glow with light and power.

This tension between freedom and order remains at the heart of United Church worship. Though worship practices are diverse, there are common patterns across the country; though there are no prescribed forms, there are service books and hymnals sanctioned by the General Council. This essay explores these commonalities and differences and poses the particular question: How has worship in the United Church of Canada been influenced by its Methodist heritage?

The "Classical Period"

By the end of World War I, Sunday worship in Canadian Methodist, Presbyterian, and Congregational Churches was remarkably similar—the "hymn sandwich" pattern typical of Free Church tradition: praise, prayer, praise; scripture, prayer, "notices," offering; praise, sermon, prayer, praise, benediction.[2] Methodists began with a doxology, said the Lord's Prayer after the opening invocation, and tended to place the intercessions before rather than after the scripture lessons. As hymnody formed the backbone of Methodist worship, organs and choirs were much in evidence. Communion was celebrated quarterly, the liturgy being a truncated version of the *Book of Common Prayer*; some Methodists came forward to kneel, though the introduction of individual communion cups was putting an end to that practice. The love feast had all but disappeared and camp meetings had evolved into evangelistic campaigns; watchnight and covenant renewal services were still occasionally observed. Much of Canadian Methodism was rooted in American Methodist Episcopal practices and in the British Methodist offshoots (Primitive Methodist, New Connection, Bible Christian) rather than mainstream Wesleyanism; except in a few instances, then, Canadian Methodism was never very "liturgical." Urban congregations were moving away from the simple enthusiasm of frontier worship patterns, however, in favor of more formal liturgies which included the chanting of canticles and other elements of service music.

Presbyterians began with a "prefacing" ("Let us worship God"), relied heavily on the metrical psalms, and said the Lord's Prayer at the conclusion of the "long prayer." Since the resolution of the organ controversy of the 1860s and 1870s, hymns were generally accepted as at least supplementary to the psalter and choirs were also much in evidence. Worshipers sat to pray and stood to sing (a reversal of nineteenth-century practice) and the "lining" of psalms by a precentor had disappeared. Communion was observed at least twice yearly (in some congregations, quarterly) and the "communion season"—a five-day series of preparatory services before and a thanksgiving service after—was on the wane. The chalice had given way to individual communion cups; grape juice and pre-cut pieces of bread were the standard elements.

Congregationalist worship tended to follow Methodist and Presbyterian patterns, the Congregational Union being by far the smallest of the founding denominations.

Patterns of Sunday worship, then, were characterized less by denominational differences than by urban-rural preferences. Larger churches tended toward more sophisticated services; rural and small town congregations preferred simpler patterns of worship. In all three denominations there persisted a tension between those who desired more formal liturgical patterns and those who cherished the simplicity of former days. This tension was exacerbated by the publication of the 1930 *Hymnary* and the 1932 *Book of Common Order*.

In the preface to the *Hymnary* Alexander MacMillan, full-time secretary of the Committee on Church Worship and Ritual, noted the Committee's twofold purpose:

> The larger aim . . . has been to offer a collection of spiritual songs widely representative of the Hymnody of the Church Universal. . . . Canticles of the ancient Church, translations and transfusions of early and mediaeval Greek and Latin hymns, songs of the time of the Reformation . . . and a rich appropriation from the treasures of modern hymnody. . . .
>
> A second purpose . . . has been to provide a hymnody true to the genius, history, and tradition of the Communions which now compose The United Church of Canada.

The *Hymnary* was a truly remarkable collection. Three things should be noted, however. First, "the Hymnody of the Church Universal" meant, by and large, those fashions current in Great Britain in the 1920s (the rise of liturgical hymnody through the influence of the Oxford movement, the understanding of "proper hymnody" advanced by Robert Bridges, the elevation of the folk song by Ralph Vaughan Williams, the popularization of the *faux bourdon*). Second, there was a distinct lack of Canadian content, especially when compared to previous Canadian hymn books. Third, there was a considerable bias in favor of Presbyterian material and practice.[3] This last was the subject of considerable controversy, not so much over the preponderance of Presbyterian material as over the impending loss of gospel hymnody—dear to the Methodist heart—and the decision (in the original draft) to follow traditional Presbyterian practice and place the metrical psalms in a group at the beginning of the book. A compromise was eventually reached on both counts. A section entitled "The Gospel Call" was included and the metrical psalms, though remaining as a unit, were placed at the conclusion rather than beginning of the hymnody portion of the book.

Two trends which would be significant in the development of United Church worship did find a place in the book. The *Hymnary* included a section entitled "For Little Children" and an index of "Hymns for the Young," as well as a number of hymns reflecting the influence of the social gospel and generally classed, in the terminology of the day, as "Hymns of the Kingdom." Also included were a selection of prose psalms intended for unison or responsive reading, a section entitled "Canticles and Other Parts of Divine Service," and several prayers. Here is perhaps the greatest contribution of the *Hymnary*. Despite the initial controversy, ultimately the book became an important liturgical resource to United Church congregations, forming their patterns of service music and use of the prose psalter.

The *Book of Common Order* was an equally remarkable document. Richard Davidson, "father" of the *Book of Common Order*, described the Committee's task:

> There were two interests to be kept in view. (1) In the first place, there was the conservative interest. Whatever was alive in any one of the three churches, whatever was cherished because of its place in actual devotion ought not to be abandoned. . . . (2) In the second place, there was a catholic interest. . . . [We] were bold to claim all

the ranges of devotion as our Christian heritage; . . . we were convinced that there was nothing more important for the newly-organized body than that it should hold to the middle of the great stream of the Church's worship.[4]

The first services in the *Book of Common Order* are two Directories for the Public Worship of God. Though the compilers claimed that "the first Directory has the structure of Morning and Evening Prayer,"[5] a closer parallel is found in the first Order for Public Worship, Morning Worship I, of the 1922 Canadian Presbyterian *Book of Common Order*. The key is the term *directory*; both the Presbyterian and United Church orders are ultimately derived, not from Morning Prayer but from the *Westminster Directory*. Davidson and the Committee believed, however, that the original model for Reformed worship was not the daily office but the eucharist (as in Knox's *Genevan Service Book* and the first Scottish *Book of Common Order*). This pattern had been thwarted by history, first by the *Westminster Directory* and then by the exigencies of worship on the North American frontier. We must begin to recover our heritage, Davidson argued; we must recapture a balance between the "Liturgy of the Word" and the "Liturgy of the Table."[6] The second directory, then, has a three-fold structure: The Introduction, The Word of God, The Fellowship of Prayer, restoring the original ante-communion pattern of non-eucharistic Reformed worship. Davidson argued that this directory should be placed first in the *Book of Common Order*, but common Methodist, Presbyterian, and Congregationalist practice prevailed.

The first Order for the Celebration of the Lord's Supper demonstrates even further the Committee's breadth of scholarship. Methodist and Presbyterian communion liturgies differed considerably. Davidson claimed that the problem was solved by adopting "the Presbyterian structure" with the "Methodist (that is, Prayer Book) words . . . fitted into it."[7] But there was a larger principle at work here; the issue was not simply to amalgamate two quite different communion orders, but to do so with a view to the tradition of the "Church catholic." So the *Book of Common Order* service is a unified order of word and sacrament (rather than communion being tacked on to the end of the normal Sunday service), the fourfold shape of the communion has been restored (the communion liturgy begins with the offering, and the fraction comes after the eucharistic prayer), and the prayers are drawn from the "entire range of Christian devotion."[8]

Perhaps the most interesting observation to be made about the first communion order is that the compilers were obviously aware of the liturgical developments in Great Britain which culminated in the (ultimately rejected) *Prayer Book as Proposed in 1928*.[9] There is a remarkable similarity between the Alternative Order for the Administration of the Lord's Supper in the *Prayer Book as Proposed* and the first Order for the Celebration of the Lord's Supper or Holy Communion in the *Book of Common Order*. It appears that the United Church committee and the English Prayer Book revisers were working with common sources. But the Canadian committee went far beyond the English, producing an even more "catholic" liturgy.

This "catholic interest" is of overriding concern in both the *Hymnary* and the *Book of Common Order*. MacMillan, Davidson, and their colleagues saw themselves as liturgical reformers. Like the sixteenth-century reformers before them, they understood the task of reform as reaching back into the past to reclaim lost tradition, appropriating its richness for a new situation. The principle of "ordered liberty" was paramount, but let that "order" be the best the church has to offer!

During the 1930s and 1940s worship in the United Church of Canada was affected by several societal trends. Changing patterns of recreation shifted the emphasis away from Sunday evening, and Sunday morning became the principal focus for public worship. Children were gradually excluded from the regular worshiping community as Sunday school came to be scheduled at the same time as "church," and "junior congregations" became popular.[10] A distinct United Church liturgical year developed, with a double focus on Christmas and Easter but including numerous quasi-religious "special days" (Mother's Day, Empire Day, Rally Day, Thanksgiving Sunday, Temperance Sunday, Remembrance Day, etc.).[11] A post-Second World War emphasis on evangelism led to the publication of a separate volume of gospel hymnody, *Songs of the Gospel* (1948).[12] Clergy dress evolved, and it became increasingly popular for ministers to wear Geneva gowns and clerical collars. Church architecture favored the "neo-gothic" with split chancels and the communion table considerably removed from the people.

By the 1950s worship patterns in the United Church had stabilized. After the trials of the Depression and the War, the United Church of Canada was rapidly becoming *the* Canadian Church. Expansion into the suburbs produced congregations with no noticeable ties to the founding denominations, union negotiations were under way with the Evangelical United Brethren, Anglicans, and Disciples of Christ, and the work of MacMillan, Davidson, and others had produced a more liturgically-minded clergy. An editorial in the *United Church Observer* noted:

> The people of The United Church . . . have been hungering and thirsting after colour and beauty in their churches, and form and dignity in their worship. . . . Older ministers may go into the communion service without a *Book of Common Order*, but the younger men . . . follow the book. . . .
>
> It may be that . . . the younger men are paying more attention to their robes and their hoods than to their sermons, and becoming more concerned for . . . liturgical correctness . . . than for the souls of the unchurched . . . ; it may be that there are all sorts of criticisms to be made of the present trends. But the fact is there are trends. . . .
>
> The youth of The United Church, the younger ministers and the young married people . . . have felt that they have been missing something. . . . They have been starved for the beauty which the Roman Catholic, the Greek Catholic, the Orthodox, and the Anglican takes for granted.[13]

A typical 1950s Sunday service began with an introit ("Holy, holy, holy," *Hymnary* 1, v.1), call to worship, invocation, and hymn of praise. All joined in a confession of sin (*Hymnary* 771) and a responsive psalm concluding with the sung Gloria Patri (*Hymnary* 754, tune: Ham). The scripture readings were followed by an anthem; children left for Sunday school after an address to the young and a children's hymn. The "pastoral prayer" culminated in the Lord's Prayer (*Hymnary* 760, tune: Langdon), followed by announcements, presentation of the offering, and the Doxology (*Hymnary* 625, tune: Old 100th). A hymn preceded the sermon, and a prayer afterward recapitulated the main points. The service concluded with a hymn, benediction, and three-fold Amen (*Hymnary* 770, tune: Danish). When communion was celebrated, the communion hymn was most often "Here, O my Lord, I see Thee face to face," the first three verses before communion, the last four after. The sacrament was served by the elders in a carefully regulated fashion to worshipers seated in the pews; in many congregations, the elements were taken by all simultaneously.[14] It was a "liturgical" service,[15] common (with only minor variations) across the country. United Church worshipers knew they were in a United Church. But this classical period was coming to a close; the 1960s would usher in an astounding ferment in United Church worship.

The "Period of Transition"

Two developments in the 1950s heralded the changes which would occur in the 1960s and 1970s: the publication of the Revised Standard Version of the Bible and the introduction of the Gestetner copying process. The RSV broke the stranglehold of the King James Version on the language of United Church worship. In 1962 the New English Bible (New Testament) appeared and voices were raised across the Church claiming that the language of worship was "archaic." Clergy were beginning to print "contemporary" prayers and modified liturgies in congregational orders of worship. The General Council instructed the Committee on Church Worship and Ritual to revise the *Book of Common Order*.

Initially the issue of archaic versus contemporary language focused on the proper address to the deity. The Minutes of the Committee record in 1966 that "about half the ministers in Western Canada were already addressing God as 'You.'"[16] But the debate soon escalated beyond the question of "thee" and "thou." What was really at issue was the theological content of liturgical language. A typical Minute reads:

> With regard to the Intercessory Prayer . . . the constant repetition of "And in thy mercy answer" was questioned. "This is a view of God that says you have to beg his mercy at every juncture as if you were before a judge who might mitigate the sentence." So said Miss Christie. She was supported by Mr. Atkinson who continued, "Yes, 'mercy' is not a useful word in liturgy anymore. . . ."[17]

Even the Executive of the General Council questioned the language used in the draft orders presented in 1968:

> "World without end" in the Gloria Patri—Is this scientific? "His resurrection from the dead and ascension on high, we confess"— There was a comment that "this concept of levitation is unacceptable." There was objection to "as God's dear children—this is hardly suitable as an address to adults."[18]

A second concern was the matter of encouraging congregational participation. Throughout the 1950s there had been calls for some method by which worship material could be available in the pews. Having been instructed by the General Council to proceed also with a revision of the *Hymnary*, the Committee initially decided to include

liturgical material in a revised hymn book. By 1965, however, negotiations with the Anglicans had progressed to the point where it was
determined that the new hymn book would be a joint Anglican-
United Church venture. This put the original plan in jeopardy.
Having already agreed that the title "Book of Common Order" was
itself an archaism, it was decided that there would be two books
produced: a *Service Book for the use of ministers conducting public worship*
and a *Service Book for the use of the people.*[19]

The fundamental issue in the creation of the *Service Book* was the
question of the shape of the services. It was generally agreed that the
second directory of the *Book of Common Order* (Introduction, Word of
God, Fellowship of Prayer) should provide the basic structure for the
ordinary Sunday service. Now the Committee determined that *all*
orders would be based on this structure, and that the first to be
included in the new book would be those for the celebration of the
Lord's Supper. The Committee settled on a threefold format for the
communion service: The Approach, The Word of God Proclaimed
and Acknowledged, The Word of God Enacted; for the ordinary
Sunday service without the sacrament the format would be: The
Approach, The Word of God, The Response.

The first Order for the Celebration of the Lord's Supper demonstrates the considerable advance in liturgical scholarship since the
publication of the *Book of Common Order*. The Approach begins with
scripture sentences, a prayer of approach "appropriate to the season
of the Christian Year," and a hymn of praise. The general confession
is a contemporary rendition of the Confiteor, followed by silence, the
Agnus Dei, and an assurance of pardon (the confession had been
removed from the communion liturgy in keeping with the Committee's intention that the sacramental service be eucharistic rather than
penitential).[20] The Word of God Proclaimed and Acknowledged
begins with a prayer for grace ("appropriate to the season of the
Christian Year") and includes two scripture readings separated by a
psalm, the sermon, creed (optional), and a hymn. The intercessions
are a contemporary rendition of the supplications from the Liturgy
of St. John Chrysostom (in litany form), followed by the announcements. The Word of God Enacted begins with an invitation (rather
than exhortation) and the peace. The offering is gathered during the
communion hymn and the rubrics encourage that the elements be
brought forward along with the gifts of money. The "prayer of
thanksgiving and consecration" begins with the Sursum Corda and

includes the response throughout: "Glory be to thee, O Lord." The oblation and doxology are said in unison, and the prayer concludes with the Lord's Prayer. After the communion the service proceeds to the post-communion prayer, hymn, commissioning (a new addition), and blessing. The people are encouraged to join in the Amens throughout.

The second order is a colloquial version of the first, its short, simple sentences giving rise to the appellation, the "Dick and Jane order."[21] An example of this style is found in the rendition of the Collect for Purity:

> O God, how mighty you are.
> You know all that is in us,
> all that we hope for,
> all that we try to hide.
> Fill us with your Holy Spirit
> that our thoughts may be clean.
> Help us to love you with all our being
> and to show by our actions
> that we are truly your people;
> through Christ our Lord.

Two innovations were a rubric describing how the peace may be physically exchanged and the direction that the "people shall remain standing" for the communion prayer (a practice never commonly observed in United Church congregations). A third order reproduced the first order in the *Book of Common Order*; a fourth was designed for use in "the home or a small group," recognizing the growing house church movement of the 1960s.

The second set of orders are services for initiation, the compilers arguing that these also must be complete services of word and sacrament.

Of the two Orders for Public Worship, the first is a revision of the second directory in the *Book of Common Order*. The service begins with scripture sentences rather than a hymn; the Collect for Purity has been replaced by a "prayer of approach"; the confession is more explicit and is followed by private confession, the Kyrie and an assurance of pardon; and an offertory prayer has been included and a commissioning inserted before the blessing. The second order replicates the first directory in the *Book of Common Order* with similar minor adjustments.

The *Service Book* marks a considerable change in United Church worship patterns. Despite the Committee's insistence on the unity of word and sacrament, the nomenclature defined each movement in terms of *the Word*: The Approach is to *the Word*, *The Word of God* is Proclaimed and Acknowledged, *The Word of God* is Enacted; in the ordinary Sunday service the Response is to *the Word* (contrast the second directory of the *Book of Common Order* in which the third movement is entitled not The Response but The Fellowship of Prayer). Coupled with this was a shift toward human rather than divine action: *we* approach the Word; *we* listen for the Word . . . acknowledge the Word . . . respond to the Word (these are actual titles from certain "gestetner orders" of the 1970s). Even the change in designation of the opening prayer, from adoration or invocation to approach, underscores this shift. (In "home-grown" prayers, the tendency was to describe those doing the approaching rather than the One approached; the emphasis was on human feelings and actions.) This was intensified by a concretization of language. As the compilers noted, "the aim has been to shun the generalities . . . of the past and to emphasize the particularity and concreteness characteristic of our age."[22] So the general confession became particular confessions followed by silent (i.e., private) confession. This concretization of language led to an overriding concern with "getting our theology straight," and the emphasis on *the Word* tended to produce an abundance of words.

Throughout the *Service Book* is found the rubric: "appropriate to the season of the Christian Year." In support of this a Table of Lessons was included. As the compilers noted, however, "the structure does not correspond precisely with that of the traditional Christian Year. Its logical order . . . is that of the Apostles' Creed." The year was divided into four seasons: Creation, Christmas, Easter, and Pentecost, and "begins, as it effectively does in most congregations, on the Sunday after Labour Day."[23]

The emphasis on congregational participation was perhaps the most significant contribution of the *Service Book*. The compilers noted that "Christian worship is something which Christians do," so provision was made for the presentation of the elements and the exchange of peace in the communion and there was "an effort . . . to relate worship to the action of the Christian in the world" through concluding each service with a commissioning. "The word 'liturgy' literally means people's work," the compilers wrote:

> This indicates that the celebrant at public worship is not the minis-
> ter but the people. The minister presides over the people's worship
> ... [but] the worship is not his alone. It belongs to the whole
> community. . . .

To this end prayers may be said in unison or with congregational
responses, and congregational members may read scripture or lead
in prayer. Finally, the compilers noted the publication of a "people's
book" containing "the basic services, a collection of prayers and an
arrangement of the prose psalms."[24]

The inclusion of the prose psalter in the "people's book" was
necessitated by Anglican participation in the *Hymn Book*. Anglicans
chanted the psalms, United Church congregations read them responsively; the psalter, then, could not be included in a common
book. One hundred psalm selections were translated by two Canadian Old Testament scholars (the Committee could not agree on
either the RSV or NEB), and were arranged for several voices:
minister, choir, lay leader, congregation, etc. But not all congregations
purchased copies of the people's book. Though some substituted
Leslie Brandt's *Psalms Now* (a contemporary paraphrase), others lost
altogether the tradition of reading the psalms responsively.

The *Hymn Book* was published in 1971, a Canadian book for a
Canadian Church that was not to be. In the matter of music the book
was indeed truly Canadian, containing "the work of more Canadian
composers than any hymn book that has preceded it";[25] in the matter
of texts the record was not quite so substantial. In a discussion of a
report of the hymn book subcommittee to the Committee on Church
Worship ("Ritual" had been dropped from the title in 1968), the
"question was raised as to whether this new book was really justified.
It was pointed out that 10% of the hymns would be in the current
language of our day,"[26] but the Committee was not convinced:

> [The] discussion reflected, as one member put it, "Dismay at one
> end of the spectrum and lack of enthusiasm at the other." . . . "Some
> of these so-called new hymns date back to Isaac Watts. There are
> probably only 15 or 20 hymns that you could call contempo-
> rary." . . . "The new book is for the 'purist.' The change that has
> taken place in this committee over the past ten years has not been
> reflected in the hymnary sub-committee."[27]

Though the concern of the Committee on Church Worship was
that the new book was not sufficiently contemporary, many United
Church members felt that the subcommittee had eliminated all the

"good old hymns." An article in the *Observer* encapsulated the response: "Some are angry because it includes 'Lord of the Dance.' . . . Others are angry because it does not include 'Onward Christian Soldiers' or 'How Great Thou Art.'"[28] The problem was, once again, the definition of "proper hymnody." The subcommittee claimed that: "What you want to say . . . has to be sound theologically, in words of good literary quality, and sung to a tune of good musical quality."[29]

Apart from the exclusion of old favorites and controversy over hymns such as "Lord of the Dance" and "Now thank we all for bodies strong" (". . . and for the sacrament of sex that recreates our kind"), the chief complaint was that familiar words were set to unfamiliar tunes. The problem was that Anglican and United Church congregations sang different tunes for the same hymn. Often, however, the subcommittee chose a tune not familiar to either, one that had "more musical merit" or "better fitted the meaning of the words." The subcommittee seemed simply to misjudge the musical requirements of ordinary congregations. One member wrote:

> Perhaps the most important . . . decision was to use a different tune for each individual hymn. . . . As a result there are only about three dozen tunes in *HB71* which appear more than once. . . . (When tunes do appear twice they are often set in different keys and sometimes with different harmonizations.) This is in considerable contrast to, say, *The Hymnary 1930* in which the tune "St. Flavian" appeared no less than nine times.[30]

Familiar harmonizations disappeared as well, partly because of copyright costs, and partly because the subcommittee believed that many "of the older hymn tunes . . . suffered . . . from inferior harmonizations."[31]

One innovation that was generally welcomed was the lowering of the pitch of the hymns to accommodate untrained voices. The decision to eliminate the Amens, however (to "discourage congregations from mourning to a slow wailing stop"), created considerable controversy, as did the decision to produce a words plus music edition only ("too awkward and unwieldy"). The benefits of providing worshipers with music was largely nullified by the matching of familiar words with unfamiliar tunes and the general re-harmonization. Choirs reverted to the old harmonies and organists chose to play different tunes than those provided; the provision of words and music in the same book simply intensified the frustration.

Perhaps the most far-reaching problem with the *Hymn Book* was its lack of United Church service music. Three communion settings were included (the part of the service the United Church did not sing) along with settings for the daily office and fifteen canticles. The Gloria Patri, Lord's Prayer, Aaronic Benediction and threefold Amen were included, but to unfamiliar tunes. With the elimination of the traditional settings, many United Church congregations ceased to sing any part of their liturgy other than the hymns themselves.

The *Service Book* and *Hymn Book* by no means tell the entire story of the 1960s and 1970s. Many patterns of church life in the 1960s were the opposite of the 1950s: membership began to decline, clergy were leaving the ministry, young people were rebelling. The New Curriculum (a major United Church Christian education program) introduced historical criticism to lay people; theologians declared that God is dead or at least that what we needed was a "religionless Christianity." The General Secretary of the Church wrote in 1967:

> In a rash moment, I said recently that . . . the next five years may well make or break The United Church of Canada. . . . Ministers find their time monopolized by running the machinery of the pastoral charge. . . . They find it difficult to bring a genuine experience of worship to the congregation.[32]

There were some, however, who were determined to explore new ways of worshiping. By 1969 the *Observer* was reporting:

> The hottest thing in the United Church right now . . . is experimental worship. . . . The manager of the Ryerson Bookstore reports that "books on modern forms of worship are our fastest moving line."[33]

The ferment originated on university campuses where chaplains sought to stem the flow of young people from the Church. Soon young couples and singles were forming house churches, meeting in each other's living rooms for study, informal worship, and to plan "action projects" in the community. Children were invariably included. In some congregations a once-a-month "contemporary service" became common; in larger churches contemporary worship was held at 9:30 a.m., traditional worship at 11:00 a.m. Increasingly, however, experimental worship became confrontational. According to the *Observer*, the chair of the newly created national Celebration Committee responded to a church member who pleaded, "Why can't we do things the way we used to?" with the assertion that "to be a

Christian is to be radical, to upset, to cause confrontation." The article described several contemporary "celebrations":

> Memorable Sunday mornings . . . include the one when a hang-man's noose hung in front of the cross—a vivid reminder of capital punishment. . . . Then there was the morning everyone received a lump of play-dough. "People were invited to offer their creativity to God.". . .
> During Lent, three Sunday mornings were devoted to each of the mind, the body and the soul. . . . On the Sunday of the body, a physical education teacher had people standing in the pews doing exercises. Breathing, . . . diet and sensuality came up, and the minister was even heard to say that he enjoyed sex with his wife. . . .
> Then there was the Sunday of "those damn balloons.". . .[34]

The mandate of the Celebration Committee was to provide resources for contemporary worship. An annual *Celebration Catalogue* eventually evolved into the thrice-yearly *Getting It All Together: A Packet for Worship Planners* (the name was changed to *Gathering* in 1983) which assembled locally-produced worship material for dissemination throughout the Church. By 1980, however, the Celebration Committee and Committee on Church Worship had been amalgamated, the dichotomy between "contemporary" and "traditional" was on the wane, and the *Service Book* was becoming entrenched within the worship life of the United Church of Canada.

The "Ecumenical Convergence"

Though a significant number of congregations retained an order of worship reminiscent of the first directory of the *Book of Common Order*, by the early 1980s many were following the 1969 *Service Book* pattern. For some the tendency was to "produce a new prayer book every Sunday." Typically the service began with a responsive call to worship and unison prayer of approach. After a hymn of praise, a unison or responsive prayer of confession was said, sometimes followed by silent prayer and a (printed) assurance of pardon. The practice was now virtually standard that children were present for the first part of the service, and the word section began with a children's story and hymn. After the children left for church school there would be scripture readings, an anthem, and the sermon. The Response began with a "hymn of response," a creed might be recited followed by announcements and offering. Prayers of thanksgiving and intercession (often in litany form) and the Lord's Prayer led to a final hymn and (responsive) commissioning and benediction. The only service music remaining might be an offertory song and some form of choral dismissal (varying from congregation to congregation).

Communion was celebrated with increasing frequency and was more often associated with the major festivals. The distinctive character of Advent was observed through the introduction of Advent wreaths and candles; palms began to appear on Palm Sunday and seder meals on Maundy Thursday; Pentecost was reclaimed as a significant celebration. Quasi-religious special days remained popular, increasingly oriented toward social concerns (Peace Sabbath, Environmental Sunday, First Nations Sunday). Though some congregations experimented with the re-introduction of wine, grape juice remained the usual communion element. Increasingly, however, a common loaf was used, and by the end of the decade reception by intinction became a recognized United Church option. Communion practice varied (coming forward to stations, remaining in the pews, gathering in a circle) from season to season as well as from congregation to congregation.

With the depopulation of Sunday schools in the late 1960s and 1970s, attitudes toward the participation of children in worship began to change. By the 1980s the United Church was experiencing a wave of interest in "intergenerational worship" with children included for the entire service in some congregations on a regular basis. Though efforts failed in 1983 and 1988 to change the Basis of Union (the constitution of the Church) so that children might be officially welcome at the table, by the end of the decade the practice was unofficially widespread.

Perhaps the most controversial issue in the 1980s was the "inclusive language debate." The *Service Book* and *Hymn Book* had been published before concern about inclusive language became widespread. In 1981 Guidelines for Inclusive Language were issued by the General Council offices encouraging clergy and congregations not only to avoid gender-specific human language, but to avoid gender-specific language for God as well. Though in the early years this led to a considerable amount of "God this" and "God that," gradually new metaphors for the Divine became common. This trend, however (aided by personal computers and copying machines), led to an increasing reliance on lengthy printed orders of worship that included the texts of hymns as well as prayers.

110

Clerical clothing was changing. Though the popularity of gowns, academic hoods, and clerical collars had waned in the 1960s (in keeping with emerging understandings of the ministry of "the whole people of God"), by the late 1970s albs and stoles were appearing, as were banners and various antependia in seasonal colors. This emphasis on the drama of the Christian year was enhanced by the introduction of the Common Lectionary in 1983. By the late 1980s the majority of United Church congregations were using the lectionary, supported by a popular lectionary-based Christian education resource, the *Whole People of God* curriculum.[35]

These trends were in keeping with what was becoming known as the "ecumenical convergence" in worship. The compilers of the *Service Book* had been keenly aware of developments in the Roman Catholic Church following publication of *Sacrosanctum Concilium* by the Second Vatican Council in December 1963: the recovery of the role of the laity in worship, the introduction of hymnody, the use of the vernacular, an emphasis on biblical preaching, a simplification of the Christian year, the restructuring of the eucharistic prayer, and the strengthening of the relationship between worship and mission. By the 1980s a new family of liturgical resources was appearing in the Canadian Churches: *The Roman Missal* (Canadian Conference of Catholic Bishops 1974), *Lutheran Book of Worship* (1978), *Book of Alternative Services of the Anglican Church of Canada* (1985), the Canadian Presbyterian *Word and Sacraments* (1987), and the United Church's *A Sunday Liturgy* (1984).

In the preface to *A Sunday Liturgy* the Working Unit on Worship and Liturgy (successor to the Committee on Worship) wrote: "The 'Sunday Liturgy' is not, in reality, a book. It is something that is *done*."[36] Emphasizing the unity of word and sacrament, the Working Unit outlined the shape of the service:

> There are two focal points or "meeting places" in the service: under the Word and around the table. These are the two main sections, the Service of the Word and the Service of the Table, which follow immediately upon the introductory or Gathering section.[37]

The Gathering consists of a prelude, greeting (all stand as the "presider greets the community with scripture sentences appropriate to the season and/or the following dialogue: The grace of our Lord Jesus Christ. . . ."), a hymn of praise, "prayer of the day" (seasonal

111

collect), and (optional) invitation to confession, general confession, silent prayer, Kyrie, assurance of pardon and "act of praise" (doxology, hymn, or anthem). The Service of the Word consists of an Old Testament lesson, Psalm, Epistle lesson, hymn/canticle/anthem, Gospel lesson (each "lesson" concluding with an appropriate dialogue), sermon and "responses to the Word" (silence, a creed, hymn, baptism, reaffirmations of faith, testimonies, announcements, gathering of concerns for the "prayers of the people," etc.). Rubrics for the prayers indicate that a "lay member . . . or diaconal minister may lead these prayers" and list appropriate subjects for intercession (the church universal, world, local community, those in need, the departed). The prayers may be in the form of a litany with responses and concluding collect.

The Service of the Table offers two alternatives. The first, for Sundays on which communion is to be celebrated, proceeds from the peace and presentation of gifts to one of seven eucharistic prayers, the Lord's Prayer, fraction, communion, and post-communion prayer.[38] On non-eucharistic Sundays the same format is followed: peace, presentation of gifts, a prayer of thanksgiving (which may be based on the shape of the eucharistic prayer: greeting, Sursum Corda, preface, Sanctus–Benedictus), concluding with the Lord's Prayer. Both options close with the Sending Forth: a hymn, blessing, and dismissal (spoken by a lay leader or diaconal minister). *A Sunday Liturgy* proposed, then, what the *Book of Common Order* and *Service Book* had never been able truly to achieve: a unified service of word and sacrament, the form of which was followed even on non-eucharistic Sundays. Though some congregations were following this order by the end of the 1980s, most retained the *Service Book* Approach-Word-Response pattern for the ordinary Sunday service, inserting one or other of the eucharistic prayers from *A Sunday Liturgy* on communion Sundays.

By the mid-1980s the problem of music resources for United Church worship was becoming acute. Many congregations had printed their own songbooks but there was a growing awareness of the implications of copyright infringement. In 1987 a task group in the British Columbia and Alberta and Northwest Conferences produced a supplement to the *Hymn Book* entitled *Songs for a Gospel People*. The intent was to provide a sampling of four categories of hymnody in preparation for the eventual production of a new hymnary: "heritage" hymns not found in the *Hymn Book*, edited from the standpoint of inclusive language; hymns found in the *Hymn Book* but edited and set to more familiar tunes; a "large selection of songs that have become popular since 1971"; and a small selection of "the best of the new hymnody." A broader genre of service music was introduced and particular attention was paid to "the needs of intergenerational worship." Twenty texts in French were included, along with a selection of hymns in other languages reflecting the cultural diversity of the United Church.[39] The book sold phenomenally well and is at present used, in conjunction with the *Hymn Book*, in a majority of United Church congregations.

By the end of the decade it was generally recognized that the Common Lectionary, the drama and color of the Christian year, inclusive language, a mix of traditional and contemporary hymnody, the participation of "the whole people of God" in worship, and the intimate relationship between worship and mission had become enduring factors in United Church worship. In 1990 the General Council authorized the preparation of a "comprehensive" hymnworship resource. The committee responsible understood this to mean a combined resource which would include liturgies "for Sunday, the Lord's Supper, Baptism and Renewal of Baptismal Faith, Weddings, Funerals and a collection of prayers for congregational use," a selection of approximately six hundred hymns, a selection of service music, and a psalter. The hymns would be both traditional and contemporary, "careful attention" being given to material "suitable for use with children, hymns and songs which express the experience of women, and hymns which acknowledge . . . our francophone, native and ethnic congregations."[40]

In 1993 *Voices United: A Sampler for Congregations* was produced and tested throughout the Church. The *Sampler* included hymns, service music, and five psalm selections demonstrating a variety of styles. The *Sampler* was well received. When the Hymn-Worship Resource Committee presented drafts of liturgical material to the General Council in 1994, however, the Council rejected the concept of combining hymns, service music, psalms, and liturgical material in one resource. It appears, at this point, that two volumes will be produced, the first to include hymns, service music, psalms and occasional prayers, the second to include a range of models for the Sunday service, celebration of the sacraments, weddings, funerals, and daily prayer, combined with educational material.

Conclusion

The question remains: How has worship in the United Church of Canada been influenced by its Methodist heritage? The bias in the *Hymn Book* and *Book of Common Order* was clearly Presbyterian. In part this can be explained by the fact that the process of liturgical reform was considerably more advanced in the pre-union Presbyterian Church than in the Methodist Church, Canada.[41] Of greater significance, however, is the fact that only two-thirds of Canadian Presbyterians entered union. In the first years of its life the United Church was engaged in an acrimonious struggle with the non-concurring Presbyterians over who would be recognized, internationally, as the continuing Presbyterian presence in Canada. It was important that United Church worship patterns at least *appear* to be Presbyterian. The Committee claimed, on the other hand, that the Methodist heritage had been preserved in the affinity of the *Book of Common Order* with the *Book of Common Prayer*. Certainly the wording of a number of the prayers would have been familiar to Canadian Methodists; the chief reason for the Committee's extensive use of the *Book of Common Prayer*, however, was more likely its fervent desire that there would soon be a further church union, this time with the Church of England in Canada.[42]

In the 1930s and 1940s the major concern of former Methodists in the new Church was the lack of gospel hymnody in the 1930 *Hymn Book*. Though a "Gospel Call" section had been included, the hymns in this section amounted to only 6 percent of the total. It was not until the Committee on Church Worship and Ritual was virtually forced to produce *Songs of the Gospel* in 1948 that a significant collection of gospel hymnody was available to United Church congregations.

The central worship controversy during the first decades of the new Church's life was the often furious debate waged between "anti-ritualists" and "ritualists." Occasionally a letter in the Church paper would be signed by a "former Methodist" such as this one commenting on the *Book of Common Order*:

> [F]ew people know there is such a book. I have never yet heard a minister mention it. They know that those who follow John Wesley in his fight for freedom from formality in worship would revolt.[43]

There seems to have been a popular misconception that Methodism, by definition, was anti-liturgical. The evidence suggests, however, that there were as many anti-ritualist former Presbyterians as anti-ritualist former Methodists, and that some former Methodists were in favor of a modest amount of "ritual":

> Born of Methodist stock going back to the time of Wesley . . . I have . . . a warm feeling of approval for the beautiful and fitting liturgy of the Church of England. I cannot say from experience that I would not weary of the repetition, but I do not think so. On the other hand I have had a life-long experience with the "long prayer" . . . and in comparison the ritual has for me a more intimate appeal.[44]

The anti-ritualism/ritualism debate was an expression of the "ordered liberty" tension within United Church worship. In the early years it focused on the dichotomy between formalism and enthusiasm. By the 1960s the focus was shifting to a tension between those with a conservative (i.e., conserving) interest and those who believed that worship must reflect the language and patterns of contemporary culture. The *Service Book* aligned a conservative formalism with a post-enlightenment rationalist approach to language and imagery; those who favored "experimental worship" aligned the libertarian-ism of the 1960s with a similar post-enlightenment approach, albeit with the beginnings of a post-modern stress on the involvement of "the whole person" in worship. Both approaches demonstrated a loss of symbolic consciousness. In an increasingly secular culture, traditional forms and symbols had lost their power: rationalists responded by explaining the symbols away; experimentalists by substituting "contemporary" forms and symbols.

By the 1980s a new tension was emerging in the ordered liberty debate. Those who favored "a new prayer book every Sunday" continued to argue that "we must get our theology straight" or that "worship must be expressed in the language and patterns of contemporary culture." Increasingly, however, there was a movement toward a reclamation of symbolic consciousness (recovery of the Christian year, vestments, a transformed sacramentalism). In 1983 the *Observer* reported:

> With all the ponderous inevitability of a ship coming into harbor, worship is changing in The United Church of Canada. . . .
> "In contrast to 20 years ago, there is a heightened awareness of what worship is," says the Rev. Harold King of Westville, N.S. "These days worship tends to be more liturgical. There is more color and involvement. . . ."
> This new era is different from the '60s and '70s with their

mind-blowing experiments in worship. What is coming into harbor today has the heartfelt support of many lay people. It is a time of radical traditionalism.[45]

This "radical traditionalism" is at the heart of the ecumenical convergence. As Davidson and his colleagues attempted to reappropriate the richness of the tradition for their day, the ecumenical convergence attempts to do so for this day. But more is involved here than simply a recovery of historic forms and symbols. Some have called it a "subversive orthodoxy."[46] In the best tradition of liberative theology, the question is one of a critique of power. Who has control: the individual minister, the local congregation, a national Church committee, the General Council? Or is there something larger to which we are responsible? Given the principle of "ordered liberty," is it possible for *order*, based on the historical/ecumenical tradition, to liberate worship from individual whim and the narrowness of local context? On the other hand, is it possible for the *liberty* of contextualization to free tradition from its natural tendency to rigidity and open it to the fresh winds of the Spirit?

There is a dialectic here between order and liberty, tradition and contextualization, which honors the experience of the past yet remains open to the experience of the future. The United Church of Canada has not solved the ordered liberty debate. It remains committed, however, to living in the tension. As the Committee on Church Worship and Ritual wrote almost seventy years ago:

> In our worship we are rightly concerned for two things: first, that a worshipping congregation of the Lord's people shall be free to follow the leading of the Spirit of Christ in their midst; and second, that the experience of many ages of devotion shall not be lost, but perserved,—experience that has caused certain forms of prayer to glow with light and power.

Chapter 7

Word and Table:
The Process of Liturgical Revision in the
United Methodist Church, 1964–1992

Hoyt L. Hickman

A Complex Ancestry

The complex ancestry of United Methodist worship is clearly seen in our weekly Sunday service, and we must understand that heritage in order to consider how the service has changed since 1964.

In 1784, when North American Methodists were preparing to form the Methodist Episcopal Church, John Wesley sent them an adaptation of the *Book of Common Prayer* (1662) entitled *The Sunday Service of the Methodists in North America*.[1] Among its services were complete texts for Morning Prayer, Evening Prayer, the Litany, and the Lord's Supper. Also included was a simplified calendar of the Church year with a lectionary for Morning Prayer, Evening Prayer, and the Lord's Supper, as well as appointed collects and psalms. Wesley advised ordained elders to administer the Lord's Supper every Lord's Day.[2]

On the other hand, in the letter to the North American Methodists that accompanied his book, Wesley wrote:

> As our American brethren are now totally disentangled both from the State, and from the English Hierarchy, we dare not intangle them again, either with the one or the other. They are now at full liberty, simply to follow the scriptures and the primitive church. And we judge it best that they should stand fast in that liberty, wherewith God has so strangely made them free.[3]

We have struggled with the implications of this mixed message ever since.

In 1792, under Bishop Francis Asbury's leadership, the Methodist Episcopal Church abandoned most of Wesley's resources for Sunday worship, including the texts for Morning and Evening Prayer, the Litany, and the first part of the Lord's Supper (what we now call the service of the word), as well as the calendar and lectionary, collects, and psalms. In their place the *Discipline* directed: "Let the morning-service consist of singing, prayer, the reading of one chapter out of the Old Testament, and another out of the New, and preaching."[4] The text for the latter part of the Lord's Supper (what we now call the service of the table) was retained.[5] This left American Methodists with a flexible, oral Sunday service rather than a fixed text, except when the retained Lord's Supper texts were added following a preaching service.

The Lord's Supper came to be held monthly or quarterly, rather than every Lord's Day, for a combination of reasons whose relative importance scholars still debate. There were in the early years few ordained elders to administer the sacrament, and most congregations had access to the service of an elder only when the presiding elder held quarterly conference. Methodists were also influenced by customs of monthly or quarterly communion in other denominations and by a prevailing enlightenment rationalism that considered the sacraments (as material vehicles or symbols of divine agency) much less important than preaching. Again: tying the Lord's Supper to the reading of a fixed text made it less popular among Methodists because it was uncongenial to their oral culture and was a jarring change of style from their preaching services. Their displeasure might be compounded when, to keep the service from being too long, preaching and other familiar acts of worship were shortened or omitted. Another reason: the heavily penitential texts, particularly when combined with warnings against taking communion unworthily, may have been regarded as oppressive for every Sunday use and considered more suited to an occasional service of penitence and renewal.

During American Methodism's most rapid growth in the early nineteenth century, Sunday services of singing, free prayer, scripture reading, and preaching seemed to fit the needs of Methodists very well. Methodists so contributed to, and were shaped by, the American culture that they became in their own eyes, and often in the eyes of others, the most American of denominations.

American Methodism's success in the early years, however, became its handicap later. As industrialization, immigration, urbanization, and growing sophistication changed the United States, the Methodists tended to remain self-satisfied with their success and be ambivalent about adapting to these changes. In Sunday worship as in other matters, Methodists quarreled among themselves over whether and how to change with the times.

Some Methodist congregations during the nineteenth century—especially its latter half—gradually added elaborate buildings for worship, choirs and organs, trained musicians, more sophisticated hymns and anthems, recitations of the Lord's Prayer and the Apostles' Creed, sung responses such as the Doxology (with the Thomas Ken text) and Gloria Patri, and responsive readings. Late in the century a few churches contracted with printers for service bulletins on special occasions or even for every Sunday. In successive editions of the Methodist *Discipline* during the century, the instructions for Sunday services, and by the end of the century actual outlined orders of worship, followed the pattern set by these congregations. Some proponents of this movement were even attracted by the Order for Morning Prayer in Wesley's *Sunday Service.*[6]

American Methodists had never entirely forgotten the great festivals of the Christian year; during the nineteenth century they gave increasing emphasis to such days as Easter, Christmas, and Palm Sunday. Growing commercial promotion of mass-produced goods for Christmas gifts and Easter wear found a ready response among many newly affluent Methodists.[7]

Many Methodists resisted these developments. Numerous congregations adhered to the old ways or adapted their services in a different direction; one example is the use of a revivalistic pattern where the sermon was preceded by a song service featuring music based on popular or folk musical styles. In congregations where services were becoming more elaborate and formal, some persons found such worship unsatisfying and worshiped less formally but with more satisfaction in Sunday school assemblies, Sunday evening services, midweek services, and revival meetings. Controversies often pitted pastors against musicians, and either or both of these leaders against many in their congregations. Resulting compromises often produced Sunday services about which everyone had mixed feelings and no one was enthusiastic.

These developments continued through the early and middle twentieth century. The 1905, 1935, and 1966 revisions of the *Methodist*

119

Hymnal contained more and more sophisticated hymns and orders of worship that looked increasingly like adaptations of Anglican Morning Prayer followed by a sermon. The 1935 and 1966 hymnals added, as an alternative to the shorter Lord's Supper text basically used since 1792, a fuller text adapted from Wesley's *Sunday Service* that included a service of the word as well as of the table. Books of worship published in 1945 and 1965, as well as the 1966 hymnal, contained resources for the days and seasons of the Church year, including a lectionary. Buildings were increasingly constructed or remodeled with divided chancels, usually more for reasons of aesthetics and fashion than for theological or functional reasons; but the resulting effect was to make worship more formal.

Resistance to such trends continued. Many congregations refused to use the official hymnal and instead used commercial hymnals featuring popular gospel songs and choruses. Even the denominational publishing house found it advisable to publish such songbooks as the *Cokesbury Worship Hymnal*,[8] used by many congregations for the Sunday service and by many others for Sunday school, evening, or midweek worship. Mimeographed or printed bulletins came into more general use, making available orders of worship and texts better adapted to local preferences and specific occasions than those found in the official hymnal or book of worship. While many pastors used the 1945 and 1965 worship books as a resource, attempts to get Methodists to use a book of worship in the pews utterly failed.

Nevertheless, when the 1964 General Conference adopted the *Hymnal* (1966) and *Book of Worship* (1965), there was general complacency about Sunday worship. Changes in the nineteenth and twentieth centuries had been gradual, the new books represented a fine tuning rather than a rethinking of tradition, Methodists who preferred less formal worship were settled into their own traditions, and diversity and discontents seemed manageable.

The Calls for Reform

Underlying the process of worship reform between 1964 and 1992 was a series of developments that challenged the old assumptions.

Methodists, long identified so closely with American ways, felt keenly the culture shocks rocking American society—new styles and fresh creativity in both secular and Christian music; increased ethnic consciousness and pride; awareness of racism, sexism, and other forms of discrimination; changes in the English language; technological developments that were radically changing American culture as well as opening up new worship possibilities; and an increasing proportion of the population whose cultural assumptions did not match those underlying traditional worship.

Second, Methodists became aware of great changes taking place ecumenically and liturgically. These included the radical reform of Roman Catholic worship after the Second Vatican Council, the liturgical reforms in other Protestant and Anglican denominations, the movement of evangelical and charismatic congregations from traditional to contemporary styles of informal worship, a new vigor in ethnic worship, and an explosion of Christian musical creativity in many styles.

Third, the 1968 union of the Methodist Church and the Evangelical United Brethren Church into the United Methodist Church was a watershed event, liturgically as well as otherwise. The Evangelical United Brethren Sunday service had a tradition similar to that of the Methodists but with distinctive features that now became part of a common heritage. The Evangelical United Brethren *Hymnal* (1957) and official Ritual (last revised in 1963) were extensively drawn upon in worship revision after 1968. The United Methodist Church was a new denomination that needed its own *United Methodist* hymnal and liturgy, building upon two heritages but boldly going beyond both.

Fourth, by 1968 there was already widespread dissatisfaction with the official hymnals and liturgies of both former denominations. New as these were, they were already perceived as out of date. Even congregations with a history of loyalty to an official hymnal were heavily supplementing it with contemporary music and acts of worship, drawn from diverse sources or composed locally.

Fifth, both United Methodist and ecumenical scholars pointed out that United Methodist Sunday services did not incorporate the results of recent scholarship and that gradual liturgical changes in the nineteenth and twentieth centuries had compromised the Wesleyan heritage as well. The use of Scripture in Sunday services had sadly declined from what had been prescribed by Wesley or early American Methodists. Preaching was commonly disconnected from Scripture. Eucharistic theology was eroded by rationalism, and the Lord's Supper was celebrated infrequently.

121

The profound rethinking of worship that was needed could not be done quickly. Recognizing that the relatively new Methodist and Evangelical United Brethren hymnals and worship books could not be replaced in the near future, the first United Methodist General Conference in 1968 reaffirmed the official status of these books and gave the task of working toward a new hymnal and worship book to a Commission on Worship.[9] The Commission, which in 1972 was incorporated into the General Board of Discipleship, developed a long-range plan involving the widest possible research, survey, consultation, and trial use. This plan took twenty-four years to carry out and resulted in the *United Methodist Hymnal* (1989) and the *United Methodist Book of Worship* (1992).[10]

The first step was to learn what was happening in local congregations and what they wanted to enable and shape their worship. Several findings emerged.

Many United Methodists wished to continue using the Sunday service resources in the official hymnals and worship books. There was general agreement that these should be supplemented, not replaced. In the years that followed, even after new worship resources had been enthusiastically adopted by many United Methodists, it was still evident that certain beloved traditional texts should be retained as options in the *Hymnal* (1989) and *Book of Worship* (1992). One example is A Service of Word and Table IV, in which traditional Methodist and Evangelical United Brethren communion texts have been retained in a form adapted for present-day use.[11]

Numerous United Methodists also prized their freedom to be creative, wished to follow local or ethnic customs, and wanted resources that opened up to them creativity and cultural diversity from outside their own congregations. These desires profoundly shaped the liturgical revision process and the resulting Sunday service resources, including the introduction of recently written and ethnically based hymns in the *Hymnal*.

A large and growing segment of United Methodists also wanted carefully developed worship resources. Many were aware that other Christian denominations were experiencing worship renewal and that their liturgies were converging toward common patterns that reflected increased knowledge of biblical and early Church worship as well as sensitivity to the needs of Christians in the late twentieth century. Many United Methodists challenged their denomination to develop resources reflecting this ecumenical Christian renewal, while at the same time maintaining a connection with the United Methodist heritage and the ideal of liturgical freedom. This challenge was accepted, and a process was begun to develop such resources.

A New Text for the Lord's Supper

The first fruits of this process was a new text for the Lord's Supper in which an entire order of service, uniting word and table, was set forth. It was introduced as the opening service of holy communion at the 1972 General Conference, and after an extremely favorable reception there it went on during the next eight years to sell more than two million copies, though the text itself was "unofficial" for the denomination. In 1980 a revised edition appeared which was also widely used. A further revision in 1984 was officially adopted by the General Conference and is substantially what appears in the *Hymnal* (1989) and *Book of Worship* (1992) as A Service of Word and Table I.[12]

The successive revisions of the United Methodist text were similar to the new eucharistic texts being adopted by other Christian denominations, just as the former Methodist and Evangelical United Brethren texts were similar to the older eucharistic texts of other denominations. The language was modern rather than archaic, Cranmerian English. The traditional pattern of a service of the word followed by a service of the table was recovered. The service of the table was simplified into a fourfold pattern of taking, blessing, breaking, and giving the bread and cup, following the fourfold shape of the liturgy recognized by the English Benedictine Gregory Dix.

The corporate dimension of the celebration is more evident within the new texts. Communion (*koinonia*) is not only with God in Christ but also with one another, since the Lord's Supper is the family meal of Christians. The leader and people greet one another as an opening act of worship and, according to the textual revision of 1980, the gathering of the people prior to the formal greeting is also seen as a part of the worship. The worshiping community as a whole is invited to lift praise and petition in prayer. Not only individual sins but the corporate sins of the Church are confessed. In the spirit of Matthew 5:23-24, the peace of Christ is exchanged with one another immediately before the offering. Beginning with the 1975 printing, language was revised to be inclusive of women as well as men.

The joyful tone of the new service, emphasizing praise and

thanksgiving, contrasts with the heavily penitential tone of the older services. Multiple confessions of sin and unworthiness are shortened to a single invitation-confession-pardon sequence, which by 1984 is followed by the peace and offering to make a five-step process that leads naturally to thanksgiving and communion. The Lord's Supper is to be *celebrated*.

Underlying this change of tone is a more comprehensive theology, best understood by studying the thanksgiving (blessing) over the bread and cup, which by 1980 is called the Great Thanksgiving. The 1972, 1980, and 1984 editions of this text are printed at the end of this chapter. This Great Thanksgiving, like recent prayers of great thanksgiving in other denominations, restores the unity of what in the early Church had been a single prayer but in later centuries became fragmented into several separate prayers.

The post-1972 texts follow the ancient three-part West Syrian structure typical of modern great thanksgiving prayers in other denominations. This pattern was adopted partly for ecumenical reasons and because of its great antiquity but principally because in present-day United Methodism, where trinitarian doctrine is poorly understood and under attack, such a structure is ideally suited to express a strong and balanced trinitarian theology. The prayer addresses God the Father, and its first part to the Sanctus ("Holy, holy, holy Lord") gives thanks for creation and the covenant with Israel. In the second part "we offer ourselves in praise and thanksgiving" for redemption through Christ and the new covenant. The third part invokes the Holy Spirit to rest and work upon the people gathered and upon the elements, petitions the Holy Spirit for sanctification, and looks forward to the consummation of all things. To clarify this structure, the acclamation "Christ has died, Christ is risen, Christ will come again" was moved in 1984 to become the transition from the second to the third part.

This joyous celebration of all God's mighty acts of salvation contrasts with the preoccupation with Jesus' death that gave previous communion texts a somber tone. By 1984 the text speaks of Jesus' death not as a separate event but as part of his passage through suffering and death to resurrection:

> By the baptism of his suffering, death, and resurrection, you gave birth to your Church, delivered us from slavery to sin and death, and made with us a new covenant by water and the Spirit.

124

The biblical feminine imagery of the God who "gave birth" and "delivered" complements the address to "Father."

The whole service places increased emphasis on the Holy Spirit. Developments ranging from biblical and historical scholarship to the charismatic renewal movement showed that the Holy Spirit plays a greater role than was expressed in previous Protestant and Roman Catholic liturgies. It is in the power and unity of the Holy Spirit that the Lord's Supper is a remembrance (anamnesis) of the past, a resurrection meal with the living Christ, and a foretaste of the heavenly banquet. Restoring the invocation of the Holy Spirit to the place in the great thanksgiving that it had in the early Church, and which it never lost in the eucharistic prayers of Eastern Orthodoxy, represents a major advance in eucharistic theology.

Theological distinctions and emphases were nuanced as the revision process went on. The 1972 petition, "Help us to know in the breaking of this bread and the drinking of this wine the presence of Christ who gave his body and blood for mankind," became in 1984: "Make [these gifts of bread and wine] be for us the body and blood of Christ, that we may be for the world the body of Christ, redeemed by his blood."[13] The 1972 petition for unity read: "Make us one with Christ, one with each other, and one in service to all mankind." In 1975 "mankind" became "the world," not only to be gender-inclusive but also from an ecological concern for the whole world rather than simply human beings. In 1984 "service" became "ministry," to include both justice and service ministries.

There are other expressions of social concern, in the Great Thanksgiving and elsewhere, that were missing in older Lord's Supper texts. Older texts said nothing about Jesus' ministry prior to his passion, but the 1972 text gives thanks that he "healed and taught" and "ate with sinners." The 1984 text, drawn in part from Jesus' own statement of his mission in Luke 4:18-19, declares:

> Your Spirit anointed him to preach good news to the poor, to proclaim release to the captives and recovering of sight to the blind, to set at liberty those who are oppressed, and to announce that the time had come when you would save your people. He healed the sick, fed the hungry, and ate with sinners.

Elsewhere in the service the prayer of confession, the litany for others (1972) and its equivalent in the *Book of Worship* (1992, #495), and the prayer after receiving communion all acknowledge a Christian mandate to social ministry.

In 1984, parts of the Great Thanksgiving were rewritten in response to complaints that its language had departed too far from prayerbook English and was too brusque. The first sentence with its abrupt "Father," for instance, was replaced by a sentence from the Episcopal *Book of Common Prayer* of 1979 ("It is right, and a good and joyful thing. . . .").

A New Structure for Sunday Worship: Word and Table

After the 1972 "alternate text" for the Lord's Supper, the next step in the process was the production of the book *Word and Table* that appeared in 1976 proposing a new structure for Sunday worship as a whole. This underwent a first revision in 1980, and was then further revised in a form officially adopted by the 1984 General Conference.[14]

The book begins with "A Basic Pattern of Worship," which after the 1980 and 1984 revisions appears as "The Basic Pattern of Worship" in the *Hymnal* (1989, p. 2) and *Book of Worship* (1992, p. 15), where it is basic for all orders of service including the rites for marriage and funeral. The Basic Pattern has the following shape:

ENTRANCE

The people come together in the Lord's name. There may be greetings, music and song, prayer and praise.

PROCLAMATION AND PRAISE

The Scriptures are opened to the people through the reading of lessons, preaching, witnessing, music, or other arts and media. Interspersed may be psalms, anthems, and hymns. Responses to God's Word include acts of commitment and faith with offerings of concerns, prayers, gifts, and service for the world and for one another.

THANKSGIVING AND COMMUNION

In services with Communion, the actions of Jesus in the Upper Room are reenacted:
    taking the bread and cup
    giving thanks over the bread and cup,
    breaking the bread, and
    giving the bread and cup.

SENDING FORTH

The people are sent into ministry with the Lord's blessing.

The order may be seen as an updating of the flexible Sunday service instructions found in the Methodist *Discipline* from 1792 to the late nineteenth century, and this flexibility extends to the Lord's Supper. Pastors and congregations are not bound to a fixed text for the service of the table but may celebrate in an oral style or with locally composed texts. The fourfold pattern of taking, blessing, breaking, and giving the bread and cup is made explicit.

Orders of worship following this basic pattern, both with and without the Lord's Supper, are found in Chapter 1 of *Word and Table*. Together with the basic pattern itself, they make it clear that the full service of word and table is normative for Sunday worship, though they recognize that most United Methodist congregations do not celebrate the Lord's Supper every Lord's Day as Wesley advised. When there is only a service of the word, it is implied that there ought to be a yearning for its completion at the Lord's Table.

These orders, which evolved through 1980 and 1984 revisions to "An Order of Sunday Worship Using the Basic Pattern" in the *Hymnal* (1989, pp. 3–5) and *Book of Worship* (1992, pp. 16–32), represent a rethinking of the whole concept of orders of worship as they had appeared in Methodist official books for the past century. "An Order" (note the indefinite article) shows some of the variety possible within the Basic Pattern and is a guide for those who plan, not an order for the congregation to follow. It is assumed that a congregation's worship service, planned according to its needs, will be ordered by a bulletin or by announcement.

Chapter 2 of *Word and Table* is an introduction with a biblical, historical, theological, and practical rationale for the pattern, and Chapter 3 is a commentary on each item in the orders of worship. These chapters were revised in 1980 and 1988.[15] Much of their content appears in pages 13–32 of the *Book of Worship* (1992).

Chapter 4, "The Great Thanksgiving: Its Essential Elements," is a guide for pastors who compose their own great thanksgivings. It was revised in 1981 and reprinted in 1987 as part of two other books.[16] A further revision of this guide is scheduled to appear.

Included in Chapter 5 are an ecumenical calendar for the Christian year and lectionary, adapted by the Consultation on Church Union (COCU) from the calendar and three-year lectionary developed by the Roman Catholics, Episcopalians, Lutherans, and Presbyterians. The calendar and one-year lectionary in the *Book of Worship* (1965) and *Hymnal* (1966) were out of harmony with ecumenical usage, and the lectionary was rarely used. There was already widespread United Methodist interest in using some version of the new ecumenical lectionary as an alternative. As will be discussed below, this proved to be an idea whose time had come.

The ecumenical texts offered in Chapter 6 had been translated from the original Greek or Latin by the International Consultation on English Texts (ICET), and included the Lord's Prayer, the Apostles' and Nicene creeds, and the opening dialogue and Sanctus in the great thanksgiving. Later these were revised by ICET's successor, the English Language Liturgical Commission (ELLC). When they appeared in the 1980 and 1984 revisions of the Lord's Supper service and in the *Hymnal* and *Book of Worship* they were revised in the light of these ecumenical developments.

New Resources for the Christian Year

From 1979 to 1986 a series of books was published with resources for the observance of the Christian year.[17] Their contents, in revised form, are found in the *Book of Worship* and in the *New Handbook of the Christian Year.*[18]

These resources are based on the ecumenical calendar and lectionary, which continued to evolve after 1976. The Consultation on Common Texts (CCT), with members from the major North American Protestant denominations and the Anglican and Roman Catholic Churches, took over from COCU the task of developing an ecumenical calendar and lectionary, and in 1982 offered a Common Lectionary for a period of trial use. The United Methodist Church formally advocated its usage in 1985. The development of a definitive lectionary was then done by CCT in cooperation with the worldwide ecumenical English Language Liturgical Commission (ELLC), which completed the Revised Common Lectionary just in time for it to be included in the *Book of Worship* (pp. 224–37).[19]

The acceptance and employment of this lectionary has been extraordinary, with most United Methodist pastors reporting that they use it at least some of the time. Because of general biblical illiteracy, the Church needs more reading and preaching of the Bible in worship. A lectionary is a tool for helping a congregation over time to hear the whole story and teaching of the Bible. While there are other ways to accomplish this end, there are great practical advantages in using a lectionary. The existence of an ecumenical lectionary has prompted numerous writers and publishers to produce a wealth of homiletical, liturgical, and musical resources keyed to lectionary usage. The revitalization of the service of the word was seen as a priority in United Methodist liturgical renewal, and the calendar and lectionary have proved crucial to that end.

Rejuvenation of the service of the table is more difficult, given generations of neglect, but here the Christian year is also crucial. A single inflexible text such as A Service of Word and Table I is well suited for occasional use, but for frequent or even weekly use there needs to be provision for more variety. Some pastors can accomplish this by taking advantage of the freedom to compose their own printed or oral liturgies; but this may be difficult, especially in the case of the great thanksgiving.

While the need for seasonal or occasional variation in the great thanksgiving has usually been met by providing "proper prefaces" prior to the Sanctus, United Methodists chose instead to produce entire great thanksgiving prayers that focus upon the day, the season, or the occasion.[20] Once it was determined that the first part of the great thanksgiving should deal with creation and the covenant with Israel, it became evident that some, but not all, seasonal variations are appropriate in that location. Seasonal emphases relating to Christ and redemption are more appropriate to the second part of the prayer. And in keeping with the trinitarian shape of the prayer, seasonal petitions relating to the Holy Spirit, sanctification, and the Christian hope are more appropriate to the last part of the prayer. The seasonal great thanksgivings in the *Book of Worship* (1992, pp. 54–77) provide variety in appropriate parts of each prayer while including an invariable core text for continuity. Services of Word and Table II and III in the *Hymnal* (1989, pp. 12–16) facilitate the use of these seasonal great thanksgivings as well as other great thanksgivings which the pastor may discover or create.

The resource books for the Christian year in the Supplemental Worship Resource (SWR) series also included introductory information about the days and seasons of the Christian year, seasonal acts of worship for every part of the service, and whole special services for days like Ash Wednesday, Passion/Palm Sunday, Holy Thursday, Good Friday, and the Easter Vigil. The acts of worship and entire orders of service were revised after trial use and included in the *Book of Worship* (1992, #238–#431).

Toward Multicultural Resources

Another group of publications reflected the fact that United Methodists in the United States represent many ethnic groups and speak many languages. The 1976 General Conference directed that supplemental hymn and song books for worship be produced with special attention to ethnic diversity, and this was done.[21] There was full freedom to use resources native to each culture, without obligation to translate or adapt resources published in English. Sunday service resources, influenced by what was being done in English but reflecting distinctive cultural heritages, appeared in languages such as Korean and Japanese.[22]

Spanish language resources for Sunday were developed by a process parallel to that used for English language services. After several supplemental resources had been published and given trial use, Sunday services in Spanish as well as English were submitted to the 1984 General Conference and there were made equally part of the official Ritual of the Church.[23]

The *Hymnal* (1989) and *Book of Worship* (1992) were in turn greatly enriched by ethnic resources. Both books allow for the possible use of texts in a language other than English. This signifies that we are joining in worship not only with congregations of a diverse denomination but with the Church of all times and all places. It suggests that the native language of the Christian community is the language of Pentecost, the day the Church was born: all languages mutually understood.

Inclusive Resources for a Diverse Denomination

Congregations now have in the pews the *Hymnal*, and those who plan and lead worship also have the *Book of Worship*. What do these books say to United Methodists, both those who have in diverse ways been calling for reform and those who are relatively satisfied with existing resources and traditions?

The services produced after 1972 represent an earnest attempt to combine authenticity with relevance, orthodoxy with inclusiveness, while being faithful to Scripture, to the teachings held in common by the ecumenical Church, and to both the Methodist and Evangelical United Brethren branches of our Wesleyan heritage. In an attempt to enrich and expand, but not replace, our distinct Wesleyan heritage, participation in the process of worship resource development came from all the diverse factions within the denomination and from United Methodist and non-United Methodist liturgical scholars. Biblical and Wesleyan orthodoxy was considered a living, growing tradition, not a static system. By affirming liturgical freedom and local creativity, it was acknowledged that no official book can meet all the needs of every congregation, and that during the lifetime of these books the denomination and its congregations will develop in unforeseen ways.

As the English language itself is changing, language issues were especially challenging. Beloved texts in archaic English have been retained, together with new texts in modern praise and prayer language. Books by their very nature cannot supply language for worship in an oral style, but the *Hymnal* and *Book of Worship* repeatedly affirm oral worship styles as legitimate options for United Methodists. Strenuous efforts have been made to use language that is inclusive and non-discriminatory.

Language for God was a highly controversial issue. Scriptural terms such as Father and Lord have been strongly reaffirmed, while a wide variety of inclusive and feminine images for God—found in Scripture or harmonious with Scripture—has also been included and affirmed as legitimate for United Methodists.

How successful the *Hymnal* and *Book of Worship* have been in all this should be judged, not by reference to any single service, but by examining all their Sunday service resources. These include the Sunday service options indicated by introductions, commentary, and rubrics as well as texts; the hymns and service music; the general acts of worship; and the lectionary, psalter, and whole range of resources for the Christian year.

Liturgical and Theological Foundations for a New Day

As we move into a new millennium, the new Sunday service resources embody a series of assumptions significantly different from those made in the recent past.

The Sunday service, when holy communion is not celebrated, is treated as a service of the word. This is considered a more faithful and fruitful interpretation, both of Wesley's *Sunday Service* and of our preaching service heritage as outlined in books of *Discipline* beginning in 1792, than was the attempt during the past century or so to

131

develop the Sunday service into an adaptation of Anglican Morning Prayer and sermon. On the one hand, morning prayer is recognized as a service in its own right and made part of a revived "Orders of Daily Praise and Prayer"[24] rather than being made, in awkward combination and tension with preaching, the main Sunday service. On the other hand, a service of the word is a unity that makes clear the integral importance of Scripture and preaching, with Entrance leading naturally to Proclamation, closely connecting Scripture and sermon to encourage biblical preaching and thereby strengthen the sermon. The Entrance—with "greetings, music and song, prayer and praise"[25]—can be brief or elaborate, formal or informal, and can be anything from an opening song service to Anglican-style liturgy.

The Lord's Supper is the completion of a unified service of word and table. It is neither an add-on to the Sunday service nor a service whose pattern from beginning to end is different from other Sunday services. Preaching is not to be deemphasized and remains crucial when holy communion follows. Word and table are not like the ends of a seesaw, where as one end goes up the other goes down; on the contrary, they strengthen each other.

In these Sunday service resources there is a fuller and more balanced trinitarian theology, celebrating not only redemption but also creation, sanctification, and eschatology. The work of the Holy Spirit in particular receives increased recognition.

The fuller eucharistic theology expressed in the great thanksgiving and its seasonal variations can help congregations see how fitting the Lord's Supper is every Lord's Day, as Wesley so clearly saw. A sermon proclaiming any aspect of the Gospel to a Christian congregation on any Sunday of the Christian year can appropriately lead into holy communion. Rather than exhorting pastors and congregations to more frequent communion, the new eucharistic resources help pastors so to celebrate holy communion that congregations will want communion more often.

Using these resources and this expanded liturgical freedom will not in itself bring renewal to the United Methodist Church or any of its congregations; only God can do that. But if faithful planners and leaders of worship use and interpret the resources with discernment and wisdom—and if congregations worship with openness, expecting great things from God—channels might be unclogged for new inrushings of the Spirit. Congregations, even the United Methodist Church, might experience a new Pentecost.

The Great Thanksgiving

1972 Text	1980 Text	1984 Text
The Lord is with you.	The Lord be with you.	The Lord be with you.
And with you also.	**And also with you.**	**And also with you.**
Lift up your hearts.	Lift up your hearts.	Lift up your hearts.
We lift them up to the Lord.	**We lift them to the Lord.**	**We lift them to the Lord.**
Let us give thanks to the Lord our God.	Let us give thanks to the Lord our God.	Let us give thanks to the Lord our God.
It is right to give him thanks and praise.	**It is right to give him thanks and praise.**	**It is right to give our thanks and praise.**
Father, it is right that we should always and everywhere give you thanks and praise. Only you are God. You created all things and called them good.	Father, it is right that we should always and everywhere give you thanks and praise. Only you are God. You created all things and called them good.	It is right, and a good and joyful thing, always and everywhere to give thanks to you, Father Almighty, creator of heaven and earth.
You made us in your own image.	You made us in your own image.	You formed us in your image and breathed into us the breath of life.
Even when we rebelled against your love, you did not desert us.	Even when we rebelled against your love, you did not desert us.	When we turned away, and our love failed, your love remained steadfast.
You delivered us from captivity, made covenant to be our God and King, and spoke to us through your prophets.	You delivered us from captivity, made covenant to be our Sovereign God, and spoke to us through your prophets.	You delivered us from captivity, made covenant to be our sovereign God, and spoke to us through your prophets.
Therefore, we join the entire company of heaven and all your people now on earth in worshiping and glorifying you:	Therefore, we join the entire company of heaven and all your people now on earth in worshiping and glorifying you:	And so, with your people on earth and all the company of heaven we praise your name and join their unending hymn:
Holy, holy, holy Lord, God of power and might, heaven and earth are full of your glory. Hosanna in the highest. Blessed is he who comes in the name of the Lord. Hosanna in the highest.	**Holy, holy, holy Lord, God of power and might, heaven and earth are full of your glory. Hosanna in the highest. Blessed is he who comes in the name of the Lord. Hosanna in the highest.**	**Holy, holy, holy Lord, God of power and might, heaven and earth are full of your glory. Hosanna in the highest. Blessed is he who comes in the name of the Lord. Hosanna in the highest.**
We thank you, Father, that you loved the world so much you sent your only Son to be our Savior.	We thank you, holy Lord God, that you loved the world so much you sent your only Son to be our Savior.	Holy are you, and blessed is your Son Jesus Christ.

1972 Text	1980 Text	1984 Text
The Lord of all life came to live among us. He healed and taught men*, ate with sinners, and won for you a new people by water and the Spirit. We saw his glory.	The Lord of all life came to live among us. He healed and taught, ate with sinners, and won for you a new people by water and the Spirit. We saw his glory.	Your Spirit anointed him to preach good news to the poor, to proclaim release to the captives and recovering of sight to the blind, to set at liberty those who are oppressed, and to announce that the time had come when you would save your people. He healed the sick, fed the hungry, and ate with sinners.
*"Men" omitted in the 1975 printing.		
Yet he humbled himself in obedience to your will, freely accepting death on a cross. By dying, he freed us from unending death; by rising from the dead, he gave us everlasting life.	Yet he humbled himself in obedience to your will, freely accepting death on a cross. By dying, he freed us from unending death; by rising from the dead, he gave us everlasting life.	By the baptism of his suffering, death, and resurrection, you gave birth to your Church, delivered us from slavery to sin and death, and made with us a new covenant by water and the Spirit. When the Lord Jesus ascended, he promised to be with us always, in the power of your Word and Holy Spirit.
On the night in which he gave himself up for us, the Lord Jesus took bread. After giving you thanks, he broke the bread, gave it to his disciples, and said: Take, eat; this is my body which is given for you.	On the night in which he gave himself up for us, the Lord Jesus took bread. After giving you thanks, he broke the bread, gave it to his disciples, and said: Take, eat; this is my body which is given for you.	On the night in which he gave himself up for us he took bread, gave thanks to you, broke the bread, gave it to his disciples, and said: "Take, eat; this is my body which is given for you. Do this in remembrance of me."
When the supper was over, he took the cup. Again he returned thanks to you, gave the cup to his disciples, and said: Drink from this, all of you, this is the cup of the new covenant in my blood, poured out for you and many, for the forgiveness of sins.	When the supper was over, he took the cup. Again he returned thanks to you, gave the cup to his disciples, and said: Drink from this, all of you, this is the cup of the new covenant in my blood, poured out for you and many, for the forgiveness of sins.	When the supper was over he took the cup, gave thanks to you, gave it to his disciples, and said: "Drink from this, all of you; this is my blood of the new covenant, poured out for you and for many for the forgiveness of sins.
When we eat this bread and drink this cup, we experience anew the presence of the Lord Jesus Christ and look forward to his coming in final victory.	When we eat this bread and drink this cup, we experience anew the presence of the Lord Jesus Christ and look forward to his coming in final victory.	Do this, as often as you drink it, in remembrance of me."
		And so, in remembrance of these your mighty acts in Jesus Christ, we offer our-

134

1972 Text	1980 Text	1984 Text
		selves in praise and thanksgiving as a holy and living sacrifice, in union with Christ's offering for us, as we proclaim the mystery of faith.
Christ has died, Christ is risen, Christ will come again.	**Christ has died, Christ is risen, Christ will come again.**	**Christ has died, Christ is risen, Christ will come again.**
We remember and proclaim, Heavenly Father, what your Son has done for us in his life and death, in his resurrection and ascension. Accept our sacrifice of praise and thanksgiving, in union with Christ's offering for us, as a reasonable and holy surrender of ourselves.	We experience anew, most merciful God, the suffering and death, the resurrection and ascension of your Son, asking you to accept this our sacrifice of praise and thanksgiving, which we offer in union with Christ's offering for us, as a living and holy surrender of ourselves.	
Send the power of your Holy Spirit on us, gathered here out of love for you, and on these gifts.	Send the power of your Holy Spirit on us, gathered here out of love for you, and on these gifts.	Pour out your Holy Spirit on us, gathered here, and on these gifts of bread and wine.
Help us to know in the breaking of this bread and the drinking of this wine the presence of Christ who gave his body and blood for mankind.*	May the Spirit help us know in the breaking of this bread and drinking of this wine the presence of Christ who gave his body and blood for all.	Make them be for us the body and blood of Christ, that we may be for the world the body of Christ, redeemed by his blood.
* "Mankind" changed to "all" in the 1975 printing.		
Make us one with Christ, one with each other, and one in service to all mankind*.	And may the Spirit make us one with Christ, one with each other, and one in service to all the world.	By your Spirit make us one with Christ, one with each other, and one in ministry to all the world, until Christ comes in final victory and we feast at his heavenly banquet.
*"Mankind" changed to "the world" in the 1975 printing.		
Through your Son Jesus Christ, with the Holy Spirit in your Holy Church, all glory and honor is yours, Father. Amen.	Through your Son Jesus Christ with the Holy Spirit in your holy Church, all glory and honor is yours, Almighty Father, now and for ever. **Amen.**	Through your Son Jesus Christ, with the Holy Spirit in your holy Church, all honor and glory is yours, almighty Father, now and for ever. **Amen.**

Chapter 8

Divine Grace, Diverse Means: Sunday Worship in United Methodist Congregations

Don E. Saliers

Midway through the final decade of the twentieth century, questions about theological substance and liturgical style are playing a significant role in debates about the character and mission of the United Methodist Church. The past twenty-five years have witnessed remarkable changes in how local congregations worship. Many voices, reflecting the ever-widening diversity within the North American Churches, have joined the conversation about what makes Christian worship authentic, true, and relevant. Responding to the current discussion of the tension between "traditional" and "contemporary" styles, one lay person puts sharply the issue of relevance and identity: "We have become so pluralistic, both in worship styles and theology, that visits to several United Methodist churches in a given area is like visiting churches of different denominations."[1] Yet, as this essay will demonstrate, questions of unity and variety, and of whether there is something distinctive about United Methodist worship, are not new.

There is something richly diverse yet elusive about the worship life of present-day United Methodist congregations. If we were to visit a random sampling of ten local churches on any given Sunday morning, we would more than likely find a half-dozen different styles, and perhaps three or four different orders of worship. In part, this diversity would be a function of geographical and sociological factors. The typical "feel" of a suburban white congregation at worship is quite distinct from that of a mixed ethnic inner city or an African American congregation, even if the orders of worship are similar. Sunday morning in a rural church in south Georgia would be closer in many respects to a neighboring Baptist congregation than it might be to a rural church in South Dakota, surrounded by Lutherans. A congregation served by a multiple staff will have a distinctive "professional" feel in comparison with a neighboring United Methodist congregation where most of the leadership is supplied by lay volunteers. All of these contrasts are part of the religious landscape of North American Protestantism. This is simply to observe that Christian worship is always culturally embedded and embodied, although the theological and liturgical implications of this have come only recently to general awareness.

But such contrasts are not the only factors at work in the wide diversity of United Methodist worship practices. Of crucial importance are three other factors: the freedom of the pastor to shape and direct worship, the continuing influence of certain dominant patterns from various periods in Protestant worship in America, and the late twentieth-century ecumenical cross-influences and convergences. The varied character of Sunday worship among United Methodists also reflects the fact that Methodism is still, despite its predominantly middle-class membership, the most "representative" American mainstream denomination, exhibiting a wide spectrum of social and cultural groupings and regional diversity. Eighteenth-century North American Methodists inherited a mixed tradition from the very outset; subsequently there has always been a strong proclivity toward liturgical pragmatism.

This essay will explore the patterns and characteristic features of Sunday morning worship in light of the particular historical and contextual factors which bear upon contemporary practice and theology. After examining some of the formative historical factors, I will focus on the social and cultural ethos which shapes United Methodist worship today, including the twentieth-century liturgical reforms. In particular, attention will be given to the ways in which the *United Methodist Hymnal* (1989) and the *United Methodist Book of Worship* (1992) are now resourcing and reshaping future directions of Sunday worship. Finally, some implications and proposals will point in the direction of a United Methodist theology of worship.

Historical Touchstones to the Character of Methodist Worship

From the beginnings of Methodism in the American colonies, geography, social and economic conditions, and political persuasions all played important roles in shaping both the patterns and the ethos of Sunday worship. The cool reception given to John Wesley's original attempt to supply a form of Sunday worship was the initial signal of the surprising history to follow. In 1784 he sent from England the *Sunday Service of the Methodists in North America with other Occasional Services.*[2] But the pattern for Sunday morning itself—Morning Prayer and an "Order for the Administration of the Lord's Supper" which included a sermon in the ante-communion—did not take hold in the hearts, minds, and bodies of Methodists in America, in part because of its character as a revision of the Church of England's *Book of Common Prayer* of 1662. For a brief while in the cities of the eastern seaboard such as Baltimore, Philadelphia, and Charleston, Wesley's intention survived, but by 1792, the year following Wesley's death, the *Sunday Service* as a worship book for regular Sunday mornings was set aside.

In his *Christian Worship in Transition*, James White speaks of early English Methodist worship as "combining a formal eucharistic life with the informality of field preaching, joyful hymnody, and extempore prayer. In many ways it was a blend of Anglican and Free Church traditions seasoned with a strong dose of pragmatism."[3] In that brief characterization he captures something of the uneasy tensions which have marked the path of Methodist worship in the United States. John and Charles Wesley's theological and spiritual grounding in the 1662 Prayer Book, and the treasury of Charles' eucharistic hymnody, did not transfer into the emerging American nineteenth century; but the informal, enthusiastic side of the Methodist movement flourished. The pattern of Wesley's "Sunday service" was set aside, although the "occasional services" that were included in the book of 1784 survived in variously modified forms. These came to be printed, not in the people's hymnals or in a separate worship book, but in the preachers' *Discipline* throughout the nineteenth century. Thus rites for baptism of infants and adults, holy communion, weddings, funerals, and ordination were preserved, to which were eventually added services for dedicating a church building and for receiving persons into church membership.

White provides a brief overview of four different "cultural eras" between the 1870s and 1975 which have shaped the patterns and ethos of four distinct periods in Protestant worship. As we shall see, various strands of Methodism have been, and still are, deeply influenced by one or more of these eras. The first period, spanning fifty years, reflects nineteenth-century revivalism. The second and third periods belong to what he calls the "era of respectability": a concern for aesthetic enhancement of worship stretched from the second decade of the twentieth century through the Second World War, and a concern to recover the Reformation and the historical roots of Methodism marked the years from 1945 to the early 1960s. The fourth era results from the splintering of American society in the mid-sixties—the era of diversity and pluralism.[4]

But what were the emerging patterns of Methodist worship during this hundred-year period? In an insightful essay, L. Edward Phillips identifies four distinct patterns which are corollary to White's general typology: the revival pattern, the Sunday School pattern, the Anglican-aesthetic pattern, and the Word and Table pattern.[5] A brief description of each will help us understand how particular worship patterns arose, and why they are still practiced in various modified forms today. In fact, the study of any given congregation of significant membership will reveal, almost as in an archeological dig, the presence of several historical understandings of how worship "ought" to be done. The previous eras live on in the multi-layered memory book in typical United Methodist congregations.

First, the revival pattern. It was westward expansion of the nation across the Appalachians that produced a dramatic change in the understanding and practice of worship. Itinerant preachers established circuits of small gatherings, preaching to the scattered non-literate population. Everything had to adapt to the conditions of the frontier—preaching style, singing, praying, the frequency of the sacraments, the role of the laity, and the organization of local assemblies of believers. This was at one and the same time a sociocultural and a theological shift. Soon the widespread practice of gathering large numbers together for an annual camp meeting developed. Whatever "worked" to bring about a vital experience of converting grace was employed. White offers a deft description of Methodism on the frontier:

> Sedate and fixed forms did not recommend themselves in such situations, but spontaneity and excitement did. For frontier people, freedom was important and structures not. So the frontier devel-

oped forms of worship that were demonstrative and uninhibited, abounding with shouts and exclamations and fervent singing. . . . [People] responded to worship that allowed them to shout their feelings about what the preacher was saying or engage in physical movements such as the altar call, at which converts were summoned to come forward to be welcomed at the communion rail.[6]

Here we see a lively, enthusiastic picture. While not identical with the frontier, later forms of urban revivalism, twentieth-century television evangelism, and the worship forms encouraged by the church growth movement show remarkable continuities with features of the original camp meetings.

The chief aim of the revivalist pattern and style of worship is conversion. Worship is understood and practiced as a means to the end of bringing individuals to saving experiences, known as saving souls. Based on the elements of the camp meetings and related forms, the pattern of the revival service emerged. It was Charles Finney, especially in his *Lectures on Revivals of Religion* which was first written in 1835 and revised in 1868, who established the basic pattern of the revival in subsequent American tradition. His "new measures" included the various practices or elements of worship which had worked on the frontier. His point was a simple one: if evangelists had the right methods for worship, they would produce the right results. So, protracted meetings of several days were designed; the "anxious" bench, specially trained choirs, song leaders, and climactic altar calls became the fixed elements of the revival. Arguing that God had not given any particular measures for worship, his approach was purely pragmatic. While short on historical understanding and theological depth, Finney nevertheless appealed to a deep strand in the American character—free individual response to powerful group religious experience.

The lasting legacy of the revivalist tradition is a three-part service of worship. The normal Sunday service throughout most of the nineteenth century and on into the twentieth for a majority of Methodists was a service of praise and song, still referred to in many churches as the "preliminaries," followed by a sermon called "the message," and concluding with an altar call and intense prayer at the altar. This became a standard form and practice in city churches as well as rural. When this pattern became more formalized, as in the joint 1905 *Methodist Hymnal*,[7] the "Order of Public Worship" contained an opening musical voluntary, hymn, the Apostles' Creed,

141

prayer (concluding with the Lord's Prayer), an anthem by a choir, the Old Testament and New Testament lessons with the Gloria Patri in between, the announcements, and an offering. Then, following a hymn, the sermon was preached. The service then concluded with prayer, a hymn, and the invitation "to come to Christ." Many local United Methodist churches, especially in the South, continue to use this pattern most Sundays. Subsequent hymnals, including the 1964 hymnal of the Methodist Church, maintained the rubric "Invitation to Christian Discipleship," although the practice of altar calls was modified and even neglected in the intervening years. However, simplified versions of this practice still exist.

The tripartite pattern of the earlier revival tradition could even be found in Sunday evening prayer services in a vast majority of Methodist congregations by the late nineteenth century. The former Evangelical United Brethren traditions also brought a Sunday evening service of this form to the merger of 1968.

The second major pattern of Sunday morning worship emerged from the Sunday school movement in the American churches. By the end of the nineteenth century, the Methodist Episcopal Church, the Methodist Episcopal Church, South, and the Methodist Protestant Church had some form of Sunday school pattern. I recall vividly my own childhood participation in a small orchestra that played for the morning assembly in my small town congregation. Before classes, for both children and adults, we would play an opening voluntary. The Sunday school superintendent would then informally welcome everyone, offer an extempore prayer, then lead us in singing several favorite hymns and songs of praise. Occasionally a particular "theme" was set forth in a brief meditation, and all were dismissed to their respective classes, to the accompaniment of the orchestra. Following the classes, we reassembled to take a collection of money to supplement the class offerings and to read a scripture lesson. We concluded with singing and a "prayer of benediction" before the main Sunday service began.

Here we note that the Sunday school assembly had its own distinctive elements. It was lay-led, and included a considerable interaction between leader and the congregation, with increasing focus on teaching and nurture, rather than building toward a call to conversion. Despite its informality in leadership style, there was a strong ritual character present in this pattern, seen especially in the collection, the development of "special music," and the processions to and from the assembly space. The celebration of special days—such as Bible Sunday, Youth Sunday, Rally Day, Mother's Day, and Father's Day—constituted a distinctive calendar. Even after the rediscovery of the calendar and lectionary of the Christian year in the twentieth century, the "thematic" keeping of time characteristic of Sunday school worship has persisted in the regular Sunday morning practices of congregational worship as well. Thus, the ritual and educational character of this second pattern provides, to this day, an alternative to the dominant revival pattern.

Many church buildings of the latter third of the nineteenth century, especially in cities and towns, were constructed to accommodate the Sunday school movement, typified in the "Akron plan" of church building. White offers the following description:

> Organ pipes, choir, pulpit platform, altar-table, and communion rail were tucked in descending order in a corner, surrounded by semicircular pews on a sloping floor. Adjacent Sunday school space could be opened by sliding doors on festive occasions, revealing the school's central space for opening exercises and classrooms on floor and balcony levels.[8]

This highly functional design has shaped worship life in countless United Methodist congregations throughout the twentieth century.

We have already alluded to the emergence at the end of the nineteenth century of an expanded order of worship. When this was first printed in the hymnal of the Methodist Episcopal Church shortly after 1896, considerable protest was raised by many who were well-formed by the revivalist and Sunday school services. A new sensibility was taking shape which led to the third pattern which has influenced United Methodist Sunday worship. With the advent of wealthier, settled, urban life came a growing sense of respectability. Despite many who preferred the lively, more informal style of the revival or the Sunday school, the gradual introduction of liturgical elements from the Episcopal tradition (and, in some regions, the Lutheran tradition) emerged. These included organs, altar candles and acolytes, more formal prayers, robed choirs, and eventually a divided chancel arrangement. This third pattern, still followed by many today, was, in effect, a rearranged form of Anglican Morning Prayer, followed by church notices, an offering (now often accompanied by anthems or organ voluntaries), the sequence of hymn—sermon—invitation, and a concluding hymn with benediction. This is the pattern Phillips calls the "Anglican aesthetic."

In contrast to the two previously sketched patterns, this one appeals to a sense of beauty in the sanctuary and in the order and tone of worship. Depending upon printed bulletins for the congregation, this pattern represents a move toward dignified reverence and artistic enhancement in the Sunday assembly. The tone and flow of the service were aimed to appeal to "good taste." The rough-hewn vitality of the "saw-dust trail" of conversion was perceived to be less relevant to an aspiring denomination. One cannot help thinking that the emergence of pentecostal and the persistence of revivalist patterns among churches of lower economic status helped to secure the dominance of the aesthetic pattern in middle-class Methodism from the 1920s through the mid-1940s. But the notion of worship which offers "our best" to God continues to shape the sensibility and the actual practices in many United Methodist churches.

The development of extensive church music programs contributed greatly to the ethos of the Anglican-aesthetic pattern. Many churches came to be known and well-attended precisely because of the grandeur of the architecture, the "beauty" of the worship, the classical sacred music, and the learned style of the preaching. In this way, Methodism inherits and continues to practice a modified Anglicanism, born more of the nineteenth-century Oxford movement ideals than of the Church of England legacy of the eighteenth-century Wesleys. It can be said that the two primary elements of Methodist worship are music and preaching, set in a less rigid liturgical environment than the Anglican traditions, but with strong interest in how the arts serve to enhance the worship experience. In many respects this third pattern sees communion with God mediated through the aesthetic experience of common worship—whether by professionally oriented choirs and organists, or by local amateur talent.

There is a fourth distinctive pattern which has emerged in the past twenty-five years which can be called "Word and Table." This represents a quite different search for roots than did the restoration of Reformation and Wesleyan morning prayer patterns in the 1940s and 1950s. This pattern is a result of the ecumenical ferment following the Second Vatican Council. But it is also a product of the era of pluralism and the rise of a larger diversity of traditions. In terms of the longer history of United Methodism (and its various contributing traditions such as the Evangelical United Brethren) this pattern is newer. Yet it is based upon some of the earliest Church traditions which were recovered as the result of an intensive period of liturgical reform and renewal among all the major Christian communions. During the late 1960s and throughout the 1970s nearly every denomination—Lutherans, Episcopalians, Presbyterians, United Church of Christ, and Methodists, along with some Reformed churches—revised their hymnals and worship books. Among United Methodists, this Sunday pattern of Word and Table first appeared in 1972. Known as "The Sacrament of the Lord's Supper: An Alternate Text," it was the cornerstone of a remarkable publication of new worship resources, the "Supplemental Worship Resources."

The most recent period of liturgical reform and renewal has raised basic theological, pastoral, and spiritual issues for many churches. Co-mingling with such ecumenically and historically based reforms have been a challenging range of other pressures as well, including the critique of much "traditional" Christian worship from feminist and liberationist perspectives.[9] At the same time, new phenomena such as the church growth movement and the resurgence of a vigorous evangelicalism have put other questions to all these inherited patterns. The tensions between identity and relevance, evangelical and sacramental understandings of worship, and the relation between Sunday liturgy and the mission of the church in the world are all alive in significant ways in the present era.

The Ethos of United Methodist Worship Today

Because United Methodism is not a confessional Church in the Lutheran or Reformed sense, nor does it legislate liturgical uniformity, the patterns we have reviewed often exist side by side within and among local congregations. The reforms of the past quarter-century have nevertheless brought about a noteworthy shift in theology and practice among United Methodists. The preface to the new *United Methodist Book of Worship* (1992) states that that book and the *United Methodist Hymnal* (1989) are "the cornerstones of United Methodist worship."[10] This is certainly true at the official level, since the word and table pattern for Sunday morning, and the various services based on this pattern, such as the rite of baptism, are authorized by the General Conference.

At the same time, however, many local churches, not informed about or concerned with the most recent reforms, do not yet use these resources. In some local congregations one still finds a version of the 1905 service outlined in the previous section. In others the perspective and style of the pastor seem to control the pattern and style of worship, which leads to various results. The *Book of Discipline* of the United Methodist Church requires that pastors of local churches "oversee the worship life of the congregation" and that members of those churches are to participate in the planning process.[11] However, when the laity are not involved, the organization of worship often reflects the pastor's own background and training. Consequently in these churches there is often a clash of worship patterns and styles between those of the pastor and the inherited worship practiced by the congregation over a period of time. This is not always a conflict between the Word and Table pattern and the revival or Sunday school patterns, though this may be true in rural and more homogeneous congregations that have a strong sense of local history. In some larger churches the tensions have been mitigated by the adoption of different patterns and styles for the early and later Sunday morning services.

In a study of thirteen United Methodist congregations conducted in 1992–1993, I discovered a fascinating range of actual practice on Sunday mornings. Among them one notes all four of the patterns emerging in the history of Methodist worship: revival, Sunday school, more formal modified Anglican, and Word and Table. Let us visit one of these churches to get a concrete "feel" for Sunday morning in a 1200-member suburban United Methodist congregation.

The following description, part of a research report written by Larry Golemon, is of an actual worship service representative of the worship hours of 8:30 a.m. and 10:50 a.m.[12] These may be called "average" services, following the more or less standard order which has emerged in this church over the past twenty years. The early service usually follows the same order as the second, but uses a piano instead of the large pipe organ, and does not involve the choir. The congregation at the early service usually has a number of younger families, some older members, and some young adults. The sermon tends to be more informal at the 8:30 a.m. service.

The 10:50 a.m. service begins with a time for meditation and some form of music, usually an organ voluntary. Some people listen intently, though many carry on friendly conversation during this time. The senior pastor or an associate pastor, with preaching robe and stole, welcomes the congregation and makes a number of announcements. Then the congregation is invited to stand for a responsive call to worship that is printed in the bulletin. This is often related to a major theme of the day, and varies in style from formal to colloquial. A hymn of praise usually follows, and the congregation sings loudly if the hymn is familiar. This contrasts with the earlier service, in part because the choir leads out vigorously on all hymns. A unison prayer comes next, led by the associate pastor or a lay liturgist, and everyone is seated. This opening section of the Sunday service moves quite smoothly. A "variable space" usually follows the opening prayer, which is the place where most baptisms, teacher recognitions, presentations of Bibles, or similar special events relating to the educational or mission program of the congregation take place. In some cases this has an informal and quite personal character.

The central section of the service, identified in the bulletin as "Proclamation" begins with a prayer for illumination by the appointed reader of the Scriptures—often a lay person. Occasionally a psalm is used, but often the lector reads through two lessons, following each with "This is the Word of the Lord," to which the congregation responds, "Thanks be to God." One of the church's choirs then offers a gradual anthem or motet, often from the "classical" choral repertoire, but not exclusively; the youth choir offers a more contemporary range. The congregation stands for the reading of the Gospel and makes the same response to the lesson as before. There often follows a hymn which is related to the sermon text. After all are seated, the preacher of the day moves into the pulpit, offers a prayer, and begins. The preaching style is usually conversational, tied to one or more of the lectionary readings. Preaching themes characteristically weave together two or more of the following topics: traditional Christian theological teachings, worship practices, congregational issues, social concerns, and personal piety. In a survey of the congregation, nearly 60 percent indicated they thought the predominant style was that of "biblical interpretation."

The concluding part of the worship service, identified as the "Response of the People" in the bulletin, begins with a pastoral prayer led by whichever of the pastors has not preached. The prayer typically includes thanksgivings, often for events in the congregation or in the wider public; petitions for the sick and the troubled; and concerns about specific issues facing the congregation, the university with which the congregation is associated, or the city and the nation. The offering is then announced and taken while one of the choirs

147

sings an anthem that is longer and more ambitious than the first. The director, who along with the choir is placed visibly before the congregation in the chancel, conducts with flair and precision. (Members interviewed speak of their great appreciation for the choir, and some name choral anthems as the "spiritual highlight" of worship. Others are less affected, and have cited elaborate choral anthems as examples of how the church has become more of a "spectator church" in the past ten to fifteen years.) A vigorous doxology is then introduced and sung as the ushers bring the offering to the pastor who stands in the center of the chancel. Following a brief prayer of thanksgiving, the final hymn is sung, and the benediction is given—often extemporized along certain themes in the sermon or in the service as a whole. The service concludes with an organ voluntary—often in grand style. Occasionally the pastor will invite the congregation to sit for this, though the majority of the people are already up and greeting one another before moving out of the sanctuary.

Children play a prominent role in the 10:50 a.m. service through participation in choirs, special recognitions, ministry as acolytes, and attendance with their families. Children's sermons occur once a month or less often. The inclusion of children has been quite intentional on the part of the staff, and is, for the most part, well received by the congregation.

Holy communion is celebrated on the first Sunday of the month, and additionally on occasions such as Christmas Eve, Epiphany, and Maundy Thursday. This practice reflects a major trend in United Methodism during the past fifteen years. In a recent survey of 135 churches, I found that 102 of them now celebrate the Lord's Supper on the first Sunday of the month, with many celebrating more frequently, and 25 having the sacrament at one of their services each Sunday. This is a remarkable shift in practice from the standard quarterly communion which predominated for well over a century in the Methodist tradition, itself being a practice originating primarily from circuit-riding days and the older "quarterly conference."

Holy communion is observed in a variety of ways. Until the recent reforms, the most characteristic mode focused on individual reception at the altar rail. The elements, in trays holding small glasses and on plates with bread in pre-cut cubes, were served by the pastor from behind the rail. The liturgical forms were often quite brief, though a significant number of churches used the "official" longer form thereby representing continuity with the Anglican tradition.

The mood was penitential and reverent, usually without congregational singing during the communion rite. With the advent of the Word and Table Sunday liturgy, first in 1972, and now with its flexible number of seasonal great thanksgivings, some significant shifts in mood and manner of communing have emerged. Four practical features of the new services are worth noting: (1) a new sense of the joyful thanksgiving character of the service; (2) an emerging appreciation for a variety of ways to serve and receive the bread and wine; (3) the singing of hymns by the whole congregation during the communion rite itself; and (4) the way in which the sacrament, over time, unfolds new dimensions, as each aspect of the Church year unfolds. In other words, the United Methodist Church is experiencing a recovery of the ancient balance between word and sacrament, though this is an uneven process, with significant reluctance to change on the part of many local congregations who have not had appropriate pastoral leadership or education in the new hymnal or knowledge of the *Book of Worship*. What we clearly note here is the way in which the Word and Table pattern, though embodied in quite different styles, has begun to make an impact on the operational theology in the churches.

The local church mentioned above has a strong Sunday school program. One of the adult classes, a group that has been together for over forty years with the same Sunday school teacher, conducts its own worship exercises, very much reflecting a modified Sunday school pattern from the late nineteenth and early twentieth centuries. There is a period of informal singing, mostly older gospel songs and a few hymns from the *Cokesbury Hymnal*.[13] Informal announcements and sharing are also part of the pattern, followed by Scripture, extempore prayer for the members and other concerns, and the lesson. There is a concluding song and/or a blessing. Like several other congregations I studied in Georgia and South Carolina, the long-time members of the church (the "pillars") are members of well-established classes which have their own version of Sunday worship, with a contrast in pattern and style from the sanctuary gathering which precedes or follows the class. This keeps a strong bonding and sense of identity for the group, and has nurtured many over a sustained history.

All of this illustrates the fact that, within United Methodist Sunday worship, each of the patterns named, however modified or even mixed, has an important role to play. Especially noticeable are the distinctive bodies of song and styles of prayer which characterize differences. In the case of Sunday school worship, the strong lay leadership contrasts sharply with the clergy-dominated main services. At the same time, increasing use of lay readers, servers, and leaders of prayer in the sanctuary is also having an impact on the perception and participation of the larger congregation.

The "Contemporary" Debate

In recent workshops and conferences I find United Methodist pastors and laity increasingly concerned and puzzled about "contemporary worship."[14] This phrase has been with us at least since the mid-sixties, a time of widespread suspicion of traditions in general. In many places, now thirty years later, pastors, musicians, and lay leaders of our congregations are at odds concerning "contemporary" versus "traditional" worship patterns and styles. The following remarks attempt to sort out some issues facing us as we search for theologically informed wisdom.

Three practical questions keep surfacing: (1) How can we "liven up" our Sunday morning worship? (2) How can worship form a deeper spirituality? and (3) How can Christian worship "target" the unchurched? In several congregations I know well, the solution to these questions is to provide some kind of "contemporary" or "alternative" service. Some large churches offer attractive Sunday gatherings which are aimed explicitly at "seekers" while offering more specifically Christian liturgy for others on weekday evenings. All such efforts are aimed at a perceived need to make worship relevant and effective.

Yet I am struck by how different the three questions are. Each requires more theological thinking than we tend to give them. First, to make Christian worship "alive" may or may not involve dispensing with "traditional" forms and styles. It certainly does not mean departing from the biblical, prophetic, and sacramental force of the Gospel. Liturgy come to life does, however, ask for more prayerful and careful planning and preparation of the assembly than I encounter in many churches. "Being alive" in worship means being alive to God and to the mystery of gathering in the name of Jesus. There is a theological root issue at stake. We can be "lively" with words, music, and relaxed styles of being together which may have little to do with an encounter with the Holy One of all creation. I can easily substitute what I'd *like* to experience in church for that which challenges me and bids me participate in a saving mystery beyond my cultural assumptions.

The first question is asked by those who experience their "standard" (what we've "always" done) Sunday worship to be lifeless and boring. Here the problem may be that a "traditional" Sunday service actually lacks tradition, that is, the lively sense of joining the church's praise and vulnerability to God "at all times and places." We may regard Christian tradition as the culprit when, in fact, it is our own culturally captive style or familiarity in worship which is the source of lifelessness.

I shall never forget one of the first occasions in which our service of baptismal renewal was celebrated in Buckhannon, West Virginia. Afterwards a laywoman exclaimed, "Was this a sacrament or a revival? I couldn't tell the difference!" She had rightly understood that the quality of celebration, the vivid sense of Holy Spirit in ritual action, a fresh word—sung, preached, and prayed—was a function of a deeper baptismal tradition being recovered in new form.

The current debate is often about style, the sense of presence, and the particular manner in which worship is led and enacted. If too "formal" or "stuffy," worship is quickly associated with being "high church." This is unfortunate, for some of the most moving and experientially alive worship is found in churches which have a strong sense of form and tradition. The problem lies in assuming that form and freedom are mutually exclusive. I have been especially impressed in a number of African American churches in the Methodist traditions where spontaneity occurs because of a deeply shared liturgical pattern. Could it be that in such contexts the whole congregation as well as the pastors and musicians have a sufficient sense of being "at home" in the forms and patterns in order to permit improvisation and variety? The real issue is: what forms and patterns done with integrity create the possibility of "life" and "experiential freedom"?

Perhaps the response to "boring worship" is precisely not to turn away from the larger Christian tradition, but to explore it critically and to develop new eyes and ears for its surprises. This does not deny the "contemporary" in the sense of fresh texts, music, and prayer forms. These are needed for relevance to what deeply afflicts and enhances our lives. The *United Methodist Hymnal* and the *Book of Worship*, whatever their limitations, contain challenging and life-

151

giving new resources, conjoined with biblically based and histori-cally informed rites.

Relevancy is often short-lived when sought through currently attractive techniques, rather than through mutual growth and edifi-cation. I struggle with Dean William Inge's observation that the church which marries the spirit of the age becomes a widow in the next generation. Ah, yes, and the church which fails to live as it prays and sings is orphaned from a living tradition.

The second question turns upon the difference between what a consumerist culture wants and what we need at the center of our being as children of God. What we want is not necessarily what we need. The more we learn about the way of Jesus, the more our wants and desires are re-formed and given new direction. The quest for relevance can lead us into cultural captivities of various sorts: psy-chological, ideological, and socioeconomic—that is, into the tyranny of the contemporary. To be captive to what is merely current is the fate of societies who lose a critical sense of history and deep memory. We live in a society that finds it increasingly difficult to distinguish between immediacy of feeling and emotional depth. So music used in stores and over the telephone creates easy feeling; music which expresses praise or repentance or joy in the midst of tribulation must touch down into deeper aspects of the human soul. So "What Won-drous Love Is This" or "For All the Saints" will elicit more durable emotion, while recent easy-listening religious music may not.

We have all been in quite plain worship with no choir or organ where the singing and the praying have been powerful because of the authenticity of the style of leadership and participation. There, nothing was casual and thoughtless, and the congregation was attentive to what was said and done. I have been in liturgically elaborate services where the well-dressed, well-mannered gathering seemed to be there more for aesthetic enjoyment than for encounter with the living God. But the reverse can also occur: a plain style which misses the spiritual needs of many, and a vibrant liturgy with enough range to speak to many different sensibilities.

The question about "contemporary" versus "traditional" is not about giving people what they want. Rather, authentic faith is shown by the way the *content* of what is said, sung, and prayed, is linked to the *style* of leadership and congregational participation. When lead-ership calls attention to itself (whether "folksy" or pompously for-mal), and where the assembly has no ownership of the forms and content, Christian worship is in danger of cultural captivity of one form or another—and indeed may not speak to the real needs of the worshiping community.

This leads to the third question. The people of God are called to evangelize—to so live and speak Christ that others will know the saving grace of God and be liberated to live as members of Christ's Body in this world. But such evangelism cannot be done only in Sunday worship or simply in occasional revivals. The problem with the revivalist tradition and its "contemporary" update is not that it is unappealing, or even that it employs a range of relevant words and music, but that it tends to treat the worship of God as a means to another end: a pragmatic tool for evangelism.

Wesley spoke in certain contexts of the Lord's Supper as a "converting ordinance," and I am convinced of his point. But this cannot mean that we simply use the sacrament as a tool for conversion. Rather, in authentically celebrating the holy meal, and in offering our best in the "sacrifice of praise and thanksgiving" to God, real witness will be shown. We must learn to use the rubric "Invitation to Christian Discipleship" in more than a perfunctory manner. We should plan for genuine times and places of altar-prayer and provide appropriate forms for a converting response of faith. But corporate worship of God is not a means to something other than what it is: the glorification of God and the sanctification of all that is creaturely.

I see no incompatibility between vital evangelism and bringing our best to Christian worship in the long run. But we need to unburden the Lord's Day of trying to do too many things at once, including evangelism. Far better are faith-sharing groups, work projects, common ministries, and study for inquirers—all brought to disciplined small groups modeled on the Wesleyan class meetings. Let the quality of our life and work bring its prophetic presence and witness to our worship. More persons are convinced that Christianity is real when they see the quality of concern, commitment, and responsible facing of the complex issues of life and death, than when they are given spiritual entertainment. But we are not mistaken in longing for more honesty and joy, for more imagination and thanksgiving and reality in Christian worship.

We should not blame the larger historical traditions of Christian liturgy for what the "lack of time for church" has done to our Sunday mornings. The secret to deeper evangelical dimensions in our assembly for word and sacrament is authentic style, coupled with more thorough teaching and experiential learning. To reach those "out-side" the church, many of whom are "inside" our congregations longing for vital worship, is to regain the inner connection between liturgy and life. This means recovering the whole economy: the principal Lord's Day service of word and table, daily prayer (corporate and devotional), more challenging patterns for conversion and baptism (rites of Christian initiation adapted to our contexts), opportunities for healing (physical, mental, spiritual), and the range of occasional gatherings such as love feasts, house prayer, and Bible study. How we worship at funerals and weddings will also witness. Above all we need to create "teaching occasions" for the learning of new *and* old hymns, psalms, forms of prayer, and ritual actions.

The tension between "contemporary" and "traditional" forms of worship masks a much deeper set of theological and pastoral issues, some of which I have suggested here. But worship is also an art requiring skillful leadership. If integrity is the aim rather than simply "updating" or "making our services more lively," then pastors, together with musicians and lay leaders, must dig far more deeply still. To lead worship which has depth, durability, and relevance to the tensions and human needs of our present age is to have more poetic and biblically informed imagination, not less. It is to become more critically aware of the theological content of what we say and sing and do. When these are once again at the heart of our struggle to guide and to celebrate the Gospel, then we will see how each congregation and each culture (or sub-culture) may discover its own form of excellence. Then we can be liberated from our various cultural captivities.

Conclusion: An Emerging Theology of Worship

The new *Hymnal* and *Book of Worship* represent, for the great majority of United Methodists, resources pointing us toward a resilient theology of worship.

In assessing the present status of Sunday morning worship among United Methodists, we have emphasized the wide range of diversity in orders and styles. Yet, if we should ask about what is essential, a picture of more continuity may yet appear, despite the rich range of styles suggested above. I venture to suggest that a basic theology of worship is now emerging, especially in light of the recent hymnal and the adaptability and flexibility at the pastoral level of our new services.

First, at the heart of Methodist worship and life is the central claim of the grace of God freely offered in Jesus Christ, made alive in the Holy Spirit. Our new rites—from the service of word and holy communion, through the reformed baptismal services (including "confirmation") to the daily prayer services and various "rites of passage" (healing, weddings, funerals, etc.)—show forth a basic trinitarian theology of the life of God with us. It is unmistakably there in the prayers of thanksgiving, both at the table and at the font of baptism. Continuing discussions about the adequacy of inherited language concerning "Father," "Son," and "Holy Spirit" are revealing new dimensions of what has been suppressed, and what early, strident critique has neglected.

Second, Methodist worship will continue to be grounded in the whole of the Bible. From the beginning, Wesley, and then Asbury and others in the American churches, insisted on coverage of both Old and New Testaments. The reformed rites, with their vigorous insistence on the whole sweep of God's creating, redeeming, and consumating work, will deepen our being "people of one Book," to adapt Wesley's phrase. Far from being a narrow or dogmatic biblicism, this aspect of our worship has already brought about a rebirth of sustained biblical study. The very fact of an adequate three-year lectionary, if entered into by pastor and people alike, re-centers the Word of God in reading, singing, preaching, and praying. This is found abundantly as the principle undergirding the *Hymnal* and the *Book of Worship*.

Third, we have always, at our best, been committed to social holiness. The *United Methodist Hymnal* makes a significant theological statement in its ordering of the hymns, and especially in combining hymns of personal and social holiness together. Thus the Methodist heritage of linking liturgy with mission, and word and sacrament with social responsibility to carry on Christ's ministry in the world, is highlighted.

Fourth, an important dimension of our emerging theology of worship is the integration of word, sacrament, and vital experience. Here we do well to remember that the Wesleys were accused of two great extravagances by the Anglicans of the eighteenth century: "enthusiasm" and "formalism" (or "sacramentalism"). They were "sacramentalists" to some because of their insistence on the centrality of the means of grace and the frequency of eucharistic celebration. They were "enthusiasts" because they were convinced of the need for genuine religious experience which shapes daily life. At our best, United Methodists are both enthusiasts and sacramentalists.

We are not at our best when we are polemical or fearful or defensive. When United Methodists become huddled into particular interest groups, we are diminished. If we choose to oppose sacraments and prophetic word, if we think evangelism and catholicity are opposite ways of being faithful, or if we cut the link between personal and social holiness in either direction, or deny the diversity of our gifts in the one Christ, we gradually drift and die. Our calling is to be a witness to the tradition in its richness.

This is a season in which we have a brand new opportunity not to be polemical, but to be irenic. In our *Book of Worship* and our *Hymnal* we have a richness of liturgical forms and breadth of hymnody that clearly invite an evangelical freedom and growth. If we can now approach the task (and the gift) of renewal from a genuinely inclusive sense which aims at an authentic synthesis of our history with the larger marks of the Church, then we are on the way toward the wholeness of worship and life which is truly in praise of God and in service to the new creation. Only then will we use the new liturgical resources well. Only then can we begin to understand ourselves as part of the one, holy, catholic, apostolic Church, with special gifts for its evangelical life of continuing reform. Even more, we can address the deepest yearnings of generations yet unborn for truth and for authentic human community. For the One celebrated in, with, and through the appropriate use of our liturgical tools is the One who stands in our midst, saying still, "Behold, I make all things new."

Chapter 9

"Under Our Own Vine and Fig Tree": Sunday Morning Worship in the African Methodist Episcopal Church

Vinton R. Anderson

The African Methodist Episcopal Church Heritage

On a Sunday morning in November 1787 at St. George's Methodist Episcopal Church in Philadelphia, Richard Allen and other Black Methodists who had been pulled from their knees while at prayer walked out in protest, declaring, "We will worship God under our own vine and fig tree." That experience triggered a movement which subsequently led to the formation of the first national African American institution in the new world.[1] The founding of Mother Bethel in Philadelphia, the sacred citadel of faith and freedom for African Methodists,[2] established a place where former slaves could exercise social and political authority based on their understanding of the Gospel. They had heard the itinerant preachers proclaim that "God shows no partiality, but . . . anyone who fears him and does what is right is acceptable to him" (Acts 10:34-35), and that "there is no longer slave or free . . . for all of you are one in Christ Jesus" (Galatians 3:28). A tradition of inclusiveness in worship began, for Black Christians had now removed the wall of separation and affirmed in practice the Gospel imperative to "go into all the world . . . to every creature."

Worship in the African Methodist Episcopal Church has its basis in a theology of liberation which springs from the event of 1787.[3] To talk of worship in the African Methodist Episcopal (A.M.E.) context is to reflect on a history of oppressed people who for more than two centuries have fostered a philosophy of self-help and self-determination. Out of their peculiar struggle they have crafted a theology of liberation which affirms freedom for the total person. There can be no spirituality for A.M.E.s that excludes the well-being of body, mind, and soul. Therefore, we continue to testify, "I looked at my hands, and they looked new. I looked at my feet, and they did too." Our worship on Sunday morning centers on Jesus, the anointed one, who "bring[s] good news to the poor. . . . proclaim[s] release to the captives and recovery of sight to the blind, . . . let[s] the oppressed go free, . . . proclaim[s] the year of the Lord's favor" (Luke 4:18).

In attempting to catch the essence of the African Methodist Episcopal heritage and to convey that legacy to their constituency, the bishops in 1976 included the following statement in the Episcopal Salutation: "The liturgy and worship forms must reflect the peculiar content of our religious experience, therefore reinforcing and reaffirming our authenticity and legitimacy as African Methodist Christians."[4] Obviously the bishops intended to be clear about their position to incorporate African American cultural elements into corporate worship. This inclination would be a corrective to those who tended toward a Euro-American mind-set and would somewhat run counter to the view of Daniel A. Payne and others who strongly embraced the Euro-American Methodist form. Payne, elected a bishop in 1852 and greatly revered by his denomination as the apostle of education, had resisted the use of spirituals, calling them cornfield ditties. In Payne's autobiography, *Recollections of Seventy Years*, he labels those who participate in slave songs and the ring shouts as "ridiculous and heathenist."[5]

It should not be thought, however, that A.M.E. bishops a hundred years later are diametrically opposed to Payne's judgment for his own day. There still remains a respect and appreciation for the Euro-American heritage, and it is coupled with a sense of Black pride and the determination for an identity with one's African roots. The 1976 Episcopal Salutation further avers:

> That the A.M.E. Church must be committed to identify itself with a value system which has grown out of the Black experience with God, and not the adoption of another culture imposed on Black people. That value system should interpret the intervention of God within the Black context and the historical pilgrimage of Black people. Our church must be in the role of enabler, and free people from the false values which make them ashamed of themselves and their heritage, and equip them with the understanding and freedom to deal with their life-conditions and decision-making process.[6]

It must be understood, then, that worship on Sunday morning in an African Methodist Episcopal church is a response of praise and thanksgiving to a powerful God who has brought Black people from a mighty long way, whose journey toward freedom is placed alongside the exodus from Egypt and the *via dolorosa*. Worship celebrates a faith learned in the crucible of adversity. It remembers the biblical story and recognizes the more recent past of a particular people: the Middle Passage, the blacksmith shop, the plantations and the cotton fields. So, we sing, "My soul looks back and wonders how we got over."

What must it have been like when the time came to walk out of St. George's sanctuary? What courage must have been required? The Black Methodists were a people who had been trapped by a system which had dictated their very existence, had directed their every move and controlled their destiny. Now they were set free to pursue their Christian pilgrim journey in an environment of their own choosing. What must it have been like in the blacksmith shop, transformed into the "house of God" at that first worship service in 1794? We, who are African Methodists, can imagine what it was like for them by acknowledging our own exuberance and relief when we tread on holy ground each Sunday morning, ground which represents our own place of refuge from an unfriendly world.

While it was clear that the Allenites could now say about their place of worship, "This land is our land," Richard Allen had no intention of breaking away from the Methodism which had so greatly affected his life. In fact, he said in his journal:

> We were in favor of being attached to the Methodist connection; for I was confident that there was no religious sect or denomination [that] would suit the capacity of the colored people as well as the Methodist; for the plain and simple gospel suits best for any people; for the unlearned can understand, and the learned are sure to understand; and the reason that the Methodist is so successful in the awakening and conversion of the colored people, [is] the plain doctrine and having a good discipline.[7]

Richard Allen was, in fact, keeping with the tradition of Methodism as defined by John Wesley in his appeal to common people, his commitment to social change, his fervor in evangelism, and his opting for freedom and spontaneity in worship. Allen may have been affected by the tradition of "a heart strangely warmed" and Wesley's contention that to be an "altogether Christian" required both a love of God that "engrosses the whole heart" and a love for the neighbor.[8] These images of Christian virtue and behavior, taken from the father of Methodism and coupled with Allen's African heritage characterized by attentiveness to spiritual matters and a quest for freedom learned in the slave environment, provided the necessary ingredients for the formulation of Sunday worship in an African Methodist Episcopal Church.

As early as 1801 Richard Allen had published *A Collection of Hymns and Spiritual Songs* for use in the fledgling society now set on a course to proclaim God's salvation, liberation, and reconciliation.[9] That work, along with Allen's directive in 1817 (following the Methodist Episcopal Church *Discipline*), "Let the morning worship consist of singing, prayer, reading of a chapter out of the Old Testament and another out of the New Testament, and preaching," shaped the sum, substance, and style of Sunday worship for the generations of A.M.E.s which followed. This informal order of service was the seed for the more formal order which grew to become the solid trunk for Sunday worship in A.M.E. churches.

For more than a century, A.M.E.s have gathered for worship heralded by the words, "I was glad when they said unto me, let us go into the house of the Lord. Our feet shall stand within thy gates, O Jerusalem." The suggestion of gladness, announcing our presence in God's house to worship God, indicates that joy and praise are two predictable expressions related to the worship experience. Gathered as the people of God, we become fully aware of the multiplexity of social and personal issues which surround us, and we seek to reconnect with God and each other as we rediscover gladness despite the difficult journey.

A.M.E.s hardly congregate without remembering the great distance God has brought Black people, and without celebrating social and political victories which intertwine with present struggles for personhood and self-esteem. Just as sure as we come to meet our God at our holy meeting-place, believing in God's power to change the world and therefore advancing the concept of "justice and equality for all," we come also to each other in our vulnerability, risking ridicule and seeking approval. We come singing, "Nobody knows the trouble I see; nobody knows but Jesus."

James Cone, in *For My People*, describes how on Sunday morning theological, social, and economic realities converge over a period of several hours as worship, and states that:

160

Worship, therefore, is not primarily an expression of the individual's private relationship with God. It is rather a community happening, an eschatological invasion of God into the gathered community of victims, empowering them with "the divine Spirit from on high," "to keep on keeping on" even though the odds might appear to be against them. In the collective presence of the poor at worship, God re-creates them as a liberated community that must bring freedom to the oppressed of the land.[10]

Worship Styles

It is generally felt by A.M.E.s that there is a common thread which weaves together the peculiar content of our worship, and allows African Methodists to be at home wherever they worship in faithfulness to the Christ-event and the Wesley-Allen legacy. It cannot, however, be said that worship in general in our context is monolithic.

There is a quality of connectedness among A.M.E. churches, but the flavor of worship may differ from setting to setting. No single picture describes our Sunday worship, yet there is order in what we do. Worship may be explosive, unpredictable, joyous or doleful, formal or spontaneous, contagious or sterile, or a combination or variation of all the above. For example, in one congregation the worshipers may be quiet and meditative, the music subdued; in another, worship may be more spirited and up-tempo. A third congregation may worship in the highly-spirited charismatic style with lots of instruments and loud joyful sounds. But in each case the congregation always knows what follows. The gamut can run from traditional to ultra-contemporary, but in some mysterious way a formal structure gives shape to the unpredictable moments. By the grace of God, the Sunday worship experience in an A.M.E. church may empower persons and the congregation. The community's gathering provides the setting, attitude, and the substance for the Spirit of God to indwell and to energize so that the work of Christ may be continued in both individual and community.

A colorful array of worship styles exists in the African Methodist Episcopal Church family. In Bermuda, the British influence is merged with the American as worshipers lustily sing hymns from the Anglican tradition and gospel songs of American origin. The order of worship is distinctly African Methodist and there is an appreciation and use of classical anthems as well as spirituals and contemporary choruses. Spontaneity is by no means squelched but congregations want and expect a well-planned service with sermons that appeal to their hearts and minds. Many churches broadcast over the radio and during the week it is common to hear parishioners discussing aspects of a particular sermon.

In South Africa, where African Methodism is flourishing and where the A.M.E. Church has been present for one hundred years, the order of worship serves as a guide, for spontaneity is natural and uninhibited. Rich vocal tones swell as South Africans sing hymns and anthems. One may hear a children's choir render an a capella version of "Cast Thy Burdens Upon the Lord" from Handel's oratorio *Elijah* or listen to an entire congregation joyfully harmonize their version of "Guide Me, O Thou Great Jehovah." Several languages may be sung at one time, but all in beautiful harmony and often without instruments. With the singing there is always body movement, and the dancing is joyful and unfeigned. In extreme cases younger people may jump several inches from the floor in continuous rhythm to the music. Dance frequently attends the offering of money, which is regarded as a time of celebration: worshipers may dance to the table, put their money down, and dance back to their seats, some-times going to the table more than once. The offering, then, can take an unplanned amount of time, but it is clearly one of the high points of the service.

Regional differences can be found in worship styles within the United States. In South Carolina, a "hotbed" of African Methodism, the members of the churches in the "low country" are known to have a style all their own. A common practice is the syncopated clapping which accompanies the music and is used as a response to the sermon when it has hit home. Dancing in the aisles with intricate steps even by someone who may look too old and unsteady to move can set the onlooker to wondering how it is possible. A.M.E. worship in Alabama still includes the mournful tones of the call and response songs and of many old spirituals and songs that may not be heard elsewhere. In some areas it is not uncommon to see somone "get happy" and "walk the benches." The latter is a practice in which a person seems to float on air while walking on the back of each pew as if in a trance. Deep in the coal mine areas of West Virginia, African Methodism has another flavor. Worshipers still follow the order of service, but their music is what many of us call "hill-billy" with banjo accompaniment and country-style singing. Churches in urban cen-ters with their magnificent pipe organs and large choirs still have space for gospel singing and for testimonies and emotional outbursts called "shouting." Many worshipers bring with them to the city remnants of their religious upbringing from the rural South.

Despite a variety of worship styles, such as those found among A.M.E.s in Canada, West Africa, or the Caribbean (with its calypso beat and local color), the churches honor an A.M.E. order of worship.[11] Whether east or west, north or south, Sunday A.M.E. worship should be identifiable because it generally follows a prescribed order of service. Thus local expressions and an established worship pattern define who we are as children of God and as spiritual descendants of Richard Allen.

Those who prefer a freer or a non-structured style of worship may not perceive what A.M.E.s cherish about uniformity and linkage with our history and the early Church. For while we revere our own uniqueness, we can never forget that we as a communion are one member of the Body of Christ, and consequently yoked with other communions whose history and worship, like ours, has its roots in the first-century Church. As is true for other Christians throughout the world, A.M.E.s share in biblical traditions and the ancient liturgies of the Church. Consequently, worship is not detached and unrelated to what other Christians do. Proclaiming the Word of God and administering the sacraments are central to our life and witness. We have been deliberate about embracing elements of worship which celebrate our ecumenicity and have been intentional about engaging in worship that has liturgical integrity and theological relevance. Hence, worship is seen as purposeful movement toward a goal which is intensely spiritual and fulfilling. Albert W. Palmer may lend support to our notion of order and discipline in worship, pointing to the sixth chapter of Isaiah as a pattern for public worship.[12] Even in our own denomination, when some argue that worship is too controlled and the Spirit often muzzled in periods of rejoicing, there is also agreement that a fine line exists between allowing for spontaneity and maintaining order.

I have found a helpful response to the concern expressed for freedom and structure in the imagery of Ezekiel's vision of the valley of dry bones:

> And as I prophesied, suddenly there was a noise, a rattling, and the bones came together, bone to its bone. I looked, and there were sinews on them, and flesh had come upon them, and skin had covered them; but there was no breath in them. . . . I prophesied as

He commanded me, and the breath came into them, and they lived (Ezekiel 37:7, 8, 10).

The passage shows the essential relationship of structure to substance. Until breath, the *ruach* of God, enters our frames, there is no life. Likewise, a framework is necessary to receive God's *dunamis* or power, namely, the Holy Spirit.

The A.M.E. Church seeks to be authentic to Christian tradition and its own heritage through a diversity of forms and styles of music, its prayer, preaching, and fellowship. The *A.M.E. Bicentennial Hymnal* (1984),[13] and the amended version, the *A.M.E. Hymnal* (1986)[14] along with the *Book of Worship* (1984),[15] were intended to be faithful to universal principles of worship and yet perpetuate the tradition unique to our own worshiping congregations. They include the three-year lectionary adopted by the Consultation on Church Union (C.O.C.U.) and other liturgical services developed within the C.O.C.U. family.

The A.M.E. Commission on Worship and Liturgy, in its preface to the *Book of Worship*, refers to the denomination as constituting a "liberating and reconciling people." In response to the perceived assault on what had been essential in worship, the preface stated:

> [We] must be open to explore new styles without dismantling all that is old. . . .
>
> It should provide both clergy and lay persons with a meaningful worship guide in the dual task of nurturing the community of faith and calling Christ to the attention of the unbeliever. . . .
>
> It is our deepest hope that this instrument . . . will stimulate liturgical renewal and worship integrity, as well as a measure of uniformity amongst worshipping African Methodists. It is our prayer that from its use a fresh movement of the Spirit will move upon our Zion.[16]

The Order of Worship

Primary, in both the *Hymnal* and the *Book of Worship*, is the Sunday Morning Order of Worship. In a typical worshiping congregation, the order of worship would be as follows:[17]

The Prelude
The Introit (if desired)
The Processional
The Doxology

The Call to Worship

The Hymn of Praise

The Prayer and Choral Response

The Anthem or Song by Choir

The Scripture Lessons

The Choral Preface to the Decalogue

The Decalogue (often abridged or summarized)

The Gloria Patri

The Choral Selection

The Benevolent Offering

The Announcements & Parish Concerns & Recognition of Visitors

The Sermonic Selection or Hymn

The Sermon

Prayer (The Lord's Prayer chanted, all kneeling)

The Invitation to Christian Discipleship

The Affirmation of Faith

The Offering and Choral Offertory

The Doxology or Hymn

The Benediction

The Recessional

The Postlude

A few aspects of the Sunday order of worship that are firmly held by African Methodists must be mentioned. It should be noted that the Doxology (the text by Thomas Ken) is twice sung in the service, at the beginning and at the end, but using alternate tunes (often Old 100th and a gospel tune). Perhaps its placement in both locations symbolizes the parameters of the celebration event. The in-between time, which may be substantially extended depending on the Spirit's energizing, validates the observation that, for Black people, linear time is not important—experience is. For some worshipers, as long as the Spirit is high, "Church" goes on and they are content. Yet for others, the extended duration of the worship service is a bone of contention. The tension exists around the notion that the Holy Spirit is an agent of order, and therefore constrains as well as excites. What must be admitted is that congregations, too, have personalities, and that variable very much prescribes the character and model of the service.

The call to worship normally used is a standardized compilation of passages from the Old Testament and is as follows:

M: I was glad when they said to me, "Let us go to the house of the Lord!" Our feet shall stand within Thy gates, O Jerusalem!

P: For a day in thy courts is better than a thousand. I had rather be a doorkeeper in the house of my God than to dwell in the tents of wickedness.

M: Because of the house of the Lord our God, I will seek thy good.

P: Those that be planted in the house of the Lord, shall flourish in the courts of our God.

M: Blessed are they that dwell in thy house. Lord, I have loved thy habitation, the place where thy glory dwelleth.

P: For the Lord is in his holy temple, let all the earth keep silence before him.

M: Let the words of my mouth, and the meditation of my heart, be acceptable in thy sight, O Lord, my strength and my Redeemer.

P: O sing unto the Lord a new song, for he has done marvelous things! Make a joyful noise unto the Lord, all the earth, sing praises!

Alternative calls to worship are encouraged for special days, but they often supplement the regular opening sentences.

In many of the smaller congregations a lay member is often asked, without warning, to offer the morning prayer extemporaneously, and with reverent pride the petitioner lifts the congregation to the throne of grace. In that prayer might be heard a familiar expression which predates the emancipation of Black slaves in America and is a recognition of God's inclusive nature: "He is a father to the fatherless, and a mother to the motherless." Lay leadership in morning worship is highly acceptable in all of our congregations. In addition, there are designated special days for full lay leadership, such as Men's Day, Women's Day, Missionary Day, Children's Day, Youth Day, and Lay Witness Day.

The Decalogue or Ten Commandments with choral responses, ending with the greatest commandment in the words of Jesus (Matthew 22:37-40), has long usage among A.M.E.s. Two short versions are also utilized, an abridged text and the summary of the law. It is placed in the order of service after the reading of the Old and New Testaments. In some liturgical circles, the recital of the law would be considered ill-placed following the reading of the Gospel, but in A.M.E. worship it fits. The use of the Decalogue has promoted moral fortitude and ethical principles easily understood by a Two-Thirds World people in a First-World context who need a set of religious rules to guide their progress.

The altar call which has become prevalent in our second century is a significant component of Sunday worship. While not done on a regular basis in all of our congregations, this period of contrition and gratitude is for us a liberating act, reminding us of our former bondage, and reinforcing in us a determination to be inwardly and outwardly free. During the altar call, the congregation kneels and lays before the altar (communion rail) those needs and situations which plague both individuals and community, thereby functioning as an occasion to search for wholeness and to find healing. This element of worship is placed to meet the particular emphases and needs that arise from the Sunday service.

Our congregations have continued the practice of an invitation to discipleship, during which the unsaved and the unchurched are presented the opportunity to respond to God's good news of salvation in Jesus Christ. It is sometimes referred to as "opening the doors of the church." At this time in the service, persons are welcomed into the gathered community of those who have said "yes" to Jesus, and the invitation is issued to others to unite with the congregation to do Kingdom work. There are three categories of candidates for membership into the Body of Christ in African Methodism: (1) confession of faith/new converts; (2) Christian experience/baptized Christians from other churches; and (3) letter of transfer/Christians from other A.M.E. churches. Those who confess Christ for the first time and choose membership in the A.M.E. Church, after completing a course of instruction, are baptized as a sign of new life through Jesus Christ. After baptism, there is a three-month probationary period during which the candidate attends new membership training classes. The culmination of the process is the Order for Receiving Persons into Full Membership which includes "the right hand of fellowship," a lively ritual which welcomes and introduces new members into the local church.

Another aspect which cannot be overstressed is the time of announcements and congregational concerns. For the A.M.E. Church, as in other historic Black Churches, the major forum for sharing community concerns is the local church. It is a time which affirms, perhaps more than any other, that the sacred and the secular are indivisible. Critical issues are always laid before the congregation. The church is *the* arena for disseminating information whether it be regarding social unrest, a display of racism, criticism of unfair economic policies, the identification of community representatives for public office, the advancement of the cause of young people, the preservation of the Black male and family solidarity, the H.I.V./A.I.D.S. crisis, or the promotion of ecumenical relations. So, the announcements, congregational and community concerns, and even the acknowledgment of visitors are by no means incidental to worship. Those segments become the focus around which the gathered community seeks God's corporate blessing and engages each worshiper in mission and ministry. It may be at this time or following the sacraments that the church is led into an act of fellowship and celebration which can be a powerful manifestation of *koinonia*. The act of fellowship in some settings is called "passing the peace."

The Sacraments

In all that we do at Sunday morning worship, nothing diminishes the centrality of the sacraments. In the vernacular of our Church community, one might be heard to say, "Chile (child), you know I can't miss my communion."

The eucharist, referred to in most of our churches as Holy Communion or the Lord's Supper, is usually administered on the first Sunday of each month (and on other occasions) to commemorate, with great thanksgiving, what God has offered to us through the life, death, and resurrection of Jesus Christ. In observance of the Lord's Supper, our foreparents composed the well-known spiritual "Let Us Break Bread Together On Our Knees."

The elements of unleavened bread and unfermented juice of the vine (in some cases sacramental wine) are administered by ordained clergy, offered to all baptized believers, and received by persons kneeling at the altar rail. If persons are unable to kneel, they receive communion while either sitting in the pews or standing at the altar. There is meticulous care of the table exercised by the women whom we have designated as stewardesses. The altar rail and the table are dressed in white linen, spotlessly clean, creating an aura of reverence.

In the *Book of Worship* there are two orders for holy communion.

One is the "traditional" order when the sacrament is administered at the conclusion of prayer, scripture, and the preached word. The other order is called the Service of Word and Sacrament; it is more clearly conceived of as a unit.

The A.M.E. Church baptizes infants, children, and professing believers; all are believed to be biblically authenticated. In no wise is re-baptism allowed. The sacraments are a response to the Word and a sign of our new freedom in Christ Jesus. Those persons who are of age and have not been baptized may choose one of three modes: sprinkling, pouring, or immersion. Sprinkling and pouring are done at the altar rail. Immersion may take place in a heated pool which is a part of the architecture of the local church, or it may be done in a borrowed pool at a sister church, in a rented pool, in a river or lake, or at the seashore. Sometimes it becomes an occasion for an afternoon service.

The Setting for Worship

The place dedicated for the worship of God in the A.M.E. tradition can be a rather unpretentious and tiny facility with few furnishings and conveniences, or it may be a spectacular edifice—gothic or contemporary—with seating capacity up to three thousand and decorated with accoutrements. It may be a simple frame or cinderblock structure laid out and built by members of the congregation, or it could be a structure of concrete, steel, brick, or stone carefully designed by an architect and built by the finest craftspersons. The space also may be an acquired facility purchased as the result of an open occupancy housing market after the majority community has taken flight to new suburbs and Blacks have moved in. The sanctuary may be a converted Jewish synagogue, or it may be a building formerly occupied by a white congregation. A transformed supermarket, office building, or movie theater might also become a place for worship. In each and every location, whether small or large, decorated or plain, A.M.E. people "come into God's House, to magnify the Lord, and to worship Him."

The arrangement of Sunday morning worship is affected by a number of different factors: a distinct understanding of time is found in Black cultures; yet there are also the pressures of the clock in western societies; and each worshiping community has its space needs and logistical considerations. Some of the larger congregations may hold as many as three Sunday morning services on a regular basis. Other congregations hold at least two morning services. In at least one of our mega-churches, the third service begins at noon. In still other congregations, the worship day is completed with an evening service. It is also true that the spiritual fervor of Sunday morning services may carry over into afternoon fellowship services, which are a characteristic phenomenon of the Black Church. These fellowship services may be either inter- or intra-denominational.

The Ethos of Worship

This ordered spiritual journey, called the order of service, is carefully planned and executed by committed and inspired persons, both clergy and lay, and rekindles the worshiping community with a spirit that runs "from heart to heart and breast to breast." Together, clergy, choir, ushers, altar pages or acolytes, and other appointed worship leaders do their work in the presence of Jesus and under the inspiration of the Holy Spirit. The hopes and dreams of the gathered community are reborn in worship, and they depart to be the Church scattered, often as a lone voice in the struggle for social identity and for true citizenship as children of God.

Even with all of the sublime euphoria penetrating the abject frustration of a minority people, there is still an air of expectancy as the worship service begins. The clergy may vest in a pulpit gown trimmed with kente cloth of African design, in cassock and surplice, or in an alb, and wear either a kente stole or a stole in the color of the particular liturgical season. The clergy, choirs, and acolytes in procession, the ushers strutting about, and the stewards and trustees, deaconesses and stewardesses all filing in with faces aglow, announce the grandeur of the occasion. The congregation waits: a diverse people from all stations of life, from common laborer to corporation executive, artisan or professional, all equalized in their "Sunday-go-to-meeting" clothes. They've come to praise the Lord, often with hung-down heads, or heads "bloody but unbowed," seeking solace for the soul, food for thought, direction for life decisions, something to hold on to in the week to come.

From this description of worship on Sunday morning, with its praise and proclamation, with the combination of head and foot worship (hand clapping and foot patting) as a demonstration of collective pathos, the questions to be asked are: Have they worshiped

God "in spirit and in truth"? Have the people been stirred and stretched? Has the service been inclusive and multigenerational in its appeal? Have the defined goals for a planned celebration of authentic and indigenous expression of the faith been met? Have the people been nurtured?

In order to reflect on this reality from the A.M.E. perspective, attention is drawn to three prominent symbols: the cross, the pulpit, and the anvil. The cross is for those who struggle for survival with dignity, an inexorable sign of God's loving care in Jesus Christ—the Jesus who understands all about us because Calvary is no strange place. The pulpit and the anvil might indeed be synonymous. Together they symbolize the strength of the Word, the place where God's Word is pounded out in tuneful, stentorian tones, and sometimes with whooping and dynamic gestures. Because the pulpit is central in A.M.E. worship, preaching is central, and the preacher who is sent by the bishop knows full well that, above all else, he or she is expected to preach the Word. No matter that the preacher's theology may be fundamentalist, conservative, neo-orthodox, or liberal, there must be in his or her preaching some validation in the existential situation. Exhortation without logic is unacceptable; preaching without practice is inconsistent and therefore not believable.

As in other communions, A.M.E.s debate the effectiveness of Sunday morning worship on the basis that preaching lacks quality. Sometimes it is argued that worship is not nurturing: there is too much performance; there are too many clichés; and, it is without empathy. It might also be contended that the service is too preacher-centered, and that the style is too manipulative with a bent toward eliciting applause or creating a "feel good" syndrome. Or the opposite may be the case: that the preacher is not sufficiently involved and is dry and insipid.

The criticism may also refer to the music: that it lacks sufficient variety or is too loud, or the tune is too worldly, or the lyrics are inappropriate. Nevertheless, numerous types of choirs sing with exhilaration, though with varying degrees of proficiency and employing a variety of musical genres. Some find reason to criticize how and when the offering is received or simply complain about whatever is uncomfortable, saying, "It is not the way we have always done things."

What cannot be contradicted is that when there is a well-prepared and balanced A.M.E. order of worship, where there is a synchronizing

171

of the sacred and the secular, when thought and action are merged, when there is an emphasis on a faith that never doubts, then all the people of God are embraced and fed by the Holy Spirit. When such an event is held, spontaneity is not preempted by formalism. Animation does not negate genuine vitality, and a climate of bliss does not circumvent the sharing of legitimate emotions, such as pain, emptiness, sorrow, disappointment, and anger.

Sunday morning A.M.E. worship is "a foretaste of glory divine." It takes seriously the needs of the human family, and it understands that all the answers are not determined by human effort, and that salvation depends on our God. The well-known cliché "after a while and by and by" is not irrelevant. For while we are convinced that there must be some respect due us in this world, we cannot allow our vision of a home "beyond this place of wrath and tears" to vanish. Not all of our dreams and hopes and aspirations will be consummated this side of the Jordan; there will always be one more river to cross.

The African Methodist Episcopal Church has at its masthead the motto, "God Our Father, Christ Our Redeemer, Man Our Brother." In 1992 there was an amendment to the third phrase, so that it now reads "Humankind One Family." Sunday morning worship, though designed, implemented, financed, and supported by Black people, is in actuality the Body of Christ proclaiming the universality of the Church's mission and ministry. We pray without ceasing Jesus' high priestly prayer, "that [we] all may be one" (John 17:20). We adhere to the Pauline passage that we are "neither male nor female" by honoring the presence of ordained men and women who preach and preside at the Lord's Table. We follow the doctrine and discipline of the A.M.E. Church as a rule of faith and life. Above all else, we invite and embrace all of God's children. Although our worship together on Sunday morning is always a reminder of that oneness in Jesus Christ, it is unequivocally a celebration of the culture of Black people and of the God who has called us to be.

Chapter 10

From Simplicity to Multiplicity: Sunday Worship among Free Methodists

Douglas R. Cullum

Worship in the Free Methodist Church has been shaped by a particular package of traditions and movements, some of which are shared with the other branches of North American Methodism. Each successive stage in the development of the denomination has been influenced in important ways by the religious and cultural currents of the day. These traditions and influences will be examined from the founding of the denomination to the present.

Nineteenth-Century Origins

The issue of worship figured prominently in the Free Methodist Church's originating struggle in the mid-nineteenth century. While it would be anachronistic to say that the early leaders of the new denomination conceived of their struggle as having to do with it as an isolated issue, they regularly insisted that worship was part and parcel of their central set of concerns. For the early Free Methodists, worship was intimately related to piety and ethos. That is, true worship was seen as the gracious and inevitable result of a well defined and experientially embraced religious belief system.

A Rigorous Simplicity: Early Free Methodist Piety

To understand the piety of early Free Methodism is to understand a great deal about the Free Methodist people of the nineteenth century and their worship. They were a single-minded people who sought rigorously to order every aspect of their lives around what they understood to be the central features of the Christian Gospel. Three aspects of early Free Methodism's commitment to gospel simplicity, which are firmly rooted in the Methodist, Frontier, and Holiness traditions of Protestant worship, offer insight into the piety of nineteenth-century Free Methodism.

First, with regard to doctrine, early Free Methodists embraced a piety that was experientially focused and soteriologically grounded. A primitivist impulse figured prominently among the leaders of the early Free Methodist movement. "There are," wrote Benjamin Titus Roberts, "many sincere and earnest persons throughout the land, anxiously inquiring 'for the old paths.' Dissatisfied with being outer-court worshippers, they are desirous of 'dwelling in the secret place of the Most High.'"[1] The doctrinal simplicity of Roberts and the other framers of native Free Methodist theology called for a re-appropriation of what they understood to be the soteriological heart of biblical religion. It was this they found wanting in the prevailing expressions of Christian faith.[2]

With soteriology at the heart of their theology, the Free Methodist presentation of the Gospel had as its goal the personal experience of God's saving grace. Evangelical conversion was a vital component of Free Methodist soteriology. B. T. Roberts promoted an "experimental religion" which he understood to be the "foundation and life of practical piety, as well as the indispensable condition of final salvation."[3] The doctrine of Christian holiness was given special attention, not as a department of theology distinct from the doctrine of salvation, but as the epitome of experimental religion and the source of spiritual power for a life of practical and ethical piety.

Free Methodist doctrinal piety demanded that nothing should be permitted to divert the focus of one's life away from the gospel call to "a deep and genuine religious experience." The Church was to do all it could "to secure a return to Gospel simplicity and purity wherever there ha[d] been a departure from them."[4] This aspect of nineteenth-century Free Methodist piety was a formative factor in the Church's conception and practice of worship. As an heir of the Frontier tradition, the Free Methodist Sunday service was conceived primarily as a means to an end. It included singing and preaching which were designed to call congregants to the personal experience of Christian conversion. But the desired end of Free Methodist worship was not simply the conversion of the unchurched; worship also focused on the ongoing Christian life. As a proponent of the ethical demands of the Wesleyan/Holiness tradition, the Free Methodist Church understood Sunday worship as an opportunity for worshipers to experience personal and corporate progress in the life of sanctification.

A second aspect of early Free Methodism's commitment to gospel simplicity may be described as an egalitarian piety. The leaders of the Free Methodist Church of the founding era insisted that the transforming life of the Gospel was available for all and therefore must be offered without regard for status or race. It was this doctrinal and disciplinary focus that was at the heart of the social positions taken by the denomination at its formation. The slavery of human beings, the holding of membership in oath-bound secret societies, and the practice of the pew rental system—each of these was perceived to compromise the simplicity of a gospel message which was intended to be for all people alike. The egalitarian piety of the early Free Methodist Church engendered a disciplinary rigor that had far-reaching ramifications for the experience of corporate worship. The nascent group's unrelenting opposition to the system of renting church pews may serve as an example.

Roberts and other leaders addressed the evils of the pew rental system throughout the founding era of the denomination, focusing their argument on the theological claim that God's universal offer of salvation is of a piece with the divine lack of partiality toward human beings.[5] For example, Roberts insisted that "every arrangement of the sanctuary of God" should be a means of demonstrating and teaching the essential equality of all people. The church was to be the place where the rich and poor knelt down together and where everyone would "be made to realize that the Lord is the maker of them all."[6] Such a goal was not achievable as long as the pew system prevailed. Nor were Free Methodists convinced that the injunctions of the Gospel could be satisfied either by the practice of reserving a designated block of seats for those unable to afford pew rents, or by the establishment of "plain mission-houses, sustained by the wealthy, for the poor."[7] Both of these practices were interpreted as an insult to human dignity; the poor could not be expected to advertise their poverty every time they came to worship. The same concern extended to those in the lower and middle strata of the socioeconomic hierarchy who could not afford the luxury of a paid seat at church. These, Roberts insisted, would stay away from worship rather than expose their economic standing to the humiliation of public scrutiny.[8]

Thus, the people of the early Free Methodist Church contended that the practice of supporting churches by means of pew rents effectively denied the essential equality of all persons, which they believed was at the heart of the Gospel message, and replaced the egalitarian standards of the Gospel with the "aristocratic principles" of the world. True Christianity, the early Free Methodists urged, "is the most thoroughly democratic institution in the world. It utterly abhors the spirit of the caste."[9]

The early Free Methodist piety of gospel simplicity also had an eschatological focus. In fact, it was an eschatological, or "other-worldly," sort of piety that was at the heart of the day-to-day routine of Free Methodist life. The rhythms of their corporate life were calibrated by the one great hope of their existence: future and final salvation. Anything which, in their view, did not contribute to being prepared for eternal life was to be rigorously avoided. Such a commitment had a dramatic effect on the people, places, and patterns of Free Methodist worship.

The Free Methodist faithful of the nineteenth century were challenged by their leaders to make their relationship with God and its ultimate culmination in heaven the all-consuming focus of their lives. They were exhorted that this simplicity of purpose demanded a radical separation from the practices of the world.[10] Virtually everything—from their manner of dress and the employment of their leisure time to the details of church architecture, fundraising practices and forms of worship—was to be regulated by their solitary passion to be prepared for eternal life. Free Methodists insisted that the world's encroachment on the Church and in the lives of its members must be strenuously resisted. The inroads of the world were seen in the ever-increasing popularity of "pic-nic religion." They were convinced that pleasure and "conviviality" ruled the day.[11]

Nor did the trend toward a "religion of beauty" among some mid- to late-nineteenth-century Protestants go undetected by the early Free Methodists.[12] Their response held no hidden surprises: the increasingly aesthetic inclinations of the mainline Churches were interpreted as accommodations to the tastes of the world and as sure indicators that modern Christianity was moving away from being "the power of God unto salvation" and rapidly becoming just another "one of the fine arts."[13] The appropriation by much of mainline Protestantism of large blocks of the Church year and the use of Christmas trees, Easter flowers, and sophisticated music to attract the people, were all regarded as dangerous drifts away from a truly

176

spiritual religion. The rage for fine church edifices caused Free Methodist leaders to reiterate their position on the stewardship demands of gospel simplicity. Costly churches, they argued, tended to exclude the poor, rendered necessary the assistance of the wealthy, and were utterly inefficient in the economy of the Gospel.[14] Biblical principles of simplicity, as well as the old Methodist *Discipline*, were pointed to in support of their stance that church edifices should be "plain and decent . . . and not more expensive than is absolutely unavoidable."[15] The Free Methodist General Conference of 1882 formally articulated the Church's position that "all houses of worship are to be plain, without steeples and no more expensive than absolutely necessary."[16]

The "other-worldly" mind-set of the early Free Methodist people permeated the rhythms of their corporate life. The annual calendar was not structured by the seemingly abstruse demands of the Christian year, but rather by a handful of very earthy events which they believed would aid them in their preparation for life eternal. Among these were camp meetings, quarterly meetings, love feasts, watchnight services, and class meetings. But at the very center of the Free Methodist experience of Christian faith was a commitment to Lord's Day sabbatarianism.[17] Church leaders taught that the Sabbath should be received as a gift of God. As such, the Sabbath took on a nearly sacramental character in the weekly routine of the Free Methodist faithful.[18] The Puritan value of completing all arrangements for the Lord's Day no later than Saturday night was recommended, so that the joy of the "holy Sabbath morning" might break in "upon the Christian, whose 'waking thoughts are bright with God's praise.'"[19] No work was to be performed except that which was indispensably necessary, and persons were to refrain from causing others to commit the sin of Sabbath breaking.[20] The Sabbath, then, was to be kept free from all secular distractions, so that it might be set apart exclusively "for rest and devotion to spiritual things."[21]

The Sabbath was believed to be a day in which God brought physical, spiritual, and emotional renewal to a weary world. Free Methodists saw the Sabbath as the divinely ordained means of providing respite from the work-a-day world.[22] For the believer, however, the primary benefits of the Sabbath were spiritual and emotional. "It is a dam," they were exhorted, "that God has thrown across the stream of worldliness every seven miles to check the rapidity of the current and make it navigable. Break down the dam and you rush in ruin."[23] Thus, the Sabbath was hailed as the most important day of the week; it was to be received as a true means of grace.[24]

Early Free Methodist Worship

The experimental, egalitarian, and "other-worldly" piety of the early Free Methodists was the engine that drove their experience of worship. Free Methodist disciplinary guidelines for Sunday worship were a direct carryover from the 1856 *Discipline* of the parent body, the Methodist Episcopal Church. Sunday morning worship followed the typical frontier-influenced Methodist pattern of singing, prayer, scripture reading from both Testaments, and preaching; the Lord's Prayer and the apostolic benediction (2 Corinthians 13:13) were additionally prescribed. Sunday gatherings for worship also included afternoon and evening services, the main staples of which were singing, prayer, and preaching.

Lively singing among early Free Methodists was encouraged as a significant form of congregational participation in worship. The Free Methodist Church adopted the statement of the Methodist Episcopal Church *Book of Discipline* (1856), "Of the Spirit and Truth of Singing," but with the addition of one weighty sentence: "In no case let there be instrumental music or choir singing in our public worship."[25] The early leaders of the Free Methodist Church believed that these restrictions were part of the distinctive witness of true Methodism. By the end of the nineteenth century, rumblings against these restrictions and in favor of choirs and instrumental music began to be heard. Yet, the General Conference of 1898 solidly affirmed the denomination's historic position and explained it in *A Digest of Free Methodist Law*, which was prepared and published by order of that same Conference:

> [Singing] is a means of grace that the church cannot afford to delegate to a select number. It is a part of divine worship in which all should be free to unite. Congregational singing is universal in the Free Methodist Church. The tendency of choir singing and instrumental music to monopolize this branch of worship, to produce lightness and irreverence in singing, and to create strife and discord, is so great that their use in our public worship is not allowed.[26]

The absence of choirs and musical instruments did not deter Free

Methodists from joyful singing as an integral part of their practice of worship. Their first hymnal, *Hymns for the Use of the Methodist Episcopal Church* (1849), was borrowed from the parent Church without revision. In the late 1860s, the use of the MEC hymn book was augmented by *Spiritual Songs and Hymns for Pilgrims*, compiled by B. T. Roberts. This collection contained a wide variety of songs and enjoyed sufficient popularity to demand the publication of several revised editions. By 1878 the book contained 199 songs. In 1883, the *Hymn Book of the Free Methodist Church* was published, a words-only collection of 868 songs and hymns, which the compilers claimed were "some of the choicest hymns in the language" as well as "orthodox, evangelical, and generally of an elevated style and character."[27] The use of this volume was enhanced and complemented in 1890 when J. G. Terrill published a new edition of Philip Phillips' *Metrical Tune Book* keyed to the hymn numbers of the Free Methodist *Hymn Book*. After Terrill's death, yet another edition of the *Tune Book* appeared, entitled *Metrical Tune Book with Hymns and Supplement*. The newest edition featured the addition of 290 songs "for camp-meetings, class and prayer meetings, Sabbath-schools, children's meetings, missionary meetings, and some choice selections for funerals."[28]

Fervent prayer was also a prominent feature of nineteenth-century Free Methodist worship. Almost all prayer in public worship, by clergy and laity alike, was extemporaneous. The use of written prayers was a salient part of Free Methodist worship only in its occasional services. Though originally found in separate disciplinary chapters, the occasional services were soon grouped together to form a single chapter entitled "Ritual," which included orders for baptism, the Lord's Supper, ordination, matrimony, and burial of the dead.

Baptism and the Lord's Supper were only occasional events in the Sunday worship experience of the Free Methodist people. With the absence of any disciplinary requirement, baptisms took place rather sporadically and on an as-needed basis. The service of baptism was guided by two forms: one for the baptism of infants and one for the baptism of adults. Adult candidates for baptism or the parents of the infant to be baptized were given the choice of the modes of immersion, sprinkling, or pouring. While steadfastly maintaining its commitment to infant baptism, the Church made alterations which underscored the responsibilities of the parents and the expectation that the child would come to a personal experience of conversion at an appropriate age.[29]

The sacrament of the Lord's Supper in nineteenth-century Free Methodism was viewed as a high and holy occasion. It was normally celebrated at least once a quarter, and often served as the culmination of the quarterly meeting. In addition, the Lord's Supper was a regular climactic feature of Free Methodist camp meetings.[30] The Sunday service of holy communion functioned as an extension of the ordinary pattern of worship. On such days it was permissible to omit the reading of the two chapters from scripture which was normally a part of the preaching service. With the exception of the substitution of an extemporaneous prayer for the prescribed post-communion prayer of thanksgiving and Gloria, the Free Methodist liturgy was adopted verbatim from the Methodist Episcopal Church. As such, the earliest order of holy communion in the Free Methodist Church was a direct descendant of Wesley's *Sunday Service*, and it proved to be very resistant to change, though the elder was authorized to omit, if time constraints demanded it, any part of the service except the prayer of consecration. The small amount of tinkering with the communion liturgy that successfully won approval in the General Conferences of the nineteenth century was driven by a concern that the Church's formal prayers be in agreement with its commitment to the doctrine of Christian perfection as articulated by the Holiness movement.[31]

Vigorous preaching was the focal point of nearly every Free Methodist service of Sunday worship. Time-honored Wesleyan advice gave Free Methodist preachers their purpose and method for preaching: "1. To convince, 2. To offer Christ, 3. To invite, 4. To build up, and to do this in some measure in every sermon."[32] But it was the urgency of the harvest that gave Free Methodist preachers their passion to proclaim the Gospel in a manner that would draw people to saving faith. The preacher was not alone in this task, for the Church also authorized the licensing of persons to the office of exhorter. The role of the exhorter was not to do the regular work of preaching, but rather to offer timely words of admonishment and persuasion in order to help worshipers make practical application of biblical truth. This would often take place at the end of the regular sermon and would lead to a time of prayer for conversions at the close of the service. It was this focus on a personal and life-changing experience that was the goal, not only of Free Methodist preaching, but also of the worship service as a whole.

Twentieth-Century Developments

Because of the significance of the founding era in shaping the denomination's core piety, the experience of nineteenth-century Free Methodism is the essential backdrop against which the developments of the twentieth century must be observed and evaluated. The evolution of worship in the Free Methodist Church of this century has been affected by the Church's identification with or participation in certain religious positions and trends. The following survey is threefold: two major periods in which there was observable development are highlighted, and a final set of observations is made with regard to the more current influences and challenges of the last two decades.[33]

Second-Generation Free Methodism

The half-century following the death of B. T. Roberts (d. 1893), the leading figure in the denomination's founding era, was a crucial time in the development of Free Methodist identity. A new generation of leaders, most of whom had worked closely with the pioneers of the first generation, took up the challenge of articulating the distinctives of the denomination as it moved into the twentieth century. Free Methodist writers of this period exhibited a great concern to demonstrate their Church's faithfulness to its Methodist heritage. Moreover, they interpreted the essentials of what it meant to be a Methodist in terms of the theological and life-style distinctives of the American Holiness tradition.

A pivotal year was 1910, the fiftieth-anniversary year of Free Methodism's existence. This milestone gave rise to a significant amount of reflection about the mission and purpose of the Church which set the tone for the remainder of the period. A special semi-centennial issue of the denomination's weekly paper, *The Free Methodist*, appeared in August of that year. A major theme was the rehearsal and interpretation of Free Methodist history as the providential continuation of original Methodism. J. S. MacGreary's lead article claimed that the parent Church had drifted away from its moorings of primitive Methodism and that the early leaders of the Free Methodist Church had no choice but to organize in order to carry out the divine plan.[34] The denomination felt somewhat vindicated in its triumphal spirit when, only a few months later in the Fall of 1910, the Genesee Conference of the Methodist Episcopal Church voted to restore the ordination parchments of B. T. Roberts and the others who were expelled in the schism of 1858–1859. The Free Methodist Church was represented at the occasion by Roberts' son, Benson H. Roberts. In his address to the Conference, the younger Roberts stressed the common roots which the two denominations shared with other branches of Methodism in America, while at the same time making a firm claim for the need of the distinctive contribution of the Free Methodist Church. The gift that the Church had to offer was understood as a unified package that presented primitive Methodism and the themes of the Holiness movement as one and the same.[35]

Though the Church underwent a measure of theological refinement in the three decades following the 1910 celebration, it is abundantly clear that the doctrine of Christian holiness as the special inheritance of Methodism was firmly embraced throughout this period. It was in this commitment that the Free Methodist Church of the second generation found its identity. In their pastoral address of 1939, the bishops of the Church discussed the place of Free Methodism in relation to three religious trends of the day: ecumenism, congregationalism, and pentecostalism. The ecumenical movement was interpreted as a trend toward "mediating tolerance and a liberal inclusiveness" which could only serve to blur denominational distinctiveness. The Uniting Conference of Methodism's three major groups which occurred earlier that year was lifted up as an example of the leveling influence of ecumenism. "The smaller bodies," said the bishops, "were forced to yield vital points" of denominational conviction. The trend toward independent congregationalism was seen as a competitive undercutting of time-tested denominational stability, while pentecostalism was charged with promoting excessive emotion as a substitute for authentic faith. In the face of these religious forces, second-generation Free Methodism reaffirmed its commitment to exist as a distinctive witness.[36]

The major liturgical accomplishment of this period was the publication of a new hymnal which would serve the denomination for the next forty-one years. The new hymnal was also an achievement in church cooperation. A representative from the Wesleyan Methodist Connection served on the hymnal commission and the volume was adopted by that denomination as its official hymnal. Issued in 1910, the new *Free Methodist Hymnal* included 738 hymns with musical notation. In their introductory address, the bishops of the Church commended the hymnal commission for the prominence the hymnal gave to the hymns of Wesley (there are 235 Wesley texts), its emphasis on Christian experience, and its suitability for revival services and camp meetings. The hymnal's front pages offered an order of worship based on the guidelines of the *Discipline*, with the structure of: singing, prayer, Lord's Prayer, scripture lessons from both Testaments, singing, notices, collection, sermon, prayer, singing, doxology, and apostolic benediction. The significance of this order resides not so much in the components of worship it includes, which were largely set forth in the *Discipline*, but rather in the rubrics it offers in addition. The service was to begin "exactly at the time appointed" and worshipers were to "kneel in silent prayer on entering the sanctuary." All singing was expected to be from the *Free Methodist Hymnal* with the people standing. The posture of prayer for both minister and congregation was kneeling, the people, presumably, facing the pew. A special, and surprising, feature of the 1910 hymnal was the inclusion of twenty-nine selections in a section entitled "Occasional Pieces, Chants, Doxologies." Included among this assortment of service music were evening hymns, a wedding hymn, table graces, seven chants including a plainchant of the Lord's Prayer, and five doxologies.

Evangelicalism in the Wesleyan Tradition

The current period in the history of the Free Methodist Church may be said to have begun sometime in the late 1930s. As the denomination moved closer to its century mark it experienced the normal process of maturation and institutionalization. The most salient event in cementing the mature identity of the denomination was Free Methodism's participation in the organizing convention of the National Association of Evangelicals in May 1943. Free Methodist Bishop Leslie R. Marston was elected to serve as the Association's first vice-president and Seattle Pacific College president, C. H. Watson, was placed on the Board of Administration. In 1944 Bishop Marston became the NAE's second president. Similarly, throughout this period, the predominant emphasis of the denominational leadership and official publications has focused on the mandate of evangelism. Early Methodist history has been reread with a view to discovering its implications for evangelism and renewal, and the theme of Christian holiness has been articulated more consciously in the light of the Great Commission.[37]

The Free Methodist Church's self-conscious alignment with mainstream American evangelicalism has resulted in both a moderating and broadening of Free Methodist piety. The denomination's earlier monothematic stress on the doctrine of Christian holiness has come to be interpreted more in line with a developmental understanding of the process of salvation. The harshness of the earlier era has been tempered by the desire to cooperate with other denominations on the basis of a more broadly conceived evangelical faith, rather than on the basis of holiness theology alone. The Church in this period came to identify itself clearly as an evangelical denomination in the Wesleyan tradition.

The forty-year span from 1939 to 1979 saw significant developments which affected the Sunday worship experience of Free Methodist people. Evolution took place in three main categories: music and hymnody, the theology and practice of worship, and sacramental services.

Music and Hymnody

The matter of instrumental music and choirs in public worship finally came to a head and found resolution in the middle third of the twentieth century. Every General Conference from 1931 through 1955 found it necessary to make some decision concerning this issue. In 1931 the restrictions were upheld, but an exemption from the rule prohibiting instrumental music was granted for "foreign-speaking churches or missions in the United States, Mexico and Japan." In 1935 a resolution to remove all restrictions was defeated by a wide margin. Likewise in 1939, a proposal to allow the use of instrumental music as a local option was rejected. But in 1943, the General Conference finally voted to permit the use of instrumental music, with the proviso that each local church must adopt the measure by a two-thirds vote, and that the annual conference in which the church was located must have approved the use of instrumental music by a majority vote. This change of position allowed the utilization of only one instrument, either organ or piano, and use of choirs in public worship remained proscribed. The final resolution came in 1955 when all restrictions were removed: the restriction against choir singing was eliminated, and the use of musical instruments, of any number or kind, was left to the discretion of each local congregation. An important result of Free Methodism's saga with regard to the use of choirs and musical instruments was that it helped the denomination hammer out its understanding of the role of the constituent elements in the public worship event. "The purpose of music in divine service," declared the new paragraph of the 1955 *Discipline*, "is to inspire and to sustain worship. Therefore, participation in musical exercises, vocal and instrumental, shall seek to contribute to reverent and exalted worship and not to the display of talent, however excellent."[38]

Two new hymnals guided the Church's music in this period. In 1951 *Hymns of the Living Faith* was published as a joint venture with the Wesleyan Church of America. It was a collection of 579 hymns, sixty-three of which were the work of either Charles or John Wesley. The largest part of the hymnal was its section on "The Christian Life" which included 231 songs and hymns. Sprinkled throughout the volume was a generous sampling of service music, including hymns for the opening and closing of worship, morning and evening hymns, a handful of doxologies, and a section of hymns for use in sacramental services. Congregational participation in corporate worship was aided by the inclusion of forty-nine scriptural passages for responsive reading and twelve selections for unison reading. A glimpse of the variety of Free Methodist worship experiences current in the period may be seen in the desire of the hymnal commission that the new hymn book would "serve the complementary purposes of the church's more formal Sunday worship on the one hand, and the brighter and more buoyant church school, mid-week prayer and evangelistic services on the other."[39]

In late 1967, the Free Methodist and Wesleyan Methodist Churches agreed to begin work on another cooperative hymnal, but the formation of an official commission had to wait until the Wesleyan and the Pilgrim Holiness bodies had finalized their merger in 1968. The project continued until the publication in 1976 of *Hymns of Faith and Life*. The 567 hymns of the new collection included sixty-eight Wesley texts. Special features of the hymnal were its inclusion of both the Free Methodist and Wesleyan services of holy communion, the Covenant Service, and a collection of eighty-six congregational readings which were designed to be used as responsive, antiphonal, or unison readings. Among the hymn texts designed specifically for use in the structuring of worship were calls to worship, responses, doxologies, and amens.[40]

The Theology and Practice of Worship

Music was not the only arena in which development was taking place in the years 1939–1979. Free Methodists were also wrestling with their understanding of the theology and practice of worship itself. In the years preceding the General Conference of 1955 and continuing through the General Conference of 1974 there was considerable ferment with regard to the question of the purpose, style, and architecture which most appropriately represented the ethos of the Free Methodist Church. The denomination's participation in the sphere of mainstream American evangelicalism in the mid-1950s seems to have forced it to struggle with how it would look and act in relation to other evangelicals. As was happening in many denominations in mid-century North America, numerous church buildings were being constructed among the Free Methodists. The fact that a few of these new churches opted for divided chancels in their sanctuary space caused a considerable stir among the delegates of the 1955 General Conference. Because they were unable to come to an agreeable resolution of the issue on the floor of Conference, the denomination's Board of Administration was authorized to draft a new statement for the *Discipline*. The resulting statement was revealing, both in what it deleted and in what it added. The existing requirement of plainness and simplicity in the erection of churches, as was noted above, had been a part of the *Discipline* since 1882. The Board of Administration's new statement for 1955 removed the rule against the building of churches with steeples, added a sentence about the need for architectural and interior designs which would contribute to the centrality of preaching, and effectively softened the precept on plainness by allowing that church buildings themselves ought to be pleasing additions to any community. This disciplinary position on church architecture remained essentially unchanged in the years that followed.[41]

Also in 1955, an important new paragraph was added to the *Discipline* which placed Free Methodism unequivocally in the Free Church tradition with its declaration that "public worship in our churches shall be free and non-liturgical in form." In addition, it emphasized the primacy of preaching as the preferred method of both Christian nurture and evangelism in the service of worship. Finally, the new paragraph recommended the use of an architectural style that would ensure "a central pulpit position for the preaching

186

of the Word."[42] The forthrightness of this statement engendered a significant amount of soul searching among the denomination's leaders concerning the nature of Free Methodist worship. A conversation had begun, but it would be nineteen years before a new statement on the purpose of worship would find its way into the pages of the *Discipline*. The first adjustment came in 1964 when the sentence which recommended the placement of the pulpit in a central position was deleted, though, as noted above, the statement of the later section of the *Discipline* that church architecture should "contribute to a distinctively evangelical simplicity and reverence in worship which makes the preaching of the Word central in the service" was retained.[43]

In 1974 sweeping changes were made in the *Book of Discipline*. Perhaps the most significant change was that the denomination's Articles of Religion were rewritten. Among the alterations was the removal of the classical statement, "Of Rites and Ceremonies of Churches," which American Methodism had inherited from Anglicanism through Wesley. The substance of this deleted Article was now inserted as a new introductory paragraph in the disciplinary section on "Christian Worship." This change, along with the rewriting of the whole section, resulted in an effective counterbalance to the bold positions taken in 1955. The new initial sentences reaffirmed the denomination's earlier position that "rites and ceremonies of the church are to be accorded respect" and that no individual member should "willfully or purposefully disregard the rites of the church." Moreover, the declaration of 1955 that Free Methodist worship should be "free and non-liturgical in form" was replaced with the more moderate statement that "public worship in our churches shall seek a balance between freedom and form."[44] A final major change in this disciplinary chapter was the addition of a new statement on the purpose of worship. The following is the 1974 revision of the paragraph on the "Order of Public Worship," which has been maintained in each successive *Discipline* through 1989:

> The Sunday morning corporate worship service should provide four basic results: (1) to provide opportunity for the praise of God; (2) to give worshipers insight into the will of God; (3) to lead individuals to commit themselves personally to God's revealed will; and (4) to strengthen the dedicated person to perform the will of God. To accomplish these desired results, each service should include congregational singing, reading from the scriptures, pas-

toral prayer, the Lord's Prayer, and preaching. The apostolic benediction is recommended for dismissing the congregation.[45]

A final event of this period which was an important factor in the
evolution of the denomination's theology and practice of worship
was the publication in 1976 of *The Free Methodist Minister: A Service
Book*. Compiled and edited by Lloyd H. Knox, this small volume of
ninety pages pulled together the sections from the *Book of Discipline*
on the ministry, worship, and fellowship, as well as the denominational rites for reception of members, baptism, holy communion,
marriage, and burial. The book also offered a selection of "Scriptures
for Various Usages," including passages for use in public worship:
ascriptions of praise, benedictions, offertory sentences, and calls to
worship. In addition, new forms of worship for special occasions in
the life of the church were made available. Free Methodist clergy now
had at their disposal a Service of Christian Commitment (Membership Covenant), an order of service for Love Feast/Breadbreaking,
and services for use in the dedication of churches, parsonages, and
hymnals. The significance of the volume was that, for the first time
in the denomination's history, it put into the hands of the Free
Methodist parish minister a book to be used in worship in addition
to the Bible, hymn book, and *Discipline*.

Sacramental Services

The Free Methodist liturgy of holy communion has been more
resistant to change than many other parts of the Church's tradition.
The main service in use in the late twentieth century was, with only
minor variations, the same as was used in the earliest years of the
denomination's existence.

The same restraint has not been the case with regard to the
sacrament of baptism. The Free Methodist Church's self-embraced
identity as a denomination in the American evangelical tradition
seems to have been at least one precipitating factor in alterations
which were made in the service for the baptism of infants. In 1974
two substantial modifications were made. First, the rite, which had
not been materially altered since 1882, was rewritten. The resulting
product was a service that sounded theologically more like an order
for infant dedication than infant baptism. The second change made
explicit what the first only implied. The following momentous new

rubric was added which officially authorized the practice of infant dedication in the Free Methodist Church:

> If the parents wish this to be a dedication ceremony, the pastor shall substitute the statement of baptism with the following words: "We, your pastor and your parents, dedicate you, *Name*, to God and the service of his kingdom, in the name of the Father, and the Son, and the Holy Spirit. Amen." [When dedicating, water shall not be used.][46]

This metamorphosis in Free Methodism's practice of baptism was finally complete in 1985 when the foregoing rubric was removed, and a Service of Infant Dedication appeared alongside the Service of Infant Baptism. The current practice of the Free Methodist Church is to offer both services. This position represents an uneasy compromise after a number of years of struggle. As early as 1964, after having heard reports that some were refusing to baptize infants and insisting rather on a service of dedication, the bishops of the Church found it necessary to issue a formal reminder to Free Methodist clergy that they were under disciplinary obligation to perform services of infant baptism.[47] Moreover, in the years prior to the General Conference of 1985, Church leaders cautioned the denomination that it was in danger of being influenced toward the loss of its heritage "by the Baptistic branches of the church."[48] Nonetheless, the Free Methodist Church has historically exhibited an uncanny ability to remain united despite a certain level of internal tension and theological ambiguity.

Post-1980 Developments and Influences

The foregoing account of the development of the denomination's position on the baptism or dedication of infants is symbolic of the mind of the Free Methodist Church as it entered the last two decades of the twentieth century. It is, perhaps, too early to determine whether forces at work within the present-day Free Methodist Church are competing traditions or creative tensions. What appears certain is that the Free Methodist Church of the late twentieth century is in the process of defining its own kind of pluralism. The process of the denomination's institutionalization has progressed in such a manner that there is a rather stable core of commonly embraced evangelical faith. That is, the Free Methodist Church stands clearly in the tradition of historic orthodoxy with regard to the essentials of Christian faith and teaching. But given this basic theological core, the Free Methodist denomination is presently at a stage in its development in which traditional boundaries are being tested and pushed outward. The issue of public worship is no exception. The denominational publications of this period have regularly included articles on the subject of worship which reveal the presence of a wide variety of popular opinion with regard to the practice and purposes of worship.[49] The following sketch is an attempt to document the items which have had the most bearing on the course of Free Methodist worship in the most recent fifteen years.

Church-Growth Principles and Neo-Pentecostalism

The commitment of the Free Methodist Church to an evangelical and experiential piety was the lifeblood that flowed through its veins from the earliest days. Rather than allowing it to dissipate, the Church's leaders have given intentional effort to strengthening this commitment in the last half of the twentieth century. For example, in 1985 the Pastoral Address of the denomination's bishops affirmed that evangelism was the "number-one task" of the Free Methodist Church.[50] As a child of the Frontier tradition and an older first cousin of the Pentecostal tradition, it would be very unlikely indeed for the Free Methodist Church not to have any kinship with the modern-day offspring of these traditions. The primary source for the dissemination of church-growth principles and methodology has been the denomination's Department of Evangelism and Church Growth. This agency has aggressively sought to communicate principles of effective church leadership to the pastors, church planters, and laity of the denomination. This has been accomplished by means of newsletters, training manuals, conferences, and seminars. One of the key parts of this program has been a teaching component on the kinds of worship that are believed to attract unchurched people. Among the ideas that have been advanced are a worship style that is relevant to needs of the people, worship that is contemporary rather than traditional, and worship that is seeker-sensitive, celebrative, and "characterized by faster-paced music and high energy."[51]

The primary influence of the neo-pentecostal movement has come in the area of music. Many Free Methodist Churches are now using the style and resources of the praise and worship tradition as either a part or all of the Sunday morning music experience. These elements include the employment of song sheets or projection equipment in addition to, or, in some cases, in place of the hymnal. Some congregations have regular worship bands, usually composed of lay volunteers who accompany or lead in worship with a wide variety of instruments, including keyboards, guitars, and percussion instruments. In some of the larger churches where there are two or more Sunday worship services, one of the services will often be contemporary in style, and the other more traditional.[52] The influence of these movements is a widespread phenomenon across the face of Free Methodism in the United States, with some convinced that this part of the American religious scene is evidence of authentic revival.

Publication of The Pastor's Handbook

In 1982 the Board of Bishops published the first edition of the *Pastor's Handbook of the Free Methodist Church*. New editions were issued in 1986 and 1991. Edited by Bishop Clyde E. Van Valin, the *Pastor's Handbook* was a substantial text of pastoral resources that made up for what was lacking in the smallness of its forerunner of 1976, *The Free Methodist Minister*. The new book was a loose-leaf volume with three major categories of material: The Pastor as Leader of Worship, The Pastor as Shepherd, and The Pastor as Administrator. Among its resources for use in the planning of public worship were suggested orders of worship, a lectionary, calls to worship, invocations, offertory sentences, benedictions, and closing prayers. Its pages included all of the approved rituals for use in the Church. In addition to the regular liturgies of the Church, some of the special services were an order for the Love Feast, a Service of Prayer for the Healing of Human Hurts, the Renewal of Marriage Vows, and various services of installation and dedication. A significant feature of the *Handbook* was its inclusion of teaching materials.

The bishops' intention for the volume was that it would "assist pastors to better understand and implement the basic pastoral functions as interpreted by the mission and practice of the Free Methodist Church" as well as help clergy identify the denomination's "patterns and prudentials."[53] Thus, what the bishops presented was essentially a mini-course in Free Methodist pastoral theology. Among the book's instructional materials were an exposition of the purpose of worship, guidelines for song leaders and ushers, a Free Methodist perspective on preaching, advice about children at the Lord's Supper, and guidelines for conducting funerals or memorial services. For the purposes of this survey, the most important of these was the statement on the purpose of worship. It began with an affirmation of the priority of worship: "The worship of God is the most noble experience known to humanity. It is also the most important activity in the life of the church." It emphasized the importance of a balanced view of worship in the Free Methodist tradition, one which would value both objective and subjective, ordered and spontaneous expressions of divine worship.[54] While the suggested orders of worship included in the *Handbook* did not break any new liturgical ground, they were helpful in presenting practical examples of how the disciplinary guidelines might be employed in relation to other aspects of public worship, such as announcements, the affirmation of faith, the offering, choral anthems, special music, and the invitation to Christian discipleship.

The Lectionary

For the first time in the history of the denomination, the General Conference of 1979 authorized the production of a lectionary for use in Free Methodist churches. The task was assigned to the denomination's Study Commission on Doctrine, which gave the primary writing responsibility for the project to one of its members, Paul W. Livermore. The completed lectionary was field-tested by twelve pastoral leaders across the denomination in the Spring of 1984. It received the approval of the 1985 General Conference, and was finally published in the 1986 edition of the *Pastor's Handbook*. Though based on the Common Lectionary, the Free Methodist lectionary was a new production especially adapted to the emphases of the denominational calendar. One of the most significant features of the project was its inclusion of a generous amount of officially sanctioned teaching material offered for the first time to the clergy of the denomination. Its presentation in the *Handbook* included not only an explanation of the lectionary itself, but also an exposition of the calendar and seasons of the Christian year, and a practical guide for the use of the lectionary in Free Methodist worship. Even though it does not appear that the lectionary has been widely used in the weekly routine of Free Methodist worship in the United States, its official status and its prominent presence in the *Pastor's Handbook* (thirteen pages are given to the lectionary material) are indicators of the continuing vitality of a classical catholic sensitivity in the denomination.

The Adoption of a New Hymnal

In the years following the 1976 publication of *Hymns of Faith and Life*, there was growing concern that the hymnal was not meeting the needs of the denomination. Concerns centered around the large number of unfamiliar hymns, the alteration of some of the old favorites, and the paucity of both gospel and contemporary songs. In 1985 the General Conference heard these concerns and adopted a resolution that a new hymnal be commissioned within four years. Although it proved impossible to realize directly, this decision resulted in an important change in Free Methodist hymnody. For the first time in its history, with the exception of the earliest years when it continued to use the Methodist Episcopal Church hymn book, it turned out that the Free Methodist Church adopted an existing non-Free Methodist hymnal (which also meant that for the first time since 1910 the Free Methodist and Wesleyan denominations did not produce a joint hymnal). In 1989, on account of economic as well as other considerations, the *Hymnal for Worship and Celebration* was adopted as the official hymnal of the Free Methodist Church. With its "Foreword" penned by pastor and radio Bible teacher, Charles R. Swindoll, this hymnal was a clear product of the best of generic American evangelicalism. By special arrangement with the publisher (Word Music), a supplement of Free Methodist materials was bound at the back of the hymnal. These pages included a "signature" of thirty-nine hymns and songs characteristic to Free Methodists, as well as the denominational liturgies for the sacrament of the Lord's Supper and the Covenant Service. Free Methodists now had at their disposal over 760 hymns, including a generous collection of service music, yet only twenty-seven of the total number were authored by either Charles or John Wesley.

Alternative Liturgies for the Service of Holy Communion

In 1985, the Study Commission on Doctrine was directed by the General Conference to prepare a new order of holy communion which could serve as an alternate to the historic ritual of the denomination. As a result of the work of the Commission, two new rituals were prepared and adopted by the General Conference of 1989. These were first published in the 1991 edition of the *Pastor's Handbook*. One of these, entitled "The Lord's Supper: A Biblical Liturgy," was designed by committee member Lloyd H. Knox. As its title suggests, it was a liturgy of responsive readings and prayers constructed entirely from scriptural passages. The other new order of holy communion was adopted as the official Alternate Ritual. Crafted by Study Commission member Paul W. Livermore, this new liturgy was intentionally rooted in the liturgical resources of the second through the fourth centuries. The structure of the liturgy was presented in a way that would assist clergy in the ordering of the service by means of the two basic units of the liturgy of the word and the liturgy of the table. The significance of the Alternate Ritual was that it provided the Free Methodist Church with a liturgy that owed its main shape to the classical liturgical tradition, thus opening the door for the first time to a sacramental theology and practice which pre-dated Cranmerian Anglicanism.[55]

Conclusion

The Free Methodist Church of the twentieth century has become a denomination that is constantly pushing at the boundaries of its identity. Whether consciously or otherwise, the Free Methodist Church continues to be in the process of defining its own kind of pluralism. The worship practices of the denomination are held together by a core of Methodistic piety that itself has been shaped in important ways by the American experience. Their evangelicalism bears the marks of both Wesley and the nineteenth- and twentieth-century varieties of evangelicalism. Free Methodists can be both revivalistic and formal. They draw not only on the Holiness movements but even on Anabaptism. They move not only in neo-pentecostal but also in more catholic directions. Free Methodists are both Methodist *and* American.

Chapter 11

Ten Thousand Tongues Sing:
Worship among Methodists in Korea[1]

Edward W. Poitras (Pak Tae In)

Western visitors to Methodist worship in Korea often comment, "Even though I can't understand a word, I feel right at home in this service!" Indeed, Sunday morning worship in most Korean Methodist churches is a cousin of the worship patterns introduced into Korea by missionaries from the United States. While there are some differences, the form and content of public worship remain close to those first imported into Korea over a century ago. There are challenges to this pattern, especially from a generation of young Christians in search of more distinctively Korean expressions of their faith, yet it is unlikely that there will be major changes in the near future.

Early Methodist Worship Experiences in Korea

When the pioneer Methodist missionaries from the United States began to settle in Seoul in 1885, the government banned evangelism, restricting Christian work to education and medical treatment. That did not completely deter those missionaries from quietly preaching and secretly baptizing converts. Because of government restrictions, Methodist worship in Korea began among foreigners, expanded to include Korean observers, cautiously brought in Korean converts, then finally emerged as unrestricted public worship.

Worship with Koreans was conducted at first in secret, in homes with the shades drawn.[2] Marking a significant development in the story, Henry G. Appenzeller of the Methodist Episcopal Church and one of the first missionaries, wrote in his diary for 1887:

Sunday, October 23, we had the first communion service ever held by Methodism in Korea. . . . We used our liturgy and all took an

195

earnest part. O what a privilege to thus break the bread of life unto these people! May our hearts feed on it with thankfulness.[3]

It is significant that the earliest expressions of the missionaries' joy and satisfaction are related to baptisms and the sharing of worship and holy communion with Koreans. The missionaries took heart when the Korean government made little effort to inhibit their evangelistic efforts.[4]

The official ban on public preaching was not evenly enforced and did not last long, so Korean Christians were soon able to express their faith freely in open worship. In a service of worship at Christmas, 1887,[5] Henry Appenzeller preached his first sermon in Korean. He admits, "I did not write it, but gave the ideas to my colporteur, Mr. Choi, and he put them into proper Korean."[6] The order of worship was simple, and certainly represents an early form of Methodist worship for Korean believers. "The service in full" was recorded by Appenzeller as follows:[7]

1. Baptism of Kim Myong Ok

2. Hymn

3. Prayer by Dr. Scranton (read)[8]

4. Lesson from 2nd Matthew

5. Lesson from 2nd Luke (read by Dr. Scranton)

6. Sermon[9]

7. Lord's Prayer

8. "Nearer my God to thee"[10]

9. Benediction

Although the early missionaries saw the need for trained Korean leaders, they were often reluctant to transfer pastoral and other leadership responsiblities to their Korean colleagues.[11] This meant, among other things, that determining the forms of worship remained mainly in the hands of the foreign missionaries for many years.

The missionaries saw the need to communicate effectively with ordinary Korean people, so were quick to produce Bible translations in collaboration with Korean colleagues, and to make use of *onmun*, today called *hangul* script, a phonetic writing much easier to learn than the traditional Chinese ideographs.[12] In spite of that cultural awareness, however, the missionaries seem to have given little attention to the appropriateness of western worship patterns or related cultural forms, such as architecture, church furniture, or music. Just as they had translated the Bible, they translated hymns and used familiar nineteenth-century American Methodist worship services,[13] simply putting everything into the Korean language as best they could. Even western hymn tunes were imported directly into Korean worship.

The early missionaries believed that there was a great difference between the religious rites of old Korea and the Christian worship they had introduced. Appenzeller noted "the absence of love in their worship. Fear is the motive power of their worship. . . . *We hear the voice of Love—we are full of joy. The heathen are without hope.*"[14] While the missionaries may be said to have introduced the forms of worship without much self-consciousness, they were much concerned to convey love, joy, and hope through the worship experience.

Later the Korean churches related to the Methodist Episcopal Church and to the Methodist Episcopal Church, South, each produced translated versions of the books of *Doctrines and Discipline*, and the orders of worship were translated verbatim for use in Korean Methodism.[15] When the Korean Methodist Church became autonomous in 1930 and produced its own *Doctrines and Discipline*, the Methodist Episcopal Church, South's custom of including an order of public worship under the heading "The Means of Grace" was retained. The order of worship in the Korean *Discipline* follows the basic outlines contained in both versions of the imported *Discipline* in use at that time,[16] but it is reduced to simple rubrics and has been stripped of fuller explanations.[17]

The order of Sunday worship for the united, autonomous Korean Methodist Church appears as the last in a series of seven "means of grace for church members," following baptism, holy communion, private and family prayer, attendance at revival and Bible study meetings, participation in class meetings, and participation in prayer meetings led by the pastor. The text of the service is as follows:[18]

Attendance at public worship (The morning and evening gathering of church members for worship every Sunday at the church)

1. Silent prayer (Music)
2. Hymn
3. The Apostles' Creed (Sunday morning)
4. Prayer (The Lord's Prayer)

5. Old Testament (Psalm)
6. Hymn (or Sacred Music)
7. Offering (Prayer)
8. Announcements
9. Hymn (or Special Music)
10. New Testament Reading
11. Sermon
12. Prayer
13. Closing Hymn
14. Benediction
15. Silent Prayer (Music, Dismissal)

Some accommodations were made to Korean customs, however, and although most of them seem quaint today, they revealed the impossibility of introducing Christian practice into Korea without some degree of adjustment to local circumstances. The early missionaries, for example, usually constructed western-style church buildings of red brick with slate or metal roofs, but frequently provided separate doors for men and for women.

Early in Korean Methodist history, missionaries like Henry Appenzeller thought it important to construct western-style buildings for both churches and schools. These structures, with their brick walls, rectangular design, and sash windows (often with neo-Gothic arched shapes) stood out among the Korean buildings with their thatched or curved tile roofs, sliding paper doors, and central courtyards. Appenzeller raised the money from the United States to build the first church building in Seoul, the Chong Dong First Methodist Church, which was completed in 1897 and still stands. The first building for Paichai School for Boys stood on a hill nearby and was also conspicuous for its western lines. Appenzeller was proud of these buildings, and felt that they expressed the spirit of the missionary work he and his colleagues were conducting in Korea.[19] The other early Methodist churches in Seoul were also brick buildings in the western style. These physical monuments symbolized the uncritical attitude of the early missionaries toward the amalgam of Christianity and western, specifically nineteenth-century American culture, which they affirmed and taught.

Later missionaries and their Korean colleagues sometimes favored using Korean architecture. In the towns such buildings would have curved tile roofs, with an open interior adapted to worship use. In the rural areas they would more often be thatched cottages, or a room or two in a farmhouse, opening up to a porch, thus permitting greater participation when the rooms were small. Pews or chairs were not used in the early buildings, Korean or western, and racks were provided in the entries for shoes, which were removed upon entering. Worshipers often carried cushions with them for prolonged sitting on the floors, especially in cold weather.

Inside, the women and men were expected to sit separately, men on the left and women on the right, facing the altar. Even though the missionaries had come from the United States and Europe, where older customs of gender separation had mostly been abandoned in Christian worship, in Korea it became customary for the men and women to be separated during worship following the strict Confucian social codes.[20] In some settings this prescription was met by hanging a curtain down the center of the room, with the preacher standing beyond its edge where he could see and address both sides. There were also instances of L-shaped places of worship where the preacher would stand at the intersection and thus be visible to both parts. In some cases the missionary or male pastor would baptize by thrusting his hand through a hole cut in a sheet in order to avoid setting eyes upon a woman convert.[21]

The missionaries soon began to teach Bible, Christian history, and some theology, but their usual habit was to transmit without adaptation what they had learned and to translate the western textbooks that they thought best expressed the heart of Christian faith and tradition. This tendency only served to reinforce among the early Korean Christian leaders an almost unquestioning devotion to those western forms of Christianity with which the missionaries were familiar. It is hardly surprising that Korean Methodist worship patterns continued to follow those in the *Doctrines and Discipline* of both the Methodist Episcopal Church and the Methodist Episcopal Church, South, in the United States.[22]

Korean Methodist Worship Today[23]

As with other churches in the Methodist family today, there is considerable variety in Korean Methodist worship patterns, ranging from a more informal, flexible style to a more elaborate liturgical form.[24] The principal service of worship for the week is usually at 11:00 a.m. on Sunday morning, and is almost always the most complex and formal order of service. In larger churches there may be several Sunday morning services, and often different groups regularly attend particular services, with an earlier service frequently oriented toward youth.[25]

Almost all churches still ask their members to attend services on Sunday morning, Sunday evening, and Wednesday evening. Daybreak prayer meetings each morning and weekly class meetings are optional, but attendance is encouraged. In the countryside there is more participation in the full range of meetings, especially by women, but in the cities only the most devoted core of members comes to evening, weekday, or especially daybreak meetings.

A typical Sunday morning service begins with a prelude played on an organ or piano, with wide variations in the type of music. In rural areas the prelude, if any, would probably be a selection from the hymnal played on a reed organ, perhaps functioning as an accompaniment when the worship leader calls for a time of silent preparatory prayer. In larger urban churches preludes might well consist of classical western sacred music, and could even include instruments, such as a string ensemble. Some of the largest city churches, the megachurches which take pride in their large memberships, are able to support large choirs and even orchestras, often with professional vocalists and instrumentalists participating.

In earlier days it was customary for the congregation to sing hymns as they gathered and waited for the hour of worship, sometimes with one of the members acting as leader. In rural areas this pattern is still followed, usually with a long series of hymns requested by members. These favorites are often nineteenth-century American hymns, long familiar in Korea.

Most churches today will follow the prelude with a call to worship. Some churches do not use a call to worship but begin the service with the opening hymn. In most places, except for the largest and most sophisticated, all elements in the service are announced by the worship leader, who is most often the pastor. Many churches, however, now include lay persons as worship leaders or readers, or employ assistant pastors who usually function as presiders when the senior minister preaches. In some churches the choir and worship leaders wear robes and process, and this more formal style of worship seems to be spreading in the towns and cities, but in many smaller congregations the leaders and choir simply enter through doors in the front of the sanctuary.

The sanctuary arrangement, whether with separate pulpit and lectern to the sides (in split-chancel arrangement) or with a central pulpit, would seem familiar to many non-Korean Methodists, down to the furniture and robes. Large churches tend to have imposing, elaborately decorated chancel furniture, and as finances permit, more and more churches are installing stained glass windows and pipe organs in their neo-Gothic or contemporary western-style buildings. The suggestion of authority is not accidental, since the pastoral style tends to be quite authoritarian in Korea. The symbolism of wealth and power is obvious, perhaps since South Korea has in the last forty years grown from a struggling, war-torn nation into a formidable economic powerhouse.

Korean hymn singing is impressive. As a general rule everyone sings with gusto and conviction. Sometimes the influence upon intonation of the traditional Korean five-tone scale can be obvious, especially in the rural areas. Even in small churches there is usually a choir, generally of young people, and while the voices may be untrained and the works limited to the hymnal, the singing is enthusiastic and expressive of living faith.

The nineteenth-century American gospel hymns seem still to be among the most popular choices for worship, although many of the more formal, sedate western hymn tunes also appear frequently. In recent years increasing numbers of Korean compositions have entered the hymnals.[26] Even ten years ago congregations seem to have avoided using these unfamiliar hymns, but they are growing rapidly in popularity throughout the Korean Methodist Church.

After the first hymn, many ministers will next recite a prayer of invocation, often using a verse or two from the Psalms or another passage of scripture. This may be followed by the Apostles' Creed or the Korean Creed, if the church tends toward a more formal style; otherwise it would be unusual to find any creed in the order of worship.[27] In some churches where the creeds are used, they may be recited with the congregation seated.[28]

During the next sequence of scripture reading or readings, prayers, and an anthem or solo, there can be considerable variation. Some pastors will often include more than one scripture lesson, perhaps reading from both the Old and New Testaments, but in many, perhaps most, cases there will be only one reading, the text for the sermon of the day, which is most often from the New Testament. Although a lectionary for the Church year has been published by the Korean Methodist Church,[29] there seem to be few Methodist churches following a regular cycle of scripture for use in worship. Occasionally a lay reader will read the scripture for the service. When there is more than one reading, the usual pattern is for one of them to be a responsive reading from the hymnal, and this is sometimes led by a lay person. The readings in the hymnal include passages from the Psalms, Old Testament, and New Testament, with some designated for special occasions such as Thanksgiving (see below), Christmas, and Easter.[30]

The hymnal used in Korean Methodist churches is an ecumenical collection used by most Protestant groups in Korea except the most theologically conservative; these have their own hymnal which is more weighted toward western nineteenth-century gospel hymns. Some revisions in the language of frequently recited liturgical materials were introduced in the ecumenical hymnal, then withdrawn because so many felt the new words were unsuitable, perhaps because they were unfamiliar.[31] There has also been resistance to introducing recent Bible translations such as the "New Translation" (*Saeponyok*, 1967) into worship or the responsive readings in the hymnal.

The principal morning prayer, or pastoral prayer, is usually led either by an associate minister or an elder in the congregation. Korean Methodism has church officers called "elders" somewhat like Presbyterian elders, an office which was introduced when all Protestant groups were forced into one body during the Second World War when Korea was under Japanese rule. Elders have considerable responsibility and stature in Korean Methodist churches, and sometimes act as substitute preachers for weekday services.[32]

The Korean style of leading in public prayer is usually emotional and intense. The voice is soft and restrained at the outset, gradually building in volume and intensity, until a series of long rhythmic arches carries the sequence of petitions through to a gradual denouement. Congregational interaction is at its greatest during the time of prayer, with many "amens" voiced from all segments of the congregation. Ordinarily much time is devoted to praying for the church and its activities, for the hour of worship and its constituent parts, and for the needs of the families in the church. Here the ethnocentricity of the Korean people becomes obvious, as Christian faith is usually invoked for the salvation of the nation and the reunification of the Korean peninsula. There is seldom much intercession for the world Church, other nations, or world needs.

In some churches, but not the majority, there is routinely a time when the whole congregation prays aloud together.[33] In many churches such prayer is more apt to be practiced in smaller, less formal services, such as the evening or daybreak prayer meetings. This congregational free-voiced prayer has become popular at revival meetings, which are a regular occurrence in most local churches. This custom does not seem to be a recent importation into Methodism, for it has been in use in Methodist churches for many years, predating the rapid growth of Korean Pentecostalism. These prayers can be quite unnerving for one unaccustomed to them, for they are often shouted or wailed in a loud voice, and the combined sound in a large group can be quite overwhelming. A bell is often kept on the pulpit and may be rung to signal the end of these spoken prayers.

The sermon is usually considered to be the heart of the service. There is considerable variety in preaching styles, but the most frequently heard is a presentation that depends heavily upon the mode of delivery. The traditional Korean oratorical style employs long sentences, rapid speaking, shouting with an elevated monotone punctuated by changes of pitch and speed, and a direct appeal to the emotions. An effective preacher will make skillful use of storytelling, and will draw upon the riches of the language through repetition, onomatopoeia, rhythm, and metaphor.[34]

Sermons are sometimes expositions of Biblical passages,[35] but seem more often to be topical, though the subject matter usually consists of aspects of Christian faith or life, rather than issues of social or political interest. The content of the faith as preached is apt to fall toward the conservative end of the theological spectrum, to be Bible-centered, and to be concerned with morals, even though Methodism is more theologically inclusive than most other Korean Protestant groups. Most pastors take a strongly exclusivist stand on relations with other religions. Christians are often reminded that the only way to salvation is through faith in Jesus Christ.

In urban congregations where educational and social levels are higher, some preachers tend to moderate the older rhetorical style and present more logical appeals delivered in a calmer, more restrained style of speaking. In general, sermons seldom last less than thirty minutes, often much more, although city preachers have responded to the time pressures of urban living and have become more concise. Most sermons end with a prayer, often quite long and complex, which usually includes an appeal to decision or to response to the message of the sermon.

The microphone has become almost ubiquitous in Korean churches, so that even in small meeting places the sound is often amplified to an uncomfortable level. This can be especially noticeable when the pastor, choir director, or worship leader stands at the microphone during congregational singing and produces a piercing tone which can discourage the congregation from its singing potential. Since Korea, like Japan, has thoroughly embraced technological culture, it no longer seems appropriate to consider the use of electronic amplifiers, closed-circuit television, and video-recorded services, or computers in churches as a "western" influence. Such things are no longer identified as being an importation into Korea.

Methodist services differ in the placement of the announcements and greetings. They can come early in the service, frequently precede or follow the offering, or may follow the sermon. Visitors are often introduced, perhaps given a ribbon or some form of identification, and the congregation is encouraged to greet them. This is a point in the service where evangelism and the bringing of friends and neighbors are often stressed.

There is usually some form of music played or sung to accompany the offertory; the offering is brought forward by the ushers, the Doxology is sung, usually to Old 100th,[36] and the pastor or worship leader prays as the offering is presented before the altar. Etiquette requires that money be given in envelopes in Korea, so most people will bring their offerings in envelopes unless the church provides them. One custom frequently observed is the presenting of special offerings and thank offerings in envelopes with an explanation written on them. These are sometimes kept apart from the Sunday offering and given to the pastor, who then reads the envelopes, noting the giver and the occasion for which they have been given.[37] There is usually an additional prayer after the reading of these envelopes, with a special invocation of blessings upon the givers and their families. Tithing is common in most churches, and it is not unknown for a congregation to give half the year's church budget in one offering at the autumn thanksgiving service.[38]

Baptisms are usually performed at Easter and Christmas. There is a preparatory period during which prospective members are given a series of lessons, usually by the pastor, about the Christian faith and the Methodist tradition.

Holy communion is observed infrequently in most Korean Methodist churches, perhaps twice a year. Grape juice is more often used than fermented wine, as the Korean Protestant churches have generally taken a strong stand against alcohol.[39] Before bread became easily available in recent years, cake was often used in the service.[40] Nowadays a few are experimenting with Korean rice wine and rice cake in the communion service, but these attempts are still rare.[41]

In general the atmosphere in many Methodist communion services might seem quite casual to the western observer. The pastor may well give sundry instructions to the congregation during the ritual, and the juice is often poured into the small cups on the communion table from a small tea kettle by the sacristan. Many traditional Korean religious rituals are quite informal and relaxed, and that background may be an influence upon Christian observances.

The benediction is always pronounced by an ordained minister, and when one is not present the service is usually closed by a congregational recitation of the Lord's Prayer. Though it is seldom heard in urban churches today, it was once common to sing the Doxology to the tune "Sessions" before the benediction. The benediction often assumes special importance in the Korean service, for the pastor usually recites it with great intensity and gravity, arms extended over the congregation, with the implication of an indispensable intermediary role of the pastor in the conferring of grace.[42]

All in all, a Korean Methodist service of worship on Sunday morning will usually prove to be a lively, emotional, often intense experience in which the preacher has exhibited great exertion and the congregation has participated actively. One of the best attestations to this vitality is the fact that Sunday morning worship often draws an attendance larger than the membership rolls of the church. Not only do members take seriously the responsibility of attending, but people hesitate to become full members until they are confident they can shoulder the obligations of Christian commitment.

Recent Explorations into New Korean Worship Forms

Korean attitudes toward cultural importations have been ambivalent for well over a century. Before that, Korea had long exhibited a strong xenophobia, leading to its old designation as the Hermit Kingdom. This isolationism was dominant until the late nineteenth century when, after a long series of internal political struggles, the nation finally opened its doors to the western world.

The acceptance by so many Koreans of Christianity and its western cultural accoutrements mirrors the ambivalence many Koreans feel toward western culture. While there are many who uncritically adopt foreign ideas and ways, there are advocates of strict adherence to traditional Korean customs and values, and in recent years they have been outspoken in both politics and religion. Students demonstrating on behalf of western-inspired democratic reforms have often made use of Korean shamanist sacrifices, and have revived the satirical masked dances through which their ancestors wryly commented upon the social scene. Thus Christianity with its western forms is rejected by some as a foreign intrusion, and accepted by others as an appropriate religious system for Koreans.

As part of a widespread cultural movement, especially among artists and students, there has been in recent years a tentative exploring of the use of traditional Korean cultural forms in Christian worship. This is distinct from the gradual trend toward including Korean tunes and rhythms in hymnody. Probably the most widely known and accepted has been the use of traditional *pansori*, a form of sung and spoken solo dramatic recitation performed with a single drum accompaniment. These ballads use old poetic texts and are rendered with great vocal virtuosity in a storytelling genre which is captivating for any Korean audience. Christian poets have set some Bible narratives to the form, and well-known Christian *pansori* performers have rendered them in stage performances as well as within the context of worship, usually in special services where the singing takes the place of the reading and sermon. Old Testament narratives such as the Joseph story have been successful, while narratives from the Gospels are also popular.

Christians have also been using chancel drama and liturgical dance in Korea, though these forms have not been widely adopted. Although many of the newer works are not specifically traditional in form, elements from traditional Korean music, poetry, dance, and dress have made their way into them. Korean cantatas for worship have been written, but in most cases they are contemporary adaptations of Korean themes and not traditional in sound or form.

Some rather interesting theological debates in Korea during

recent years have had a direct impact on worship. One has concerned the translation of the Bible. Several new translations have appeared during the last generation, all of them in varying degrees using contemporary Korean.[43] This is a delicate issue, though, since Koreans still use several different levels of formality when speaking. How polite should St. Paul be when writing to the Corinthians? Should Jesus speak to his followers like a past Korean sovereign addressing his subjects? How honorific should the language be when it gives narrative descriptions in the Bible?

On the whole, most Protestants in Korea, including the Methodists, have resisted using the newer translations in worship, preferring the familiar cadences of the earlier, more formal rendering. As with the King James Bible in English-speaking lands, the dignity of the traditional resonates with many believers, and the resistance to newer translations is probably greater in Korea than in the west. There has also been a "Common Translation" produced by a joint committee of Roman Catholics and Protestants in Korea. This was a landmark achievement in ecumenicity, but the translation, while used uniformly by Catholics, has not been accepted in most Protestant churches. Several western paraphrases, such as the Living Bible, have been translated into Korean, and seem popular with young people.[44]

A related debate has swirled around the Korean terms used by Christians to refer to God. The word *hananim* was customary for many years and appears in the older Bible translations. In recent years, however, there has been a movement to revive another old Korean term, *hanunim*, and this version has appeared in some worship guides and is the one used in the Common Translation.[45] Acrimonious debates have raged within Methodism over which of these terms is "orthodox," and at present both terms are in widespread use. Similar, though less intense, debates have taken place over the terms used for the Holy Spirit, *songyong* and *songshin*.[46] Despite the explanations of some theologians, both of these debates seem to be resolving themselves largely as matters of changing taste and custom.

Many churches still use such cultural anomalies as Sallman's *Head of Christ* as decorations, even in their sanctuaries, but others are turning to Korean calligraphy of Biblical texts and traditional Korean art to depict Christian themes. A few architects have ventured into the application of Korean traditional forms adapted to modern Christian use, some of them quite effective, but most recent church buildings continue to be a pastiche of Gothic and contemporary western themes.

There are some creative and exciting explorations being made in Korean Christianity today which seek to mine the rich local cultural traditions, but most Christians are content to continue with familiar western ways. This tendency reinforces the judgment of Aloysius Pieris of Sri Lanka, who feels that Christianity is *in* Asia, but not yet *of* Asia.[47] Despite that reservation, however, it is evident that Korean Methodism has responded to the heart of the Gospel and has become a vital part of the mainstream of authentic world Christian history.

Chapter 12

Chinese, Tamil, and English Congregations: Sunday Worship of the Methodist Church in Singapore

Swee Hong Lim

"Not by might, nor by power, but by my Spirit, saith the Lord" (Zechariah 4:6) was the text of the first sermon preached on the shores of Singapore by a Methodist, Bishop James M. Thoburn of the Methodist Episcopal Church in the United States. On the occasion of this first evangelistic meeting in 1885, it was also reported that Miss Julia Battie played a recently unpacked organ, the Reverend William F. Oldham served as usher and handed out hymn books, and Mrs. Anna Thoburn led in the singing.[1] Having seen this eyewitness account of the first Methodist worship service held in Singapore, one might wonder whether Methodist worship in Singapore would ever come to develop a unique character. How is the practice of Methodist worship in Singapore different from that of Methodists in other parts of the world? What makes Methodist worship there different from that of other Christian denominations present in Singapore? To understand how Methodist worship developed in Singapore, it will be helpful to present briefly the history of Methodism's establishment on the island.

The First Century of Methodism in Singapore

Methodism first came to Singapore in the late 1800s through the work of pioneering missionaries from Australia, Britain, Germany, and the United States. These missionaries had first set their sights on India and China, but in God's mysterious way, they were led into this part of South East Asia. Chief among those who were instrumental in the start of the Methodist movement in Singapore were Thoburn and Oldham as well as Charles Phillips, an English layman who founded the Christian Institute which served as the first center for Methodist ministries in Singapore.[2] According to Bobby Sng's analysis, the Methodist movement in Singapore gained much of its foothold through an emphasis on indirect evangelism by establishing schools that included a component of Christian formation (largely through attendance at chapel worship).[3]

Prior to the arrival of Methodism, other Christian bodies such as the Armenians, Anglicans, Presbyterians, and Brethren were already on the island. Attempts to evangelize the native population had not been very successful, and worship services were mainly directed toward the small Caucasian minority who understood the English language. Occasionally, chapels were founded that met the needs of the growing number of Asians, mainly Chinese and Indians, who were not indigenous to the island and were already believing Christians before they immigrated for economic or other reasons.[4]

In these early years most, if not all, of the hymns used for worship had their origin in the western hemisphere and were made accessible to native Asian worshipers through translation. Within the Methodist movement, the Englishman W. G. Shellabear was well known for his fluency with the Malay language and appears to have been involved in the process of translating hymns into the Malay language—Bahasa Melayu—by 1888.[5] Research also shows that the Anglicans, through the effort of the Reverend William Henry Gomes in 1872, also embarked upon the process of making prayers and hymns accessible to Asian worshipers in both Bahasa Melayu and Hokkien (a Chinese dialect).[6] However, no attempts were made at that time to create or discover indigenous hymns or worship forms that might be meaningful or beneficial to the local population.

It was not until 1930, under the episcopal leadership of Bishop Edwin F. Lee, that indigenization of worship was first raised as an issue in the *Malaysia Message*,[7] the official publication of the Methodist Church at that time. Though the work of Bishop Lee in recruiting church leaders of Asian descent was significant, its impact on worship services remains uncertain. At this time, the Methodist Church in Singapore had two kinds of churches. The English-speaking churches ministered to those who understood the English language. Apart from the Caucasians, the English-speaking churches also included a small proportion of Tamils (from India and Ceylon) and Chinese who had the command of the language. Their services featured western leadership in all aspects of the liturgy. At the same time, there were other churches that had services conducted in the vernacular, either Malay, Tamil or Chinese.[8] In time to come, the autonomous Methodist Church in Singapore was to find itself organized linguistically. Today, in fact, the three Singaporean Methodist annual conferences are organized generally according to linguistic distinctions: the Chinese Annual Conference (CAC); the Emmanuel Tamil Annual Conference (ETAC); and the Trinity Annual Conference (TRAC) for English-speaking Methodists.

While the English-speaking churches borrowed resources directly from the west, the other churches drew their resources from India and China. This refers not only to the people who were trained to minister to these local congregations, but also to the hymns that they sang and the Bibles that they read: all came out of translation efforts based in India and China. While the resources for worship may have come from China and India, these were not indigenous creations but translations from the west. The form of the worship services was similar to those customary in American Methodism at the time. In general, the situation in Singapore was such that almost everything was "imported," and this borrowing still prevails to the present day, even in worship.

In the 1930s, the Chinese-speaking churches received a revival through the work of Dr. John Sung which greatly entrenched the conservative and fundamentalist theology of the Christian faith within the vernacular-speaking churches. The western-led English-speaking churches, on the other hand, became liberal-oriented as they continued to receive ministers from seminaries of that orientation.

By the 1970s, charismatic renewal began to penetrate Methodism through its educational system.[9] From then on, there was a gradual shift in the theology of the Church from the predominant liberalism to evangelicalism. Likewise in worship, that time saw the beginning of the praise worship commonly associated with the renewal/charismatic movement. This form of worship first occurred on school grounds as students of Methodist schools began to adopt this movement and its practices in their Christian fellowship groups; subsequently it spread to Sunday Schools and youth meetings. Before long, students who were renewed by this movement became leaders of the church. The movement eventually gained a foothold inside the church sanctuary as people began to see lives touched and

211

radically changed. Truly, this encounter with the charismatic renewal movement brought a change in the manner in which worship was organized in churches.

Apart from the charismatic movement, the organization of the church along linguistic lines has been the other crucial factor in the development of worship in Singapore. This is because each of the three linguistic groups reacts differently to various influences within the Christian world. In turn, these influences ultimately shape the manner in which the linguistic groups view worship and the theology behind it. This point will be elaborated later.

Present-Day Methodism

As one approaches one of the many Methodist churches scattered throughout this island city, one cannot help but imagine that all Christians in Singapore must be from the middle and upper class of the society. This conclusion would be supported by the presence of well-dressed worshipers, the traffic congestion experienced outside the church grounds, and the chaos within the car parking area. Upon entering the church, one would be confronted with the need to make a choice of what type of worship service to attend. No longer is worship a one-service affair in which the worshiper has no choice. The present trend in the worship life of the Church in Singapore, particularly among the English-speaking congregations, is to make available as many worship formats as possible to the worshipers. Variety in worship services could be as simple as different languages or as drastic as different worship forms. The tradition of division by language lines between annual conferences no longer fully corresponds to linguistic realities. Some TRAC churches have developed services in Mandarin, Hokkien, Malay and, for resident Filipinos, Tagalog, while some CAC congregations have introduced English services.

However, this concept of variety in worship is still very much western-oriented. This is to say, innovation within worship is still very much influenced by what comes from the west. For example, the preference for bands in contemporary worship has a lot to do with people who are brought in to conduct contemporary Christian music seminars,[10] and the audio and video materials that are imported for sale in Christian bookshops. On the other hand, within Methodism there is a slow but sure growth of interest in liturgical worship that reaches deeper into historic Christianity as well as in the development of Asian worship forms. The brief existence of an association of the Order of St. Luke is a clear sign of the emerging trend for liturgically-oriented worship.[11] For example, the Reverend Lorna Khoo, while pastor of the Methodist Church of the Incarnation, at times used adapted Church of South India and early Christian practices to make the baptismal service of that congregation distinctive. While liturgy and liturgical inculturation have not been major concerns for theological institutions based in Singapore, this writer has had, on a few occasions, the opportunity to present to seminarians a discussion about Asian worship, thanks to invitations from some teachers who feel that liturgical issues are an important aspect of theological training.[12]

Having the opportunity to host the 16th World Methodist Conference in 1991 was a major boost to the development of indigenous worship materials in Singaporean Methodism. For once, we were encouraged to present our distinctiveness to the rest of Methodism; that generated a sense of self-searching which gave an opportunity for the creation of worship in a different direction, that of "incarnational" worship, seeking to express Christ through our culture rather than removing our cultural traditions to accommodate the Christian message.

In dealing now with Methodist Sunday worship in Singapore, we will focus on the forms of worship (traditional and contemporary), music in worship, the message preached, and the Lord's Supper.

Forms of Worship: Traditional and Contemporary[13]

In Singapore, worship formats can be broadly divided into two types, the traditional and the contemporary (samples of these services follow). The traditional form shares its roots with other Methodist churches throughout the world. Printed worship bulletins and the hymnal (containing ritual texts in addition to hymns) allow the congregation to participate in the various aspects of worship. The observance of the liturgical year provides an important framework for the traditional service. Prior to the late 1980s and early 1990s, the traditional service was always considered the "main" morning worship service of the church. Major events in the life of the congregation, such as dedication or commissioning services, are still usually

213

held within the traditional service. Contemporary services were usually relegated to evenings as an "informal" service.

But this norm has more recently been replaced by another that holds both types of service as of equal importance. This has been achieved in some larger churches by holding the two types of services at the same hour. Consequently, baptism and some forms of dedication services are shared equally between the traditional and the contemporary services or conducted simultaneously. At the largest and oldest church, Wesley Methodist, whenever guest preachers of importance are present, it has been the norm to have the preacher in the traditional service and to have his/her message transmitted by closed-circuit television to the contemporary service. This form of sharing the same preacher while having two different forms of worship at the same time is unique to this church.

Contemporary worship, which has its origin in the praise worship commonly associated with the charismatic movement, displays an absence of a printed worship order, though sometimes the various segments within an order of worship may be indicated. In Singapore, this form of worship is commonly known as the "Prayer and Praise" service. In this form of worship, the printed bulletin is replaced by the use of transparencies on overhead projectors. Choruses and essential rituals like the baptismal and eucharistic rites are projected upon a screen for the congregation to follow. Other features of this service are the use of extempore prayers, hand lifting, and clapping. Generally speaking, a sense of flexibility seems to dominate this form of worship. Discussion has been under way recently at Wesley Methodist Church about the possibility of introducing a worship folder for the contemporary service which would contain announcements, words of encouragement, testimonies, and possibly a brief summary about the thematic focus of worship for that Sunday's service.

These two forms of services—the traditional and the contemporary—are usually found in churches that hold multiple services on Sundays. Churches that do not have multiple services tend to use the traditional form of worship but may include a section where contemporary songs are sung. The placement of this particular section within the worship format is very much a pastoral decision; the "Prayer and Praise" component may be located before the choral introit, just before the pastoral prayer or an intercessory prayer, or immediately before the sermon. The "Prayer and Praise" is usually led by a separate worship leader, and depending upon the skills of the worship leader and musicians, the songs may be arranged in the form of a medley. There are some Methodist churches that use only the traditional service and sing only from the hymnal, though this is becoming rare in Singapore. Most Methodist churches supplement their hymnals with hymns and choruses from other sources.

In terms of duration, the traditional service would take an average of about one hour and fifteen minutes. The contemporary service would take slightly longer, depending on the time given for singing, extempore prayers and prophetic utterances, and the sermon preached. Churches that hold these two forms of worship simultaneously usually attempt to regulate the length so that they end at about the same time.

Music and the Arts in Worship

Organizers of contemporary services usually work toward getting a band together rather than utilizing a single organist or keyboardist, and they prefer soloists or small choral groups singing contemporary Christian music with accompaniment tapes rather than a choir performing Bach chorales. This form of worship transcends linguistic barriers and as such can be found in all three annual conferences. There have also been attempts to incorporate the use of dance and drama into worship services, innovations which have been more successfully introduced into the contemporary type of service.

Traditional worship services employ larger choirs with a repertoire ranging from J. S. Bach to Tom Fettke. Flexibility can be found in the traditional services of many congregations, as there have been developments such as the introduction of additional instruments to supplement the organ and piano. Most of these instruments are associated with the orchestra of the west. But this growth of instrumental music is experienced primarily in churches that have the resources of voluntary trained musicians possessing a sense of ministry. No less important is the presence of a capable lay person who is a musician, or a minister keen on music, in directing this form of music. The concept of a full-time church musician to direct the music ministry has yet to take root within the Methodist tradition in Singapore.

Asian instruments are not commonly found in worship except for significant events of the church as a whole, such as the combined worship service held on Aldersgate Sunday for all three conferences. Nevertheless, it has been reported that the tabla, a pair of drums from India, is beginning to make inroads in the worship life of some ETAC churches. The absence of Asian instruments may be attributed to a general feeling that instruments commonly associated with worship in other faiths are inappropriate for use in Christian worship. At issue here is whether these instruments belong to a particular religious culture or subculture, or are indeed part of a broader social culture. Another factor: A number of instruments are not used for Christian worship because no one has attempted, or been able, to introduce them into the church worship context on account of a lack of technical skill or ability for playing those instruments. Most teachers of Asiatic instruments are not Christians, and the sharing of musical knowledge and technique between Christian and non-Christian can be quite awkward. An additional reason for the absence of Asian instruments is the reluctance of many Asian Christians to "recover" their own cultural tradition (what was once labeled "heathen" during missionary days) for the Christian faith. This hesitation could also be attributed to the manner in which the Gospel was transmitted to the local population in the early days of Methodism: Christian worship was clothed in western dress; few attempts were made to incorporate elements from the local culture.

In terms of music resources, the English-speaking churches are presently making a transition from the *Methodist Hymnal* (1966) to the *United Methodist Hymnal* (1989), both borrowed from the United Methodist Church in the United States. Wesley Methodist Church was among the first to be introduced to this new resource and certain theological and musical objections were initially encountered. Nevertheless, the new hymnal has now found its niche in several churches, although strong sentiment continues for the *Methodist Hymnal* of 1966, especially its holy communion ritual. Some churches have even continued to use this ritual in spite of the changeover to the new hymnal.

Choruses from *Hosanna!* (USA), *Scripture in Songs* (Australia/New Zealand), *Songs of the Vineyard* (USA), and *Songs of Fellowship* (UK) are popular in the contemporary services of most TRAC churches as well as in CAC churches that hold English services.[14] In the CAC churches, two hymnals, the *Hymns of Praise* and the *Hymnal of Universal Praise*, seem to dominate the churches in their traditional services.[15] These hymnals have their origin in Hong Kong, and a high percentage of

216

the hymns are translated texts set to traditional western hymn tunes. However, efforts are being undertaken in Hong Kong and Taiwan to promote ethnic Chinese material for Christian worship. Attempts are also being made by lay members of ETAC churches to write their own choruses and hymns for worship.

Local sacred music compositions are not thriving, first, because of the traditional dependence on worship material coming from overseas. Nevertheless, there is an interest in the writing of choruses and hymns for specific occasions such as National Day, church anniversaries, and other significant occasions of the church.[16] Second, there are not many trained and professionally active composers writing for the Methodist Church.[17] Music composition is commonly seen as a hobby and not a crucial aspect in the music ministry of the church. Attempts by the General and Annual Conferences to encourage song writing through competition and festivals have not proven very successful. There is a need for the Church to explore ways and means of encouraging the growth of this area especially if it seeks to be a contributor to the growth of global worship in Methodism.

One possible way of ensuring the growth of indigenous creations is to develop a network whereby such new works can be commissioned, published, and presented. For the moment, there have been efforts undertaken by local churches to explore non-traditional music sources for their worship services. The Methodist Church of the Incarnation (MCI) is well known for its adoption of the use of "May God's love abide with you" in several different languages for a sung response to the benediction.[18]

Scriptures and the Sermon

Scripture is read from the pulpit and the majority of churches have only one reading, though some churches use three or four readings that include a Psalm. Unlike the Philippines, where scripture readings are usually assigned to lay people, Singapore Methodist churches tend to place the scripture reading directly before the sermon, and so it is preferable to have the preacher read the lesson, particularly since the biblical passage is often the basis of the sermon.

In dealing with the sermon, one is immediately struck by the evangelical and generally conservative stand. A majority of the pastors feel that the most significant purpose of their sermon is to encourage discipleship and promote Christian living. Other purposes identified include the transmission of basic Christian doctrine, invitations to mission and evangelism, and conflict reconciliation. Sermon series are a popular form for pastors; sermons are also developed by attention to theme, to the lectionary, or to the day/season in the liturgical year. Most sermons are preached by ordained ministers of the church, though lay people have been invited to the pulpit during significant events of the church's life such as Youth Sunday, Women's Society for Christian Service Sunday, and Missions Sunday.

The Holy Communion

The administration of communion takes several forms within the Methodist Church in Singapore. Once again, the ritual and the act of communion fall within the purview of the pastor of the local church and are very much dependent on the minister's personal inclination; in some cases, they become an opportunity for innovation! Most pastors and congregations have adopted the communion orders found either in the 1989 *United Methodist Hymnal* or in the *Methodist Hymnal* of 1966. Other churches do not strictly observe the established rituals, but create their own services using the hymnals as a guide; this is true for some CAC congregations. In general, Sunday communion is celebrated monthly. Some congregations conduct a weekly communion service on a weekday in addition to the monthly Sunday celebration.[19]

The most common form of communion is this: following the consecration, the congregation is invited to come forward, and the people are given the elements separately while kneeling. Each "table" of communicants is "dismissed" by a prayer before they rise from the altar area. Two prominent variations exist on this basic model. In one form, the congregation comes forward, receives the elements while standing around the altar, and departs following a table dismissal prayer. The other form allows for the congregation to come forward and receive both elements simultaneously from the pastor and the assisting communion stewards. After reception, they may move toward the altar to stand or kneel for some moments, consuming the elements before returning to their seats. In this instance, there is no table dismissal prayer.

Some churches have also adopted intinction as a method for communion, but this is slow in gaining popularity. Another method allows for the distribution of the elements to the congregation who remain in their seats. The words of distribution (e.g., "The body of our Lord Jesus Christ broken for you. . . . take, eat, and remember. . . .") are said, and the minister and congregation consume the elements together.

There have been some attempts to introduce wafers (for bread) and wine. While some churches have moved into this relatively easily, some churches still prefer freshly baked bread cut into cubes and grape juice. Some attempts have been made to introduce Asian food and drink for the communion elements, but without much success.

The Question of Inculturation

One possible reason for the difficulty in introducing the Asian perspective in worship is that Singapore is heavily influenced by the west in her practice of Christian worship. The fact of the matter is, Christianity is but one of several religions found within this city state and the only thing that sets Christians apart from the other faiths is its characteristic of "forsaking the past." Traditional Chinese ancestral worship, Islam, and Hinduism place great emphasis on building one's faith upon one's traditional roots, and on a sense of community. But the missionaries who first came to our shore fostered the growth of a community that was to transcend traditional cultural ties. Indirectly, this has led to the abandonment of traditional ties of family and existing community with its inherent "heathen" practices. In the eyes of the local community, converts to Christianity are regarded as outcasts who have betrayed their rich past for a "foreign religion." This gives rise to the forming of a church community that lacks the foundation of relating to one's racial tradition. At the same time, this new community is seen to have its link with brothers and sisters in the outside world who are seemingly "superior."

In this way, one can easily understand why invited Christian ministers from overseas are highly esteemed, far more than the minister Singaporeans have in their own church. By the same token, the worship tradition that the overseas speakers introduce and promote would seem far superior to the local one. This is especially so in the English-speaking congregation. The situation just described was present not only in the early days of Methodism in Singapore but is still very much the case today. As much as inculturation is cherished in the churches of other countries, it is facing an uphill fight in the worship tradition of the Methodist Church in Singapore.

The Future of Methodism

As we approach the year 2000, there is a sense of anticipation of what the future will hold for Methodist worship in Singapore. Can the traditional and the contemporary forms of worship coexist or shall we see the amalgamation of the two diverse worship forms into one? Will there be a blooming of liturgical worship that is presently dormant? Will the future see the demise of any interest in indigenous worship and the potential it has for making an impact in the global Christian realm? What about the organization of the Methodist Church along linguistic lines when most churches of the three annual conferences seem to overlap in language use in worship? Will this change, and if so, how will it affect the way Methodists worship in Singapore? Will the Methodist Church in Singapore continue to be the recipient of the worship tradition from the west, or will it take on the role of a catalyst for a new Asian worship tradition, or must we first be accomplished in the "western" aspect of our worship and music before we can move on into exploring our Asian identity? The answer to many of these questions lies in the hands of the ministers and lay persons who will take leadership in the years to come and their personal theological convictions relating to the purpose of worship and church music. It is an exciting moment as the Methodist Church in Singapore looks forward to an era where the possibilities are so varied.

Types of Worship Service

Traditional Form of Worship

This type of worship features the use of a printed worship bulletin which may include the text of a call to worship, unison prayers, and hymn numbers. At times, the prayer of the liturgist is also written out. Following is a sample of a traditional worship service taken from Wesley Methodist Church:

NINTH SUNDAY AFTER PENTECOST—MISSIONS SUNDAY
24 July 1994—9:15 a.m. Service

WE PREPARE

Time of Silence (organist plays softly)
Choral Introit: "As the Sun doth daily rise"   adapt. by Horatio Nelson

WE UNITE IN PRAISE

Call to Worship
    Leader: Come to Me, all you who are weary and are
        carrying heavy burdens.
    People: **I will give you rest.**
    Leader: Take my yoke upon you and learn from Me.
    All: **You will find rest for your souls.**
Hymn of Praise: "Wonderful Words of Life"   UMH 600
Affirmation of Faith   UMH 594
Gloria Patri   UMH 71

.... IN PRAYER

Prayer Hymn: "Spirit of the Living God"   UMH 393
Silent Prayer
Prayer on behalf of all
Organ Response

.... IN SHARING

The Sharing of God's Peace
Concerns of the Church
Dedication of Missionaries supported by Wesley
Tithes and Gifts to God
Choral Offering: "Jesus Saves"   arr. by Don Hustad
Doxology   tune: Owens

.... IN LISTENING

Hymn of Preparation: "Thy Word is a lamp unto my feet"   UMH 601
Scripture Lesson: Acts 8:1-8
Sermon: "The Chosen and the No Choice"   The Revd. David Wang

.... IN SERVICE

Hymn of Dedication: "Go forth for God"   UMH 670
Benediction: "Ye shall be witnesses"
Organ Postlude
Prayer Ministry at the altar
Note: UMH = *United Methodist Hymnal*

Contemporary Form of Worship or "Prayer and Praise"

This worship form is marked by its spontaneous nature, in that it does not use any printed material aside from that which is projected onto a screen by an overhead projector. This is a sample of a 7:30 p.m. "Prayer and Praise" service from Wesley Methodist Church at which communion is celebrated:

Welcome   Pastor Peter Wong
Opening Songs (2 or 3 songs may be used)   Worship Leader
Invitation to Communion   Pastor
Confession (using overhead projected transparencies)
Offertory Song: "We bring sacrifice of praise"
Doxology (tune: Owens)
Communion Ritual
    (pastor's discretion on which ritual to use)
Songs in Preparation:
    "Father in Heaven how we love You"
    "Lamb of God"
Prayer of Humble Access (using overhead projected
    transparencies)
Distribution of Elements (worship leader leads in
    communion-oriented choruses)
The Lord's Prayer
Sermon   Guest Preacher
Benediction   Pastor Peter Wong

Samples of Indigenous Music

The following pages present samples of music composed by the author and currently in use in the Methodist Church in Singapore.[20]

Still for Thy Loving Kindness

Charles Wesley, 1740

Swee Hong Lim

1. Still for Thy lov - ing kind - ness Lord, I in Thy tem - ple wait, I look to find Thee in Thy Word, or at Thy ta - ble meet.
2. Here in Thine own ap - point - ed ways, I wait to learn Thy will; Si - lent I stand be - fore Thy face, and hear Thee say: Be Still!
3. Be still and know that I am God; 'tis all I live to know; To feel the vir - tue of Thy blood, and spread its praise be - low.
4. I wait my vi - gour to re - new, Thine i - mage to re - trieve; The veil of out - ward things pass through, and grasp in Thee to live.

O Lamb of God

Traditional

Swee Hong Lim

Gently with slight lilt (♩=88)

Holy, Holy, Holy Lord

Traditional

Swee Hong Lim

Ho-ly, Ho-ly, Ho - ly, Lord God of hosts. Heav'n and earth are full of Thy glo - ry.

Glo-ry be to Thee, O Lord most high. Bless-ed is He that com-eth in the name of the

Lord. Ho-san-na in the high - - est. A - - men.

Memorial Acclamation

Swee Hong Lim

Christ has died, Christ has ri - sen,

Christ will come a - gain!

Amen

Swee Hong Lim

A - men. A - men.

A - men.

Chapter 13

A Singing and Dancing Church: Methodist Worship in Kenya and Zimbabwe

Paul W. Chilcote,
with Katheru Gichaara and Patrick Matsikenyiri

By the time we reached Ntakira we were already three hours behind schedule. The bus had been late in picking us up. The roads were more dangerous than usual because of unexpected repair work. About two hours into our journey some repair work had to be done on the bus itself. Needless to say, many of us were anxious about our failure to arrive on time to the preaching engagements in rural Methodist churches that had been previously arranged. How would people respond to the circumstances? Wanting to have a positive experience of worship with African brothers and sisters in Christ (for most of us a first-in-a-lifetime opportunity), how would our unintentional inconveniencing of would-be friends color the event? As we approached the central church of the circuit, none of us knew what we would encounter. I think most of us expected an empty church with disappointed Methodists ready to begin the return journey to their homes. Nothing could have prepared us for what lay ahead.

When we turned off the dirt road into the church compound, we were awestruck by the scene before our eyes. Men, women, and children literally covered the ground. Most of them were sitting: women in one area, men in another. Youth engaged in conversation here and there, but more generally pulsated to the rhythms of music sung in quiet yet confident tones. Children ran to and fro or rested in their mothers' laps. I think my first reaction was, how could they be so patient? And then my mind swiftly flew to images of family, community, celebration, and life. As the hundreds who had gathered caught sight of the bus, the serene atmosphere immediately burst into a kind of excited frenzy. The sounds and rhythms we had heard from afar exploded as the singing turned (as I was later told) to exultant praise of God. The mass of people was now moving, dancing, expressing their faith in their own unique way as disciples of Jesus Christ in Africa. We were overwhelmed!

Before the formal service of worship began, we were ushered into a large hall for a meal. And eating could not take place until our hands were washed. Two women stood at the door: one with a pitcher of warm water, the other with a clean white towel. No one was allowed to forgo this important ritual of hospitality, an act of welcoming that made each participant feel important, loved, and clean. No one had to explain to us what tremendous sacrifice many had undertaken to provide the food for us which awaited on the tables. It was a feast of love, lovingly prepared for honored guests. The service of worship which followed was an alternating series of songs and prayers and testimonies, all held outside for lack of space within, which led us to and prepared us for the preaching of the Word. Once the preaching (which we were invited to do) was complete, the dancing began. An individual woman began the chorus (an adapted Meru hunting song, I was told), but she was quickly joined by other women, young and old, and then by men. The circle of dancing believers expanded slowly but surely with each beat of the drum. In the end, no one was excluded. All joined in the celebration of life, one circle, one family, linked arm in arm, singing the praises of the God who had brought us together and made us one in Christ. This was my first experience of worship on a Sunday morning, nearly three hours north of Nairobi, Kenya, in the heart of rural "Methodist country" among the Meru people.

About four years later I had the opportunity to visit Zimbabwe for the first time and looked forward to the worship experience I was to have there in Mutare, in a congregation appropriately known as Hilltop United Methodist Church. As we made our way through Sakubva, one of the "high density suburbs" of this third city of the nation, I was struck by the way in which the church was situated atop a small *kopje* (or hillock) in the center of this sprawling mass of people. From the heights above we could look down upon hundreds of small homes which housed the urban poor of the area. We could hear the sounds of children crying, of young boys playing soccer in a small area cleared for that cherished activity, of drums beating, and voices singing as residents were called to their various places of worship in homes and churches and open fields.

I wasn't able to form an immediate impression of the congregation because I was whisked away to the pastor's chamber behind the chancel. I could already hear singing though, and once again began to feel the spirit and vitality of worship in this African setting. When we made our way through the back door, situated behind the pulpit, I was overwhelmed by sheer numbers. A cruciform structure, Hilltop Church was packed in all directions. The mature women of the congregation, many of them sporting the uniforms of their beloved *Rukwadzano* (women's) organization, filled the transept to my left. Elder men balanced off the scene to the right. The central nave was filled with youth, as younger brothers and sisters pressed their way into the balcony to the rear. The pastor, later to be a student of mine at Africa University, nodded almost imperceptibly to one of the men to our right, and the singing began. Following a solo introductory phrase, instruments of various sizes and shapes accompanied the congregation as all joined the exultant song. Pastor Magamba leaned over and whispered, "He's our 'song-leader.' He's good."

At least three things impressed me greatly in this, my first, opportunity to worship among the United Methodists in Zimbabwe. First and foremost was the music. The singing of these Methodists appeared to be effortless; it simply flowed from the center of their being. While translated English hymns were used in parts of the service, the extemporaneous outbursts of song which punctuated their worship here and there revealed a certain abandon, a celebrative spirit before the presence of God that could do nothing other than burst forth in song. Secondly, I was impressed by the way in which they prayed. When the time of prayer was announced, the congregation stood, turned, and knelt, facing their seats, hands folded and raised with elbows resting on their chair or bench. I don't suppose it was the position so much as the unison action and movement that struck me so profoundly. Here was a community, a family, united in prayer. Thirdly, as in all African worship I have experienced since that time, I was impressed by the overwhelming presence of children and youth. On this particular Sunday, the overflow from the balcony was ushered to the area beneath the pulpit where all took their places on the floor, woven mats spread out carefully by the women in anticipation of their arrival.

Such are the impressionistic memories of my first encounters with two specific Methodist communities at worship. While narrative description and analysis hardly do justice to the dynamics of African worship in the Methodist tradition (video materials such as the Roman Catholic production, *The Dancing Church*,[1] penetrate more directly to the realities), a focused study of this nature marks an important initial step in what must be a lengthy journey.

First, then, some preliminary observations and comments about methodology. The African continent is immense. United Methodism (the product of both American and indigenous evangelistic activity) is organized into thirteen Annual Conferences in eight different nations, most of which have been liberated only recently from English, French, and Portuguese colonial bonds. British Methodism extended its missionary influence into at least as many nations south of the Sahara; and traditions that trace their roots back to the Wesleys in one way or another are pervasive. The diversity of the Methodist tradition in Africa, not to mention Christianity in general, is sometimes overwhelming. This situation, of course, makes it impossible to say much of anything in general about the nature of Methodist worship on the continent. Moreover, the study of worship among the various African Christian traditions, with the exceptions, perhaps, of Roman Catholicism and the African indigenous or independent traditions, is in a nascent stage.[2] In view of these circumstances and for the purposes of this essay, I have chosen to invite two African colleagues to reflect with me upon their personal experience of and involvement in Methodist worship in their own specific contexts.

Patrick Matsikenyiri has been recognized internationally for his major contributions to the development of African Christian music. A layman of the United Methodist Church in Zimbabwe, he presently serves as Lecturer in African Music and Culture at the newly established Africa University, the first United Methodist-related institution of its kind on the continent. Katheru Gichaara, a pastor of the Methodist Church in Kenya, is presently engaged in doctoral studies at Emory University. Having served for some time as secretary of the Africa Association for Liturgy, Music, and the Arts (AFALMA), his primary interest in liturgical studies has carried him into broader discussions related to the interfacing of theology and culture. As a team, therefore, we represent both British and American Methodist traditions, laity and clergy, and two specific and very different cultural contexts of African Methodist worship. Reflecting upon our experiences in Kenya and Zimbabwe, we hope to present something of a case study of worship in these particular settings and offer some preliminary observations for future reflection, discussion, and practice.

A Kenyan Safari

Methodism in Kenya is caught up, like other Christian traditions in Africa today, between "modernism," sometimes seen as synonymous with "westernism," and the indigenous African heritage that informs the African personality and cultural consciousness. The creative tension that has resulted from this struggle for identity has given birth to a distinctive, albeit elusive, religious tradition on the continent—African Christianity.

The imaginative journey (safari) upon which we now embark has its setting in a rural congregation of the Methodist Church in the East African Republic of Kenya. The day is Sunday. It is a very special day for the worship of *Murungu* (God) in Meru. The local people have been looking forward to this day all week. The service is supposed to begin at 10:00 a.m. The pastor who is responsible for ten congregations is the preacher for the day in this particular church. Lay (local) preachers will serve the other nine congregations. These men or women have received basic instruction in the art of preaching and have passed the preacher's test administered by the Church. Their only other special qualification is that they are literate (at least in the local language and/or dialect). All have expressly professed the Christian faith.

The pastor occupies a very special place in the society. Among the Meru of Kenya, this community/religious leader stands in the cultural tradition of the *Mugwe* of Meru. According to Meru custom, it was the singular duty of the *Mugwe* to offer blessings before major sacrifices were made or expeditions taken, but he also functioned as a prophet, diviner, and "king" whom the people consulted in order to receive guidance in all community and personal affairs. The Meru people believed that the left hand of the *Mugwe* was especially potent when stretched to bless or to curse. The Methodist minister in the community is viewed by many as an heir to the *Mugwe* powers, especially now that the traditional *Mugwe*'s dominant role in the community is diminishing with the encroachment of "modern" attitudes and customs.

It is 10:00 a.m. on Sunday and the minister/pastor has arrived at the local church for the morning worship service which may include adult baptism and holy communion. By 10:15 a.m. only the congregational leaders and a few of the members have trickled in. The minister, trained and socialized in "western ways," who looks at the clock rather than the shadow of the sun, is a little impatient. The congregational leader, known by all as the chairman, reassures the pastor that his people will yet come! The pastor is tactfully reminded that according to the African way, time is not meticulously watched nor carefully measured, as may be the case in other parts of the world. There is less urgency, less government of life by time. Perhaps he remembers what John Mbiti, one of Africa's prominent theologians, once said: "Unlike the west where time is a commodity which must be utilized, sold, and bought, time in Africa has to be created and produced."[3] For the African it is the event that is important. As long as the event takes place, then all is well. Time is not so much quantified as qualified. And this traditional worldview will operate, more often than not, in the Sunday morning service of worship of the Methodist congregations.

By 10:30 a.m. the pastor feels comfortable enough to begin the service. Most of the people have arrived by now. There may be a few who will come later, but what matters to them is that they come at all. Sunday morning worship stands in the time-honored tradition of "clan gathering." In the clan gathering, every adult member of the community felt constrained to attend. This event was always special because it involved the invocation of the deity. It was an event heavily laden with rituals and traditions, with words and actions that reached back to generations long gone but not forgotten. Increasingly, with the passage of time and the many changes that have occurred in independent Kenya, indigenous spirituality and the traditional instruments of worship have found their rightful place in the worshiping life of the Church, though they are inevitably reconfigured and adapted for Christian use. In the traditional milieu, clan gatherings and structured worship occurred only intermittently, often before the planting season, after harvest (for thanksgiving), or before a hunting or a raiding expedition. In the Christian tradition, God is ritually and corporately approached in new and more frequent rhythms.

In Methodist worship in Kenya, just as in the traditional rituals and observances of the Meru people, everybody takes an active part. Nothing could be more foreign to the African mind than the idea of a withdrawn observer who remains aloof and studiously watches the others. This is not to say that people are not reflective of what they are doing. Rather, they are "participant/observers" who both act within and meditate upon the inclusive community of God's people in worship. Such an attitude and practice reflects the traditional heritage in which everybody in the community was an active participant in the ritual dance and in other physical actions that made worship real and relevant. Ritual movement, action, and gesture in the traditional society retained and communicated the community's memory.[4] "Inclusive participation" ensured the continued life of that community.

Thus the church, in addition to being a locus of worship, plays another important role: it is a place for social interaction. In the villages of Kenya there are very few telephones, and not many people have cars, so communication with friends and relatives takes other forms. If someone wants to see another person, the best place to "catch" him or her is in the church. It is also in the church that important messages from community leaders and others will be announced; therefore one who fails to attend church might miss something important. This communal existence is captured by John Mbiti's famous transposition of Descartes' "I think, therefore I am" into "I am because we are; and since we are, therefore I am."[5]

In most cases, the pastor of a Methodist congregation in Kenya will open the service of worship by reading from the vernacular translation of the inherited English liturgy, *Ndwimbo cia Kwinira Murungu.*[6] In addition to the hymns and services directly translated from the British Methodist *Hymn-Book* and *Book of Offices* which constitute the bulk of the volume, this collection also contains a few songs that employ traditional local tunes and rhythmic styles, e.g., *Nguri* (youth dance), *Kigaru kia Ekuru* (a festive women's song), and *Rwimbo rwa Maketha* (harvest hymn). While *Ndwimbo cia Kwinira Murungu* is the standard book of worship for the Methodists of Meru, not every member of the congregation owns a copy, nor is a copy available to every participant in common worship. In fact, there is only one copy for about every five worshipers. Similarly, even fewer participants own their own Bibles. A few people may be seen carrying individual booklets, perhaps one of the gospels. These were common before the Bible in its entirety was published in the Kimeru language in 1964.[7] The Scriptures are often studied, however, in family groups or in home and church fellowships, which enhances the communal nature of the Book. Those who are illiterate listen intently as the Scriptures are read and commit them to memory. The same thing can be said of the order of service. The Meru people, coming out of an essentially oral cultural tradition, are able to recite the creeds and other frequently repeated liturgical pieces with great ease.

Even a casual observer will note that the fixed forms of the "foreign" liturgy, however, inevitably create a feeling of alienation among those gathered for worship, for at least two reasons. First, the liturgy has a strange ring in the ears and minds of the people. The images it conjures do not excite them. In the traditional milieu, for instance, the Meru people addressed God from the heart, praising God spontaneously for concrete acts accomplished in their midst. They would invoke and praise the God of concrete and tangible physical features, e.g., Mount Kenya, the Nyambene ranges, and the Kazita River. Second, the fixed forms of the imported book of worship are used without taking advantage of the provisions for improvisation. The people are forced to follow a rigid order of service, with a mode of worship that seems strange. Worship acts that involve the entirety of the participants, that are kinetic as well as verbal, emotive as well as contemplative, find little place in the inherited liturgy from the west. One hopes that, when the worship book being compiled by the Methodist Church in Kenya is completed, it will draw from the rich, holistic spirituality of African culture.

The morning service will come to life once again, therefore, as soon as the pastor abandons the foreign liturgy and invites the people for extempore prayers and other informal concerns. Perhaps more than any other period within the experience of worship, this is the time the worshipers begin to feel that they are in the presence of God. Common items for prayer and praise include the concern for the sick of the community; the perennial dependence of an agrarian people upon the rains (especially during periods of drought); the acquisition of school fees for children and the successful completion of exams; crops and livestock; government; and common life. The Scriptures will then be read. Nearly always a passage from the Old Testament precedes a selection from the Epistles. The people usually stand for the reading of the Gospel. It is common for the readers to be younger members of the congregation, not only as a visible incorporation of the growing generation into the body of believers, but because of their literacy and "youthful eyes."

Most of the stories of the Bible, particularly those of the New

Testament and Jesus' ministry, are well known to the members of the congregation. They have heard them time and again or have seen them acted out in concerts and dramas. The part of the Bible, however, that interests most of the people and resonates with the Meru cultural ethos is the Old Testament. The Meru people are intrigued by the parallels they immediately discern between themselves and the children of Israel. The two cultures have many common aspects. Indeed, the central story of exodus from Egypt and settlement in Canaan has its counterpart in Meru mythology. In the original Meru flight from an island called Mbwaa (thought to be Shungwaya on Kenya's coast), the liberated people of God cross the Iria Itune (literally Red Sea, but most likely the River Tana which originates on Mt. Kenya and drains into the Indian Ocean) under the leadership of Koome Njue, whose rod parted the water. The Israelite story of hardship at the hands of the pharaohs is parallel with the Meru plight under the Nguu Ntune (those who wore red clothes).[8] The imagery of the sacrament of baptism, in addition to its initiatory elements, inevitably enhances this coincidental similarity of origin, belief, and cultural practice.

It has been some time since his last visit, so, following the proclamation of the Word, the pastor will invite forward "those to be baptized" who come escorted by their sponsors. Before this day of baptism, the candidates will have completed up to six months of instruction on the doctrines and church procedures of the Methodist Church.[9] The pastor interrogates the candidates earnestly: "Do you renounce the devil with all of his works?" And subsequent to an affirmative response, "Do you then accept Christ as your personal savior and wish to be baptized?" Again, the candidate answers, "Yes." The candidate is accepted as a full member of the Church and is invited to receive the sacrament of holy communion for the very first time. A solemn spirit of awe—a sense of the dramatic—fills the passing moments. The sign of the cross is generally made upon the forehead of the initiate.

High value is placed upon baptism by the Methodist in Kenya, who takes it as a rite comparable to that of the traditional ritual of initiation. In this African "rite of passage," a group of initiates banded together and visited their relatives to announce their impending ritual event and collect gifts. On the morning of initiation all the candidates were chased into the river, stark naked, to wash away the "blemish" of youth. Then the actual initiation took place amidst much singing and other celebrative chants. Each candidate was conducted into seclusion by a ritual "father" or "mother" whose duty it was to instruct the initiate into proper manhood or womanhood. Men were thereafter invited into the many councils for the defense of the society and taught the secrets of what it meant to be a Meru man. Women were socialized into the place of women as mothers of the Meru people.

This rite symbolized nothing less than the complete metamorphosis of the individual. Once initiated, the neophyte was allowed to marry and partake of societal rituals. Having endured the trials of ritual circumcision, a male was considered a "mature Meru." At baptism, the Meru Methodist Christians see themselves in this same light. Water is used at baptism as a sign of washing away sins, just as water, in the tradition, washed away the "blemish" of youth. The signification of the cross upon one's forehead is an "indelible mark" of incorporation into Christ and the Church, just as one joined the social-religious milieu of the Meru through the indelible mark of circumcision. The candidate in both cases is given a new name, thus discarding the old and putting on the new to signify new birth (2 Corinthians 5:17).[10]

When administered to adults, the sacrament of baptism in the Kenyan Methodist tradition always culminates with the celebration of the eucharist. The British Methodist missionaries forbade children and persons who had not been confirmed into full membership of the Church to partake of holy communion. Perhaps this tradition has been carried forward to the present because of the sacrificial associations of the rite which also find a parallel in earlier Meru custom. The eucharist is the paschal feast at which the sacrifice of the Lamb is remembered and celebrated as a thanksgiving to God in the context of all God's mighty acts of deliverance. Interestingly enough, it was common among the Meru, once they had fulfilled their parental obligations and seen their children through the rites of initiation, to offer a sacrifice of thanksgiving to God. The sacrificial animal in this rite was a lamb of one color (therefore without blemish). Rich parents could replace the lamb with a black bull which was eaten by the parents' age-mates.[11]

The baptism of infants in the Meru Wesleyan tradition is as important as the baptism of adult believers. The infants are brought to church after the pastor or some senior member of the congregation has had time to visit with each family of the children to be baptized.

The pastor will invite everyone in the family to participate fully in the ritual process along with their infant child. During the service of baptism the pastor asks both the parents and congregation to promise that they will lead exemplary lives so that the infant will want to emulate them.[12] Each candidate is baptized in the name of the Trinity, marked on the forehead with the sign of the cross, presented to the congregation as a new member of the Body of Christ, blessed and returned to the parents. The rite of confirmation will normally follow when the candidates are between eleven and thirteen years of age and after they have received serious instruction in the Christian faith.

Whereas adult baptism is seen in the light of traditional rites of circumcision, infant baptism is regarded as related to the traditional infant name-giving. In Meru culture, the naming of a child was always considered to be a community as well as a family affair. Boys were received with five ululations or trills, while girls received only four. On the eighth day the child was ready to be named. The naming ceremony was enacted at the place of seclusion where the newborn remained for the first week of life. The crossing of the front door into the outside world on the eighth day symbolized passage from name-lessness into the community of the Meru people. The child was given a name and therefore became a person. The Meru, in fact, believed that you became a person only when you had received a name. Meru Methodists, therefore, cannot help seeing a connection between belonging to the Christian community and the fact that infants, in baptism, receive a "new name." Popular Methodist belief held, until very recently, that you only became a Christian when you acquired a "Christian name," many of these names being of European origin without obvious connection to the Christian faith.

At the end of the morning service of worship, the Meru women will lead the congregation with the singing of *Gikubua Kiatho* ("the feast has been wonderful") which is a song of thanksgiving. And the minister, whose black robes are reminiscent of the *Mugwe*'s black mantle and his ritual black staff, will bless the people, lifting his arm just as the *Mugwe*'s left hand was extended in the ritual blessing of the people.[13] After the service, which lasts from one and a half to two hours, many people will linger around the church grounds, socializing with their friends and relatives. In the Methodist Church in Kenya, the liturgy is increasingly a celebrative ritual of life. While the proclamation of Christian faith and practice in the Wesleyan tradition has transformed and shaped the lives of the Meru people, the rediscovery of indigenous African spirituality (especially in this post-colonial era) has greatly enriched Methodist worship, making it real and relevant in the lives of the people.

A Sojourn among United Methodists in Zimbabwe

Among the Shona-speaking peoples of Zimbabwe there is a saying, "If you can talk, you can sing. If you can walk, you can dance." This is a powerful way of saying that the entire being of the African must be involved in worship. Even the simple act of going to church, for most United Methodists in this setting, means that they will walk to church, many kilometers in some cases. The worship of God begins there, in the journey with brothers and sisters, uncles and aunts, neighbors and friends, and is inevitably punctuated with periods of singing and dancing along the way.

When a Shona believer enters the sanctuary, he or she gives a silent prayer of gratitude for a safe journey and good health. After prayer he or she will join with other believers who sing both from their hymn books (generally the *United Methodist Hymnbook* of the Zimbabwe Annual Conference) and from a common repertoire of powerful "short songs" (oftentimes inaccurately referred to as choruses). Youth, men, and women provide guidance as song leaders and help create a worshipful atmosphere. The song leaders are powerful, innovative people. As the congregation becomes more involved, the members express enthusiasm: one can read the inner feelings of joy in each face. When a song moves into the second stanza, the shaker and the drum are set into motion. The congregation spontaneously rises to its feet and begins to sway. The song leader can creatively adapt songs to the situation by improvising or by relating verses to current community, national, or world affairs. This aspect of worship moves the congregations with meaningful emotion.

Africans are a singing people; music is an integral part of African life. In many cases manual work and chores are accompanied with music in the background. When lifting a heavy log from one place to another, workers sing to the rhythm of the physical labor. Music plays a prominent role in the pounding or threshing of corn. It is not a surprise, therefore, to discover that a large portion of worship life in Zimbabwe is devoted to music. Music is regarded as central to any worship experience. This can be seen clearly in the various elements of a typical service of Sunday worship, which usually will include most of the following components:

Chipangidzo che Rusando (Order of Service)

Procession
Invocation
Hymn
Creed
Pastoral Prayer, concluding with the Lord's Prayer
Choir
Responsive Reading (Psalm)
Gloria Patri
New Testament Reading
Announcements
Offering
Choir
Sermon
Prayer
Hymn
Rukudze (Praise Hymn)
Benediction
Silent Prayer

Procession

The choir, lay leader, minister, and those taking part in the service get ready for the procession as the congregation sings. The choir then breaks into a song of its own during the procession until all are in place. The procession itself often involves rehearsed and cherished rhythmic movements, and is drawn from traditional African tunes related to the life of the people. A good example of such a song is Jesu Tawa Pano ("Jesus we are here"; the text and tune are given at the end of this chapter).[14] Characterized by their repetition and driving rhythms, such tunes move the congregation as a united body into this sacred time. The minister formally calls the people to worship and the service continues. The choir sings an anthem before the first hymn is sung by the congregation. Music permeates the opening moments of worship as the people of God "pray twice" in song.

Prayer

Before the first prayer, the congregation usually sings the *Kuhuhudza* (calling), invoking God and informing God that they are ready to hear the Word. This lyrical invocation is deeply imbedded in the soul of Shona people; its origin lies in the pastoral life of herders, and it specifically relates to the herding of cattle. Often isolated from one another in the bush, head boys would determine a special "call" described as a *kuhuhudza*. This was a unique, musical cry, understood only by those involved. *Kuhuhudza* for Christians, therefore, is a special call to God. It is a very powerful way of calling upon the presence of the Lord, reminiscent, perhaps, of the intimate imagery reflected in Jesus' own words concerning his sheep (John 10:1-6, 14). A typical *kuhuhudza* is developed extemporaneously by the leader:

> He he Touya kwamuri mambo (Oh, we come to you, Lord)
> He he he (Oh, oh, oh)
> He he Toite royi zano (Oh, what advice shall we take
> [please give us one])

The Lord's Prayer then follows the general prayers of the people.

The older members of the congregation highly esteem the position of kneeling whenever they pray. This creates in people, they believe, a great sense of humility. When individuals walk into church they often kneel in the aisle in order to offer themselves to God in prayer before they take their place in the benches or pews. When the time of prayer is announced, therefore, it is not uncommon to see people moving into the kneeling position in readiness for the prayer. This act derives from the notion that whenever we come before the presence of a *Mambo* (king), we humble ourselves. Believers feel that the same should apply to God each time people pray. It is the custom in most United Methodist churches, if chairs or pews are present, to turn and kneel, facing the seats. Following the prayers, a choral anthem precedes the proclamation.

Preaching

After the reading of the Bible, a hymn is sung to invite the preacher forward in order to begin the sermon. Most preachers are lay men and women who lack formal theological training. Many of the preachers are charismatic. To Africans, a powerful preacher is one who is energetic and whose voice projects and conveys conviction. A sermon that is situational and addresses issues that are current within the community, district, province, and nation will catch the attention of the congregation. But it is assumed that the sermon has its roots in a relevant biblical text. As the preacher moves to the pulpit, the congregation has been prepared and is ready to hear the Word. When people feel inspired during the sermon, they break spontaneously into spirited song. One member after another will join in, and soon, the entire congregation will be on its feet, swaying, clapping, and singing. The preacher is left with no option but to stop preaching and join in the singing. Tears appear on the cheeks of some of the parishioners as an expression of joy and gratitude, a reflection of the sustaining power of God. Only the Holy Spirit is in control at this time. The shaking of hands as a way of affirming each other's faith and commitment is a common feature during this powerful singing. Women will even make some small controlled rhythmic jumps and ululate in response to the singing by the congregation and the message delivered. And the congregation will not sit down until the one who began the singing brings it to an end.

At the conclusion of the sermon, a song leads the congregation into prayer yet again. During the singing, people often move forward to the pulpit area to kneel and pray. Prayer, at this point in the service, is generally spontaneous and open to all who feel called upon by the Holy Spirit to "offer their sacrifice" to God. At the conclusion of this time of prayer, the people once again sing as they move back to their places.

Offering

Giving is an expression of gratitude to the Lord for all the blessings that have been bestowed on the individual and the community. The introduction of a special service of thanksgiving at the time of harvest has helped to improve pledges to the church. Usually in July, individuals bring in a part of what they have harvested from their fields. Local churches, districts, and the Annual Conference now set high giving goals which churches proudly meet as they feel positively challenged by such celebrative practices. Gifts are often brought forward by special groups within the congregation and presented with singing and drama. The money is then used for operational and building purposes. Many people invite church leaders to come and collect a beast for the church as an offering to enhance the festive nature of the community event. In addition to harvest, people now give thanks to the church for their birthdays and wedding anniversaries. When people receive promotions at work they feel grateful and share their joy with the church. These practices have increased the church's resources and remind the congregations of their essentially communal nature.

Sunday morning worship ends as it began, in song. Singing will carry the congregation from corporate worship to proclaiming the message they have heard in their daily living. Since many worshipers walk far distances to attend worship, it is not unusual for clusters of friends and family to sit together before their return journey, sharing food, conversation, and Christian fellowship. For some, Sunday worship will be, necessarily, an all day affair, but a day anticipated with great joy and expectation.

A number of factors continue to influence the worship and music of United Methodism in Zimbabwe. Sunday worship, in some areas, carries with it the legacy of camp meetings linked to the previous history of the Methodist tradition in this region. In the past, it was not unusual for the church in Zimbabwe to have camp meetings which lasted as long as ten days. The meetings were the highlight of annual worship experiences among the churches. This heritage left a trail of strength which has enhanced present worship in the life of the Methodist tradition. The Annual Conference continues to have a program of revival meetings organized by the different groups of the Church, including youth, *Rukwadzano rwe va dzimai* (United Methodist Women), and men's meetings. These revivalistic services generally last from Wednesday to Sunday morning. The goals of these meetings are to enrich the parishioners' faith and enable them to appreciate the working of the Church. In fact, for each group, the revival meeting functions as the focal point around which all of the planning for the year is structured.

A wide range of music is exchanged and shared at these meetings. Song leaders from different districts, circuits, and churches take turns leading music as people gather for the service. This is the time worshipers learn many new songs to take back to their churches. This prelude to revival, as is the case in normal Sunday worship, ensures sound preparation of the congregation for the preaching to follow. During this period people express joy, and sing with gratitude for the safety they have experienced and God's care between revivals. Revival meetings generally include highly structured programs where people meet in small groups and give testimonies. It is during these testimonies that many souls are saved and people reaffirm their faith. Revival meetings have become a strengthening phenomenon for the Church at large. Individual Christians go back to their churches renewed in spirit and able to share with the rest of the congregation when they get back home.[15]

Since the late 1950s, music in the church has taken a major turning point to meet the aspirations of Africans. When the Church came into Zimbabwe, missionaries did not take time to learn and understand the music of the people they were going to evangelize. They condemned the music of the people and the use of drums in church and preferred established European and North American hymn tunes and hymn texts. Hymns like Heber's "Holy, Holy, Holy" were introduced into the nascent worship life of the African Church. These songs were sung rigidly, from the African point of view; and even more unfathomable to the African, without movement.

So the Africans were forced to live two lives at once. When they were in church they had to sing like missionaries and when they got home they were free to sing with liberty of movement in the accompaniment of the drum, the shaker, and the rattle. This situation continued to prevail for most of the time African nations were under colonial rule. When the political emancipation of colonized Africans came, however, the need for liberation in worship was also felt keenly within the churches. The need to assert an African identity and to proclaim renewed pride in one's culture was pervasive. Innovative women in the church, and in the United Methodist Church in particular, started to improvise tunes for some of the translated texts which were in the hymn books.

One of these hymns, *Kuita basa rake pano* ("To do his will"), was particularly popular. The women would follow the original tune for seven verses. Then, creatively, they would start to sing *Ndindindi ndindi, ndindi vanamai imi* ("Oh, oh, oh you mothers") with movement and ululation in the process. The women's faces would light up with joy and expression. New verses would be invented, reflecting with deep emotion the particular needs of the community and the situation. This, and many other examples, made a number of missionaries realize that there was need to address the new context of the life of the church. Some missionaries were now commissioned, in fact, for a specific task: to study the cultures of the people and to begin to incorporate relevant songs from the cultures of the people into their worship.

The first missionary sent by the Board of Global Ministries of the

United Methodist Church to embark upon this task was Dr. Robert Kauffman. After a study visit throughout Africa, he settled down in Zimbabwe and organized workshops in which he encouraged old people to sing some of the songs that they used to sing for activities like hunting, threshing corn, and fishing. One of these was a hunting song, *Baya wa baya*. After the old people had joyfully sung it to the workshop participants, the missionary asked all participants to help "fit" a biblical text to the tune. This is the precise way in which *Ngatikudze Musiki* ("Let us praise the Creator") was composed. The tune and the rhythm set forth by the drum are essentially unaltered forms of the ancient hunting song (the hymn is printed at the end of this chapter).

This is how many musicians began to get interested in composing African Christian music. In 1964, the first African-based songs were added to the Zimbabwe Annual Conference hymn book when it was going through revision. From that time until now, Zimbabwean United Methodists have been singing songs like *Ngatikudze Musiki*, along with Euro-American hymns like "Amazing Grace" (with innovation in order to make them as lively and appealing as possible), thereby transforming the whole worship experience in the church.

African Christians within our tradition are rediscovering how to sing and to dance in their praise of God.

Some Concluding Observations

In 1854, Thomas Birch Freeman, the renowned British Methodist missionary to Ghana, reported to his Missionary Society: "If our Public worship in Cape Coast is not heaven come down to earth, it is pretty nearly that of England come to Africa."[16] In today's post-colonial, post-independence situation in Africa, no question burns with greater intensity than this one: What does it mean to be African *and* Christian? And that question touches, perhaps, more directly upon the worship of African Christians than on any other area of Christian praxis. In spite of the urgency of this question, and its particular liturgical manifestations, it is surprising that so little has been done to address creatively the issue within the life of the Methodist tradition. While other Christian communities have devoted much effort toward these ends, especially Roman Catholics since Vatican II, Methodists (like most of their Protestant counterparts) lag far behind.[17]

Over a decade ago, Ghanaian Methodist Kwesi Dickson spoke

with some urgency about preaching in the African context. "What this should consist in," he wrote, "given the change in context from Europe to Africa, was not raised in the missionary period, and to our knowledge it has yet to be seriously raised."[18] Unfortunately, that statement rings as true today as it did in 1984, and not only with regard to preaching in particular, but with regard to worship in general. A few prophetic voices have recently penetrated the silence. A large portion of Mercy Oduyoye's "theological reflections on Christianity in Africa," for example, addresses the issues of indigenization and inculturation. "The earth is the Lord's and everything in it too," she exclaims, "and on this foundation Christianity is coming to grips with the external manifestations of African culture."[19] Zablon Nthamburi of Kenya offers a "strategy for indigenization" in *The African Church at the Crossroads*, particularly drawing attention to the successes of the African indigenous Churches, in general, and the Kimbanguists in particular.[20] More practical guidance to the Church is offered by Canaan Banana of Zimbabwe who has called for the "decathedralisation of the Eucharist" and the discovery of "authentic African expressions of worship" for a Church that is truly "the People's Church."[21] More voices need to be added to these within the life of the Methodist tradition.

It is impossible in the scope of these reflections to launch fully into the ocean of this central issue with its many unexplored inlets where the waters of culture not only lap almost imperceptibly at the shore, but just as often crash relentlessly upon the immovable bedrock of Christian tradition. What we can hope to do, however, is point to some salient themes that both require further study and potentially contribute to the enrichment of the global Methodist tradition.

Music and Dance

In his early efforts to articulate a theology in Africa, Kwesi Dickson observed:

> Singing and dancing are a very important feature of life in Africa; these twin activities go on in joy and in sorrow, at worship and at play. Hence a service of worship would have much less meaning if it did not centre round a significant amount of the kind of stirring music that generates religious emotions.[22]

As a tradition born in song, Methodism needs to reflect more intentionally upon the centrality of music in the life of the African Church.

245

How does the "lyrical" and "kinetic" theology of the African Church form, inform, and transform our faith? What further steps need to be taken within the life of the Methodist tradition, both in and outside Africa, to liberate singers and dancers for Christ?

Drama and the Sacred

For the African Methodist, gestures and bodily movements, like dance, are natural and liberating. Worship is the place, whether in procession, in greeting, in sacramental acts, or in the proclamation of the Word, where divine drama is reenacted within the life of the community of God. While pastors are encouraged to follow the liturgical rhythms of the Christian year, most congregations are only beginning to develop a sense of the divine drama reflected in the seasons of the inherited "calendar." Here is a tremendous resource for the church as the African acts out redemption with enthusiasm and desire. For the African Christian, the supernatural is ever present and ever directing the drama of life. The rhythm of the day and the cycle of life belong to God. Is there not something extremely worthwhile for all of us to rediscover in the rhythmic abandonment of the self to God in this safari of faith? Intimately related to these concepts of drama and the sacred is the concept of time. Suffice it to say here, that whereas African Methodists are not always "on time" (in the western sense of the expression), they are quite often "timely."

Community and Meals

In his discussion of communal meal traditions among the Shona, Canaan Banana draws together a number of these salient themes:

> Other forms of fellowship and communion in the traditional Shona life are seen from youngsters (adolescents) when the youths of a village gather together in partnership for *madzamira/mahumbwe/ amadlwana* (role playing). They gather at night when there is moonlight (*jenaguru*) and share food in common. *Humwe/nhimbe/ilima* (communal work) is another form of fellowship and communion among the Shona/Ndebele. At this *jakwara*, people of a village come together and do some work for a particular member, either ploughing, weeding or fencing the fields. They are bound together by a common purpose, common ancestors, and a common culture. . . . Ritual dances like *majukwa, shangara,* and *doro remukwerera* are part of this communion and fellowship.[23]

In spite of the fact that meals are at the very center of African culture and that the eucharist, our family meal of thanksgiving as Methodist Christians, was at the center of the Wesleyan revival, the two have not been put together constructively in the Methodist settings of our experience. How exciting it would be to discover new means of celebrating "our meal" that enhance our experience of true community, that emphasize the intimate connection between liturgy and life, that explore the fuller ranges of meaning made possible in the confluence of biblical text and African context![24] There is much to be explored here, and perhaps a revolution in worship to be anticipated in the re-formation of community around meal.

The full effects of serious reflection upon worship and liturgy are yet to be appreciated in the Methodist churches of Africa. Time and energy must be devoted to this critical task. In its music and dance, in its ability to perceive and act out the great divine drama in the midst of human history, in its profound sense of community *katika safari* (in the journey) with Jesus, and in so much more, it has treasures to enrich a global Church.

Samples of Indigenous Music

The following pages present samples of indigenous music currently in use among Methodists in Africa.

Ngatikudze Musiki

From a hunting song

Parts 2, 3, and 4 may be omitted.

3. Ndiye anotipa zano Rekuita zvakanaka Mambo Mukuru.
4. Ndiye akatipa Jesu Kuti azotiponesa Mambo Mukuru.
5. Tanga tigere mudima Zvino tava murujeko Mambo Mukuru.
6. Kuti tikatora Jesu Hatiohasoshayi chiro Mambo Mukuru.
7. Vaparidzi udzai vanhu Kuti Jesu anotida Mambo Mukuru.
8. Ti-tunga-mirei Tizagara naBaba Mambo Mukuru.

Ndovimba

Patrick Matsikenyiri

Jesu Tawa Pano

Patrick Matsikenyiri

Je - su   ta - wa - pa-no;   Je - su   ta - wa - pa-no;
Je - sus   we are here;   Je - sus   we are here;

(except last time) Mam-bo Je-su.

Je - su   ta - wa - pa-no;   ta - wa - pa-no mu   zi - ta re - nyu.
Je - sus,   we are here;   we are here   for   you.

Mbiri Kuna 'She

Refrain:

	Mbiri kuna 'She tokudza !	Praise to the Lord, praise
	E— tokudza !	Oh—, praise
	(He he he— tokudza) !	Oh oh oh—, praise
1.	Wakatuma Jesu tokudza !	He sent us Jesus, praise
	E—tokudza !	Oh—, praise
	Kuzotiponesa tokudza !	To save us—, praise
	E—tokudza !	Oh—, praise
2.	Ngatimurumbidze, tokudza!	Let's rejoice in Him, praise
	Imwi vanhu mwese, tokudza	All ye people, praise
3.	Uyai tinamate, tokudza !	Come let us pray, praise
	Mwari wakanaka, tokudza !	Gracious God, praise
4.	Anotipa zvese, tokudza !	He gives us everything, praise
	Zvakatinakira, tokudza !	That is good for us, praise
5.	Ipai zvikudzo, tokudza !	Give praise and honor, praise
	Kuna mwari wedu, tokudza!	To our God, praise
6.	Vakomana woye, tokudza !	Young men, praise
	Vasikana woye, tokudza !	Young women, praise
7.	Vanmai woye, tokudza !	Ye mothers, praise
	Vana baba woye, tokudza !	Ye fathers, praise

Chapter 14

At Chapel on the Lord's Day: Methodist Worship in the Caribbean

William W. Watty

Methodist worship, like so much else in the Caribbean, reflects a bewildering diversity. This diversity is, however, held together by two common features which are historically derived. The one is continuity with patterns which have evolved in other parts of the world and have been adapted to local conditions. Methodism in the Hispanic Caribbean is an offshoot and extension of the Methodism in the United States, whereas in the Anglo- and Francophone Caribbean and the Netherlands Antilles it is the British traditions which have persisted. All of this is to emphasize the fact that nowhere in the Caribbean will be discovered an expression of Methodist worship which is totally or even significantly indigenous in the sense that the local culture has been made the point of departure or the matrix for the emerging liturgy.

The second feature is related to the first, and that is the importance of literacy in worship. Its importance can be traced to the very origins of Methodism in the Caribbean. This particular feature appears in the journal of Dr. Thomas Coke who, on his unscheduled arrival in Antigua on Nativity morning 1786, proceeded to the chapel where a congregation of two thousand had foregathered and where he "read prayers." This "reading of prayers" suggests a form of worship according to an ordered liturgy, most likely the *Sunday Service* which John Wesley had adapted from the 1662 *Book of Common Prayer* for the use of the Methodists in North America.

From that earliest period, "read prayers" has been the normative pattern of Methodist worship in the Caribbean on the Lord's Day, for the observance of the sacraments, and at the high festivals. Indeed, until the middle of this century, it was binding on preachers to use the Order of Morning Prayer for morning worship on the Lord's Day, and that without modification or abridgment.

> Worship was marked as much by a joyous simplicity as by due form and comeliness. Methodists knew where they were and what to expect when they foregathered on the Lord's Day— either for Holy Communion with Collect, Epistle, and Gospel, or Morning Prayer with Ancient Hymns, Canticles, and Psalms. . . . Times were when the whole congregation upgraded itself to one rousing choir with harmonies ingeniously improvised, and set tunes spontaneously modified by insertions and variations, to assist that verve and vigour which made for vital participation. . . . People walked miles over hills, through bush and mud, under scorching sun, and some-times pouring rain, because they knew to whom and for what they were coming, and were seldom disappointed.[1]

This pattern broke down in the 1950s, and a period of random experimentation, individual idiosyncrasies, and confusion super-vened. The 1992 *Prayer Book of the Methodist Church* is intended to be a corrective to that unhappy departure and a resumption of the earlier tradition.[2]

The matter of "read prayers" is bound to raise the vexed question of the relevance of a prayer book for Christian worship, for not only does it suggest an inhibiting constraint upon the kind of exuberance which Caribbean worshipers are expected to typify, but it must be something of a surprise to many people to learn that, even in the period of slavery when the majority of worshipers were illiterate, prayers were "read." Its practical and positive value was, of course, the notice that was served of the commitment of Methodism to education and cultural improvement. It advertised the determina-tion that "conversion" should be not merely a religious experience but also part of a process of rehumanization from the degradation of plantation slavery. It signified the clear design that Methodists should be a literate people, able to sing their praises with under-standing as well as with hearts and voices. It is therefore not surpris-ing that it was Methodism which provided the earliest opportunities for popular education in the Caribbean, or that the first school houses were Methodist chapels, or that to this day, Caribbean Methodists differ from Methodists of other countries in that they deem it both an obligation and a matter of pride to *own* copies of the *Prayer Book*, the hymn book,[3] and the Bible which they use in public worship. The blend of religion and education could not be closer.

The problem of illiteracy can also be grossly overstated. Unfortunately it has sometimes been equated with ignorance and mental deficiency. But this is quite incorrect. Literacy and illiteracy are relative terms. One can be quite versed in the intricacies of one's own language and be totally illiterate when confronted by another language. Essentially, illiteracy is unfamiliarity with the script. It shows itself in a difficulty in writing and in reading, but not necessarily in understanding what is read and heard. Furthermore, as several cases coming out of the Caribbean will attest, it is quite possible for someone to be totally illiterate in a certain language and still be able to wax eloquent in utterance in the same language.

"Read prayers" have therefore not been a major obstacle to worship in Methodist chapels in the Caribbean. On the contrary, the retentive memory could use it to advantage. Prayers read in chapel became useful material for personal and family devotions during the week. Hymns called out "line upon line" in public worship provided the music in the home, in the field, on the road, and at the riverside. The very repetitiveness enabled worship to be all the more easily integrated into the daily round of common tasks and a liturgical pattern became etched into the religious consciousness of the regular worshiper. The flow and ebb of the seasons, the rise and fall of the calendar, with their festivals and their fasts, took on an appeal and a power of their own at the emotional level. It was much more the hymns, than the changing colors of the fabric in the sanctuary, that announced for Methodists the change of the seasons. It was taken for granted that "O come, O come Emmanuel" would be sung at the commencement of the Advent season, that the opening hymn at the 5:00 a.m. worship on Nativity would be "Christians awake! Salute the happy morn," that "Come, let us anew" would usher in the New Year, that Resurrection would resound with "Christ the Lord is risen today, Alleluia!" It was the hymns that were the wheels on which the church moved through the liturgical year, and it was the hymns, chiefly, which carried the chapel over into daily life. Nothing could be as jarring to the religious consciousness as a hymn that was sung out of season. An inappropriate sermon or the omission of a collect or a proper preface might be forgiven, but not the singing of "Hark! the herald-angels sing" in deep mid-Lent. It was not just liturgical incompetence but insensitivity to the religious consciousness. The sense of season is one of the results of "read prayers" and the religion of the *Prayer Book*.

The Place of Worship

It has perhaps already been observed that the special name of the place where Caribbean Methodists worship is "chapel." The nomenclature has nothing to do with size or architecture or historic importance or lack of these criteria. It might be an imposing ediface which adorns the city center or an unpretentious oblong by the side of the road that runs through the village. Either way it is a chapel. The original intention of the name must have been ideological and tactical. It must have been intended to accentuate the theological and evangelical distance from the parish church whether Roman Catholic or Anglican. It has been retained even in our more enlightened ecumenical times for domestic reasons. "Church" is reserved exclusively to define the connectional character of the Methodist community and to eschew congregationalism. There is no local "church" in the Methodist Church in the Caribbean and the Americas. Nor are there circuits of churches. There are only local congregations (hitherto "Societies") which meet for worship in local chapels. There is only one Methodist Church which exists locally in the shape of thousands of congregations and chapels all over the area but all constituting the one and single Methodist Church.

Chapels also betray a bewildering variety of architecture which can be categorized according to the period of construction, and whose size and interior decor might have been determined by the prevailing theology of the period and the financial resources that could be mustered. In the earlier period of the evolution of Methodism, the chapel was dominated by the raised central pulpit, varying in height above the floor from one and one-half feet to six or even seven feet depending on the size of the building. In the largest buildings, found mostly in the city centers, accommodation was improved by the addition of gallery seating either at the back or on three sides; behind the pulpit were located the choir stalls and a pipe organ. The interior design betrayed the prevailing notion of worship and the priorities which informed it, doubtless reflecting the evangelical tradition of the dominance of the Word (both read and proclaimed) over all else. The purpose of the chapel was to ensure that as many persons as possible could gather to hear the Word of God expounded and the Gospel proclaimed and also to enjoy some lusty singing led by a competent choir and organist.

More recent buildings show a change of mood and direction. For one thing they are of smaller dimensions because fellowship is far more important for worship than is theater. Secondly, the pulpit has been lowered from its eminence and placed on the side to allow greater visibility to the sacraments. Worship as a corporate experience rather than an occasion for individual satisfaction has been one of the enduring insights of the liturgical revival which has found its way into the redesigning of Methodist chapels in the Caribbean. Most of the chapels of more recent vintage are therefore not only liturgically more authentic, but aesthetically more pleasing. There is one glaring fault which is still noticeable in chapels of both earlier and later dates, and that is the short shrift that has been given to the baptismal symbols in the interior decor. It is now being gradually repaired as congregations seek to carry out the directive that in every chapel there should be a font permanently and prominently situated, to be used exclusively for baptisms, and to be always covered when not in use.

The Time of Worship

The most popular time of worship for Methodists in the Caribbean is the morning of the first day of the week or the Lord's Day. There was a time when it was rivaled and even surpassed by the evening services which followed a freer form with less formal ritual and more extempore praying. But in most parts of the Caribbean the evening service is dying out and will revive only as the evangelistic zeal revives in Methodism.

The morning hour varies widely, beginning anywhere from 6:00 or 6:30 a.m. to 11:00 a.m. on the half hour. There are two reasons for this spread. In the large city congregations, it allows for two communion services in a morning where one service, because of the number of communicants, would be of intolerable length. Also, in places where chapels are easily accessible and preachers are in short supply, it allows the minister and other preachers to accommodate two or even three services in one morning. Furthermore, in the tourist resort areas, the very early hour enables Methodists to worship before going out to work. There is more constancy in the rural areas and the hour of worship tends to be either 9:00 a.m. or 11:00 a.m.

There was a time when the two proud and sacred pieces of equipment for worship in the Methodist chapel were the organ and the bell. From most city chapels the sound of the bell is no longer heard as a means of announcing the approaching hour; but in the rural communities the bell is still rung—an early bell to remind the community that this is the day for worship, a second bell to advise that it is about time to be getting dressed, and a last bell to announce that the hour has come and worship is about to begin. Even this is not as strict as it appears, for in most rural communities the last bell will be rung not fifteen or ten or five minutes before the stated hour, but when the preacher, coming from conducting an earlier service, has actually arrived, which might be fifteen minutes late.

There is no stated duration of worship or a time given by which the service should be ended. Notwithstanding the clock which is strategically placed directly opposite to the pulpit, the congregation is at the mercy of the preacher. Caribbean congregations are a model of courtesy and propriety and will not even set their wristwatches to alarm at a given hour, much less bow out gracefully when they think they have had enough. A communion service, according to the liturgy, and depending on the size of the congregation, will last anywhere between two and three hours. Without holy communion it might be one hour and a quarter to one hour and a half. There are places where classes meet with their leaders after the morning service, and this extends the period still further, so that even if the midday meal was prepared well in advance, it would not be possible to sit down to lunch, after a 9:00 a.m. communion service, before 1:30 or 2:00 p.m. After that marathon, an evening service must be specially attractive to entice the faithful to another session.

The Worshipers

While a rural congregation is homogeneous, the Methodist city congregation is drawn from all classes—some from positions of affluence and others from situations of extreme poverty. This might not be immediately apparent to the visitor, for the Caribbean person has a sense of pride and takes worship very seriously. The best apparel is reserved for the first day of the week and therefore it is very difficult, even impossible to tell from the dress the economic circumstances of the worshipers. The importance which Caribbean worshipers attach to dress has attracted adverse comment from time to time and, if taken to extremes, deservedly so. However, it derives from a theological predisposition which needs to be understood. Methodists go to worship on the understanding that they are not

going to a picnic or a party. They are subjects going to a king. They
cannot go any old way or put on any old thing. They would not do
it for an earthly dignitary, how much more the High King of heaven?
They must prepare themselves outwardly as well as inwardly. They
must be scrupulous in their appearance. They want to feel good
when they enter the sanctuary, and to look good is to feel good. Some
will carry it to the extreme and make of worship a fashion show. But
this is not the intention of the majority of the worshipers. All they
wish to do is to give of their best. Even among the poorest there will
be a modicum of neatness. There will be nothing beyond a shirt and
trousers and a pair of shoes, but they will be clean. They are appearing before the King. And as they strive for excellence in their own
appearance, so they do with respect to their offspring. Mothers will
deny themselves the privilege of worship so that their children can
have the wherewithal—the special clothes reserved only for worship.

Nor will the worshipers enter the sanctuary empty-handed.
They will bring an offering according to their ability and the dictates
of the conscience—the poorest being the most conscientious—and
they will be coming with the books—the *Hymn-Book*, the *Prayer Book*,
and the Bible. The copies which the congregation keeps in stock are
not for members but for visitors. Members come with their own. It is
a matter of pride and dignity. They will enter reverently. They will
have been taught that, on entering a place of worship, their first duty
must be to bow in silent prayer, and if they must converse it should
be in muted tones. Preferably they should wait quietly for worship
to begin.

The Order of Worship

With the recent publication and authorization of the Methodist
Prayer Book for use in chapels of the Methodist Church in the Caribbean and the Americas, a semblance of order has returned to worship. Indeed the new complaint is that of a slavish use of the *Prayer
Book* which leaves little room for spontaneity. But, as the rubric will
show, this was not the intention. The published form of worship,
while it can be used, is also intended to be a pattern in which the
content may be adapted even while the sequence remains unaltered.
The form of worship in the *Prayer Book* has been so devised that it
can either be self-contained as a liturgy of the word when the

sacraments are not observed, or as leading to the sacraments when they are observed.[4] The order is as follows:[5]

The Preparation
    Organ Prelude
    Responsive Introit
    Opening Sentences, read responsively
    Opening Hymn
    The Collect for Purity

The Commandments of our Lord Jesus

Confession of Sin and Assurance of Pardon

Hymn ("Glory be to God on High" on festivals and eucharistic Sundays, except in Lent)

The Ministry of the Word
    The Collect of the Day
    Old Testament Lesson
    Psalm for the Day (sung or read responsively)
    Epistle Lesson
    Gradual Hymn
    Gospel Lesson
    Sermon

Apostles' Creed (Nicene Creed, on festivals and eucharistic Sundays)

The Renewal of Fellowship
    Choral Anthem
    Greetings, Courtesies, and Announcements
    The Offertory (with a choral rendition)

The Intercessions and the Lord's Prayer

Closing Hymn

Benediction

Organ Postlude

When either of the sacraments is to be observed, the rite will be inserted after the intercessions and the Lord's Prayer. The eucharistic rite begins with the passing of the Peace and a communion hymn during the singing of which an offering will be taken specially for persons in need. Next comes the thanksgiving prayer which follows the pattern of that in the British Methodist service book while using some of its own phraseology. For example, the ordinary preface moves into the Sanctus with these words:

In witness of his glory and honour, you poured out the Holy Spirit, Building up many people into one Body,

Making us living members of your holy Church,
And enabling us to stand before you to sing your praises and
     celebrate your mighty acts.
Therefore with Angels and Archangels. . . .[6]

The baptismal rite begins with the singing of a baptismal hymn (such as "Ye faithful souls who Jesus know") during which persons to be baptized will come, or will be brought, to the font.

The Mood of Worship

Such a pattern of worship might suggest dullness and a somber atmosphere, especially when it is not assisted by visual symbols to relieve the monotony. It is therefore significant that, in more recent times, some grudging concessions have been made for visual aids to worship. More and more choirs are being robed, liturgical colors are coming into vogue. Ministers are exchanging the black academic gown for the white alb or cassock with the stole and the pectoral cross. A cross can be seen on most tables and, here and there, the lighted candles. Services begin and end with a procession of choristers and ministers. The congregations now stand for the reading of the Gospel and the manual acts now form a part of the eucharistic rite.

But what has created a new mood of worship is the increased scope for participation the *Prayer Book* has offered to the worshipers. Included in its contents are suggestions for daily family devotions as well as a family service for preparation for the Lord's Day.[7] This gives the worshiper an opportunity to read the collects and the lessons beforehand and, since the lectionary is to be strictly followed and the sermon must be based on one of the lessons, a mood of expectation is awakened in the congregation.

Indeed "expectation" is a word which most appropriately sums up the mood of worship. In the midst of the usual and the expected, the unexpected can still break in. Even in the last minute fuss in the vestry and the choir room one might detect the mood of expectancy. For, in the final analysis, worship is not just "our business." It is an existential encounter with the Wholly Other whose Word is not bound by forms, whose Spirit floweth free, whose Voice can be heard even in the silence, and whose earthly house is a dreadful place because it is the gate of heaven.

Chapter 15

Singing a New Song: Developing Methodist Worship in Latin America

Simei Ferreira de Barros Monteiro

The Missionary Impetus for Methodist Worship

Methodist worship, in most Latin American countries, began as a meeting in the dwelling of the missionary or in the homes of other families. It was a simple meeting featuring chiefly hymns or songs in the official language of the country, whether Portuguese or Spanish, the reading and interpretation of the Scriptures, and prayers. In most of the countries, evangelizing activity on the part of Protestants was considered subversive as Protestant worship did not fit the reigning Roman Catholic pattern, a form of worship characterized predominantly by the Latin Mass and Gregorian chant.

The difference between Methodist worship in Latin America and worship in the countries from which the missionaries came showed itself first in the liturgical space. In some countries, such as Brazil, Methodist worship was permitted only in homes or places that lacked the outward appearance of a church building; a shed or a room in a house was not considered as a sanctuary. Even in countries where permission was granted to build Protestant churches, it was difficult to find a piece of land and succeed in buying it for the building of a Protestant place of worship, and in most cases an existing house was simply adapted as a church building. In general, these worship spaces were small, tight, without adequate ventilation, and functioned as the location for all the activities of the church. At one and the same time, this space served as a sanctuary, a Sunday School room (without dividers for the various classes), a place for parties and special meals, and even a theater for Christmas plays, concerts, and meetings. This explains, to some extent, the absence from the very beginning of an emphasis on liturgical ornaments or objects.

The Methodist missionary did not offer a message completely distinct from that presented by missionaries of other denominations. He was the bearer of the good news of a Gospel which did not claim only to save "souls" but also to show people a "new life" and thus to transform in some way a society which, in the eyes of the missionary, was idolatrous and backward. His optimistic vision was that the Gospel would be able to release the Latin American peoples from the darkness of ignorance and religious fanaticism in which they had been immersed, thanks principally to Roman Catholic "paganism." The missionaries often saw themselves as superior preachers (in comparison with the Catholic priests) and as charismatic bearers of modernity.

From the outset, it is clear that the missionaries saw the Latin Americans as "receivers" with not much to "offer." Nobody claimed to learn anything from the Latins, only to teach them. One of the missionary hymns produced in Brazil, of which there must be a version or at least something similar in the hymnals used until recently in most of the Methodist Churches in Latin America, says:

Maravilhas grandiosas outros povos têm.
Venham bênçãos semelhantes sobre nós também.

(Other peoples have great miracles.
Let such blessings come on us, too.)[1]

That is something that we are certainly not going to find in the text of a missionary hymn in Europe or North America. Those who send missionaries do not often see the wonders of God's saving work being performed first among "other peoples"; rather they are themselves the people who export such wonders for other nations.

The mentality that the Gospel brings progress to a people and a nation meant that worship, simple and bare as it was, should be centered on the sermon, the message of the Bible. The Sacred Book represented not only the Word of God but also a literate culture that one was to know how to expound and interpret, even with the difficulties of translating it into another tongue. It is no surprise that the first poetry to be produced in Brazil, either by missionaries or by newly converted persons, inclined more toward erudite than to popular language. The translation of the Bible was considered one of the best translations into Portuguese.

It is possible to prove, by documents from the missionary era, that there was a concern to preach the Gospel, or rather to convert people and to promote their education. No project was more calculated to reach the intellectual elites, and it can be shown that the object of this proselytism was to promote the liberal ideas that were then affecting the aristocratic and intellectual circles in many countries of Latin America. In this way, devotional meetings or domestic worship services could take a clear and correct form, illuminated less by the rapture of the Spirit than by the instruction of the Word. The Gospel was the preaching of the Truth. The reading and comprehension of the Scriptures provided a challenge for people with little schooling who hardly knew how to read, but within the church they blossomed and soon became preachers, Sunday School teachers, and evangelists. Parochial schools arose to promote literacy and improvement of life for the people. It was believed that the truth of the Gospel would penetrate people's minds and make them immediately desire to improve their lives; they would quit sloth and vice and start to seek education. As some of the songs in the *Hinário Evangélico* (Evangelical Hymnal) say:[2]

> Luta contra as trevas!
> Luta contra o mal! . . .
> Dar combate ao erro, à superstição,
> E salvar os homens
> Da degradação.
>
> (Fight against darkness! Fight against evil! . . .
> Fight against error and superstition!
> Save people from degradation!)
>
>
> Contudo, ainda muitos,
> Bem longe de cristãos,
> Adoram deuses feitos
> Por suas próprias mãos.
>
> (Yet many more people,
> Far removed from the Christian faith,
> Worship gods made by their own hands.)

The Sunday School soon was the center of worship activities; corporate worship and Sunday School became practically equivalent. Both in Sunday School and in worship, people sang, the Bible was read and explained, there was prayer, an offering was collected, visitors were welcomed, and the works of the church were promoted. Thus worship came to be seen as one of the "works" of the church rather than as an expression of praise or a liturgical moment. Worship became much more a place of teaching than of celebration. Identification of believers in Jesus Christ was by way of the Book, the Bible, so that Protestants were called "the Bible people." This is exemplified by the text of a children's song:

> Domingo vou à Igreja, à Casa de Oração,
> estudo a Bíblia e sei de cor os textos da lição.
>
> (Sunday I am going to church, to the house of prayer.
> I study the Bible and I know by heart the texts of the lesson.)[3]

Nowadays, an emphasis on celebrative worship—rather than on didactic worship—is found in many new Christian communities and, through their influence, in many Latin American Methodist communities. However, in research done so far, especially in Brazil, we see that the preaching, message, or sermon is still the part that is most emphasized, thereby retaining its mystique. The theology and practice of the sacraments as means of grace was and still is obscured by the elevation of the proclamation of the Word, an emphasis which, historically, was enforced by the shortage of ordained pastors and the consequent non-sacramental lay leadership.

It is certain that some missionaries, especially those who worked with children, soon perceived that it would be good to overcome the separation between the world of home, school, and street where they played, and the world of the church, especially as a place of education. "Go and teach" and "preach the Gospel" were taken as synonymous. The church as a place of learning, as a "school," could perhaps create certain links with the worldly culture. The Methodist Church in Latin America placed much importance on its educational institutions. Areas existed where there was no Methodist church but where there was a Methodist school. A worship service or even a Sunday School might be held in the school.

Patterns for Methodist Worship in Latin America: Brazil

Methodist worship, as with Protestant worship generally, was much influenced by the spread of Bibles and by the formation of lay Bible study groups which received almost no direction from trained pastors. The missionary pastor J. J. Ransom came to Brazil in 1876 and wrote a short book on Sunday worship in the preface of which he tells a little about the situation of lay groups and how he tried to help them organize worship:

> Numerous copies of the Holy Scriptures have been distributed in many places, and there are many people looking for a simple, rational form of worship, which is pure and pleasing to God. There are places where no preacher has visited and yet there is a desire for Sunday worship in an intelligible language. To all these people we make the following proposal: In whatever city, town, village or neighborhood there are ten people who commit themselves to gathering in a convenient place on a Sunday morning, or both morning and evening, let them obtain this book, and let one of them take the place of a minister, saying in a competent manner the parts that belong to him, and allotting the responses to the others, and let them say the "general confession" all together, etc.[4]

Ransom put himself at the disposal of these groups and asked that, if they had any hesitations at all, they should write to him so he could help them understand that "divine worship is not in the letter but in the Spirit."[5]

As we can observe, Methodist worship in Latin America from the missionary era had to adjust to the realities of the lack of sure direction. Already in the beginnings of Methodism there were difficulties in maintaining an elaborate liturgy. Besides the high degree of illiteracy among the people, worship books themselves were a rarity. Dr. Carl Joseph Hahn states that the Methodist Church of Brazil—and I think the same applies to Latin America in general—followed closely in the footsteps of the Methodist Churches of North America and bore the marks of its Anglican and Puritan ancestors. Worship books in Latin America generally consisted of adaptations of North American manuals made by the missionary; they restricted the rituals to special occasions such as baptism, funerals, and weddings. Many missionaries used the *Book of Common Prayer* for these occasions. The manuals for pastors also included, besides these rituals, general directions on worship such as the length of service, etc., matters that would be included later in books of *Discipline.*

Throughout Latin America there was a concern to preserve at least the rituals of the sacraments according to the model of the *Book of Common Prayer.* In the *Cânones de Igreja Metodista do Brasil* (the Canons of the Methodist Church of Brazil) of 1950, after the presentation of the order for Sunday worship (which was later changed) came this rubric:

> The order of public worship can be adapted according to the necessities of the moment, following the judgment of the leader, as long as the reverence and decency of the act is not compromised.

But in the case of the sacraments, article 311 stipulated:

> For the sake of good order in divine worship and uniformity in the administration of the sacraments, the Church has established a ritual that, except in certain circumstances set out in these canons, must be strictly observed by the officiants.[6]

Today the Methodist Church in Brazil does not have a uniform practice in worship. At present there exists a book of rites which tries to orient churches in the basic aspects of Methodist worship. Like the old manuals, it contains general directions for the pastors and leaders of the churches, chiefly in regard to specific and special services and occasions. In reality, the Methodist Church in Brazil enjoys no national coordination in the area of liturgy. The work falls to the college of bishops who call together when necessary a national working group to prepare some specific material or to revise what already exists. In general the church does not provide much guidance or direction. The basic pattern of worship or order of service follows the plan of Isaiah 6:1-8, augmented by a moment of praise after the confession of sin. This order is as follows: adoration, confession, praise, edification, and dedication. The manual contains no explanation of the theology of this order. It can hardly be said that this constitutes an official order of liturgy of the Methodist Church of Brazil, or that it has to be used every Sunday except for when baptism or the Lord's Supper is celebrated.

In large cities such as São Paolo, Mexico City, Santiago, and Buenos Aires, midweek worship services are becoming quite popular, largely because they are informal. Often called "programs," they consist, in broad outline, of a moment of adoration and praise interspersed with testimonies and prayers, and a second moment of preaching the Word, which can be concluded by a third moment of intercessions, prayers for healing, and songs. This pattern is also becoming common in the celebrations of the Catholic charismatic movement. The two movements also share other common features such as vigils and fasts.

There may be no national manual of liturgy in Brazil, but there are at present regional commissions being organized and producing liturgical resources; these are generally limited to the musical area such as, for example, collections of songs. This work aims to fill the gap left by the lack of a specifically Methodist hymnal in Brazil. The hymnal currently in use is *Hinário Evangélico*. This hymnal emerged from the efforts of the Evangelical Confederation of Brazil to unify the hymnody then in use in the Evangelical Churches of Brazil. For this reason it brings together songs from various denominational hymnals, chiefly from the first hymnals produced in Brazil: *Salmos e Hinos* (Psalms and Hymns), which was Congregational, and *Cantor Cristão* (The Christian Singer), which was Baptist. The hymns selected from these hymnals were augmented by new hymns from other hymnals and hymnodic sources such as Calvinist psalmody and Lutheran hymnody. Some hymns by Brazilian and other Latin American authors were also included, though for the most part they were scarcely poetic texts. Most of the music is of foreign origin. After several partial editions, the definitive hymnal was published in 1960. At the moment this is the "official" hymnal of the Methodist Church, although hymnals and collections of other denominations are also used.

Regarding the rest of Latin America: After a first phase of translated hymnals, there was published in Buenos Aires in 1943, at the initiative of the Central Conference of the Methodist Church in Latin America, the *Himnario Evangélico* to be used in all the countries included in the Conference. It was the first ecumenical project in collaboration with the Waldensian Church and the Disciples of Christ. What is now the Higher Institute of Theological Studies (ISEDET) exercised, through its ecumenical commitment, great influence in the development of a Latin American hymnody and the rediscovery and restoration of liturgical traditions, including the Wesleyan. It was decided in 1952, at the initiative of the Latin American Conference of the Methodist Church, to revise the *Himnario Evangélico* of 1943, which in reality resulted in a new hymnal, *Cántico Nuevo* (A New Song) of 1962. However, this hymnal does not do much to express Latin American hymnody. In the following decades, ISEDET gave the lead in a flourishing of Latin American hymnody through the work of Methodist musicians and poets, among whom can be singled out Pablo Sosa, Homero Perera, and Bishop Federico Pagura. Students from other countries living with this group found a resonance among them and together they tried to produce inculturated music for the liturgy. It was perceived that this desire was common to many musicians and poets of our churches.

The Creation of a New Song

At the time of the initial influx of missionaries into Latin America, there was no concern to address the indigenous context or, as it would have been in Brazil, the mixture of African-Brazilian religion. This absence of concern for contextualization is quite evident in the matter of Christian music. Although in England Charles Wesley had used popular tunes, some of them sung in English taverns, the missionaries did not encourage the use of Latin American melodies, especially those with a more marked rhythm. Hymn tunes were imported from North America and Europe, and these, until recently, have been predominant in the hymnals used by the Methodist Churches in Latin America. Even band instruments, so much used in popular processions and feasts, and which later the Assemblies of God Churches would so much appreciate, were in general in the nineteenth century forbidden from use in Methodist worship services, where the harmonium, the organ, or the violin were considered the only instruments worthy to accompany liturgical songs and evangelistic hymns.

Albert and Ethel Ream, Methodist missionaries in the School of Sacred Music of Bennett College in Rio de Janeiro, and who later worked in Argentina, tried to introduce the music of folk songs into the church. They published a collection of songs for children with popular children's tunes judged most "acceptable" for children to sing in church. But the church did not receive this proposal very well and few (if any) persons use these songs today. At that time, the church was hardly conditioned to accept indigenous songs as good for singing in church. Much later, some musicians tried to introduce popular rhythms into liturgical singing but it was feared this might provoke the introduction of dancing into worship, which remains unacceptable to this day.

Pablo Sosa, one of the pioneers of Latin American liturgical song, tells us that while he was studying in the United States he wanted to compose something Argentinian, and he confides:

> I asked my father in Argentina to send me a collection of tangos.
> My father sent me a selection of "old guard" tangos. I picked up

one called, I think, "The Last Sip," and I tried to set to it a religious message in English, and I came to more or less the same conclusion as (my friend) Faustini: It can't be done. Why can't it be done? We said it was because there was a breach between the religious and the secular, and we did not perceive that the breach was rather between the culture that had come to us with the Gospel . . . and our popular culture.[7]

When some of our composers dare to write a melody in our national styles, they generally try to disguise it as much as possible by means of a harmonization in the choral style. This constitutes an effort to make them acceptable to a taste acquired by the congregations after so many decades of cultural domination in the churches. Examples of this treatment can be found in the hymnal *Cántico Nuevo* from Argentina and in other Spanish-language hymnals. A clear example is the *modinha* (popular song) composed by Henriqueta Braga and which turns into a baroque chorale in the *Hinário Evangélico*, the hymnal adopted by the Methodist Church in Brazil.[8]

It is lamentable that nobody has said to the people of our churches, so efficiently taught to reject what is their own, that the "evangelical hymns" they used to sing and indeed still sing are also, for the most part, popular songs of other nations now covered by that aura of sacredness that is given to the popular style by being harmonized for organ, choir, or other erudite instrument. We do not know when all this will be overcome, now that the concept of "gospel music" is spreading through the Evangelical and Methodist churches because of the influence of pop music groups from North America or Europe, though its texts differ totally from Latin American theologies. Even the "praise groups" or "gospel bands," as they are called, which try to introduce more inculturated styles using "Latin" rhythms, are not well received, even though their theology follows the patterns of other evangelical groups.

The 1960s saw the rise in Latin America of the first movements in the struggle for the recognition of national cultures. There was discussion of the concepts of culture and of autochthonous cultures. Festivals of folkloric music arose in various parts of the continent, and new popular composers and poets influenced especially the intellectuals and political activists.

Moreover in the sixties, through the influence of the Second Vatican Council, a change occurred in the understanding of the liturgy in the Roman Catholic Church. It turned more toward the people. Folkloric music was recommended for use in each country as a model for new liturgical compositions. Thus there arose popular Masses such as the *Misa Campesina Nicaraguense* (Nicaraguan Peasant Mass), the *Misa Criolla* (Creole Mass) in Argentina, and other songs of a strongly folk tendency. There was a search for a new spirituality, less clerical, more lay.

The "celebrations" also arose in Catholic circles, and they acquired some political force and expressed faith in the God of Life who desires abundant life for all. Whether coincidentally or not, during this time interconfessional meetings of song and music were organized where not only Roman Catholics participated but also Protestant artists and musicians. These elements were very important in the search for a Latin American hymnody.

Other factors originating in the sixties have led to the production of new music. "Youth music" movements in the United States contribute in some way either to the continuance of cultural dependency or to critical reflection on the part of our national musicians who wonder whether they could not create something similar in their own countries. The growing Pentecostal movement, in part because of its identification with the populace, has had a tremendous influence upon other Christian groups, including worship practices in the Methodist Churches. With the Pentecostal movement came an emphasis on spontaneity, informality, communication in the language of the people, simple dress, oral culture, and the habit of singing from memory, especially in the Sunday Schools where "choruses" are learned.[9] One of these, taught by the missionaries in Brazil and originally in waltz rhythm but now sung in samba rhythm, goes like this:

Só o poder de Deus pode mudar teu ser.
A prova que eu te dou
é que mudou o meu.
Não vês que sou feliz
sequindo ao Senhor?
Nova criatura sou,
nova sou!

(Only the power of God can change your life.
The proof I give you is he changed mine.
Don't you see you'll be happy, in the way of the Lord?
Become a new creature, become new!)[10]

In the 1970s there arose the movement called *Nova Canção* (A New Song) which showed itself throughout the whole of Latin America and continues to sow the seeds of renewal not only from the hymno-logical viewpoint but also in the wider ambit of liturgy and theology. At this time there appeared *Cancionero Abierto* (The Open Songbook), a project of ISEDET which publishes contributions from Latin American poets and composers as well as contributions from European and North American authors.

In Bolivia, the then bishop of the Methodist Church, Mortimer Arias, wrote poems and, joining them to popular music, turned them into liturgical songs. And with the awakening of the aboriginal Quechua and Aymara to the expression of the Christian faith, there emerged aboriginal songs and a trilingual hymnal in Spanish, Quechua, and Aymara.

In Costa Rica, Federico Pagura, from 1969 bishop of the Methodist Church, has promoted the production of a songbook, *Nova Hora* (The New Hour), which includes, besides folkloric rhythms, songs in the popular styles of Latin America as well as of Europe and the United States.

In Brazil, the Methodists support this movement. The Faculty of Theology of the Methodist Church and the Methodist Institute of Higher Education, in São Bernado, São Paulo, promote meetings led by a U.S. Presbyterian missionary, Norah Buyers, who has appropri-ated for Brazilian hymnody the style of the singer Luíza Cruz. A first collection of liturgical songs appeared in 1974, *Nova Canção* (A New Song). Other collections and other names, both men and women, promoted this movement. In 1982 a new collection appeared: *A Canção do Senhor na Terra Brasileira* (The Lord's Song in a Brazilian Land). In the prologue of this little collection we read the following:

> This is the first document to contain some of our specific features. The texts speak of the life of our people, their sorrows, their sufferings and their joys, in the light of the Gospel. The human being is treated in its entirety, without division of body and soul. . . . This collection of hymns bears an experimental character. Nothing in it is final. It is a document for study . . . , which if it is of the Lord will remain (Acts 5:38-39).[11]

It seems there is always a hidden fear of breaking with a tradition that has lasted over the years and has sanctified the "other" songs that have been immortalized in our hymnals, the sacred hymns, the spiritual hymns.

The emphasis placed in the beginnings of Methodist evangeliza-tion on the salvation of the soul, on individual sanctification, concealed the message that "there is no holiness but social holiness." Today we cannot deny that there are documents and directives to guide the liturgy in this direction. There are songs written by Methodists and non-Methodists which express this dimension. But the habit of not celebrating and never singing our social engagement is so ingrained in our churches that they do not show much interest in the songs that express the involvement of the church in the "works of mercy." The final part of the service, generally called "Sending and Blessing," is usually very formal in character. A song of dismissal is sung, and the officiating minister invokes a blessing. Neither verbal forms nor appropriate songs are used to express social commitment or active engagement in the community, even though these are well accepted by our people.

We are losing the dimension of incarnation, even while recognizing that our worship needs to be more celebratory and to rejoice in the renewing and restoring presence of God. Worship is not a theological lecture hall, and the theological work which comes out of it is not verbal or conceptual but above all symbolic and relational. The Methodist way of social commitment points to a form of worship in which a theology of incarnation and martyrdom (from a people that experience a passion and death like Jesus Christ) is expressed concretely not only in hymns, prayers, and acts of dismissal but in the vision of bodies which visibly bear the suffering face of Latin America even if the suffering is not, for the moment, our own.

Then, when the Methodist Church includes in its repertory of liturgical songs the Guarani Kyrie and is challenged to sing, even imperfectly, *Orê poriahuverekó Ñandeyara*, it remembers and revives, in a much more powerful form, the Paschal mystery—much more than when it listens to the "Passion Chorale" of J. S. Bach, no matter how much more beautiful it has been taught to consider that. The Guarani Kyrie, like other indigenous songs, represents the "sacred head, now wounded" of the Latin American Christ. It is therefore a fine hymn. As the Portuguese poet Fernando Pessoa says:

> The Teio is more beautiful than the river which runs through my village, but the Teio is not more beautiful than the river which runs through my village because the Teio is not the river that runs through my village.[12]

A short while ago, the Methodist Church in Brazil produced and published a collection of songs which contains, among other things, songs made by street children. Some said that this material could not be used in the parishes because it wasn't suitable for singing by church children. Now if the children of our local churches are not able really to get to know the other children of Brazil or show their solidarity with them in song, how are we preparing them for active engagement in society and, what is more serious, how can we sing happily and joyfully if there are children suffering in the streets of our cities?

The movement in favor of an inculturated hymnody becomes provocative. It provokes discomfort in those who quietly sing the faith until they die and go to heaven, a faith that shuts its eyes and leaps into the dark. But we want to sing a faith for living and to dare to promote the reign of God in history, a faith that even in the shadows propels us toward the light of God. Today we can count a significant contribution from Methodist authors and composers in various collections both denominational and especially ecumenical. Some of these songs were created collectively in workshops for liturgy and music. Practically the whole lot of them was included in an ecumenical hymnal *O Novo Canto da Terra* (The New Song of the Earth), a collection of 201 songs edited by an Anglican, Dr. Jaci Maraschin. Many of the themes presented by the hymns are innovative: earth, body, women, and others. The authors and composers come from different areas of the church. There are clergy and laity, both male and female, students of theology, people from almost all the Christian Churches including the Catholic.[13]

The practice of organizing workshops to produce new songs has been common and effective in Latin America. The Methodist Church has organized many such workshops and seminars. In 1973 there was organized in Chile the first workshop for "group composition." Later this activity came to be a part of the program in Methodist youth camps.

We believe that the liturgy of the Methodist Churches in Latin America has been renewed chiefly by this hymnody. It has also given impulse to the ecumenical movement. It is probable that the new hymnals which are appearing now and in the future will be less sectarian, with a more comprehensive vision of what is meant by Christian hymnody or a Christian liturgical song.

We hope that more careful study of the history and theology of liturgical songs will help us discover their true origin: the people. We know that we no longer need to disguise our songs as "hymns" in order for them to figure in hymnals and be considered Christian hymnody. When studied and read in its sources, hymnody proves itself to be better, more appreciated, and more enduring precisely for being popular in origin.

> We firmly believe that we must all play an effective part in the creation of our community's song, or it will not be the song of our community. There are many levels of participation open to our creativity; some have already been discovered, others remain to be discovered. In our Latin American search to define our identity as human beings, and in the struggle to show ourselves as a people in fidelity to our Lord, we shall find the tools we need.[14]

When the people's songs were denied to the people, the mobilizing force of these songs was lost. Song and life cannot be separated any more than can liturgy and life. It is necessary that the song of life, in all its force and expressiveness, should give life and form to liturgical song. One must believe that the Creator of heaven and earth enjoys the song of the earth as much as the song of heaven. In this new perspective, the hymn will not be only that of the liturgical tradition, preserved in its form and style, but also the joint praise of all the universe in which the Latin Americans will be perfectly at home with their distinctive voices and their varied instruments.[15]

Representative Music

Of the three representative songs that follow, two were composed by the author: "Tua Palavra" ("Your Word") and "Kyrie" ("Lord, have mercy on us"). The third, the Guaicuru Kyrie "Ouve, Deus de amor" ("Hear, God of love, our cry to you"), utilizes an aboriginal melody.

Ouve, Deus de Amor

do povo Guaicuru, Brazil
adap. Simei Monteiro

Simei Monteiro

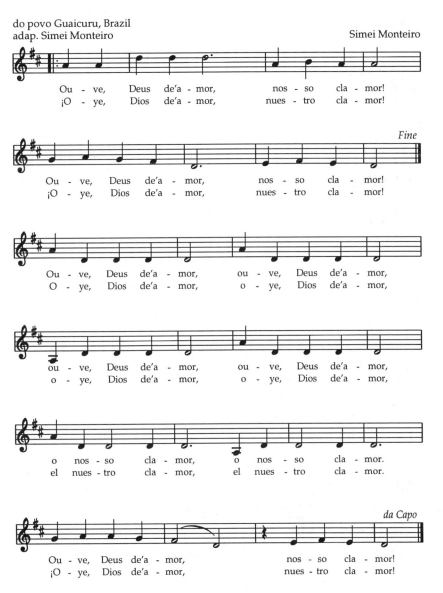

Ou - ve, Deus de'a - mor, nos - so cla - mor!
¡O - ye, Dios de'a - mor, nues - tro cla - mor!

Ou - ve, Deus de'a - mor, nos - so cla - mor!
¡O - ye, Dios de'a - mor, nues - tro cla - mor!

Fine

Ou - ve, Deus de'a - mor, ou - ve, Deus de'a - mor,
O - ye, Dios de'a - mor, o - ye, Dios de'a - mor,

ou - ve, Deus de'a - mor, ou - ve, Deus de'a - mor,
o - ye, Dios de'a - mor, o - ye, Dios de'a - mor,

o nos - so cla - mor, o nos - so cla - mor.
el nues - tro cla - mor, el nues - tro cla - mor.

da Capo

Ou - ve, Deus de'a - mor, nos - so cla - mor!
¡O - ye, Dios de'a - mor, nues - tro cla - mor!

Tua Palavra na vida
(Your Word in Our Lives)

Simei Monteiro

Tu - a Pa - la - vra na vi - da
E - sa Pa - la - bra en la vi - da
Your word in our lives, e - ter - nal,

é fon - te que ja - mais se - ca,
es fuen - te que no se se - ca,
it is a clear foun - tain flow - ing;

á - gua que a - ni - ma e res - tau - ra
a - gua que a - ni - ma y res - tau - ra
wa - ter that gives strength and cou - rage

Bb7   E7

to - dos que a quei - ram be - ber.
a to - do que ha de be - ber.
to all who draw near and drink.

2. Tua Palavra na vida/ é qual semente que brota;/ torna-se bom alimento,/pão que não há de faltar.
3. Tua Palavra na vida/ é espelho que bem reflete,/onde nos vemos, sinceros,/como a imagem de Deus.
4. Tua Palavra na vida/ é espada tão penetrante/ que revelando as verdades/ vai renovando o viver.
5. Tua Palavra na vida/ é luz que os passos clareia,/ para que ao fim no horizonte / se veja o Reino de Deus.

2. Esa Palabra en la vida/ es cual semilla que borta;/ llega a ser buen alimento/ que no ha jamás de faltar.
3. Esa Palabra en la vida/ espejo es que bien refleja,/ donde nos vemos, sinceros,/ como la imagen de Dios.
4. Esa Palabra en la vida,/ espada es tan penetrante/ que revelando verdades/ va renovando el vivir.
5. Esa Palabra en la vida,/ luz que los pasos aclara,/ muestra al final el camino/ del Reino eterno de Dios.

2. Your word in our lives, eternal,/ seed of the Kingdom that's growing;/ it becomes bread for our tables,/ food for the feast without end.
3. Your word in our lives, eternal,/ becomes the mirror where we see/ the true reflection of ourselves:/ children and image of God.
4. Your word in our lives, eternal,/ it is a sharp two-edged sword;/ dividing our lies from your truth,/ it's bringing new life to all.
5. Your word in our lives, eternal,/ is light that shines on the long road/ that leads us to the horizon,/ and the bright Kingdom of God.

Kyrie

Simei Monteiro

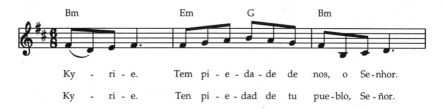

Ky - ri - e. Tem pi - e - da - de de nos, o Se - nhor.

Ky - ri - e. Ten pi - e - dad de tu pue - blo, Se - ñor.

E - le - i - son. Ky - ri - e.

E - le - i - son. Ky - ri - e.

Tem pi - e - da - de de nos, o Se - nhor. E - le - i - son.

Ten pi - e - dad de tu pue - blo, Se - ñor. E - le - i - son.

Chapter 16

Building up the House of God: Sunday Worship in German Methodism

Walter F. Klaiber

What is a typical Methodist Sunday morning service and what are the distinctive Methodist elements or patterns contained in it? It is not easy to answer these questions in regard to German Methodism for there are different feelings about this matter among different people. When, for example, people who are influenced by the charismatic movement ask for a more lively worship service with songs of praise, spontaneous witnessing, or extemporary prayers; they are often met by people who insist on preserving the genuine "Methodist type" of worshiping. What these latter mean is the order of the Sunday service which they knew from their childhood in the 1940s or 1950s: a very orderly form of worship which is led by the pastor and has a clear and almost invariable pattern.

But is this really genuine "Methodist" worship? A Methodist pastor from Brazil who has served for a year in one of our local churches recently commented, "I have not experienced any real Methodist worship since I have been in Germany." It was not possible for him to recognize any Methodist element (from his understanding of Methodist worship) in those clergy-dominated, well-planned and ordered worship experiences in which he had taken part. (To be fair to the local churches, it must be said that the German Methodist worship style could be called relaxed and informal by a *German* observer when compared with the very formal liturgy which is used in some of the Lutheran churches!)

Unlike the Roman Catholic Church, the Anglican Communion, or even the Lutherans, the Methodist tradition has not preserved a common pattern of worship which is recognizable all over the world. This holds true at least when one moves beyond the Anglo-Saxon sphere with its common liturgical culture. If we look closely at the German example, we will find that Methodist worship there too is the result of a long process of adaptation of worship to German culture and yet also of the search for an identity acknowledging both the heritage of the past and the challenge of the future.[1]

The Different Roots of Methodism in German-Speaking Central Europe

Methodism in Germany comes from several different roots.[2] Four denominations which belonged historically to the wider Methodist family started missionary work in Germany between 1830 and 1870. The pattern of these beginnings was almost always the same. Emigrants from different parts of Germany went to Britain or North America and became acquainted with Methodist preaching and spiritual life. Many of them were converted to a living faith and a new life, and as a result joined Methodist classes and congregations. They wrote back to their relatives about this experience, and on returning to Germany told their friends at home first hand and in detail how the Gospel was understood and lived by this new movement within Protestant Christianity. The governing bodies or the mission boards of the respective Methodist churches were then asked to send "missionaries" to Germany.

The purpose of their mission was not always clear. Were they meant to be evangelists who should preach the Gospel for revival within the existing Church and perhaps gather their converts into "religious societies"? Or was their calling to be missionaries whose task was to start new congregations and a "Methodist Church"? It seems that even those who were sent and those who sent them were not always clear in regard to these questions.

The first to start their work in Germany were the English Wesleyan Methodists. In 1830, Christoph Gottlob Müller (1785–1858) from Winnenden in Württemberg, who as a young man fled to England in order to avoid being drafted for Napoleon's army, visited his parents and told his relatives and friends about the Methodist way of preaching and living the Gospel. His words and his living example must have been very impressive. Soon after his visit, the Wesleyan Methodist Missionary Society was approached to send a missionary to Württemberg. After due consideration and with some reluctance, Müller himself was sent in 1833 and worked for twenty-five years as a faithful evangelist and pastoral counselor with those who were awakened by his preaching. He was clear in his conviction not to form a new Church but to gather the people who joined his work into societies within the State Church. But this had the result, as his successor observed, that the Wesleyan association consisted of "pietistic societies with a Methodist touch."[3] It was clear to some that a more distinct Methodist organization was necessary. In 1872, when in Württemberg a new legislation for religious dissenters was passed, the Wesleyan Methodist Association took the necessary steps to declare its independence from the State Church, and on January 6, 1873, the first communion service of the newly established Free Church was solemnly celebrated. For several reasons, in 1897 the Wesleyan branch of the Methodist movement in Germany merged with the Methodist Episcopal Church that had come from the United States.

The work of the Methodist Episcopal Church in Germany began in 1849. After some preliminary explorations by Wilhelm Nast, Ludwig S. Jacoby was sent as the first missionary. He started a social work among the emigrants who gathered in Bremen for their journey to America as well as a mission which soon reached many parts of the whole of Germany. His work was the most determined among all Methodist missions in Germany, and from the beginning he was clear in his intention to establish in Germany congregations connected with the Methodist Episcopal Church. Nevertheless, he was flexible enough to do only what was possible in light of the varied political and religious circumstances within Germany. Because of this stance, in February 1851, he admonished people in Saxony not to neglect attendance at holy communion in the Lutheran State Church, whereas in Bremen, where the legal position was much more favorable for the Methodists, he celebrated holy communion as early as August 1850.[4]

The first annual conference of the Methodist Episcopal Church was held in Bremen in 1856. From the beginning, the work in Germany was closely related to the strong German-speaking branch of the Methodist Episcopal Church in the United States, and a German-language edition of the Methodist Episcopal *Discipline*, including the Ritual, was used in Germany.

The Evangelical Association began its mission in Germany only one year after that of the Methodist Episcopal Church. In 1850 Johann Conrad Link from the Western Pennsylvania Conference was sent to Germany and started his work in Stuttgart. In spite of opposition on the part of the State Church, the movement soon began to grow and reached many people, especially in Württemberg.

The Mission Society of the Evangelical Association had no clear picture about the purpose of this mission at first. The intention was not to make proselytes but "to contribute to the promotion of the Kingdom of God and the salvation of precious souls" (*zur Förderung des Reiches Gottes und des Heils teuer erkaufter Seelen zu wirken*).[5] But if it would turn out that the organization of regular congregations would best serve this purpose, those responsible were prepared to pursue this method. Therefore, not earlier than 1859, the first meeting rooms were built. Local churches were organized according to the *Discipline* of the Evangelical Association from 1862, and in 1863 the first holy communion was celebrated in a worship service of the Evangelical Association. The first annual conference met in Stuttgart in 1865. Because the work of the Evangelical Association in the United States was primarily done in the German language at this time, the *Discipline*, the Ritual, and even the hymn book of the American church could be used or at least reprinted in Germany.

The last branch of the Methodist family to start mission work in Germany was the United Brethren in Christ. In 1869 a missionary was sent to the northern part of Bavaria who also found open doors in the neighboring parts of Thuringia and Saxony. But there was not much support from the denomination in the United States and this was the main reason why the congregations and the ministers of the United Brethren in Germany in 1905 joined the Methodist Episcopal Church (not the Evangelical Association as in the United States in 1946).[6]

In 1968, the two remaining members of the Methodist family in Germany, the Methodist Episcopal Church and the Evangelical Association, took part in the worldwide union between the Methodist Church and the Evangelical United Brethren. The resultant denomination in Germany is called the *Evangelisch-methodistische Kirche*, a constituent part of the United Methodist Church.

A last remark regarding the history. It is not quite accurate to speak about "German Methodism" when we deal with the first century of Methodist work in continental Europe. The exact term should be "German-speaking Methodism." Very soon after their arrival in Germany, the Methodist preachers went into Switzerland (the Methodist Episcopal Church in 1856; the Evangelical Association in 1865), Alsace, Austria, and German-speaking communities in Eastern Europe. Although separate annual conferences for the work in Switzerland had to be established very soon (1879 for the Evangelical Association; 1886 for the Methodist Episcopal Church), there were common German editions of the *Discipline*, the Ritual, and the *Gesangbuch* (hymn book) for all German-speaking Methodists until after World War II. For at least eighty years there was a common culture of worship in German-speaking Methodism.[7] Why, later on, the road divided is a very delicate question. A closer study would possibly identify as important motives for this development the European political situation, the growing adaptation to the liturgical and spiritual "climate" of the respective countries and times, and also the influence of some leading figures with strong opinions.

The Role of Sunday Worship in the Early Days of Methodism

This short overview of the origins of Methodism in German-speaking Central Europe was necessary not simply in order to give the framework for a presentation of the historical development of Sunday worship. In point of fact, if we look into the situation of the Methodist mission in its early years, it needs to be registered first of all that Sunday worship was not the center of the life of the church as it is now. The preachers traveled the country and when they found people who were ready to host them, they held meetings in private houses or sometimes in rented rooms or even banquet halls. The first step in organizing the common life of those who were awakened or converted was to establish classes. The class meetings became the core of the emerging church; they were crucial for the first Methodists and strange to those outside.[8]

Wherever it was possible, meetings on Sunday were indeed held, mostly in the afternoon or at night. When development led to the establishment of local churches, Sunday morning worship was conducted. The places where this happened often formed a "main church," which was the center of a large circuit or "charge" with many "daughter churches." Whereas in the main church there were regular worship services in the morning and the evening, the daughter churches would be served only in the afternoon or in the evening, at times different from the church hours of the State Church. Many lay preachers and exhorters assisted the traveling elder in his charge. Because people from outside the congregation normally visited the meetings in the afternoon or evening, these meetings were the evangelistic "main services" of the growing church. The worship in the morning was thought to edify the existing congregation; the meeting in the evening was intended to attract strangers and to proclaim to them the saving message of the Gospel.

In the center of both services was the sermon. Hymns, scripture readings, and prayers were seen as leading up to the message of the sermon or giving response to it.[9] Even the architectural design of the Methodist chapels was focused on preaching. At the front of almost every chapel there was a huge pulpit with stairs on both sides and a small box or table in front of it as a kind of altar. In some regions even today Methodist people say that they are going to the "sermon" when they go to Sunday worship, and for decades the official name of the normal Sunday service was the "preaching service" (*Predigt-gottesdienst*). When Methodists thought it necessary to account to others for their special worship life, they singled out the simplicity and informality of their services. They praised the fervor and depth of the singing in which the whole congregation joined (and not only the choir masters and children as in the State Church). And especially the Wesleyans and the Episcopal Methodists insisted that, therefore, the congregation should stand when singing.[10]

A typical habit for all Methodist groups during the early period was to kneel for prayer. This custom was very strange for Protestants in Germany, and Methodists were accused of yielding to Roman Catholic superstition. The posture was defended by Methodists as scriptural and appropriate to the attitude of human beings before their God.[11]

One peculiarity of the Methodist worship experience, which was very important for the life of the Church at least until the middle of the twentieth century, should not be omitted in this description. Methodists liked to gather together and to celebrate with festive worship services such special occasions as "quarterly meetings," annual conferences, dedications of churches, anniversaries of congregations or choirs, and choral festivals. In many churches there was a plethora of choirs and orchestras, and they competed in the praise of God at such times. Solos and the recitation of spiritual poems contributed to the solemnity of these worship services. Such events were living expressions of the Methodist connection and were at least as important for the life of the church and its members as the feasts of the ecclesiastical year.

The Development of the Order of Sunday Worship

Although early Methodists considered their worship services to be simple and informal, they deemed it necessary to give them some order (or to record what had developed as a kind of natural order).

The *Discipline* of the Methodist Episcopal Church (*Bischöfliche Methodistenkirche*) gives us some insight into the process of ordering. Until 1876, the *Discipline* mentions only the elements which should be present in the "Public Worship" of the Methodists: "Let the morning service consist of singing, prayer, the reading of a lesson from the Old Testament, and another from the New, and preaching."[12] In the afternoon or evening service and on the days of administering the Lord's Supper, the reading of one or both of the scripture lessons could be omitted. There are some other provisions: the Lord's Prayer was to be used on all occasions of public worship in concluding the first prayer, and the congregation was to be admonished to join audibly in its recitation. At the conclusion of each service a doxology was to be sung and the Apostolic Benediction (2 Corinthians 13:13) used in dismissing the congregation.

In 1888 the *Discipline* not only mentioned these elements but ordered them in a clear structure. The congregation was to be seriously admonished to participate actively in the public worship in singing and in prayer through the scriptural attitude of praying on the knees and through the audible recitation of the Lord's Prayer.

The *Discipline* of 1904 has a more elaborate order of public worship. It has as optional elements the Apostles' Creed after the first hymn and the Gloria Patri after the reading from the Old Testament. But whereas the order of worship of 1888 was obviously the basis for Methodist worship in Germany, it seems that the new elements were seldom used in German-speaking Methodism and therefore were omitted in later editions.

In 1928 the German-speaking conferences in Central Europe published for the first time a Ritual of their own which was not a translation but an adaptation of the American version.[13] At the beginning of the service (after the prelude) there is placed a greeting which uses the trinitarian formula (*Im Namen des Vaters, des Sohnes und des Heiligen Geistes*) or one short biblical sentence. After the Lord's Prayer, the Sanctus or another hymn could be sung. The Gloria Patri was omitted. The final blessing was put before the concluding doxology which was more generally described as a song of praise. The Ritual of the Methodist Episcopal Church in Germany of 1948[14] changed the sequence of the traditional order and put the first prayer (including the Lord's Prayer) after the scripture readings and inserted after this prayer a hymn of confession or adoration (among others, the Gloria Patri or the Sanctus were suggested).

The early editions of the *Discipline* of the Evangelical Association have no provision regarding the order of public worship. They do, however, have a lengthy section entitled "Thoughts on Singing and Praying." This corresponds to a similar section, "The Spirit and Truth of Singing," in the Methodist Episcopal *Discipline*. Whereas the Methodist Episcopal version gives some of Wesley's sober and practical advice on how to improve singing in worship, the *Discipline* of the Evangelical Association has a pastoral exhortation about the right spiritual attitude in praying and the necessity not to sing only with the mouth but also with the heart.

It is difficult to determine when the Evangelical Association in Europe for the first time defined the order of its Sunday worship. In 1952, the new hymnal of the Evangelical Association in Switzerland, called *Christenlieder*,[15] printed three different forms for Sunday worship. One is a very simple order:

Greeting
Hymn
Scripture reading
Prayer
Choir or hymn
Sermon
Verse of a hymn
Prayer
Announcements
Hymn
Blessing

Another form, based on the previous order, adds after the first hymn a short reading of scripture and the Gloria Patri, a sung Amen-response of the congregation following the first prayer, the Lord's Prayer in response to the second prayer, and a closing verse of a hymn after the blessing. The third form inserts the Apostles' Creed and the Sanctus after the first prayer. Similar forms are found in appendices to the German Hymnal of 1931 (*Gesangbuch für die Evangelische Gemeinschaft*) which were printed in the early fifties. The usual form for Sunday worship corresponds to the second version of the Swiss edition, and includes a threefold Halleluja-response of the congregation after the scripture reading and a threefold sung Amen-response after the blessing. The third form ("For Feastdays") has the Apostles' Creed but not the Sanctus.

In 1963 the Evangelical Association in Europe (which included the Swiss Annual Conference) published a new book of worship or *Agende*, the main parts of which had already been on trial use since 1957.[16] The order for Sunday worship in this publication got a slightly new pattern:

Prelude

Greeting

Hymn

Old Testament reading

Gloria Patri or corresponding hymn

New Testament reading

Threefold Halleluja or a corresponding hymn (in Lent, the Agnus Dei)

Prayer

Choir or hymn

Sermon

Verse of a hymn or choir

Prayer with the Lord's Prayer

Announcements

Closing hymn with collection

Blessing with threefold Amen-response

Postlude or concluding hymn

The order for feastdays included the creed whereas a simple version for small congregations had only one scripture reading and omitted the Gloria Patri and the Halleluja. The liturgical background of this form of worship seems to be the Sunday worship of the *Evangelische Kirche der Union*, although in a simplified form.[17] It shows the influence of the liturgical movement which through the so-called *Sing-Bewegung* (Singing Movement)[18] had a strong influence within the Evangelical Association.

After the creation of the *Evangelisch-methodistiche Kirche* through the union of the Methodist Episcopal Church and the Evangelical Association, it was no easy task to find a common order for Sunday worship. The result for the Central Conference in Germany (published in the *Agende* of 1973,[19] following a time of trial use from 1970) followed this pattern:

Prelude
Greeting
Hymn
Old Testament reading
Gloria Patri
New Testament reading
Halleluja
Creed (only on feastdays or in services with holy communion)
Prayer
Hymn of praise or adoration
Announcements
Choir or hymn
Sermon
Prayer with Lord's Prayer
Hymn and collection
Blessing and (threefold) Amen as response
Closing hymn or chorus
Postlude

The pattern clearly represents a compromise between the two constituent traditions. The Gloria Patri and the Halleluja come from the Evangelical Association. The hymn of praise after the first prayer is from the Methodists, the announcements are before the sermon as in the Methodist tradition, and the Lord's Prayer comes after it as in the Evangelical Association. This order of worship was a break with the tradition which went back to the first days of Methodist worship ordering, but it corresponds to the pattern of German Protestant liturgical tradition in Lutheran and Reformed churches.

The most recent *Agende*, that of 1991, did not change this pattern, though it suggested a time of common concern and intercession after the announcements.[20] An order that followed a similar pattern was provided by the 1981 worship book of the Central Conference of

Central and Southern Europe.[21] The main difference was the absence of a sung response of the congregation after the Old Testament reading, and the placement of the Gloria Patri after the New Testament lesson. For the former Methodist side, a most radical change was the decision that the congregation should sit during singing in order to be able to stand for prayer (having abandoned the habit of kneeling during prayer, it seemed appropriate to stand for prayer as in other Protestant churches).

The whole story shows the difficulties for German-speaking people of the Methodist tradition to find the appropriate form of worship in the context of a liturgical culture other than Anglican. The new order of worship in the *Evangelisch-methodistische Kirche* has served now for more than twenty years and has proven itself as a useful instrument for the congregations. But it does not provide a self-evident or organic unit, and pastors have to prepare very carefully their choice of hymns, readings, and liturgical verses to give the worship service a consistent and convincing profile. For many of them, that is not easy; this is one of the challenges for the future.

It is uncertain whether Methodists in German-speaking countries are aware of one detail in their liturgical tradition which makes a small but not unimportant difference when compared to other Protestant traditions. The reading from the Old Testament has been an integral part of public worship in Methodism from the beginning; in no other liturgy in Germany has this been the case.[22] Each *Evangelisch-methodistische Kirche* congregation hears the Old Testament (and not just a psalm) on every Sunday morning. Whether this has had a positive influence on the theology of our Church is a question still to be studied.

German-speaking Methodism has not developed a lectionary of its own. The Central Conference of Central and Southern Europe provides in its worship book the lectionary of the United Methodist Church in the United States as a suggestion and stimulus for the use of Scripture in Sunday worship. In Germany there is no official recommendation. Many pastors use for the choice of the text of their sermon the lectionary of the Lutheran Church which has a cycle of six years and which corresponds to the traditional emphases of the ecclesiastical year. But in principle the lessons from the Old and the New Testament and the text of the sermon (if different) are chosen by the pastor.

The Place of the Lord's Supper in the Sunday Worship

Holy communion was not an integral part of the Sunday worship in Methodism in continental Europe for more than a century. This meant no low regard for the importance of the Lord's Supper. Rather, the reverse was true: the high estimation of this sacrament and of its meaning and holiness was the reason that Methodists on the Continent were reluctant to celebrate it too often. From the early days we find in the Methodist Episcopal Church as well as in the Evangelical Association the custom to have holy communion during the "quarterly feast" which was held when the district superintendent (or his representative) visited a circuit.[23] On Saturday evening the quarterly conference took place, and on Sunday the "quarterly meeting" of all congregations of the circuit was held. The morning service included holy communion, and in the afternoon the love feast was shared. The origin of this custom may be found in the very early days of the Methodist mission when only a few ordained elders (who were also, in fact, the district superintendents) were available to administer the sacraments. But the custom was preserved until the middle of our century in many places. Good Friday and New Year's Eve also were occasions for many local churches to celebrate additional communion.

The deep respect for the sacrament was increased by the fact that there was no "open communion." In the Evangelical Association, a preparatory service for holy communion took place on Thursday evening (the *Agende* of 1963 still included a liturgy for it). The quarterly conference examined the church members, and friends of the congregation had to apply for participation in the communion liturgy proper. In the Methodist Church, the classes seem to have functioned in a similar way and the *Discipline* said: "No person shall be admitted to the Lord's Supper among us who is guilty of any practice for which we would exclude a member of our church."[24] This also included a certain oversight or examination of the communicants.[25]

The effect of this discipline was that often not all of those who attended Sunday worship took part in the celebration of the Lord's Supper. Often a hymn was sung as "transition" to the Lord's Supper and with its announcement those who intended to leave were expressly dismissed—sometimes with a special blessing.

Most congregations in the *Evangelisch-methodistische Kirche* celebrate the Lord's Supper not more frequently than every second month (a few once a month). But now all who seek forgiveness and life through the blood of Christ are invited to take part, and the "preaching service" and the "communion service" are bound together without any caesura. Normally even those who will not receive communion will stay with the congregation.

The liturgy of the Lord's Supper went through significant changes. The "Order of the Administration of the Lord's Supper" of the Wesleyan Methodists, published in 1874, one year after the denomination celebrated the first holy communion of its own, is almost entirely a translation of the liturgy of the British Wesleyan Methodist Conference or its Anglican equivalent in the *Book of Common Prayer*.[26] Even the Collect for the King was preserved—which was not problematic for use in the Kingdom of Württemberg! There were also included prefaces for the eucharistic prayer which varied according to the liturgical season, a very unusual practice for continental Methodism.

The Ritual of the Methodist Episcopal Church contained an order for the Lord's Supper that had been abridged from that formulated by Wesley in his 1784 *Sunday Service of the Methodists in North America*. The first liturgy to be adapted for the use of the German-speaking conferences in Europe (1928) made only a few changes to the pattern that had been received from the Methodist Episcopal Church in the United States. Instead of the collection for the poor and the words of scripture related to it, the order began with the recitation of 1 John 2:1-2. The Sanctus was placed after the prayer of consecration. The worship book for the Methodist Episcopal Church in Germany from 1948 retained this pattern. But the words of institution were no longer embedded in the prayer of consecration. They preceded it and the prayer itself conformed to a trinitarian shape. Also, the closing prayer was changed from a prayer for the acceptance of the sacrifice of praise and dedication to a short general thanksgiving.

The original liturgy of the Evangelical Association had a different pattern. It began with an extemporary exhortation following the lines of 1 Corinthians 11:23-29. This may be the reason why there was no recitation of the words of institution before or within the prayer of consecration. The Sanctus had its place directly before the prayer of consecration which was followed by the Lord's Prayer. In principle we find most elements of the Anglican tradition within this liturgy, but often in an abridged form and with a different wording. Not only the heading but also the content of this liturgy identify the Lord's Supper as a "Meal of Remembrance." This shows a strong Reformed influence. Nevertheless, the words which are spoken during the distribution of the elements, originating from the Anglican tradition, are consonant with an expression of the real presence of the body and blood of Christ:

> Iss das Brot, das wir brechen, zum Gedächnis, dass Christus seinen Leib hat brechen lassen . . . ; geniesse ihn im Glauben in deinem Herzen und sei ihm dankbar. . . . Trinke daraus zum Gedächtnis, dass Christi Blut für dich vergossen worden ist . . . ; geniesse es im Glauben in deinem Herzen. Sei ihm dankbar."[27]

This liturgy seems to have been in use until 1957 when a trial edition of a new worship book was published which then was approved in 1963. The order for the Lord's Supper in this book shows a total break with the previous orders. It consists of words of invitation, the words of institution, a short confession of sin followed by Psalm 51 and John 3:16, the invitation to come to the table, the traditional words which are spoken when the elements are distributed, and a psalm of thanksgiving (Psalm 34:2-9, or 23, or 103:1-5).

In the same way the *Agende* of the *Evangelisch-methodistische Kirche* from 1973 (in trial use since 1970) showed almost no traces of the traditional wordings of the Anglican/Wesleyan liturgy. Words of invitation, confession of sin and words of grace, a prayer of thanksgiving (in one form followed by the Sanctus), the words of institution, a hymn of thanks, invitation, communion, a word of sending, and a prayer of thanksgiving are the basic elements of three slightly different forms. The wording is in modern language; the text seems to have been written for this liturgy, although there may be some sources in other modern liturgies for it. The Conference in the German Democratic Republic added as a fourth form a revised version of the liturgy in the Anglican/Wesleyan tradition. Similarly, the worship book of the Central Conference of Central and Southern Europe from 1981 has as its first form a liturgy which goes back to the old Anglican/Wesleyan pattern, including the self-examination with the Ten Commandments, the Great Commandment, and a general collect. There is a second version of the order for the Lord's Supper which corresponds to one of the forms that is in use in Germany.

The new *Agende* of the *Evangelisch-methodistische Kirche* in Germany from 1991 adds to a slightly revised version of 1973 two other forms: one in the "Wesleyan tradition" (similar to that in the liturgy of the Central Conference of Central and Southern Europe) and one which was introduced by the United Methodist Church in the United States in 1972 with some additional elements from the so-called Lima liturgy of the World Council of Churches (1982).

Sunday Worship and Hymnbooks

Methodism in Britain and in the United States was known for the fervor of its singing. This was true also for Methodism in Germany. Sometimes it was said that the singing of the people in the Methodist chapel attracted more people than the preaching of the Methodist preachers. Methodists were also attacked because of the music they sang. Especially after 1870, when the *"Englische Heilslieder,"* hymns of the holiness movement in the style of Ira D. Sankey (1840–1908), were introduced and published by the Methodist minister Ernst Gebhardt (1832–1899), Methodists were accused of emotional and improper singing. The use of tunes and rhythms which resembled those of popular music was very uncommon for German Protestants although Luther had said much in favor of it, believing a variety of musical forms could be employed in the service of God.

But the official hymnals did not contain only gospel hymns; in fact, gospel hymns represented only a small minority of the hymns. In the early Methodist hymnbooks, the author whose texts are used most frequently is, of course, Charles Wesley. The *Zionsharfe* of the Wesleyans, which was published in 1863,[28] had about sixty hymns by him, which represents 10 percent of the total of 613. Pietistic hymnwriters, like Philipp Friedrich Hiller (1699–1769), Ernst Gottlieb Woltersdorf (1725–1761), Count Nikolaus Ludwig von Zinzendorf (1700–1760), and the most important of all the German hymnwriters, Paul Gerhardt (1607–1676), were also represented by a large number of hymns. The outline of this hymnbook was very simple and could be called "a little body of systematic theology":

Von Gott (God)

Von dem Menschen (Man)

Von der Kirche Jesu Christi (The Church of Jesus Christ)

Von der Zeit und Ewigkeit (Time and Eternity)[29]

We find a similar order in the hymnbooks of the *Bischöfliche Methodisten-Kirche*. In the *Deutsches Gesangbuch der Bischöflichen Methodisten-Kirche* (1865),[30] the content is given under these headings:

Lob des Dreieinigen Gottes (Praise of the Triune God)

Von Gottes Eigenschaften und Werken (God's Attributes and Works)

Von der Erlösung durch Christus, den Sohn Gottes (Redemption through Christ, the Son of God)

Von dem Heiligen Geiste (The Holy Spirit)

Von der Kirche Christi (The Church of Christ)

Von der Heilsordnung (The Order of Salvation)

Vom Sinn und Wandel der Christen (Christian Temperament and Conduct)

Von den letzten Dingen (The Last Things)

Für besondere Lebensverhältnisse (For Particular Circumstances in Life)

The next edition of 1888[31] brought only few changes within this outline. Its content of seven hundred and eighty hymns (now with music set in harmony) may be representative for the singing of early German-speaking Methodism. The hymnwriter who has the largest representation of hymns is now Philipp Friedrich Hiller (forty-one hymns), followed by Wesley and Woltersdorf (twenty-five each), Philipp Spitta (1801–1859; twenty-two) and Albert Knapp (1798–1864; nineteen).

The hymns of Charles Wesley may not have played the same role in German-speaking Methodist churches as they did in the English-speaking, particularly in Britain. The translations were very poor and not many hymn quotations are found outside the hymnbook. It is significant that the hymnal of the Methodist Episcopal Church for Germany and Switzerland, which was published in 1926,[32] has no more than six hymns of Charles Wesley of which, perhaps, only four were sung with regularity. None of these hymns is central for the theology of the Wesleys! The most frequent writer in this hymnal was again Hiller (thirty-nine hymns) followed by the Methodist writer August Rücker (1871–1952; thirty-six), Philipp Spitta (twenty-five), Paul Gerhardt (twenty-two), Albert Knapp (twenty-two) and Ernst Gebhardt (thirteen original and another twenty-five translations). The book is divided in four major parts:

I. *Der christliche Glaube* (The Christian Faith: Adoration and Worship; God's Nature and Attributes; The Revelation of God)

II. *Der christliche Kirche* (The Christian Church: Nature, Means of Grace, Institutions and Mission)

III. *Das christliche Leben* (The Christian Life: Fall and Human Corruption; Invitation and Revival; Conversion, Repentance, Justification and Assurance; Sanctification; Family and Work)

IV. *Die christliche Hoffnung* (The Christian Hope)

If we look into the hymnbooks of the Evangelical Association we will find a similar picture: the *Gesangbuch für die Evangelische Gemeinschaft*[33] has twenty-four chapters, beginning with "Gottes Wesen und Eigenschaften (God's Nature and Attributes)" and ending with "Die letzten Dinge (Death, Judgement and Future Life)." From Philipp Hiller are forty-five hymns; Gottlieb Füssle (1839–1918, the first German minister of the Evangelical Association) has thirty-nine; Benjamin Schmolck (1672–1737) contributed twenty-five; and Gerhard Teerstegen (1697–1769) has twenty-one. There is no hymn from Charles Wesley in this hymnal! In the 1931 edition[34] the picture has changed only slightly: Hiller leads (thirty-six), followed by Gerhardt (twenty-eight), Gottlieb Füssle (twenty-two), Spitta (twenty-one), Tersteegen (twenty), and Knapp (nineteen). Only two hymns are from Charles Wesley. But the table of contents looks now quite different. We find these headings:

Anbetung Gottes (Adoration of God: Praise, Thanksgiving and Prayer)

Heilige Zeiten (Holy Seasons: The Lord's Day and the Christian Year)

Gemeinde Christi und Gnadenmittel (Church and Means of Grace)

Jesuslieder (Songs about Jesus)

Die Heilsordnung (The Order of Salvation: Call to Repentance, Faith and Justification, New Birth; Peace and Joy in God; Sanctification)

Das christliche Leben (Christian Life: Love of God and our Neighbors, Discipleship)

Besondere Verhältnisse und Zeiten (Special Occasions and Times: Home, Family, Nation, Seasons, Morning and Evening)

Die letzten Dinge (The Last Things: Death and the Life to Come)

Doxologien und Schlussgesänge (Doxologies and Closing Hymns)

In the 1950s both Churches published a supplement to their hymnbooks in which they included especially hymns from the time of the Reformation and a few modern songs. The appendix for the hymnbook of the Methodist Episcopal Church (1953) had only twenty additional hymns; that of the Evangelical Association (1954) included fifty. The tendency was to depart from the nineteenth-century styles and to return to the forms of the Reformation and the Baroque. The new situation, which was very much influenced by the so-called *Sing-Bewegung* and represented by the new German *Evangelisches Kirchengesangbuch* (1953),[35] is best shown by the fact that the Evangelical Association in Switzerland published a hymnal of its own in 1952 (*Christenlieder*[36]) which contained all the ingredients of a good modern hymnbook in the Reformed tradition though with perhaps a stronger emphasis on texts from the pietistic period. This tendency continued until the new hymnbook of the *Evangelisch-methodistische Kirche* was published in 1969.[37]

Of hymnwriters in the *Evangelisch-methodistische Kirche* hymnbook, Paul Gerhardt leads with thirty hymns (out of six hundred and sixty-one), followed by Hiller (thirty), Luther (fourteen), Spitta (twelve), Rücker (eleven), Matthias Jorissen (1799–1823; ten), Knapp (ten), Christian F. Gellert (1715–1769; ten), and Jochen Klepper (1903–1942; nine). Charles Wesley is represented by six texts, as many as Zinzendorf. Ernst Gebhardt has three (and eleven translations), as many as Füssle and the Swiss Methodist Hans Jakob Breiter (1845–1893). Some of these hymns were relegated into a kind of appendix with the nostalgic headline: "Aus der Väter Tagen" (From Days Gone By).

Clearly, the representation of hymns of different authors is much broader in recent collections than in the earlier hymnbooks. As with the *Evangelisches Kirchengesangbuch*, attempts were made to return to the original form of the tunes and to omit versions which were arranged in the nineteenth century. For the people of the Evangelical Association, this was already prepared through the relatively large appendix of their old hymnbook. For Methodists, the new hymnbook looked like a totally new book—not because Charles Wesley hymns were omitted, which in fact was not the case, but because many familiar tunes and songs of the nineteenth century were no longer included. Another major change for the Methodists was the structure of the new book. It was similar to that of the last hymnbook of the Evangelical Association and of the *Evangelisches Kirchengesangbuch*, the hymnal of the Protestant churches in Germany since 1953, but formed a deep break with the Methodist tradition. The main parts are:

Das Kirchenjahr (The Christian Year)

Der Gottesdienst (The Worship of God: Praise; Thanksgiving; Prayer; Confession; Word of God; Church; Fellowship; Services; Mission)

Das christliche Leben (The Christian Life: The Way to Salvation; Experience of Grace; Discipleship and Christian Hope)

Besondere Zeiten (Special Times and Seasons)

Aus der Väter Tagen (From Days Gone By)

Soon after the publication of the 1969 *Evangelisch-methodistische Kirche* hymnbook, a trend began for singing in German churches. New songs were written which used elements from popular music or the tradition of the gospel songs combined with modern texts; some of these became very popular. Not many of them were in use for more than a short period, but in the 1980s it became evident that there was at least a core of new songs which could be used more frequently in worship services. And as did many other churches, the *Evangelisch-methodistische Kirche* published in 1987 *leben und loben* (to live and to praise) containing "new songs for the Church."[38] What was peculiar to this publication was that besides these new songs it included eight previously unfamiliar hymns of Charles Wesley that were newly translated, one hymn of Heber ("Holy, Holy, Holy"), one of Watts ("Joy to the World"), and two translations by Ernst Gebhardt of hymns by Albert Midlane and William Paton MacKay. The great surprise was that these hymns (including some by Wesley) became the most popular ones in the new songbook. For the first time we have in this edition readable translations of hymns by Wesley which really represent his theology (e.g., "Love Divine," "O for a Thousand Tongues," "What Shall I Do my God to Love"), most in the same meter as in English and with the same tune which is used in the 1966 United Methodist hymnal from the United States. This small booklet, with its 129 songs, has done more to renew the quality of Methodist singing than many previous efforts. And this again does not only mean that hymns of Wesleyan origin are sung, but that people are singing with new joy and devotion.

Present Trends and Problems

As has been indicated before, not all people in the *Evangelisch-methodistische Kirche* in Germany are convinced that the present form of our Sunday service is the best solution for the worship of the people called Methodist and especially for those outside the Church whom we hope to reach and to include in our worship services. After the introduction of the new liturgy for the *Evangelisch-methodistische Kirche*, it was soon said that the present order was a compromise that should be developed into a more consistent and self-evident form.[39] But the people who say this have very divergent ideas on the question of liturgical forms. Some argue for a broader and more consistent use of the elements from the liturgical traditions of Christianity. These persons are few in number and get little response at present. But because they are considered liturgical experts, they have nevertheless some influence and try to help the congregations to have lively worship in good liturgical order.[40]

There are others who plead for the old "preaching service" where everything that happens during the service is oriented to the proclamation of the Word of God in the sermon, either to prepare for it or to respond to it. We find the advocates of this model more in the older generation.[41]

Many people, however, would like to give more opportunity for an active participation of the people of God. Already in 1971, shortly after the union and before the final approval for the new *Agende*, Fritz Harriefeld, a prominent district superintendent, published a booklet called *Gottesdienst in neuer Gestalt* (Worship in New Forms).[42] He made a series of suggestions for a new shaping of the service as a whole, but also for singing, prayer, and the sermon, all with the intention of using forms which are suited to our time and would enable lay people to play an active role in the whole worship service. Exactly twenty years later, an article was published by Dieter Sackmann, Professor of Practical Theology at the Theological Seminary of the *Evangelisch-methodistische Kirche* in Reutlingen, in which the same ideas may be found in a more general and less radical form.[43] "Worship in United Methodist Perspective" is his subject, and he pleads for a worship experience in which is present not only the dimension of *martyria* (and by more than one witness!), but also that of *koinonia* and *diakonia*. Not much seems to have changed since 1971!

There is, however, one important new element in the discussion. In the past few years, the charismatic movement has had an impact in the congregations of the *Evangelisch-methodistische Kirche*. People who are influenced by it ask for more flexibility in the formation of worship. But they want "songs of praise" instead of hymns, space for the voice of prophecy and speaking in tongues, special blessing for people in difficult situations, and the service of healing and the celebration of God's wonders among his people. This kind of worship attracts young people, but often the traditional congregation moves out when it becomes the main service of a local church. As most German Methodist churches observe only one Sunday worship service (and cling to the ideal that there should be only one worship time for the whole congregation), compromises are difficult to achieve.

A person who visits different churches in the *Evangelisch-methodistische Kirche* would probably find diversity in the forms of worship. The visitor will witness churches where the liturgy is followed rather strictly and the pastor will speak no personal word until coming to the announcements. At other places, the basic form of the service may still be recognizable, but is enriched by planned or spontaneous additional elements such as a song by the Sunday School, a "sermon" for the children, greetings or personal communications, or the contributions of various groups from within the congregation. A few churches will have worship in a very free "charismatic" style which includes long periods with songs of praise, personal witness, and prayers of intercession and thanksgiving.

Perspectives for the Future

Christian worship, as with the Church of Jesus Christ itself, should be like a room. There has to be a dimension (height) for the encounter with the living triune God in praise and prayer, in word and sacrament. There should be a dimension (breadth) to meet other people: to share concerns and needs, to serve and to be served. (It may not be by chance that John Wesley's famous dictum "The gospel of Christ knows of no religion, but social; no holiness but social holiness" was written within the preface of a hymnbook.[44]) And there should be a dimension (length) to face the challenges of the world in which we worship and witness to God's love. These three features have found different expressions and accentuations in the history of the Church. The Methodist tradition represents one of the efforts to build up the "house of God" by Christian worship through which people are able to experience the presence of God in Jesus Christ by the Holy Spirit, to find sisters and brothers who care for one another in mutual love, and to be disciples in mission unto the world.

The history of the Methodist worship in Germany shows two faces. It is the story of a new worship experience arising from a new experience of God, a witness which was not without effect on other churches and their worship. It is at the same time the story of the adaptation of this form of worship to a general "Protestant" liturgical culture in Germany with roots in the Lutheran and the Reformed heritage. This adaptation was a source of enrichment for the Methodist worship experience, but where it was used to cover differences it has come with the danger of suppressing the distinct heritage of Methodism.

The future of Methodist worship will not be a repetition of the past, but the revival of the spirit found at the beginning. Tradition does not mean to guard the ashes but to pass on the embers! It will be our task to preserve the best of the old and to find new forms of worship able to serve as means of grace for the people of today through which they may give worthy praise to God and experience the presence of God in their lives.

Chapter 17

Methodism through the Lens of Lima

Geoffrey Wainwright

At Lima (Peru), in January 1982, the Faith and Order Commission of the World Council of Churches put the finishing touches to its convergence document on *Baptism, Eucharist and Ministry*.[1] After a distant preparation dating from the 1920s, and a closer preparation dating from the 1960s, the text was unanimously judged by the 120-member Commission to have reached sufficient "maturity" for submission to the Churches with a request that they make an "official response . . . at the highest appropriate level of authority." The questions posed to the Churches concerned

> the extent to which your church can recognize in this text the faith of the Church through the ages; the consequences your church can draw from this text for its relations and dialogues with other churches, particularly with those churches which also recognize the text as an expression of the apostolic faith; the guidance your church can take from this text for its worship, educational, ethical, and spiritual life and witness; the suggestions your church can make for the ongoing work of Faith and Order as it relates to material of this text on Baptism, Eucharist and Ministry to its long-range research project "Towards the Common Expression of the Apostolic Faith Today."

Among the unprecedentedly high figure of some two hundred Churches taking up that invitation to respond to the ecumenical proposal were ten Methodist denominations from around the globe and a further six united Churches with a variably significant Methodist component.[2] The aim of the present chapter is to display the current Methodist understanding and practice of Sunday worship, in actuality and aspiration, as these are refracted in the relevant responses to the Lima text. We can watch the Methodist Churches locate themselves in relation to the most commonly agreed statement on the chosen topics that it has been possible to achieve on the part of the most representative theological body in the world (the Faith and Order Commission draws its membership from all six continents, and from the Eastern Orthodox, Oriental Orthodox, Roman Catholic, Old Catholic, Lutheran, Anglican, Reformed, Methodist, Baptist, Disciples, Adventist, and Pentecostal traditions). We can observe where Methodists affirm the text, where they criticize it, where they avow that they can learn from it.

The Lima Text Itself

A brief description of the content of the three-part Lima text (quickly nicknamed *BEM*) is needed at the outset: first, baptism; then eucharist; and finally ministry.[3]

Beginning from the gospel record of the institution of baptism by the risen Lord at Matthew 28:16-20, the first section of the Lima text follows the manifold New Testament witness in displaying the "meaning of baptism"—in both sign and effect—as "participation in Christ's death and resurrection," "conversion, pardoning and cleansing," the "gift of the Spirit," "incorporation into the body of Christ," and "the sign of the kingdom." On the tangled problems regarding the relation of faith, water baptism, and the Spirit, the Lima text affirms that "baptism is both God's gift and our human response to that gift. . . . The necessity of faith for the reception of the salvation embodied and set forth in baptism is acknowledged by all churches"; it stresses that "both the baptism of believers and the baptism of infants take place in the Church as the community of faith"; and, while observing that "Christians differ in their understanding as to where the sign of the gift of the Spirit is to be found," it claims general agreement that "Christian baptism is in water and the Holy Spirit."

Setting the Last Supper in the context of other significant meals during the earthly ministry of Jesus and after his resurrection, the second section of the Lima text sees there the institution of the eucharist as the new paschal meal, the meal of the new covenant, which Jesus gave to his disciples for the memorial of his death and resurrection and in anticipation of the feast of the final kingdom. The eucharist is called "a gift from the Lord," and it is said that every Christian receives "the gift of salvation through communion in the body and blood of Christ." The "meaning of the eucharist" is then displayed according to a trinitarian pattern and the fivefold sequence of the ancient creeds as "thanksgiving to the Father," "memorial of Christ," "invocation of the Spirit," "communion of the faithful," and "meal of the kingdom." Touching the historically controversial questions concerning presence and sacrifice, the Lima text speaks of "Christ's real, living, and active presence in the eucharist," which is "the living and effective sign of Christ's sacrifice, accomplished once and for all on the cross and still operative on behalf of all humankind." This central section of *BEM* ends with several paragraphs on "the celebration of the eucharist," and to these I shall return.

The final section of *BEM* opens with "the calling of the whole people of God" and places the ordained ministry within that framework. The ordained ministry is regarded as a reminder "of the dependence of the Church on Jesus Christ, who is the source of its mission and the foundation of its unity." As one factor within the broader reality of an "apostolic Tradition" that is transmitted in several ways, the "episcopal succession" is proposed as "a sign, though not a guarantee, of the continuity and unity of the Church"; and it is claimed that "the threefold ministry of bishop, presbyter, and deacon may serve today as an expression of the unity we seek and also a means for achieving it."

Thus the basic content of the Lima text. Our study will concentrate on the eucharistic section of *BEM*, drawing on the other two parts only as necessary to deal with the service on the Lord's Day. In addition, however, to the fivefold understanding of "the meaning of the eucharist" already mentioned, the eucharistic section of *BEM* makes the following practical points of celebration that provoke Methodist response in matters to do with the Sunday liturgical assembly; and it is important, therefore, to have them in mind as we seek to read Methodism through the lens of Lima.

First, it is affirmed that the eucharist "always includes both word and sacrament" (*E* 3), and that, as such, it is "the central act of the Church's worship" (*E* 1).

Second, *E* 27 declares that the eucharistic rite

is essentially a single whole, consisting historically of the following elements in varying sequence and of diverse importance:
- hymns of praise;
- act of repentance;
- declaration of pardon;
- proclamation of the Word of God, in various forms;
- confession of faith (creed);

- intercession for the whole Church and for the world;
- preparation of the bread and wine;
- thanksgiving to the Father for the marvels of creation, redemption and sanctification (deriving from the Jewish tradition of the *berakah*);
- the words of Christ's institution of the sacrament according to the New Testament tradition;
- the *anamnesis* or memorial of the great acts of redemption, passion, death, resurrection, ascension, and Pentecost, which brought the Church into being;
- the invocation of the Holy Spirit (*epiklesis*) on the community, and the elements of bread and wine (either before the words of institution or after the memorial, or both; or some other reference to the Holy Spirit which adequately expresses the "epikletic" character of the eucharist);
- consecration of the faithful to God;
- reference to the communion of saints;
- prayer for the return of the Lord and the definitive manifestation of his kingdom;
- the Amen of the whole community;
- the Lord's Prayer;
- sign of reconciliation and peace;
- the breaking of the bread;
- eating and drinking in communion with Christ and with each member of the Church;
- final act of praise;
- blessing and sending.

From the viewpoint of liturgical history, it may be observed that all the features listed between "thanksgiving to the Father" and "the Amen of the whole community" classically belong to what is technically called "the eucharistic prayer" or "great thanksgiving" or "anaphora."

Third, it is recognized that "many differences of theology, liturgy, and practice are connected with the varying frequency with which the Holy Communion is celebrated" (*E* 29); and the following recommendation is made: "As the eucharist celebrates the resurrection of Christ, it is appropriate that it should take place at least every Sunday"(*E* 30).

Fourth, the Lord's Supper is presented as the meal of the faithful baptized. "As it is the new sacramental meal of the people of God, every Christian should be encouraged to receive communion frequently" (*E* 30). In any refusal of the "right of baptized believers" to communion by other eucharistic congregations than their own, "the catholicity of the eucharist is less manifest" (*E* 19, commentary). In reference to the "discussion in many churches today about the inclusion of baptized children as communicants at the Lord's Supper" (ibid.), it is further suggested that "those churches which baptize children but refuse them a share in the eucharist . . . may wish to ponder whether they have fully appreciated and accepted the consequences of baptism" (*B* 14, commentary).

Fifth, *E* 29 declares that "it is Christ who invites to the meal and who presides at it. . . . In most churches, this presidency is signified by an ordained minister. . . . The minister of the eucharist is the ambassador who represents the divine initiative and expresses the connection of the local community with other local communities in the universal Church."

Sixth, the commentary to *E* 28 reads thus: "Since New Testament days, the Church has attached the greatest importance to the continued use of the elements of bread and wine which Jesus used at the Last Supper. In certain parts of the world, where bread and wine are not customary or obtainable, it is now sometimes held that local food and drink serve better to anchor the eucharist in everyday life. Further study is required concerning the question of which features of the Lord's Supper were unchangeably instituted by Jesus, and which features remain within the Church's competence to decide."

The Various Methodist Responses

The Methodist responses are scattered through the six volumes of *Churches Respond to BEM*.[4]

The response of the United Methodist Church, issued by the Council of Bishops under the date of April 30, 1986, was one of the most thorough and one of the most positive responses made by any Church to the Lima text.[5] For the United Methodists, the grounds for evaluating *BEM* are the Scriptures and the Christian faith as interpreted and lived in the Wesleyan tradition. The Wesley brothers themselves are substantially invoked a good dozen times, whether to show how they anticipated the positions of *BEM* or could still strengthen the ecumenical convergence, or to describe how they shaped the Methodist heritage or now stand in implicit judgment on some later turns in the denominational history.

Additional responses to *BEM* were made by other bodies of United Methodism. A group of such responses, bearing some noticeable verbal resemblances to each other, came from the three Central

Conferences of Central and Southern Europe, the then German Democratic Republic (East Germany), and the then Federal Republic of Germany (West Germany).[6] These responses criticize *BEM* by appeals to the Protestant Reformation of the sixteenth century, and especially to some insights characteristic of Lutheranism. Thus the East Germans set a "scriptural" understanding of the Church as *creatura verbi divini* against an "historical" ecclesiology of "development and continuity" said to be Orthodox, Catholic, and Anglican, and they charge *BEM* with "promoting the misunderstanding that traditions of liturgical customs hold greater value than the living word of Christ itself." The Central and Southern European response finds in *BEM* "the notion of the Church as a dispensary of salvation (*Heilsanstalt*)," "the danger of a triumphalistic and authoritarian image of the Church." John Wesley is invoked by the West German response also for his criticism of mere "formal religion." For each of the sections of *BEM*, the East German response groups its reflections under two heads: "What do we agree with?" and "What do we disagree with?" The West German response follows the pattern of "Agreement," "Self-Assessment," and "Critical Objections."

The response of the British Methodist Church, approved by the Conference after formulation by the Faith and Order Committee, is an elegantly written piece of discursive theology.[7] The British Methodist judgment on *BEM* is "basically positive": in the exposition of baptism and eucharist "we find the essential matter of the faith through the ages," while the response on ministry, though "in general positive," is tempered by some "serious reservations." The British Methodists make their response out of a "doctrinal identity" that is "guaranteed by common respect for the standards" laid down in their 1932 Deed of Union (affirming the "apostolic," "evangelical faith" that is "based upon the Divine Revelation recorded in the Holy Scriptures" and "found in Wesley's Notes on the New Testament and the first four volumes of his Sermons"), "by the use of a common hymn book, a common service book and common patterns of worship, by a connexional system that ensures remarkable consistency of usage in Methodism, and by loyalty to the interpretations of the doctrinal standards given by Conference from time to time."

The Methodist Church of Southern Africa, which originated from British Methodism, affirmed much in the Lima document and indicated a need for self-criticism on its own side, while twice regretting that *BEM* for its part did not make more explicit "the necessity of personal faith for the personal appropriation of the saving work of God in Jesus Christ."[8] The Methodist Church in Ireland was concerned lest *BEM*, in dealing with the sacraments, had confused the sign with what it signifies; on the one hand, the divine agent must retain sovereignty over the *means* of grace, while on the other, faith is needed for the *reception* of grace.[9]

Some smaller Methodist Churches made shorter responses to *BEM* that do not bear directly on our subject of Sunday worship, namely, the Methodist Church of New Zealand, the Protestant Methodist Church in the People's Republic of Benin, and the Jamaica District of the Methodist Church in the Caribbean and the Americas.[10]

Responses came also from several united Churches with a Methodist component. The Church of South India (1947) and the Church of North India (1970) included Methodists of British and Australasian origin with Anglicans and Reformed as well as (in the latter case) Baptists and Brethren; the responses of these two Churches to *BEM* are much concerned with the location of the Church and of Christian worship in Indian cultures.[11] The United Church of Canada (1925) and the Uniting Church in Australia (1977) both brought together Methodists, Presbyterians, and Congregationalists; the Canadian response questions whether *BEM* has sufficently reflected "pluralism" both within and without the Church, while the Australian text affirms a "diversity" which refuses to "unchurch" variant views on several matters.[12] The responses of the United Protestant Church of Belgium and of the Joint Synod of the Waldensian and Methodist Churches in Italy each bear the stronger stamp of the Reformed tradition which outweighs the Methodist in their cases.[13]

Liturgical Themes and Ritual Practices

In this part we come to the interaction between Methodism and the ecumenical text. We are looking to learn about the Sunday worship that is described or implied in the Methodist responses and about Methodist participation in the ecumenical convergence: what Methodists are able to endorse in the Lima text, the challenges Methodists have addressed to the Lima text, and the help Methodists can find in the Lima text for a renewal of their own understanding and practice. Matters fall into three groups: the relation between word and sacrament; the conditions of admission to holy communion; and the elements to be used at the Lord's table.

Word and Sacrament

Several issues cluster around the question of the relationship, at the level of doctrine and of rite, between word and sacrament. Here belong particularly the frequency with which the Lord's Supper is observed, the liturgical structure of services both eucharistic and non-eucharistic, and the ministry of presidency and other functions in the worship assembly.

Since our chief concern is with the Sunday service of the Methodists, the basic question may appropriately be formulated thus: What is, according to Methodist theory and practice, the norm for worship on the Lord's Day? Is it a preaching service in which a complex of scripture readings, prayers, and hymnody finds its climax in a sermon? Or is it (as the response to BEM by the National Alliance of Lutheran Churches of France nicely puts it) an ellipse with two foci, the proclamation of the word and communion in bread and wine?[14]

Historically, it is clear that the most characteristic form of specifically Methodist worship has been the preaching service. At Wesley's insistence, the earliest Methodist preaching services fell outside "church hours" and were meant to complement the services in the Anglican parishes, at which Wesley encouraged the Methodists to press for more frequent communion. At the New Room in Bristol and eventually at the Foundery and then the City Road Chapel in London, however, where and when presbyters of the Church of England were available, the Methodists regularly held services of both word and sacrament.[15] And when in 1784 John Wesley sent Superintendent Coke and Elders Whatcoat and Vasey to North America with *The Sunday Service of the Methodists*, he "advise[d] the elders to administer the Supper of the Lord on every Lord's Day."[16] To the end of his life, as is shown in the so-called Korah Sermon on "Prophets and Priests" preached at Cork on May 4, 1789, Wesley held that presbyteral ordination was necessary to presidency at the eucharist, though not to the ministry of preaching.[17] While not uncontested in Methodism from early days, the link between ordination and presidency at the eucharist helped to build a habit of infrequency in many congregations, since rarely was Methodism, either on the American frontier or in the circuits of nineteenth-century England, in a position to supply a presbyteral presider Sunday by Sunday. Even when, later on, various parts of Methodism came to authorize lay presidency at the Lord's Supper, whether on grounds that persons who preached and pastored should also (be allowed to) preside or on grounds of the "sacramental deprivation" of some societies, the enlargement of permission to preside at the Lord's Table did not by and large lead to much greater frequency of eucharistic celebration. In the twentieth century, the influence of the ecumenical and liturgical movements, in a geographically and denominationally uneven way, has brought some Methodists to a more frequent celebration of the Lord's Supper and a closer approximation to Wesley's ideal of "constant communion." Given that history, how have Methodists responded to the achievements and challenges of the Lima text in the question of word and sacrament?

The responses from the German-speaking areas were the most critical among the Methodist responses (German Democratic Republic, Federal Republic of Germany, and, in part, the United Methodist Church, Central and Southern Europe). The East German response affirms the importance of "the unity between proclamation of the word and the celebration of the Lord's Supper," and the West German response recognizes that according to E 3 the eucharist "always includes both word and sacrament." But neither they nor the Central Europeans will accept that such a eucharist is, or should be, "the central act of the Church's worship" (E 1). Against what they see as a consistent tendency in Lima to "sacramentalism," all three are concerned to assert the integrity of the preaching service even when it stands alone. Nevertheless, Central and Southern Europe appears pleased to note that "the frequency of celebration [of the Lord's Supper] is increasing in our church, certainly as a result of ecumenical contact and stimulation"; and the West German text self-critically admits that "the relative infrequency of the celebration of the eucharist makes the Lord's Supper seem like a 'peripheral act' in our church's life" and declares that "the eucharist should be celebrated more often in the Evangelical Methodist Church."

The British Methodist response rejoices that, thanks to Methodist participation in the liturgical and ecumenical movements, "holy communion is now more frequent in [British] Methodist churches than it has ever been, and in many places the full order of holy communion is now established as a regular monthly service." Noting that "the history and structure of Methodism make weekly celebrations in all our churches all but impossible," the British response asks it to be recognized that "because the Methodist tradition has always meant frequent preaching services without communion, Methodists have learnt to nourish themselves on that kind of worship and many would not now wish to see the balance altered in favour of more frequent communion. They would argue that it is not now a matter of administrative necessity, but rather that the infrequency of celebration actually heightens the sense of the eucharist's importance": "A eucharist less frequently celebrated is not necessarily a eucharist less highly valued." The British Methodists reproach *BEM* with failing to discuss "the relationship between the eucharist and other forms of worship, such as the preaching service, where the eucharistic shape is present but the holy communion is not." Alluding to their *Methodist Service Book* of 1975, which provides a service to reflect "the complete order of Word and Sacrament even when there is no celebration of the Lord's Supper," the British note that "the sermon, for so long the climax of our normal worship, is now commonly moved into the centre of the service so that, after God's Word has been proclaimed, there is an opportunity for the people to respond with prayer, with confession of faith, with self-offering, and above all with thanksgiving. The idea of a eucharistic pattern in all worship is now gaining ground, although only a fraction of our services are eucharists. We believe it very important to note that many of the elements listed in *E* 27 do in fact occur in services that are not formally eucharists."

The response from the bishops of the United Methodist Church moves from self-criticism toward an observation and encouragement of liturgical renewal: "As we United Methodists regard the Church's practice through the ages, we can recognize how our own usage has fallen short of the fullness of the holy communion. Like other Protestants, we have allowed the pulpit to obscure the altar. Now, without minimizing at all the preaching of God's word, we more clearly recognize the equivalent place of the sacrament." For United Methodists, a "vigorous renewal of liturgical theology and practice in the ecumenical movement" has been conjoined with "a remarkable recovery" of the beginnings of their own tradition in the high eucharistic devotion, theology, and practice of the Wesleys; and "we intend to urge our congregations to a more frequent, regular observance of the sacrament." As to the ritual structure of the service, *E* 27 is found to contain "a comprehensive summary of the elements of liturgical action." Yet, "in many eucharistic services, including our own, some of these elements are omitted, either for reasons of carelessness,

314

neglect, or lack of informed understanding. We find in *BEM* a strong reminder to us and all churches of the value of the unreduced celebration."

The deepest question in these issues of word and sacrament concerns the understanding of Christ's presence. The German and the British Methodist responses all take issue with the statement in *E* 13 concerning the "uniqueness" of Christ's presence in relation to the bread and wine. Thus the East Germans: "We see no qualitative difference between celebration of the Lord's Supper and the proclaimed word." The West Germans: "The Lord is not any more 'present' in the feast of the eucharist than in prayer or in the proclamation of his word." The British Methodists imply a negative response to the questions they see raised by *E* 13: "Christ's presence in the eucharist is unique in the sense that every means of grace is unique, but is it unique in the sense that it is superior to all others? Does a discussion which concerns modes of the divine presence allow us to use 'unique' in a comparative sense?" The Central and Southern European response considers it "a great advance" that "the representatives of the various churches did not pressure one another to define the 'how' of the presence of Christ"; and the West German response considers that the various historical accounts of the presence mentioned in the commentary to *E* 13 "can be completely accommodated within the unity formulated in the text itself." The United Methodist bishops judge that *BEM* "succeeds in surmounting conventional disputes in this matter" and make their own striking doxological confession concerning the full service of word and sacrament: "God's effectual word is there revealed, proclaimed, heard, seen, and tasted." The Methodist Church of Southern Africa particularly welcomes the statement in *E* 12 that "since the anamnesis of Christ is the very content of the preached Word as it is of the eucharistic meal, each reinforces the other."

In welcoming the "convergence" in *BEM*'s witness to Christ's presence, the United Methodist response acknowledges the work of "concentrated liturgical scholarship and ecumenical dialogue." It singles out the recovery of the significance of "two traditional Greek words: *anamnesis* and *epiklesis*":

> In terms of the congregation's appropriation of the reality of Christ's presence, the *anamnesis* (memorial, remembrance, representation) means that past, present, and future coincide in the sacramental event. All that Jesus Christ means in his person and

redemptive work is brought forth from history to our present experience, which is also a foretaste of the future fulfillment of God's unobstructed reign. And this presence is made to be a reality for us by the working of God's Spirit, whom we "call down" (*epiklesis*) by invocation, both upon the gifts and on the people.

"All this," the United Methodist response goes on, "we find explicitly taught by John and Charles Wesley, who knew and respected the apostolic, patristic, and reformed faith of the Church." What a pity, then, that the Wesleyan *Hymns on the Lord's Supper* have been so conspicuously missing from the *lex orandi* of twentieth-century American Methodism! Whereas the hymnals of the nineteenth century contained more than a score of the 166 texts in that 1745 eucharistic collection of John and Charles Wesley (though sometimes scattered in places that rendered their sacramental reference less evident), the 1905 joint *Hymnal* of the Methodist Episcopal Church and the Methodist Episcopal Church, South, included only one (and the first verse of another), and the 1935 *Hymnal* took away even what its predecessor had; the 1966 *Hymnal* of the Methodist Church climbed from zero to four ("Author of life divine," "O the depth of love divine," "Happy the souls to Jesus join'd," "How happy are thy servants, Lord"), but the 1989 *Hymnal* of the United Methodist Church sank back to two ("O thou who this mysterious bread," "O the depth of love divine").[18]

Another historically controversial question concerns the sacrificial character of the eucharist, or (more generally formulated) the respective parts played by God and by the human participants in the liturgical action. The response of the United Methodist bishops to *BEM* states the matter thus:

> Throughout Christian history the concept of the sacrificial and atoning death of Jesus Christ has been closely related to the sacrifice of worshipping Christians in the context of the Lord's Supper. Jesus' words of institution at the last supper make this inevitable and salutary. Just *how* that relationship is to be acknowledged and interpreted theologically is a question much disputed by Catholics and Protestants, though less by Orthodox. As Wesleyans, we are accustomed to the language of sacrifice [the allusion is presumably again to the *Hymns on the Lord's Supper*]; and we find *BEM*'s statements to be in accord with the Church's Tradition and with ours. *BEM*'s assertion that "God does not repeat" the sacrificial life, death and resurrection of Christ removes the cause of past disputes.

In this connection, both the United Methodists (implicitly) and the British Methodists (explicitly) show themselves comfortable with the name "eucharist," and it is significant that these two Churches have shared in the recovery within the ecumenical liturgical movement of a full-blown "eucharistic prayer" or "great thanksgiving" or "anaphora" (a feature which even E 27 in BEM did not clearly designate). On the other hand, the German-speaking responses are uneasy that BEM should have made "eucharist," not "the Lord's Supper," the predominant designation of the sacrament: the emphasis is thereby "shifted from God's action in Christ to the celebrating congregation and its 'activity' (praising God)." Nevertheless, the West German response acknowledges that "thanksgiving and praise are neglected in our eucharistic celebration."

On the question of presidency at the eucharist, almost all the Methodist and related responses indicate that the normal practice in their church is for an ordained minister to preside. The British state that "provision is made by the Conference for congregations that suffer [sacramental] deprivation by authorizing individual lay persons to preside at holy communion in particular places." The United Methodist bishops make a similar statement and then ask a question: "In unique situations we allow unordained pastors to preside at the holy communion, while most Churches do not. How can our practice be justified, or can it not?" The British and the Germans are particularly concerned to avoid what the British call "a distinction of kind between the priestly service of the ordained ministry and the priestliness of the laity"—a distinction of which they see traces in BEM, and which would show itself in the grounds offered for the normal presidency of the ordained (presbyter or bishop) at the Lord's table and the possibility or otherwise of exceptions. While the German responses reject the notion that the ordained ministry is specially representative of Christ, the response from Southern Africa runs thus:

> We need to recognize that a eucharistic celebration is not "the assemblies' own creation or possession" (E 29) and that the presiding minister "represents the divine initiative and expresses the connection of the local community with other local communities in the universal Church." This underlines the need for the presiding minister to be recognized as widely as possible in the Christian Church, and should strengthen our resolve to limit the presidency at the eucharist to ordained ministers of the word and sacrament.

An Open Table?

Questions concerning admission to communion arise especially with regard to three cases: first, (baptized) children; second, Christians of other denominations ("eucharistic hospitality" or "intercommunion"); third, evangelization. A related matter is the communion of the sick.

All Methodist Churches practice the baptism of infants, although they vary in the grounds advanced for the practice and in the conditions of doing so. Several Methodist responses to *BEM* reflect a tendency in recent decades to admit baptized children to the Lord's Table at an earlier age than it has been (or remains) customary in Methodism to grant "admission to full membership."[19] The response of the United Methodist bishops conjoins with the admission of baptized children what may in fact be a different issue:

> *BEM*'s commentary 19 can be used to promote discussion of eucharistic participation not only by baptized children, but also by persons who are emotionally or developmentally disabled. Though we cherish cognition in matters of faith, we need to define our sacramental theology and practice for those with deficient mental capacities. We understand God's prevenient grace to be inclusive of all persons.

On the ecumenical front, Methodist Churches characteristically welcome to the Lord's Table Christians in good standing as members of other Churches with which Methodism is officially or implicitly in communion (and most would also welcome individual Christians from Churches, such as the Roman Catholic, which canonically do not admit Methodists to their own eucharistic communion). The United Methodist Church is most forthright in its recognition, with *BEM*, of the classic ecumenical insight that even official intercommunion, let alone occasional eucharistic hospitality (whether in both directions or unilateral), cannot be the final form of Christian unity: "In discussing the Church as either the universal body or a local eucharistic community, BEM calls into question the sufficiency of the denominational model of church organization. . . . Eucharistic unity cannot be divorced from the broader issue of church structure." The Uniting Church in Australia calls for

> the self-examination, repentance, and forgiveness of those who are at odds before eucharistic sharing can take place. What is needed, therefore, goes beyond the "mutual understanding" between

churches, to which *BEM* will undoubtedly contribute, to a genuine act of contrition for the hostility which so often underlies our dividedness.

In connection with evangelization, modern Methodists like to cite Wesley's designation of the Lord's Supper as a "converting ordinance." The United Methodist bishops rightly point out this phrase cannot be taken to mean that there was unrestricted access to communion in original and early Methodism: "John Wesley spoke of the eucharist as a 'converting ordinance.' Some find that to be a warrant for inviting all who seek faith in Christ but have not found it. On the contrary, Wesley, as an Anglican priest, tried to be obedient to the canons, even in a century of sacramental carelessness. He probably assumed that all people in Great Britain were baptized, and could thus come to holy communion to find conversion. In fact, in early British and American Methodism the altar was often 'fenced' for reasons both moralistic and doctrinal." Wesley's rare use of the phrase "converting ordinance" appears in fact to be limited to the time of his controversy with the Moravians in the early 1740s over their doctrine of "stillness": he urged that those who grieved for their sins, who already had some degree of faith and were seeking its full assurance, should use this and other divinely ordained and appointed means of grace.[20]

The response from Central and Southern Europe declares: "In the Methodist understanding, the Lord's Supper offers prevenient, justifying, and sanctifying grace. It is therefore not only a meal of the faithful, but it can also lead seekers to faith. This is the reason the United Methodist Church practices, as a matter of principle, open access to the Lord's Supper."[21] The East German Methodists in their response to *BEM* made much of the evangelistic mission of the Church in and to the world, and stated as a principle: "For us the right to take part in communion does not depend on baptism. Instead we see in the Lord's Supper an invitation that is open to everyone, as well as an opportunity for mission." Less controversially, the same response continues by making a couple of points that several other Methodist responses also welcome from *BEM*: the Lord's Supper "demands and promotes reconciliation and community particularly within the family of God. Having been strengthened by the eucharist, the members of the body of Christ recognize their tasks in the world in which they live and thus try to carry out their duties responsibly in all aspects of their lives."

The response of the Methodist Church in Southern Africa is one of the few among all the responses to take up the point from E 32 about the communion of the sick:

> Do we see it as a continuation of the Church's liturgy or as a type of 'private communion'? Should we not make plain that the sick are in fact sharing in the worship of the whole Church? If so, should not the person administering the elements be accompanied by other members of the congregation? And is it necessary for an ordained minister to administer the elements?

In the context of communal solidarity and cultural alienation, the Church of South India raises, without answering, two questions: "If an earnest, devoted Hindu seeker comes to the holy table, are we justified in denying the holy sacrament to him? Why do non-Christians desire the eucharist so much, while they do not show the same desire with regard to baptism?"

The Elements of Communion

The United Methodist bishops state and ask: "Since 1876, only the unfermented juice of the grape as the 'wine' of communion has been used. Does this constitute a serious ecumenical problem today? Or is United Methodist practice coming to allow a diversity of usage?"

The Church of South India declares: "The symbol should be obvious and meaningful. We have no problem with any type of bread, but it may be difficult to take the coconut water and say: 'This is the blood of Christ.'"

These two comments need to be set beside the firm declaration of the Apostolic Catholic Assyrian Church of the East (often called by others "Nestorian"): "The matter of this sacrament Christ ordained to be of wheat and wine as being most fit to represent body and blood."[22]

At one level, the issue is how the Church best expresses its fidelity to Christ's institution. Is the crucial point "eating" and "drinking," so that some flexibility is allowed regarding the food and beverage consumed? But then how much flexibility? And is sufficient ground for adaptation to be found in the desire for inculturation or for social witness to the dangers of alcohol? Or is there rather an intrinsic relation between Christ's command and the use of the very elements of the Last Supper, bread and wine, their choice by the Lord perhaps being conditioned by their biblical associations and symbolic appropriateness? At another level, the question of the elements may be framed chiefly in terms of the due recognition of both the particularity and the universality of the Gospel and the Faith. The use of bread and wine at the eucharist, in every time and place, makes a universal witness to the particular origins of Christianity while functioning also as a binding tie in the communion of the saints across the generations and the continents. On the other hand, the shift to local elements, its proponents argue, allows the universal scope of the Gospel to find particular expression in a historical and geographical variety of cultures.

Conclusion: A Matter of Experience

If one seeks a common thread, characteristic particularly of Methodism, running through most or all of the Methodist responses to the Lima text, it may perhaps be found in the notion that Sunday worship, in actuality or aspiration, is a living experience of believers in encounter with God. This shows itself in many ways.

Thus, already at the level of procedures for responding to Lima, the British relate their difficulty in deciding "what was the precise setting in the life of the Church in which the text belonged. Because of Methodist tradition, we are held together by a common life of worship, fellowship, and service, rather than by subscription to a series of articles. Consequently, when we speak of confessing the faith, we think primarily of a community addressing God in worship or a preacher proclaiming the Gospel to the world. . . . The present text requires of us systematic intellectual discussion but not an immediate response either in terms of worship or practical action." The United Methodist bishops—for all the difficulties surrounding the allegedly Wesleyan "quadrilateral" (a word they do not use!)—explicitly stated that "experience" would be one of their criteria of assessment.[23]

The German-speaking responses warn against an over-emphasis on the "objective," the "institutional," the "sacramental," to the detriment of the "subjective," the "personal." Thus from Central and Southern Europe: "Where there is no personal encounter with God, there remains only an outward religiosity, a 'formal religion' as John Wesley called it." The United Methodist bishops, while affirming both sides of the divine-human encounter, wish that *BEM* had given more attention to the experience, in the Holy Spirit, of the "subjective, personal appropriation" of God's work.

In this final connection with experience, two words of conclusion may be offered. The first comes from the United Methodist "alternate text" of *The Lord's Supper* of 1972. I refer to the sentence in the eucharistic prayer which links the words of institution to the anamnesis-oblation: "When we eat this bread and drink this cup, we experience anew the presence of the Lord Jesus Christ and look forward to his coming in final victory." This passage was abandoned by the *United Methodist Book of Worship* of 1992, perhaps because it did not fit into the rhetorical form of a prayer addressed to God; but it was a fine—and characteristically Methodist—setting of the present experience of believers in relation to the mighty acts of God in Christ and the sacramental gift of their benefits through the liturgical celebration.[24] The second point is simply to cite some wise words from the response of the United Methodist bishops: "We United Methodists need to recover the belief that the holy communion is central in our worship and life together before some other Churches will honor our statements of theological accord."

Chapter 18

Sunday Worship in the World Parish: Observations

Karen B. Westerfield Tucker

Methodism, even from the beginning, has been committed to proclaiming the Gospel to any and all who stand in need of hearing God's word of grace. The artificial boundaries of nation, class, race—and even ecclesiastical parish—were not, according to John Wesley, to be stumbling blocks in the work of mission and ministry to all the objects of God's unbounded love. In a letter dating from early in his ministry, Wesley accounts for the territorially unlimited work which he believes to have been divinely assigned him, and uses an expression that would become a catchphrase for all later Methodist endeavors in evangelism:

God in Scripture commands me, according to my power, to instruct the ignorant, reform the wicked, confirm the virtuous. Man forbids me to do this in another's parish; that is, in effect, to do it at all, seeing I have now no parish of my own, nor probably ever shall. Whom then shall I hear? God or man? "If it be just to obey man rather than God, judge you." "A dispensation of the gospel is committed to me, and woe is me if I preach not the gospel." But where shall I preach it upon the principles you mention? Why, not in Europe, Asia, Africa, or America; not in any of the Christian parts, at least, of the habitable earth. For all these are, after a sort, divided into parishes. . . . Suffer me now to tell you *my* principles in this matter. I look upon *all the world as my parish*; thus far I mean, that in whatever part of it I am, I judge it meet, right, and my bounden duty, to declare unto all that are willing to hear the glad tidings of salvation. This is the work which I know God has called me to. And sure I am that his blessing attends it. Great encouragement have I therefore to be faithful in fulfilling the work he hath given me to do.[1]

The work of mission and evangelism begun by Wesley and the early Methodists and continued through the last two centuries into the present has, in effect, created the world parish of Wesley's vision. Methodism in the late twentieth century is found in some form in all regions of the globe—from Tonga to Togo, from Mexico to Malaysia, from Poland to Peru.[2] New congregations of the Methodist family are arising in places where the denomination had not previously existed and in locations, such as the now-independent states of the former Soviet Union, where the Church had existed but was suppressed. Hence, the previous essays, for all their geographical range, are but a sampling of the liturgies and practices of Sunday worship that are celebrated by members of the worldwide Methodist family.

What, then, can be said in general about Methodist worship in the world parish? Do these Churches have anything in common other than the name Methodist? (And, indeed, for some Churches, "Methodist" is not included in their official name, as is the case for the uniting Churches.) Is there a uniquely "Methodist" identity or ethos of worship? Has Wesley's legacy for worship continued throughout and into the latter years of the twentieth century?

At the risk of over-generalizing, it can be said that worldwide Methodist worship, at its best, is characterized by a series of polarities or tensions that may be expressed in different combinations and accommodated by various means. Methodist worship may be identified as ordered and flexible, particular and catholic, traditional and contemporary, spiritual and worldly, local and global, pragmatic and perfectionist. Each of these poles, and indeed each pair of them, is valuable. The tensions they represent may in actuality all be embraced. As the previous essays have indicated, diverse styles and forms of worship, resulting from different ways of keeping these values and tensions, may be found among the churches within a particular Methodist denomination, and even within the worship life of a single congregation.

Ordered and Flexible

Resources for ordered worship have always been available to the Methodist people. Prior to the establishment of a distinct Methodist liturgical text created by Wesley's revision of the *Book of Common Prayer*, Methodists (ideally) relied upon the liturgical orders of the Church of

England supplemented by their own informal—but structured—preaching service. In Britain, the early Methodist preaching service generally took the shape of hymn singing, prayer, and scripture reading before the sermon, and hymn singing and prayer following it.[3] After 1792 and into the late nineteenth century, a similar pattern of preaching service is hinted at in the disciplinary rubric defining the normative contents of Sunday worship for North American Methodists and the regions influenced by their missionary activity. For most Methodist denominations throughout their respective histories, orders or instructions for Sunday worship have been provided either in service books and hymnals (officially and unofficially) or within general books of polity (e.g., the *Discipline*). Materials have ranged from the printing of full liturgical texts (such as those largely based upon Wesley's orders for morning and evening prayer and for holy communion) to bare outlines where only subject headings are provided. The texts or orders, as well as the resulting practice of worship, may extend from the highly complex and formal to the very simple and informal.

Methodists have always felt it important that there be at least some liturgical norm by which to gauge their worship, and in various denominations at particular times there have been attempts made to establish uniformity in liturgical practice—but always with an eye to retaining the Methodist hallmark of extemporary prayer. The desire for homogeneity in text and practice has been particularly strong in regard to the sacraments. Both historically and at present, Conferences and congregations alike have expected ministers to follow rather carefully the authorized texts for baptism and the eucharist and for the occasional services of marriage and burial. This has not been as true for the service of the word which remains the normal Methodist practice for Sunday even with the publication by many Methodist and United denominations of combined orders for word and sacrament produced in the liturgical revisions following the Second Vatican Council. Methodists have always felt somewhat free to move with the Spirit in shaping or celebrating worship. While discipline and order in worship is sought, Methodists do not wish to be overly restricted by particular patterns, modes, or forms. For this reason, liturgical texts generally are not mandated; they are recommended rather than prescribed. Even if an officially approved text is followed, it is usually judged flexible enough to allow in certain circumstances for expansion, abbreviation, or emendation.

Particular and Catholic

When they gather for worship on the Lord's Day, Methodists assemble as part of the whole Church, a Church that shares "one Lord, one faith, one baptism." Although Methodists worship with a Methodist "flavor" or "style," they nonetheless engage in *Christian* worship. Methodists may use a "Methodist" liturgy or order, but it is a liturgy that transcends confessional boundaries and is broadly ecumenical on account of its intention (the praise and glorification of the triune God) and its component parts: the singing of canticles, psalms, and hymns; the reading of scripture; the interpretation of God's Word; the praying of prayers; the recitation of creeds; and the sharing of the Lord's Supper.

The twentieth century has been a time for Methodists to recover an ecumenical awareness and to advance ecumenical conversation and cooperation. Engagement in the ecumenical movement and attention to the renewal of worship fostered by the liturgical movement have directly impacted the way Methodists pray together. As the result of affirming with other Christians a common heritage of Scripture and of liturgical traditions from the early Church, many Methodists have reappropriated for Sunday worship practices such as these: psalmody (as is especially true for the Churches where Methodists have united with Reformed denominations); the prayers of the faithful (such as the minister and the society steward lead in dialogue with the congregation according to the *Prayer Book* of the Methodist Church in the Caribbean and the Americas); and the sharing of the peace of Christ (a recovery led by the Church of South India). Liturgical texts have been developed that integrally connect word and sacrament, and efforts have been made to reinstate the eucharist as a vital component of Christian life and practice.

The reclamation of sacramental life invited by the ecumenical and liturgical movements has been accompanied by a renewed desire for "constant communion" encouraged from the reexamination of Methodism's Wesleyan origins: frequent attendance at the Lord's Table is lauded as both a primitive Christian and a Wesleyan ideal. Methodists during the twentieth century have turned to their ecclesiastical, theological, and liturgical roots; studies or reflections in Wesleyana and Methodistica that address numerous areas of the Church's life have proliferated in the last fifty years among many Methodist groups. Some of this reflection has influenced Methodist liturgical praxis in ways additional to the matter of eucharistic frequency. The simple Methodist preaching service has been used as a model for worship in church planting and church growth. There is a renewed interest in evangelical preaching that fires the heart, and in liturgical evangelism where the attempt is made to order worship in such a way that it invites the unchurched into full participation and Christian commitment. The historic Methodist classes and bands have modern counterparts which hold persons accountable for both private devotion and public worship.[4] Whether or not the reappropriation of parts of Methodism's past can determinatively shape worship at the turn into the twenty-first century remains to be seen. Nevertheless, an important product of the rediscovery of the Methodist heritage has been an awareness of a distinct Methodist identity which stands as a part of the Church catholic.

Traditional and Contemporary

Recognizing that the Holy Spirit was an active agent in the shaping of Methodist worship of the past, Methodists trust that the Spirit is also active in the present, guiding Methodist worship into the future. Hence, Methodist worship certainly strives to be in accord with the spirit of worship of former years, to be an authentic representation of the Methodist "tradition." In some places this means retaining the orders and practices of Methodist worship of earlier days. But Methodist worship also seeks to be relevant both to a modern world and to the local culture. The charge "to serve the present age" propels Methodists to discover new ways to proclaim the Gospel and to speak the language of faith in the vernacular.

Nowhere is this tension between the traditional and the contemporary clearer than in the Church's music. Methodists have always claimed the vast collection of hymns penned by the Wesleys as part of their distinct heritage (and that in spite of the fact that John and Charles Wesley died as Anglican priests) and gladly share their poetic treasure with Christians of other communions around the world. Twentieth-century Methodists still sing the Wesley hymns, although admittedly the repertoire is diminishing in some regions. Many non-English-speaking Methodists are discovering the timelessness and richness of the Wesley hymns for the first time as selected hymns are translated into their native tongue.

But Methodists also sing a new song, using the words and tunes

of Methodist and non-Methodist poets and composers of each suc-
ceeding generation; just as the Wesleys contributed to the new music
(hymnody) of their day, later Methodists have been inspired to add
to the growing and evolving corpus of Christian song. Today Methodist songwriters and hymnwriters around the world are putting the
Good News of Jesus Christ into contemporary idioms and images
using the languages of many lands and nations, and are accompa-
nying these texts with the rhythms and harmonies of many cultures.
Three Methodist musicians have contributed to this volume and
have given examples of their work; other active songwriters include
Pablo Sosa, Jane Marshall, Tomas Boström, Fred Pratt Green, Hart-
mut Handt, and Carlton Young. Both the hymns of the past and the
new songs of the present give voice in Methodist worship to God's
mighty work of salvation and attest to the ever-blowing winds of the
Spirit:

> The Church of Christ in every age,
> Beset by change but Spirit led,
> Must claim and test its heritage
> And keep on rising from the dead.[5]

Spiritual and Worldly

Wesley's notion that worship "in spirit and in truth" necessarily
includes an ethical component has been a vital inheritance.[6] Christian worship, with the primary purpose of rendering due glory to
God, has the natural consequence of forming and informing both
personal and corporate inner religion. While seeking "the things that
are above," Methodist worship strives to emphasize care for God's
creation, particularly by love of the neighbor and stewardship of the
earth; for Methodists, works of piety and works of mercy are to go
hand in hand. Spiritual growth and moral formation occur through
the disciplined life of corporate and individual prayer and praise as
well as by use of the other instituted and prudential means of grace;[7]
how and what an individual (or a congregation) prays is expected to
be shown forth in daily living. The Methodist evangelical impetus of
yesterday and today has not sought to create disciples in word only,
but has insisted, following the example of Christ, that Christian
ministry is in word *and* deed.

Faithful witness and service in everyday life is encouraged in
Sunday worship through numerous acts of the liturgy: prayers of

confession, intercession, and supplication; collects and litanies for particular concerns; and the collection of alms and special offerings. The authorized rites for Christian initiation and the Lord's Supper found in many Methodist denominations refer by text and context to the ethical dimensions of Christian discipleship. For example, several of the post-communion prayers ask that the meal which has just been shared may be a means to equip the recipients for the work of ministry.[8] Yet in spite of the availability of texts and resources identifying the connection between the work of worship and the work of the world, it is difficult to ascertain how readily what is affirmed in worship is translated into practice.

Local and Global

Because of its ability to be both ordered and flexible, Methodist worship has generally been able to include elements from the local culture, though in some places (as has been described in the essays) it has taken decades for the imported patterns and practices of worship to be inculturated. Efforts have been made, especially during the latter half of the twentieth century, to address the matter of the cultural context (or contexts) of a given community when shaping congregational worship. Indigenous musical styles, arts, architecture, gestures, postures, and symbols have been introduced, in varying degrees, into Methodist worship in different locales. But at the same time, questions have been raised regarding the uncritical inclusion of some cultural materials; worship may need to be, on occasion, intentionally counter-cultural. These issues of contextualization or localization have not been concerns solely for Methodists outside of North America, Great Britain, and Australia; they are concerns for all Methodists who seek to proclaim the Gospel in genuine and relevant ways. As the Word became flesh and dwelt in human culture, so must the Church—and its worship—become incarnate.

But worship must also be transcultural: it should reflect the wider Christian community and not be culturally confined or limited, for the God to whom praise and glory is ascribed is transcultural and transcendent. Several of the Methodist service books and hymnals recently produced illustrate such a cross-cultural quality. Prayer texts, hymns, songs, and choruses from the numerous cultural, racial, and ethnic constituencies that make up the particular denomination, are all represented in the book as are comparable resources compiled from beyond that denomination's national or regional boundaries.[9] For example, within one worship service a Methodist congregation in the United States could pray using a litany written by a Chinese Christian and sing three different songs: a hymn by the Englishman Charles Wesley (eighteenth century), an African American spiritual (nineteenth century), and a song in Spanish with samba rhythm (twentieth century). The ideal of a world parish takes on a deeper meaning and a greater significance with such sharing of resources. This sense of the broad communion of saints (Methodist and otherwise) is further accentuated by the increasing interest on the part of some members of the Methodist family in the production of a calendar of commemorations (*sanctorale*) which includes Christian notables of all times and places; the Uniting Church in Australia has already included a calendar in its most recent service book.

Pragmatic and Perfectionist

To take just one example of Methodist pragmatism: although there were variations in policy under different Soviet régimes, Methodists in Estonia generally were permitted to gather only for corporate worship; all other assemblies were limited or forbidden, and advertisement was illegal. Undeterred, they incorporated catechesis, church school, choir rehearsal, and business meetings into the framework of a two- to three-hour Sunday worship experience. The great choral tradition of Estonian Methodism owes its origin to those hard days when choirs for all ages were formed to provide leadership for worship and to serve as a forum for otherwise restricted Christian education.[10]

Estonian Methodists, like other Methodists today and in ages past, are a pragmatic people, particularly in matters related to worship. Following in the footsteps of Wesley before them, twentieth-century Methodists are prone to judge the service of worship by its results or fruits, though often this is seen more in terms of individual benefit than in regard to the corporate edification and strengthening of the whole Body of Christ or as it concerns the faithful and faith-filled worship of God. With this concern (perhaps overconcern) for the practically expedient comes a danger that the question "will it work?" will override the questions "is it appropriate?" and "is it faithful to the Gospel?" This issue is increasingly relevant for the branches of Methodism that are strongly influenced by the church growth movement and by the language of business and marketing.

There is, however, another tendency in the Methodist tradition, namely the search for Christian perfection. This has been particularly characteristic of individual spirituality, especially in the beginnings of Methodism and in some strands of the later history, as in the Holiness movements. Wherever Methodists have striven to worship God to the best of their God-given inspiration and abilities, their corporate worship has been marked by a corresponding quality. While perfectionism may carry a negative sense of overscrupulousness (such as Wesley had to reprove in those who abstained from the Lord's Table on account of their alleged unworthiness[11]), the quest for a perfect sacrifice of praise and thanksgiving, a complete offering of ourselves, our souls and bodies, is deeply written into the biblical vocation and the liturgical sensibility of Christianity. Without transgressing into aestheticism or moralism, the holiness of beauty and the beauty of holiness should characterize Methodist worship. To sing the matchless Wesleyan hymns of entire sanctification is both to pray and to commit oneself to God's perfecting work:

> God of all-redeeming grace,
> By thy pardoning love compelled,
> Up to thee our souls we raise,
> Up to thee our bodies yield;
> Thou our sacrifice receive,
> Acceptable through thy Son,
> While to thee alone we live,
> While we die to thee alone.
>
> Meet it is, and just, and right,
> That we should be wholly thine;
> In thy only will delight,
> In that blessed service join:
> O that every work and word
> Might proclaim how good thou art!
> Holiness unto the Lord
> Still be wrote upon our heart![12]

Conclusion

Even after identifying these six pairs of distinguishing features, it still may be asked, does Methodist worship truly differ from the worship of others who are recognized also to belong to the Church catholic? In matters of style, yes; but hopefully not in substance. Employing indeed a variety of characteristic styles as displayed in this book, Methodists worship the triune God—Father, Son, and Holy Spirit—whose decisive self-revelation is recorded in the Scriptures that are read and expounded in the liturgy. Methodists give thanks for the divine work of redemption in Jesus Christ and seek the pardoning grace of God for sins repented of. Methodists profess the faith confessed in the ecumenical creeds. They rejoice in the Holy Spirit over the various gifts which God bestows for the building up of the Church in every generation. Methodists intercede for a needy world and commit themselves before God to its service. They eat the bread and drink the cup as the Lord commanded his followers to do. And they sing God's praise in hymns that fuse orthodox belief and fervent personal faith.

Perhaps the best answer to the question of Methodist liturgical distinctiveness follows the line of Wesley's identification of the characteristics of a Methodist: Methodists—and their worship—are not to be substantively different from other Christians, but only from people who worship gods other than the God who sent Jesus Christ into the world for its redemption:

> By these *marks*, by these fruits of a living faith, do we labour to *distinguish* ourselves from the unbelieving world, from all those whose minds or lives are not according to the gospel of Christ. But from real Christians, of whatsoever denomination they be, we earnestly desire not to be distinguished at all. Nor from any who sincerely follow after what they know they have not yet attained.[13]

Methodists, the people of the warmed heart, have striven in three different centuries and in congregations located worldwide to worship God faithfully in spirit and in truth. Now at the dawn of the twenty-first century, their purpose remains clear:

> Give we all with one accord
> Glory to our common Lord.[14]

Tribute

James F. White:
Historian, Liturgist, and Teacher

Grant S. Sperry-White

In the course of a scholarly career spanning five decades, James White has amassed a nearly two-hundred-item bibliography embracing a wide array of subjects in the areas of history, liturgy, theology, and architecture.[1] He has written as an historian, as a participant in the renovation of Christian worship, and as a teacher at the seminary and doctoral levels. James White has been a scholar in the trenches, a figure far removed from the ivory tower stereotype pilloried today by those with little understanding of academia. His work reflects a deep concern for the liturgical and theological currents and controversies of his day, and for their effect on people in the pulpit and pew. White continues to add to this already substantial corpus, and the opinions he expresses in his writings continue to develop and change. Because of this, the task of writing a tribute to this versatile scholar is daunting.

Of course, it would be unfair to evaluate a career in which the last word has not yet been said. At this time, perhaps the most we can do is pause to take stock of some of White's most conspicuous accomplishments of the past four decades. Therefore, what follows is based on a selected handful of White's writings which I think illustrate particularly well some significant aspects of the multidimensional work of this pioneer of liturgical studies in North America. Doubtless, others with a knowledge deeper than mine of the currents of twentieth-century liturgical revision could offer a richer tribute to the life work of James White. I am nonetheless pleased to have been given the opportunity to offer these few notes on Professor White's career. They are offered with respect by one who owes his own involvement in liturgical studies to James White's writing, teaching, and continuing friendship.

Historian

James White is first and foremost an historian of Western Christian worship since 1520. Through a variety of publications for specialists and nonspecialists alike, White's writings have revealed to audiences unaware of them the riches of the history of Protestant worship. Several of his books and articles address the fairly narrow audience comprising the interpreters of the history of Christian worship in the Reformation and post-Reformation periods. At the same time, White also has written on the broader spectrum of Christian liturgical history from the New Testament period to the twentieth century in response to the needs of churches involved in liturgical revision and experimentation. At a time when churches were jettisoning the burdens of their liturgical pasts, White's historical writing argued in numerous ways for the view that a knowledge of liturgical history was an indispensable condition for liturgical revision and renewal with integrity. Put another way, White's historical work argues that the history of Christian worship reveals (to borrow a term from linguistics) deep structures with which those who plan worship must come to terms.

White also has been the major force in North America in developing the professional study of the history of Protestant worship. Through teaching and mentoring a new generation of scholars, he has helped create an academic space for the study of liturgy by Protestant students in North America. Thus in a variety of ways his work has been about the hard task of reminding the North American Christian community of the indispensability of knowing history when one attempts to talk about what Christians do when they worship.

Writing for Specialists and Nonspecialists Alike

White's historical writing covers a spectrum of subjects from works for specialists in nineteenth-century English church history, to books addressing a broad audience including seminarians and laypeople concerned about worship. White's first book and perhaps his most specialized, *The Cambridge Movement* (1962), is a revised version of his doctoral dissertation at Duke University that was directed by the historian of medieval Christianity Ray C. Petry. Its treatment of the history of the Cambridge Camden Society and its revolutionary effect upon English church architecture and worship in the nineteenth century demonstrated the influence architecture could exert upon theology, worship, and canon law. In addition, it foreshadowed the occupation with church architecture, theology, and worship reform and revision which would dominate his later writings. This first book reflects White's academic training, first as an English major at Harvard College (where his 1953 senior honors thesis was entitled "The Livery of God: George Herbert's Poetical Materials"), then at Emmanuel College, Cambridge (as a Fulbright Scholar), Union Theological Seminary, New York, and Duke University.[2]

Important as the scholarly contribution of *The Cambridge Movement* is, the bulk of White's historical writing has been aimed at a more general audience. Some may lament the fact that the next books after *The Cambridge Movement* did not continue in the same specialist vein. Yet, it is clear that White's writing in the 1980s reflected the pastoral and strategic concerns so central to his overall work, given the needs of Protestant seminary students for reliable introductory texts in history and sacramental theology. Instead of directing his scholarly and literary gifts into more narrow channels, books such as *Introduction to Christian Worship, Sacraments as God's Self Giving, Documents of Christian Worship,* and *A Brief History of Christian Worship* have allowed White to reach a much wider audience than might otherwise have been the case, and arguably a larger readership than any other Protestant author in those fields at that time. A generation of pastors and teachers in several denominations has learned its liturgical history and vocabulary through the *Introduction*, which may someday be celebrated as the foremost liturgical primer of its era. White's work has brought the history of Christian worship to those outside the fold of what he himself has termed "the liturgical establishment." Only now, at the end of a long phase of writing in the service of liturgical reform, has his work returned to a somewhat narrower focus: the history of Roman Catholic worship after the Council of Trent.[3]

A North American School of Liturgical History

One of the most significant accomplishments of White's historical work has been its part in the creation of what might be called "a North American school of liturgical history."[4] For White, the history of Christian worship in North America has been an abiding concern, because North American developments have been neglected in the past by the European scholars who wrote much if not most of the liturgical history in the first two-thirds of the twentieth century. Says White:

> If one reads the standard histories, one would never guess the contribution to liturgical history of such cultural phenomena as Jacksonian democracy, Enlightenment rationalism, or the fusion of worship and justice among English Quakers. These are of vital interest to us today in North America in order to understand ourselves.[5]

Through his teaching and direction of doctoral dissertations (on which more will be said below), James White has created a school of historical research concerned with liturgical developments in the North American setting. The development of this school, while filling a lacuna in historical research, also reflects White's recognition of the growing importance of North America as a major liturgical center whose practices are being exported to congregations in Latin America, Africa, and Asia.[6] White himself contributed a piece to the chronicle of the history of the North American liturgical scene in chapter six of his *Christian Worship in Transition*, entitled "Inside the Liturgical Establishment." In it he outlined the development of the bureaucracies responsible for liturgical revision in the Roman Catholic Church and in the mainline Protestant denominations in North America, and assessed the effectiveness of such agencies in serving the churches.[7] He concluded his evaluation with an observation which may epitomize the motivation of much of his historical work: "Best of all, we have learned to live with change without losing our historical roots and have, in many cases, affirmed our roots more securely."[8]

Liturgist

In his response to the 1983 Berakah Award given by the North American Academy of Liturgy, White confessed, "I've never been able to make up my mind whether I was primarily a liturgical scholar or liturgical activist, whether liturgical studies or liturgical life came first for me."[9] White's career reflects this unwillingness to separate scholarship from participation in the churches' worship life. The shape of his life's work has been molded in a profound fashion by the needs of the church for scholarship and revised liturgical texts reflecting the theological and pastoral imperatives of the ecumenical liturgical movements which emerged when theologians and scholars in the 1950s began to think that there was a way to move beyond sixteenth-century divisions by appealing to early Christian faith and practice.

One who carefully peruses James White's bibliography of published books will note a curious gap between the years 1967 and 1976. The pause in White's workmanlike publication schedule was on account of his immersion in the renovation of United Methodist and ecumenical liturgical texts during those years. White was involved in lectionary revision (for the Consultation on Church Union), revision of eucharistic and baptismal texts in the United Methodist Church, and tried his hand at an experiment in liturgical typography (*We Gather Together*). Along with H. Grady Hardin, Hoyt Hickman, Paul Hoon, Don Saliers, Laurence Stookey, Lawrence Wagley, and others, White played a central role in the revision of United Methodist services during the 1970s and early 1980s. The full story of White's ecumenical liturgical work remains to be told, but his part in the creation of United Methodist services for the Lord's Supper and baptism has been chronicled by Robert B. Peiffer, one of his doctoral students at the University of Notre Dame.[10] Addressing the North American Academy of Liturgy in 1983, White downplayed his role in liturgical revision, saying, "whatever leadership roles I have had to play were largely a matter of timing. Someone had to write articles, make decisions, and give speeches because most of you, who could have done these things as well or better, simply had not yet appeared."[11] Yet, it seems that White's particular gifts, training, and experience served him well for the tasks of liturgical revision and the work of making the wider Church more aware of the practical, theological, and historical dimensions of that revision.

Revision of the United Methodist Eucharistic Rite

In his response on receipt of the Berakah Award, White remarked that revision of the United Methodist eucharistic rite was the most important work in which he had participated.[12] As is well known, that revision marked a radical move away from the Anglican-Methodist tradition of the *Book of Common Prayer* eucharistic rite to a liturgy informed by the description of the eucharist in Justin Martyr's *First Apology* and in the so-called *Apostolic Tradition*, and drawing upon early Christian theologies of the eucharist. The service underwent revision eight times before its publication in 1972 as *The Sacrament of the Lord's Supper: An Alternate Text*. The process of revising White's text by committee was apparently at times difficult, and misunderstanding between White and the Committee on Alternate Rituals sometimes ensued.[13] Yet White's experience as the first person chosen to be primary author of an experimental United Methodist liturgical text proved invaluable for guiding the process of writing some fifteen subsequent texts and commentaries in the Supplemental Worship Resources series.

Within four years of its publication, nearly one million copies of *Lord's Supper* had been sold, and a new textual tradition of United Methodist euchology had been established. The precise significance of that new tradition will continue to be debated, but at the very least it is clear that White reintroduced into Protestant eucharistic prayer a sacrificial dimension not seen since Luther (inspired by the Wesleys' *Hymns on the Lord's Supper*). In addition, the 1972 and subsequent texts included the recitation of salvation history, epiklesis, and eschatological dimension so often found in early Christian eucharistic prayers but also almost totally lacking in Protestant traditions. Thus the text moved the celebration of the eucharist away from an exclusive theological focus on the death of Christ by crafting a wider euchological framework for proclaiming the content and meaning of Christ's saving work. The invocation of the Spirit signaled a return to a Wesleyan emphasis on the work of the Spirit in the Lord's Supper, and the eschatological note in the prayer also drew on a dominant theme in Wesleyan eucharistic spirituality. Finally, the 1972 text highlighted the character of the Lord's Supper as a joyful feast celebrating the resurrection, not the mournful remembrance of the death of Jesus which the Lord's Supper had become for many American Methodists.

Popularizing Liturgical Revision

White's liturgical work was not limited to the production of official texts. Much of his publication from the late 1960s was devoted to the discussion of liturgical revision and renewal in journals such as *The Christian Century* and *Circuit Rider* (a journal for United Methodist clergy). Writing articles entitled "Our Apostasy in Worship,"[14] "Methodist Kitsch,"[15] "Where the Reformation Was Wrong on Worship,"[16] and "A Protestant Worship Manifesto,"[17] White brought issues of liturgical renewal and reform to North American audiences larger than the members of the North American Academy of Liturgy.

Always ready with the potent one-liner, White's articles raised awareness of urgent theological and pastoral issues in contemporary liturgical practice. For example, in "Our Apostasy in Worship" White took aim at the common Methodist practice of not reading from the Old Testament in worship, a custom rooted in Rubric VI of the 1905 order of worship in the Methodist Episcopal Church and the Methodist Episcopal Church, South: "What Marcion tried to do in the second century, Methodists accomplished in the twentieth. The effect of Rubric VI was virtually to eliminate 38 books of God's Word from Methodist worship."[18] In "Methodist Kitsch," White began his list of such items with the warning, "At worst, I could find something to offend each of you."[19] In decrying the use of "fish food pellets or plastic wafers" at the eucharist, White suggested that "it may require even more faith to believe these artificial concoctions are really bread and wine than to believe that they represent Christ's body and blood to us."[20]

In these articles and many others, White may have appeared as a participant in a kind of liturgical guerrilla warfare, in which the sometimes striking, sometimes shocking *bon mot* served as a verbal Molotov cocktail. Another way of approaching White's popular writing is to view it in the context of the debates of the 1970s and 1980s around liturgical revision and its necessity. White used his position as a known scholar and teacher to further the aims of liturgical revision, part of which involved challenging the current practices of the churches.

Sacramental Theology

White's work in sacramental theology arose, as so much of his work has, from the needs of denominations for which contemporary systematic theological reflection on the sacraments was almost non-existent. His book *Sacraments as God's Self Giving* (1983) was born out of a cognizance of the success of liturgical revision and renewal in the 1970s, and of the need for reflection in the service of reform:

In this book, I encourage Protestants to see and listen to what goes on in the rites and ceremonial of their sacraments. . . . We must be willing to go beyond the Reformation of the sixteenth century. No longer can we rest content with the resolution of practices and understandings in that time, any more than Roman Catholics now

339

can be satisfied with that of the Council of Trent. A true catholicism cannot be limited to any century or culture. Our concern here is with reformation in the present, not reformation as past.[21]

Notable in this description of the rationale for writing a sacramental theology is White's emphasis on the ecumenical context. As United Methodist scholars and theologians in the 1970s were seeking to find common theological ground with Roman Catholics, Lutherans, Episcopalians, and others in a common heritage antedating the sixteenth century, White sought to do the same for theology of the sacraments. True to his insistence on providing an ecumenical framework for liturgical revision and theology, *Sacraments* included a response from the noted Roman Catholic sacramental theologian and historian Edward Kilmartin, S.J., White's colleague at Notre Dame.

Also noteworthy here is White's presentation to Protestants of the notion that liturgy can serve as a source for theological reflection. In other words, *Sacraments* moves Protestant theological discourse about sacraments into a more complex understanding of the relationship between the *lex orandi* and the *lex credendi*.

Liturgy and Justice

One of White's central preoccupations has been with the relationship between liturgy and justice. For White, sacramentality implies doing justice: "The Church's contribution to social justice derives largely from its power of making God's love visible in the world through the sacraments."[22] In chapter five of *Sacraments*, White notes that God's self-giving in the sacraments empowers the self-giving of Christians for others in acts of justice. He quotes the post-communion prayer of the 1972 eucharistic rite (which he authored) in support of his view:

You have given yourself to us, Lord.
Now we give ourselves to others.
Your love has made us a new people.
As a people of love we will serve you with joy.
Your glory has filled our hearts;
help us to glorify you in all things.
Amen.

At the same time, White's view of the power of the sacraments is not naive, nor content to rest in an affirmation of the complete appropriateness of liturgy as a source for theology. For White, the

Church as *semper reformanda* retains an important place in sacramental theology:

> But, even within the Church, there is an ambiguity in the sacraments, a constant danger that they may be misused as vehicles of oppression of groups who are without power to prevent such abuse. Constant scrutiny is necessary even within the Church.[23]

Questioning Reform: Recent Reflections

After so many years in the forefront of liturgical renewal, White has begun to step back from this dimension of his work and to question some of what he has done in the name of worship reform. White confessed in 1983, "In the whole process of liturgical revision, one question keeps coming back to haunt me: 'What right do we have to change the way people pray?' It is the only liturgical question that ever keeps me awake at night."[24] In answering his own question, White outlined four reasons for revision: (1) to make prayer more accurately reflect "the true nature of God and God's relation to humans"; (2) to make prayer reflect and teach justice; (3) to make prayer accessible to all; and (4) to shape prayer so that it "relates to the prayer of all Christians."[25] On a more Machiavellian note, White confided in the same address, "I was learning that a person who comes to a committee meeting with mind made up or agenda prepared has a good chance of prevailing. Planning is power."[26]

The descendant of White's work now appears in the 1989 *United Methodist Hymnal* and in the 1992 *Book of Worship*. The full legacy of White's work of liturgical revision will not be known for some decades to come, after which time others may be able better to judge the extent to which the services of the *Hymnal* and *Book of Worship* contributed to the shaping of the piety not only of liturgical scholars, but also of United Methodists in the pews. In White's view, the revisions to which he contributed were not the final word in North American Christian worship:

> Much that was done in the 1970s I think is irrevocable. Things that will endure include reading from both testaments of the Bible, the use of contemporary language, the concentration on eucharist as action, and the understanding of the eucharistic prayer as thankful proclamation of the church's faith. In time, our words will be refined and be exchanged for other words that function more adequately.[27]

In a recent article, White speaks of the tension between under-

341

standing liturgical studies as a normative discipline and understanding them as a descriptive discipline:

> The greatest conversion experience in my own teaching has come about in moving from a normative approach to a descriptive approach. After years of trying to reform United Methodist worship, I came to feel maybe I should have spent those two decades listening to United Methodists.[28]

That shift in perspective is reflected in his 1989 book, *Protestant Worship: Traditions in Transition,* in which the final chapter concludes with an acceptance of the diversity of Protestant worship traditions as a sign of God's gracious working with humanity.[29]

White's most recent ruminations, appearing at the conclusion of a significant period of liturgical revision, raise the question for scholars about the role of revision as the engine driving liturgical studies. To put the question another way, once the work of liturgical text revision is done, will liturgical studies wither away?

Teacher

Those who have had the privilege of being taught by James White know him as a generous teacher who dispenses rigorously organized lectures laced with a bone-dry wit. His passion for the sources, and his insistence upon the importance of bibliography, have modeled liturgical scholarship for dozens of doctoral students. At Perkins School of Theology White trained a generation of pastors who now serve across the United States, and he has taught for brief periods at several other seminaries in North America.

James White belongs to the first generation of full-time professors of worship in Protestant seminaries. His forty-year teaching career (which took him from the Methodist Theological School in Ohio to Perkins School of Theology to the University of Notre Dame) has been spent in large part preparing the way for the next generation of teachers of worship in seminaries and graduate programs in North America. He has monitored the teaching of liturgy in North American seminaries, and continues to advocate for the importance of the field in seminary curricula.

Doctoral Liturgical Studies

White has been personally responsible for the training of a generation of liturgical scholars, many of whom now teach in North

American seminaries, colleges, and universities. He has directed or co-directed eighteen doctoral dissertations at the University of Notre Dame, and also has taken a part in occasional teaching in liturgics in the liturgical studies program at Drew University. The breadth of subject matter and variety of traditions represented by his students signal the continuing influence of his perspectives in seminary education in liturgical studies for the forseeable future.

Teaching Worship in the Seminary

As important as his training of scholars in the field of liturgical studies is White's contribution to the formation of a significant portion of a generation of North American pastors. Through his teaching at Perkins and through his books, White has shaped and continues to shape the ways in which those responsible for pastoral leadership think about worship. A concern for linking the theoretical and practical aspects of worship has been a central element of his teaching:

> Much of the uniqueness of teaching liturgy is that theory and practice are more closely linked here than anywhere else in the seminary curriculum. That is one thing that makes it a joy to teach. One touches both the *Apostolic Tradition* and next Sunday.[30]

Concluding Prospect: A Continuing Dialogue

James White's career has coincided with the most significant period of liturgical reform in Western Christianity since the sixteenth century. What lies ahead for the history of worship in Western Christianity is, of course, impossible to foresee with the clarity we might wish. The good news is that James White's career continues into this post-reform era, and that we can look forward to more light from this scholar, teacher, and liturgist who has influenced so many in the North American Christian scene and beyond. It is appropriate, therefore, at the end of this tribute to suggest some directions in which James White's work calls the next generation of scholars, teachers, and pastors to look.

The Future of Liturgical Studies in North America

The North American liturgical scene continues to develop in the last decades of the twentieth century. Today one hears of the Liturgy of St. John Chrysostom celebrated with gospel hymns sung alongside the Cherubikon. Churches from countries once served by western missions have begun to send missionaries to the United States, bringing with them their own liturgical patterns and practices. The seekers' service has had an impact not only on churches not served by the liturgical establishment, but also on the worship of mainline denominations. The shortage of Roman Catholic priests in North America has not been reversed, and parishes are awakening to its effects on how Mass is celebrated. Feminist and womanist theologies offer not only critique of traditional Christian worship structures, but propose their own alternatives. African American Christians strive to recover pieces of their African heritages which speak to the content and conduct of worship. Some African American churches have made rites of passage central to their ministry to youth. Today's neo-orthodox and confessional movements contain liturgical implications which are beginning to unfold. This is a period of historical development of worship which cries out to be chronicled.

In the midst of this rich diversity, James White has created a space for its study and interpretation. By building a North American school of liturgical studies, White has made possible the continuing legitimacy of the study of North American Christian worship. This accomplishment is particularly significant in the face of the end of the era of liturgical revision which has driven so much liturgical scholarship in the past thirty years. White's more recent insistence on the variety of Protestant worship traditions, I think, points to a significant ideological shift in North American liturgical studies. In an age in which diversity and the integrity of cultural traditions are fundamental societal concerns, White calls future scholars to contribute to the vital work of cultural and theological interpretation through study and analysis of liturgical practices. In addition, White's emphasis, shared by other scholars, on the nontextual aspects of worship (e.g., architecture, art, music) also point to future directions for liturgical studies in a North American context.

The Continuing Work of Revision and Renewal

It would be wrong, however, to ignore or downplay the continuing significance of White's work in liturgical revision and renewal. White's teaching, writing, and scholarship initiated a long period in which Christians in North America and around the world have begun to see their worship in a broader liturgical and theological context than ever before. Far from the end of the process of renewal, the publication of the last revised service books of the mainline North American Churches marks only the beginning of a more complex process of continuing development and congregational ownership. The structures are in place; it remains for the churches to make them come alive with texts and practices reflecting their individual cultural and theological identity as well as the wider *oikoumene*. As much as in the period of revision itself, White's emphases on ecumenism and solid liturgical theology have a great deal to say for the churches in the coming decades.

One of White's greatest gifts to Protestant liturgical studies is his uncompromisingly ecumenical stance. His teaching career, work in liturgical reform, and scholarship have all taken place in the context of the wider *oikoumene*. His *Introduction* is read by Protestant, Roman Catholic, and Orthodox students, and as the first Protestant professor of liturgy at the University of Notre Dame, he has trained a generation of liturgical scholars from a wide variety of communions. In this era when it is fashionable to mourn the passing of the ecumenical movement, James White's writings exhort the Churches not to lose sight of the importance of listening to as many of the voices of the churches as possible when teaching worship and revising liturgical texts. If anything, White shows us that we have not taken the worldwide churches seriously enough in our scholarship and revision, much less in our thoughts about the content and leadership of the Sunday service.

Sometimes the results of White's ecumenical perspective are unexpected. For example, the "convergence movement" emerging in several denominations traditionally aligned with holiness and charismatic traditions signals the fruit of the ecumenical liturgical dialogue which White and others have advocated for thirty years. The blending of charismatic and holiness liturgical practices with a rich sacramental and liturgical life drawing upon the resources of the so-called classical traditions certainly signals a trend unforeseen twenty years ago. Yet White contributed significantly to it. His writings on the history of Christian worship made the riches of Christian liturgical traditions available to Protestants.

As important as the continuing ecumenical context is White's call to the churches to evaluate their texts and practices from a theological perspective. Again, given the wide variety of North American liturgical traditions, there is enormous potential here for the emergence of interesting, important reflection on sacraments and worship. In particular, White's consistent linking of justice and worship will continue to speak to the churches. His writing in this area will continue to be significant for anyone interested in creating communities who in their worship are faithful to the whole Gospel.

Conclusion

As historian, liturgist, and teacher James White has given a wide slice of North American Christianity the tools to continue the liturgical dialogue he helped begin thirty years ago. Ours is obviously a different time from the optimistic days of the 1960s and 1970s when almost anything ecumenical and liturgical seemed feasible. Yet because of James White's life work, it is possible for a new generation to believe that the dialogue can continue. Thus the ecumenical vision embodied in his writing and teaching will continue to bear fruit in the future, sometimes in startling ways. That future vitality of this vision will be the most appropriate tribute of all to the work of James F. White.

James F. White:
Complete Bibliography

Books

Notes on the Design of Methodist Student Centers. Nashville: Methodist Student Movement, 1961. 30 pp.

The Cambridge Movement: The Ecclesiologists and the Gothic Revival. Cambridge: Cambridge University Press, 1962, 1979. 272 pp.

Protestant Worship and Church Architecture: Theological and Historical Considerations. New York: Oxford University Press, 1964. 224 pp.

Architecture at SMU: 50 Years and 50 Buildings. Dallas: Southern Methodist University Press, 1966. 32 pp.

The Worldliness of Worship. New York: Oxford University Press, 1967. 181 pp.

New Forms of Worship. Nashville: Abingdon Press, 1971. 222 pp.

Christian Worship in Transition. Nashville: Abingdon Press, 1976. 160 pp. (Korean edition, Seoul, 1994).

Introduction to Christian Worship. Nashville: Abingdon Press, 1980. 288 pp.

Sacraments as God's Self Giving: Sacramental Practice and Faith. Nashville: Abingdon Press, 1983. 158 pp.

Protestant Worship: Traditions in Transition. Louisville: Westminster/John Knox Press, 1989. 251 pp.

Introduction to Christian Worship. Revised edition. Nashville: Abingdon Press, 1990. 317 pp. (Korean edition: *Ki dol kyo yeh bae hoek ip moon.* Seoul: Emmaus Publishing House, 1992. 333 pp.)

Documents of Christian Worship: Descriptive and Interpretive Sources. Louisville: Westminster/John Knox Press, 1992; Edinburgh: T & T Clark, 1993. 257 pp.

A Brief History of Christian Worship. Nashville: Abingdon Press, 1993. 192 pp.

Roman Catholic Worship: Trent to Today. Mahwah, NJ: Paulist Press, 1995. 174 pp.

Edited Works

Seasons of the Gospel: Resources for the Christian Year. Nashville: Abingdon Press, 1979. 144 pp.

We Gather Together: Services of Public Worship. Nashville: Abingdon Press, 1980. 34 pp.

John Wesley's Sunday Service of the Methodists in North America. Nashville: United Methodist Publishing House, 1984. 107 pp.

John Wesley's Prayer Book: The Sunday Service of the Methodists in North America. Cleveland: OSL Publications, 1991. 171 pp.

Co-Authored Works

(With H. Grady Hardin and Joseph D. Quillian). *The Celebration of the Gospel: A Study in Christian Worship*. Nashville: Abingdon Press, 1964, 1970, 1978; London: Epworth Press, 1965. 190 pp.

(With Hoyt L. Hickman, Don E. Saliers, and Laurence Hull Stookey). *Handbook of the Christian Year*. Nashville: Abingdon Press, 1986. 304 pp.

(With Susan J. White). *Church Architecture: Building and Renovating for Christian Worship*. Nashville: Abingdon Press, 1988. 176 pp.

(With Hoyt L. Hickman, Don E. Saliers, and Laurence Hull Stookey). *The New Handbook of the Christian Year*. Nashville: Abingdon Press, 1992. 304 pp.

Component Works in Larger Works

"Theology and Architecture in America: A Study of Three Leaders." In *A Miscellany of American Christianity: Essays in Honor of H. Shelton Smith*, ed. Stuart C. Henry, 362–90. Durham: Duke University Press, 1963.

"Motivations for Worship in Protestantism." In *Ecumenism, the Spirit and Worship*, ed. Leonard J. Swidler, 237–58. Pittsburgh: Duquesne University Press, 1967.

"The Role of Tradition in Modern Church Architecture." In *For Church Builders: A Recall to Basics*, ed. William S. Clark, 20–29. Valley Forge: Agora Books, 1969.

"The Order of Worship: The Ordinary Parts" and "The Order of Worship: The Proper Parts." In *Companion to the Book of Worship*, eds. William F. Dunkle, Jr., and Joseph D. Quillian, Jr., 11–43. Nashville: Abingdon Press, 1970.

"Baptism: Methodist" (with Raymond George); "Liturgies: Methodist"; "Matrimony: Methodist"; and "Methodist Worship: USA." In *A Dictionary of Liturgy and Worship*, ed. J. G. Davies. London: SCM Press, 1972; New York: Macmillan, 1972; *Westminster Dictionary of Worship*. Philadelphia: Westminster Press, 1979.

"Worship in Our Changing Culture." In *Worship: Good News in Action*, ed. Mandus A. Egge, 41–56. Minneapolis: Augsburg Publishing House, 1973.

"Durandus and the Interpretation of Christian Worship." In *Contemporary Reflections on the Medieval Christian Tradition: Essays in Honor of Ray C. Petry*, ed. George H. Shriver, 41–52. Durham: Duke University Press, 1974.

"Architecture: Development in the United States." In *Encyclopedia of World Methodism*, vol. 1, ed. Nolan B. Harmon, 128–29. Nashville: United Methodist Publishing House, 1974.

"Toward a Liturgical Strategy: Problems and Resources." In *Worship Points the Way: A Celebration of the Life and Work of Massey H. Shepherd, Jr.*, ed. Malcolm C. Burson, 142–50. New York: Seabury Press, 1981.

"The Great Thanksgiving: Its Essential Elements"; "Great Thanksgiving 1: From *We Gather Together*"; "Great Thanksgiving 5: A Lyrical Prayer." In *At the Lord's Table*, 11–13, 20–21. Nashville: Abingdon Press, 1981.

"Words That Hurt: Language and Justice." In *The Word and words: Beyond Gender in Theological and Liturgical Language*, ed. William D. Watley, 44–49. Princeton: Consultation on Church Union, 1983.

"Creativity: The Free Church Tradition." In *Liturgy: A Creative Tradition. Concilium*, vol. 162, eds. Mary Collins and David Power, 47–52. Edinburgh: T & T Clark; New York: Seabury Press, 1983.

"Services to Commemorate the Bicentennial of American Methodism 1784–1984." In *Methodist Bicentennial 1784–1984 Planbook: Resources and Ideas for Celebrating the Bicentennial*, ed. Boyd E. Wagner, 14–26. Nashville: United Methodist Publishing House, 1983.

"Baptism: Methodist" (with Raymond George); "Liturgies: Methodist"; "Marriage: Methodist"; and "Methodist Worship: USA." In *A New Dictionary of Liturgy and Worship*, ed. J. G. Davies. London: SCM Press, 1986; *The New Westminster Dictionary of Liturgy and Worship*. Philadelphia: Westminster Press, 1986.

"The Development of the 1972 United Methodist Eucharistic Rite" and "John Wesley's *Sunday Service* and Methodist Spirituality." In *Wesleyan Theology Today: A Bicentennial Theological Consultation*, ed. Theodore Runyon, 330–34; 403–5. Nashville: United Methodist Publishing House, 1985.

"The Eucharist and Justice." In *Eucharist and Ecumenical Life*, ed. Ronald P. Byars, 42–51. Lexington: Kentucky Council of Churches, 1985.

"United Methodist Eucharistic Prayers: 1965–1985." In *New Eucharistic Prayers: Development and Analysis*, ed. Frank C. Senn, 80–95. New York: Paulist Press, 1987.

"Liturgy and Worship." In *Encyclopedia of the American Religious Experience*, vol. 3, eds. Charles H. Lippy and Peter W. Williams, 1269–83. New York: Charles Scribner's Sons, 1988.

"Public Worship in Protestantism." In *Altered Landscapes: Christianity in America, 1935–1985*, eds. David W. Lotz, Donald W. Shriver, Jr., and John F. Wilson, 106–24. Grand Rapids: Eerdmans, 1989.

"Gottesdienst: Freikirchliche Tradition." In *Evangelisches Kirchenlexikon*, bd. 2, eds. Erwin Fahlbusch et al., 274–75. Göttingen: Vandenhoeck & Ruprecht, 1989.

"Architecture, Church." In *Encyclopedia of Southern Culture*, eds. Charles Reagan Wilson and William Ferris, 1276–77. Chapel Hill: University of North Carolina Press, 1989.

"Liturgical Books"; "Liturgical Commissions"; and "Liturgies in America." In *Dictionary of Christianity in America*, ed. Daniel G. Reid. Downers Grove, IL: InterVarsity Press, 1990.

"Traditions, Liturgical, in the West: Post-Reformation." In *The New Dictionary of Sacramental Worship*, ed. Peter E. Fink, 1272–82. Collegeville: Liturgical Press, 1990. (Reprinted in *Twenty Centuries of Christian Worship*, ed. Robert E. Webber, 72–87. Nashville: Star Song, 1994.)

"Sacraments, Ordinances and Rites, Terminology and Concepts." In *Dictionary of Pastoral Care and Counseling*, ed. Rodney J. Hunter, 1100. Nashville: Abingdon Press, 1990.

"Liturgical Movement." In *A New Handbook of Christian Theology*, eds. Donald W. Musser and Joseph L. Price, 296–98. Nashville: Abingdon Press, 1992.

"Methodist Worship." *Perspectives on American Methodism; Interpretive Essays*, eds. Russell E. Richey, Kenneth E. Rowe, and Jean Miller Schmidt, 460–79. Nashville: Abingdon Press, 1993.

"Sacred Actions Among the Churches: United Methodist Church." In *The Sacred Actions of Christian Worship*, ed. Robert E. Webber, 52–53. Nashville: Star Song, 1994.

"Gottesdienst im freikirchlichen und charimatischen Kontext." In *Handbuch der Liturgik*, eds. Hans-Christoph Schmidt-Lauber and Karl-Heinrich Bieritz, 186–94. Leipzig: Evangelische Verlagsanstalt, 1995; Göttingen: Vandenhoeck & Ruprecht, 1995.

"Methodist Churches" and "Methodist-Roman Catholic Dialogue." In *Encyclopedia of Catholicism*, ed. Richard P. McBrien, 858–59. San Francisco: HarperCollins, 1995.

"Thirty Years of the Doctoral Program in Liturgical Studies at the University of Notre Dame, 1965–1995." In *Rule of Prayer, Rule of Faith: Essays in Honor of Aidan Kavanagh, O.S.B.*, eds. John F. Baldovin, S.J., and Nathan Mitchell. Collegeville: Liturgical Press, 1996 (forthcoming).

Periodical Articles

"Christianity and the Arts: Survey of Recent Theological Literature." *Union Seminary Quarterly Review* 10 (May 1955) 47–49.

"Early Methodist Liturgical Architecture." *motive* 17 (Mar. 1958) 12–13, 19–20.

"Liturgical Architecture in Protestant Churches." *Christianity and Crisis* 18 (July 7, 1958) 98–100.

"No People and God's People." *motive* 19 (Dec. 1958) 3–8.

"Church Architecture: Some Standards." *Christian Century* 76 (Feb. 18, 1959) 196–97.

"The God Whom We Worship." *motive* 20 (Feb. 1960) 29–32.

"Church Choir: Friend or Foe?" *Christian Century* 77 (Mar. 23, 1960) 354–56.

"America's Churches." *American Legion Magazine* 70 (Feb. 1961) 14–15, 45–46.

"Some Contemporary Experiments in Liturgical Architecture." *Religion in Life* 30 (Spring 1961) 285–95.

"Next Steps in Protestant Liturgical Architecture." *Union Seminary Quarterly Review* 16 (May 1961) 365–74.

"A Good Word for William Dowsing." *Theology Today* 18 (July 1961) 180–84.

"Personal and Common." *Christian Advocate* 6 (July 1962) 6–7.

"Religion and Art: A Creative Dialogue." *Christian Advocate* 7 (Jan. 31, 1963) 9–10.

"Church Architecture and Worship." *Adult Student* 22 (July 1963) 15–17.

"Heresies of Modern Architecture." *Southwest Review* 49 (Winter 1964) 64–72.

"What Is the Liturgical Movement?" *Perkins Journal* 17 (Winter–Spring 1964) 20–25.

"Liturgy Is Evangelism." *Christian Advocate* 8 (Dec. 31, 1964) 9–10.

"The Role of Tradition in Modern Church Building." *Your Church* 11 (Mar.–Apr. 1965) 20–21, 36–40.

"Current Trends in American Church Building." *Studia Liturgica* 4 (Summer 1965) 94–113.

"The History of Christian Liturgy." *Adult Teacher* 19 (Aug. 1966) 29–46.

"A Church as a Part of the City." In *Worship in the City of Man*, 190–93. 27th North American Liturgical Week. Washington, D C: The Liturgical Conference, 1966.

"Church Architecture and Church Renewal." *Christian Advocate* 10 (Dec. 29, 1966) 7–9.

"Guidelines for Church Architecture." *Your Church* 13 (July–Aug. 1967) 20–27. (Reprinted in *Designs for Worship '68*, 3–6. Valley Forge: Agora Books, 1968.)

"The New American Methodist Communion Order." *Worship* 41 (Nov. 1967) 552–60.

"Historical Considerations for Church Builders." *Your Church* 14 (Jan.–Feb. 1968) 24–27, 58–63.

"'Lord Teach Us to Pray.'" *Twelve/Fifteen* 17 (Jan. 28, 1968) 5.

"Worship in an Age of Immediacy." *Christian Century* 85 (Feb. 21, 1968) 227–30. (Reprinted in *Dimensions in Christian Education* 19 [Mar. 1969] 22–26.)

"Worship: The Use of Symbols." *Junior Hi Times* 7 (Mar.–May 1968) 24–31.

"Training in Spirituality at Perkins." *Perkins Journal* 22 (Winter 1969) 5–9.

"The *Rationale Divinorum Officiorum* of William Durandus." *Perkins Journal* 22 (Spring 1969) 50–52.

"Changing Protestant Worship: Two Revolutions in Communications." *Living Worship* 5 (June 1969) 1–4.

"Basic Bibliography on Worship." *Work/Worship* 18 (Advent 1969) 14–23.

"Lay Participation as Leaders of Corporate Worship: A Methodist Perspective." In *The Layman as a Leader of Worship*, 69–76. Washington, DC: U.S. Navy, 1970 (Navpers 15155).

"Resources for the Study of Christian Worship in Bridwell Library." *Perkins Journal* 25 (Spring 1972) 15–18.

"Characteristics of Effective Christian Worship." *Studia Liturgica* 8 (1971/72) 195–206.

"The Sacrament of the Lord's Supper: The New Alternate Rite." *Christian Advocate* 16 (Sept. 14, 1972) 13–14.

"Should Worship be a Family Affair?" *Together* 16 (Nov. 1972) 15–16.

"Liturgy Starts With People." *Faith & Form* 5 (Fall 1972) 22–23.

"Worship and Culture: Mirror or Beacon?" *Theological Studies* 35 (1974) 288–301.

"Traditions of Protestant Worship." *Worship* 49 (May 1975) 272–82. (Reprinted in *Today's Parish* 7 [Nov.–Dec. 1975] 36–41.)

"Church Architecture of the 1970's." *Liturgy* 20 (May 1975) 151–57. (Reprinted in *Faith and Form* 9 [Spring 1976] 8–11, 25–27; and in *Cutting Edge* 5 [July 1976] 1–6.)

"Vermont and Texas: Two Different States of Mind." *The Texas Observer* 67 (Oct. 31, 1975) 21–23.

"'Worship' Outward and Visible." *Worship* 50 (Nov. 1976) 526–28.

"'New' Garb for Clergy." *Circuit Rider* 1 (Feb. 1977) 14–15.

"Keeping Time." *Homily Service* 10 (Apr. 1977) Supplement, 1–4.

"How to Eat." *Liturgy* 22 (May 1977) 35–36.

"Using Music in the New Communion Service." *Music Ministry* 9 (June 1977) 7, 26–27, 29.

"Sacraments: God's Way of Giving." *Circuit Rider* 1 (June 1977) 9–11.

"Our Apostasy in Worship." *Christian Century* 94 (Sept. 28, 1977) 842–45.

"Landmark Churches." *Vermonter: Burlington Free Press* (Oct. 2, 1977) 4–8.

"Liturgy and the Language of Space." *Worship* 52 (Jan. 1978) 57–66. (Reprinted in *Cutting Edge* 7 [May–June 1978] 1–4; in *The Roman Pontifical: Dedication of a Church and an Altar: Study Edition*, 107–16. Ottawa: Canadian Conference of Catholic Bishops, 1978; and in *Symbol: The Language of Liturgy*, 59–63. Washington: FDLC, 1982.)

"Methodist Kitsch." *Circuit Rider* 2 (May 1978) 10–11.

"Liturgy, Theology of the Laity." *Duke Divinity Bulletin* 43 (Winter 1978) 33–43. (Reprinted in *Nuts and Bolts of Worship* 11 [June 1979] 1–6.)

"Outside the Liturgical Establishment Or Who Needs Us?" *Worship* 52 (July 1978) 291–99.

"Church Architecture As If People Mattered." *Christian Ministry* 9 (Nov. 1978) 23–25.

"The Words of Worship: Beyond Liturgical Sexism." *Christian Century* 95 (Dec. 13, 1978) 1202–6. (Reprinted in *Women's Concerns Newsletter* 15 [Sept. 1981] 10–13.)

"Writing the History of English Worship: The Achievement of Horton Davies." *Church History* 47 (Dec. 1978) 434–40.

"Disappearing Building Types." *Country Journal* 6 (Jan. 1979) 70–77.

"Preaching from the New Lectionary." *Circuit Rider* 3 (Jan. 1979) 6–7.

"A Liturgical Strategy: Four Lines of Attack." *Christian Century* 96 (Mar. 7, 1979) 242–46.

"The New *Lutheran Book of Worship*." *Liturgy* 24 (May–June 1979) 37–40.

"Presidential Report." *Worship* 53 (July 1979) 379–80.

"Dramatic Worship." *Christian Ministry* 10 (Sept. 1979) 37.

"Towards a Discipline of the Sacraments." *Circuit Rider* 4 (Jan. 1980) 3–7. (Reprinted in *The Best of Circuit Rider's First Decade*, 31–44. Nashville: Abingdon Press, 1987.)

"Teaching the Arts in Seminaries." *Christian Century* 97 (Feb. 6–13, 1980) 133–35.

"The Actions of Worship: Beyond Liturgical Sexism." *Christian Century* 97 (May 7, 1980) 521–23.

"Justice and the Work of Liturgical Renewal." *Christianity & Crisis* 40 (June 9, 1980) 173–77.

"An Evolving Sacramental Theology." *Christian Century* 97 (July 16–23, 1980) 732–33.

"Signs of Vermont." *Sunday Rutland Herald and Sunday Times Argus* 5 (Sept. 14, 1980) p. 3, sect. 4.

"Making Our Worship More Biblical." *Perkins Journal* 34 (Fall 1980) 38–40. (Reprinted in *Worship Alive*, 1982.)

"Infant Baptism: Should We Continue the Practice? Yes: Why Not?" *Circuit Rider* 5 (Jan. 1981) 8–9. (Reprinted in *The Best of Circuit Rider's First Decade*, 120–24. Nashville: Abingdon Press, 1987.)

"Liturgical Scholars: A New Outspokenness." *Christian Century* 98 (Feb. 4–11, 1981) 103–7.

"A Service Book for United Methodists." *Circuit Rider* 5 (Mar. 1981) 15–17.

"The Teaching of Worship in Seminaries in Canada and the United States." *Worship* 55 (July 1981) 304–18.

"Coming Together in Christ's Name." *Liturgy* 1 (Fall 1981) 7–10.

"The Teaching of Preaching, Worship, and Music." *Homiletic* 6 (Dec. 1981) 1–5.

"A Protestant Worship Manifesto." *Christian Century* 99 (Jan. 20, 1982) 82–86. (Reprinted in *Twenty Centuries of Christian Worship*, ed. Robert E. Webber, 332–37. Nashville: Star Song, 1994.)

"Function and Form of the Eucharistic Prayer." *Reformed Liturgy and Music* 16 (Winter 1982) 18–21.

"Does Our Liturgy Reflect Our Faith?" *Circuit Rider* 6 (Mar. 1982) 3–5.

"Where the Reformation was Wrong on Worship." *Christian Century* 99 (Oct. 27, 1982) 1074–77.

"Recent Developments in Worship." *Review and Expositor* 80 (Winter 1983) 19–31. (Reprinted in *Minister's Personal Library Journal* 4 [Summer 1983] 1–8.)

"New Seasons for Worship." *Circuit Rider* 7 (Feb. 1983) 4–6.

"The Constitution on the Liturgy as Agenda for Protestant Liturgical Reform." *Modern Liturgy* 10 (May 1983) 8–10.

"Making Changes in United Methodist Euchology." *Worship* 57 (July 1983) 333–44.

"Concerning the Announcements." *Circuit Rider* 7 (July–Aug. 1983) 3–4.

"Shattering Myths About Worship." *Circuit Rider* 7 (May 1984) 4–5.

"The Development of the 1972 United Methodist Eucharistic Rite." *Doxology* 1 (1984) 14–22.

"Liturgical Reformation: Sixteenth Century and Twentieth." *Reformed Liturgy and Music* 18 (Spring 1984) 78–82.

"Worship as a Source of Injustice." *Reformed Liturgy and Music* 19 (Spring 1985) 72–76.

"Worship and Community." *Doxology* 2 (1985) 23–34.

"Why You Should Change Your Worship Setting." *Circuit Rider* 9 (July–Aug. 1985) 5–7.

"Liturgy and Community." *Drew Gateway* 56 (Fall 1985) 31–42.

"Why We Say Creeds." *United Methodist Bridges* 1 (Jan. 1986) 14–15.

"Open Letter to a Pastor." *Circuit Rider* 10 (Feb. 1986) 4–5.

"The Missing Jewel of the Evangelical Church." *The Reformed Journal* 36 (June 1986) 11–16. (Reprinted in *Mission Journal* 20 [May 1989] 3–8.)

"An Introduction to the *Book of Services*." *Doxology* 3 (1986) 39–47.

"Religious Book Week: Critics Choices." *Commonweal* 114 (Mar. 13, 1987) 158–59.

"Moving Christian Worship toward Social Justice." *Christian Century* 104 (June 17–24, 1987) 558–60. (Reprinted in *The Ministries of Christian Worship*, ed. Robert E. Webber, 463–65. Nashville: Star Song, 1994.)

"The Classification of Protestant Traditions of Worship." *Studia Liturgica* 17 (1987) 264–72.

"Sources for the Study of Protestant Worship in America." *Worship* 61 (Nov. 1987) 516–33.

"Church Growth Through Worship." *Circuit Rider* 11 (Dec. 1987–Jan. 1988) 6–7.

"Liturgical Space Forms Faith." *Reformed Liturgy and Music* 22 (Spring 1988) 59–60.

(Reprinted in *Reader: A Medley of Practical Theology*, ed. M. Hestenes. Pretoria: University of South Africa Press, 1993.)

"The State of Worship." *The Christian Ministry* 20 (May–June 1989) 11–13.

"Know Your Needs before You Build." *Your Church* 35 (July–Aug. 1989) 12–14.

"New Developments in Christian Worship in America." *The Navy Chaplain* 4 (Nov. 1989) 14–21.

"The Goal Must Be the Authentic and the Relevant." *Circuit Rider* 14 (Sept. 1990) 7.

(With James T. Burtchaell), "'Linguistic Injustice': An Exchange." *First Things* no. 8 (Dec. 1990) 11–12.

"Christian Worship in the 1990s." *Pulpit Digest* 82 (July–Aug. 1991) 70–78.

"The Minister's Bookshelf: Worship." *Quarterly Review* 12 (Spring 1992) 73–80.

"A Short History of American Methodist Service Books." *Doxology* 10 (1993) 30–37.

"Refining the Gold." and "A Conversation with Bishop Sano." *Circuit Rider* 18 (July–Aug. 1994) 10–11.

"'Forum': Some Lessons in Liturgical Pedagogy." *Worship* 68 (Sept. 1994) 438–50.

Collaborative Works

"The Sacrament of the Lord's Supper: An Alternate Text, 1972." Commission on Worship of the United Methodist Church. Nashville: United Methodist Publishing House, 1972; Revised Edition, 1981. 6 pp.

"A Lectionary." Commission on Worship of the Consultation on Church Union. Princeton: Consultation on Church Union, 1974. 42 pp.

"Historical Maps of Barnet, Vermont." Barnet, Vermont: Barnet Bicentennial Committee, 1975.

Word and Table: A Basic Pattern of Sunday Worship for United Methodists. Nashville: Abingdon Press, 1976, 1980. 80 pp.

Words That Hurt; Words That Heal: Language about God and People. Nashville: United Methodist Publishing House, 1985. 24 pp.; New Edition, 1990. 48 pp.

A Christian Celebration of Marriage: An Ecumenical Liturgy. Philadelphia: Fortress Press, 1987. 32 pp.

Abbreviations

Journal	*The Journal of the Rev. John Wesley, A.M.*, ed. Nehemiah Curnock, 8 vols. (London: Epworth Press 1909–1916).
Letters	*The Letters of the Rev. John Wesley, A.M.*, ed. John Telford, 8 vols. (London: Epworth Press 1931).
Works	*The Works of John Wesley*; begun as "The Oxford Edition of *The Works of John Wesley*" (Oxford: Clarendon Press 1975–1983); continued as "The Bicentennial Edition of *The Works of John Wesley*" (Nashville: Abingdon Press 1984—); 15 of 35 vols. published to date.
Works (J)	*The Works of the Rev. John Wesley, M.A.*, ed. Thomas Jackson, 3rd edition, 14 vols. (London: Wesleyan Methodist Book Room 1872; reprinted Grand Rapids: Baker Book House 1979).

Notes

Notes to Preface

1. See J. H. Arnold, ed., *Anglican Liturgies* (London: Oxford University Press 1939); Bernard Wigan, ed., *The Liturgy in English* (London: Oxford University Press 1962; rev. ed. 1964); and Colin O. Buchanan, ed., *Modern Anglican Liturgies, 1958–1968* (London: Oxford University Press 1968), *Further Anglican Liturgies, 1968–1975* (Bramcote, Nottingham: Grove Books 1979), and *Latest Anglican Liturgies, 1976–1984* (London: SPCK/Grove Books 1985).

2. For example, see Max Thurian and Geoffrey Wainwright, eds., *Baptism and Eucharist: Ecumenical Convergence in Celebration* (Geneva: World Council of Churches 1983; and Grand Rapids, MI: Wm. B. Eerdmans 1983). A future volume by a Roman Catholic liturgical scholar, Irmgard Pahl of Germany, will also examine the eucharistic texts of liturgical families.

Notes to Chapter 1

1. Letter to Dr. Coke, Mr. Asbury, and our Brethren in North-America (September 10, 1784), *Letters* 7:239. Copies of this letter were frequently bound in with the *Sunday Service* itself, a practice that has continued in modern reprints of the service book.

2. For a brief history of the revision of the *Sunday Service*, see two essays by Wesley F. Swift: "'The Sunday Service of the Methodists,'" *Proceedings of the Wesley Historical Society* 29 (1954) 12–20; and "'The Sunday Service of the Methodists': A Study of Nineteenth-century Liturgy," *Proceedings of the Wesley Historical Society* 31 (1957–1958) 112–43.

3. J. Hamby Barton, "A Double Letter: John Wesley and Thomas Coke to Freeborn Garrettson," *Methodist History* 17 (1978) 61.

4. "Farther Thoughts on Separation from the Church," §1–3, *Works* 9:538.

5. These criteria look remarkably like those developed for theological reflection by Methodists of the mid- and late-twentieth century who emphasize their Wesleyan "base." But see Ted A. Campbell, "The 'Wesleyan Quadrilateral': The Story of a Modern Methodist Myth," *Methodist History* 29 (1991) 92–95.

6. "Preface to *Sermons on Several Occasions*," §5, *Works* 1:105. See also Letter to William Dodd (February 5, 1756), *Letters* 3:157; and Letter to John Newton (May 14, 1765), *Letters* 4:299. Wesley makes the same claim for the other "Bible-Christians" who were members of the Holy Club at Oxford and who were given such derisive appellations as "Bible-bigots" and "Bible-moths." See Sermon 107, "On God's Vineyard," I.1, *Works* 3:504.

7. *Works* 18:171 (Journal entry for September 13, 1736).

8. "Ought We to Separate from the Church of England?" (III).2, *Works* 9:570–71. See also *Works* 22:42–43 (Journal entry for June 5, 1766)

9. While Anglicans regarded the first five centuries as authoritative, the so-called Puritans were more cautious, employing the early writings for justifications of "Scriptural" worship. Paul Marshall notes that herein is a basic disagreement between Anglican and Puritan, the issue being not *if* Christian antiquity (and the sum of Christian "tradition") is to be used but *how* it is to be read and used ("*Non Angeli Sed Anglicani*: Style and Substance in Seventeenth-Century England," *Worship* 65 [1991] 148).

10. Letter to James Hutton (November 27, 1738), *Works* 25:593. "But whatever doctrine is *new* must be *wrong*; for the *old* religion is the only *true* one; and no doctrine can be right unless it is the very same 'which was from the beginning'" (Sermon 13, "On Sin in Believers," III.9, *Works* 1:324). The period of antiquity to which Anglicans generally appealed embraced the first four ecumenical councils, the ecumenical creeds, and developing liturgies. Although Wesley had no doctrinal objection to Nicaea and Chalcedon, he believed that the moral and spiritual condition of the Church declined after the first three centuries.

11. Accounts of primitive Christianity by William Cave and Claude Fleury were recommended reading for the Methodist Assistants in 1746. See *John Bennet's Copy of the Minutes of the Conferences of 1744, 1745, 1747 and 1748; with Wesley's Copy of those for 1746*, Publications of the Wesley Historical Society, no. 1 (London: Charles H. Kelly 1896) 36.

12. "During the twelve festival days, we had the Lord's Supper daily, a little emblem of the Primitive Church. May we be followers of them in all things as they were of Christ!" (*Works* 22:441 [Journal entry for December 25, 1774]; cf. *Works* 23:441 [Journal entry for March 30, 1777]).

13. Sermon 39, "Catholic Spirit," I.11, *Works* 2:86. For a discussion of Wesley's "programmatic" use of antiquity in worship, see Ted A. Campbell, *John Wesley and Christian Antiquity: Religious Vision and Cultural Change* (Nashville: Kingswood Books 1991) 94–100.

14. "Letter to Dr. Coke, Mr. Asbury, and our Brethren in North-America," *Letters* 7:239.

15. See Nathan Bangs, *The Life of the Rev. Freeborn Garrettson: Compiled from his Printed and Manuscript Journals and other Authentic Documents* (New York: J. Emory and B. Waugh 1832) 155.

16. See Letter to Samuel Walker (September 24, 1755), *Works* 26:593; and *Works* 22:313 (Journal entry for March 25, 1772); but cf. "Ought We to Separate," *Works* 9:569, 571.

17. "A Dissenter in Wesley's time would have destroyed the Prayer Book, not revised it" (J. E. Rattenbury, *The Conversion of the Wesleys* [London: Epworth Press 1938] 216).

18. The notice is found as a preface in most extant copies of the *Sunday Service* and has been reproduced in the reprint editions. See also the Letter to Walter Churchey (June 20, 1789), *Letters* 8:144–45.

19. "It is a fundamental principle with us that to renounce reason is to renounce religion, that religion and reason go hand in hand, and that all irrational religion is false religion" (Letter to Dr. Rutherford [March 28, 1768], III.4, *Letters* 5:364). See also the various references to the use of reason in the renderings of the *Appeal to Men of Reason and Religion* (*Works* 11:37–325).

20. Rupert Davies, "The People Called Methodists; 1. 'Our Doctrines'" in *A History of the Methodist Church in Great Britain*, vol. 1 (London: Epworth Press 1965) 154. For an in-depth study of Wesley's understanding and use of reason, see Rex D. Matthews, "'Religion and Reason Joined': A Study in the Theology of John Wesley" (Th.D. diss., Harvard Divinity School 1986) 121–83.

21. Letter to Henry Brooke (June 14, 1786), *Letters* 7:333; and *A Farther Appeal to Men of Reason and Religion*, Part I, VI.12, *Works* 11:185–86.

22. "But the man of a truly catholic spirit, having weighed all things in the balance of the sanctuary, has no doubt, no scruple at all concerning that particular mode of worship wherein he joins. He is clearly convinced that his manner for worshipping God is both scriptural and rational. He knows none in the world which is more scriptural, none which is more rational. Therefore without rambling hither and thither he cleaves close thereto, and praises God for the opportunity of so doing" (Sermon 39, "Catholic Spirit," III.2, *Works* 2:93).

23. "Thoughts Upon Liberty," §16, *Works* (J) 11:37–38; Sermon 39, "Catholic Spirit," I.6–9, *Works* 2:84–85; and Sermon 127, "On the Wedding Garment," §14, *Works* 4:145–46.

24. "Thoughts Upon Liberty," §17, *Works* (J) 11:39.

25. Sermon 39, "Catholic Spirit," I.10, *Works* 2:86. See also "The Principles of a Methodist Farther Explained," III.2–3, *Works* 9:186–88.

26. See *Works* 20:163 (Journal entry for March 13, 1747); Sermon 7, "The Way to the Kingdom," I.3–5, *Works* 1:218–20; Sermon 61, "The Mystery of Iniquity," §29, *Works* 2:464–65; and Sermon 127, "On the Wedding Garment," §15, *Works* 4:146.

27. Wesley typically wore his gown and cassock even for field preaching. See *Works* 19:337 (Journal entry for September 9, 1743).

28. Sermon 39, "Catholic Spirit," II.2, *Works* 2:89–90.

29. Experience is designated as a corollary with Scripture in Sermon 123, "On Knowing Christ after the Flesh," §8, 14 (*Works* 4:101, 105), and with Scripture and reason in Sermon 14, "The Repentance of Believers," I.2 (*Works* 1:336–37).

30. Letter to Thomas Whitehead (February 10, 1748), *Letters* 2:117.

31. For a discussion of Wesley's distinction between spiritual worship and spiritual idolatry, see Geoffrey Wainwright, "Worship According to Wesley," *Australian Journal of Liturgy* 3 (1991) 5–13. Wainwright shows the trinitarian shape for Wesley of worship "in Spirit and in Truth."

32. "I would have you introduce ye Prayer-book every where, as far as you possibly can without giving *great* Offence: but I would not give *great* Offence to precious souls even for ye best of forms" (Barton, "A Double Letter," 63).

33. *Journal* 8:5 (August 26, 1789).

34. Sermon 24, "Upon our Lord's Sermon on the Mount, IV," III.4, *Works* 1:544.

35. Karen Westerfield Tucker, "Liturgical Expressions of Care for the Poor in the Wesleyan Tradition: A Case Study for the Ecumenical Church," *Worship* 69 (1995) 52–54.

36. *Letters* 3:226–28 (September 20, 1757).

37. See especially *Works* 23:292, 298, 324–25 (Journal entries for October 23, 1783, March 17, 1784, and July 29, 1784); cf. Letter to Thomas Maxfield cited in *Works* 21:397 (Journal entry for November 1, 1762).

38. See, for example, *Journal* 7:349–50 (Journal entries for December 21 and 24, 1787), and numerous entries in the Minutes of the Methodist Conferences.

39. "The Large Minutes," Q. 36, *Works* (J) 8:317.

40. "Preface to *Sermons on Several Occasions*," §3, *Works* 1:104. On the content of preaching, see Letter to an "Evangelical Layman" (December 20, 1751), *Works* 26:482–89.

41. See *Works* 19:46 (Journal entry for April 2, 1739), and "The Large Minutes," Q. 7 and 8, *Works* (J) 8:300.

42. *Works* 22:152 (Journal entries for August 9 and 10, 1768). See also *Works* 22:161–62 (Journal entry for October 22, 1768); *Journal* 7:258–59 (April 8, 1787); and "Thoughts on the Power of Music" [written 1779], *Works* (J) 13:470–73.

43. G. J. Cuming, *A History of Anglican Liturgy*, 2d ed. (London: The Macmillan Press 1982) 149.

44. Wesley uses these words to describe the 1780 *Collection of Hymns for the Use of the People Called Methodists* (Preface, §4, *Works* 7:74).

45. See Letter to Mary Bishop (October 18, 1778), *Letters* 6:326; and Letter to the Printer of the "Dublin Chronicle" (June 2, 1789), *Letters* 8:141.

Notes to Chapter 2

1. See Sermon 104, "On Attending the Church Service," *Works* 3:464–78.

2. *Minutes of the Methodist Conference*, vol. 1 (London: The Conference Office 1812) 58.

3. John Wesley, *The Sunday Service of the Methodists in North America* (London: [William Strahan] 1784). It is now most accessible, though with omissions, in the Methodist Bicentennial Commemoration 1984 reprint from the United Methodist Publishing House which includes introductory materials by James F. White. A fuller reprint was produced by OSL Publications in 1991. Wesley's text will appear in full in a future volume of *The Works of John Wesley*.

4. *Letters* 7:239.

5. For details about worship in Wesley's lifetime, see John C. Bowmer, *The Sacrament of the Lord's Supper in Early Methodism* (London: Dacre Press 1952),

especially 62–102; A. Raymond George, "The People called Methodists, 4. The Means of Grace" in *A History of the Methodist Church in Great Britain*, eds. Rupert Davies and Gordon Rupp, vol. 1 (London: Epworth Press 1965) 259–73.

6. *Minutes*, 323.

7. Ibid.

8. See John C. Bowmer, *The Lord's Supper in Methodism 1791–1960* (London: Epworth Press 1961), and C. Norman Wallwork, "Origins and Development of the Methodist Preaching Service" (M.A. thesis, University of Birmingham 1984).

9. It was published the following year: *The Book of Public Prayers and Services for the Use of the People Called Methodists* (London: Wesleyan Methodist Book-Room 1883).

10. *The Methodist Hymn-Book* (London: Methodist Conference Office 1933).

11. *The Book of Offices* (London: Methodist Publishing House 1936).

12. See Wesley F. Swift, "John Wesley's Lectionary, with notes on some later Methodist Lectionaries," *London Quarterly and Holborn Review* 183 (October 1958) 298–304.

13. Methodist Conference Agenda 1960, Representative Session, 17–38.

14. *Hymns and Songs* (London: Methodist Publishing House 1960).

15. *The Methodist Service Book* (London: Methodist Publishing House 1975). Some congregations worship in the Welsh language; successive service books are published in Welsh translations, but of course these congregations use an entirely different hymn book.

16. The four-action shape, popularized by Gregory Dix in *The Shape of the Liturgy* (London: Dacre Press 1945), is brought out clearly; this section is the only place in the book where block capitals, in red in the book itself, are used for the headings. But the reason for doing it is simply to imitate Christ's action in taking, thanking or blessing, breaking, and giving. As the taking precedes the thanking, there is no need to use during the prayer any of the old manual acts that were prescribed in 1662 and in some versions of 1784 and continued to some extent after their omission in 1882. Nor is it appropriate to regard the breaking as a sign of the breaking of Christ's body, as the Bible at John 19:36 emphasizes that no bone was broken and the addition of "broken" to "this is my body" at 1 Corinthians 11:24 occurs only in the inferior manuscripts.

17. The use of red block capitals in the book for "The Final Prayers" is probably an oversight.

18. Ronald C. D. Jasper, ed., *The Calendar and Lectionary: A Consideration by the Joint Liturgical Group* (London: Oxford University Press 1967). The evening lessons are based on *An Additional Lectionary for Use at a Second Sunday Service* prepared by the Joint Liturgical Group (London: SPCK and Epworth Press 1969).

19. *The Calendar and Lectionary*, 19–20.

20. See Bowmer, *The Sacrament of the Lord's Supper in Early Methodism*, 103–22.

21. Methodist Conference Agenda 1987, 91–93, also available as a pamphlet *Children at Holy Communion: Guidelines* (London: Methodist Church Division of Education and Youth 1987).

22. The children's groups may have been using the material in the periodical *Partners in Learning* published by the National Christian Education Council, which sometimes but not often bears some relation to the lectionary. Often the resemblance which the preacher claims to see is somewhat forced.

23. Conference Agenda 1994, 536–50.

24. *Hymns and Psalms* (London: Methodist Publishing House 1983).

25. Conference Agenda 1994, 114–23.

26. The Joint Liturgical Group, *A Four Year Lectionary: JLG2* (Norwich: Canterbury Press 1990).

27. *Lessons, Psalms and Collects* (London: Methodist Publishing House 1992).

28. The Consultation on Common Texts, *The Revised Common Lectionary* (Norwich: Canterbury Press, and Nashville: Abingdon Press 1992). For a comparison of lectionaries, see Donald Gray, ed., *The Word in Season, Essays by Members of the Joint Liturgical Group on the Use of the Bible in Liturgy* (Norwich: Canterbury Press 1988), especially 82–91, 97–115.

29. "Inclusive Language and Imagery about God," Conference Agenda 1992, 80–107.

30. *Praying Together, A Revision of "Prayers we have in Common" (ICET 1975): Agreed Liturgical Texts prepared by the English Language Liturgical Consultation 1988* (Norwich: Canterbury Press, also without the sub-title, Nashville: Abingdon Press 1988).

31. Available from Methodist Publishing House, Peterborough.

32. Conference Agenda 1988, 155–89.

33. Geoffrey Wainwright, *Doxology* (London: Epworth Press, and New York: Oxford University Press 1980).

34. *The Methodist Service Book*, B12–B14.

Notes to Chapter 3

1. *The Service of the Lord's Supper or the Holy Eucharist* (London: Oxford University Press 1950; rev. ed. 1954).

2. Louis Bouyer, "A Catholic View of the Church of South India Liturgy," *Theology* 59 (1956) 4–6.

3. Quoted in T. S. Garrett, *Worship in the Church of South India* (London: Lutterworth 1958) 17. We might note also a spontaneous comment to Marcus Ward (a Methodist on the Liturgy Committee that drafted the CSI liturgy) by an Orthodox scholar who had just witnessed a celebration of the liturgy: "You have a wonderful Liturgy" (A. M. Ward, *The Pilgrim Church: An Account of the First Five Years of the Church of South India* [London: Epworth Press 1953] 136).

4. E.g., see W. J. Grisbrooke's critique reported by Garrett in *Worship in the Church of South India*, 31–32.

5. Not only was the Liturgy Committee overwhelmingly dominated by missionaries; of the 85 letters providing input to the convenor of the Committee from 1949 to 1954, 75 are from non-Indians, either missionaries or theologians and liturgical scholars from related Western Churches who were asked for their opinions of the draft liturgy. Only one Indian, E. L. Anantarao of the former Methodist district of Hyderabad (part of which became the CSI diocese of Medak), seemed to have had serious doubts concerning the missionary domination of the process. See Michael J. Hill, "The Formative Factors in the Compilation of the Eucharistic Liturgy of the Church of South India between 1949 and 1954" (post-graduate thesis, United Theological College, Bangalore 1978), Appendix B, iv–vii.

6. Mark Gibbard, in *Unity Is Not Enough* (London: Mowbrays 1965), identifies four significant features of the liturgy: its classical shape; its corporate

character; its biblical language; its linkage with the lectionary (with Old Testament readings as well as epistle and gospel) that divides the year into Advent–Christmas–Epiphany, Lent–Easter, Pentecost, a calendar scheme that pointed the way for many Church lectionaries since.

7. Prominent Presbyterian theologians in Scotland regarded the proposed form of the Peace as "grotesque" (Hill, "The Formative Factors," 88).

8. Hill, "The Formative Factors," 91–92.

9. *The Lord's Supper or Holy Eucharist: A Revised Version* (Madras: Christian Literature Society 1972). Linguistic style was modernized; there is some abbreviation; and the litanies of intercession are quite substantially changed.

10. Cf. E. J. Lott, "Religious Faith and Cultural Diversity in India," in *Christian Faith and Multiform Culture in India*, ed. Somen Das (Bangalore: United Theological College 1987) 48–84. In the context of western culture, this is an issue to which Professor James White has contributed significant insights. See, for example, *New Forms of Worship* (Nashville: Abingdon Press 1971) 33–36.

11. Hill, "The Formative Factors," 52–56.

12. L. W. Brown, *Relevant Liturgy* (New York: Oxford University Press 1965) 4, 7.

13. Ibid., 5, 9.

14. Garrett, *Worship in the Church of South India*, 6.

15. L. W. Brown, *The Indian Christians of St. Thomas* (Cambridge: Cambridge University Press 1956) 218.

16. Garrett, *Worship in the Church of South India*, 21.

17. *The Indian Liturgy*, rev. ed. (Bombay: Oxford University Press 1948). Lesslie Newbigin, on the contrary, saw the Anglican Holy Communion of 1662 as the starting point for the Church of South India.

18. Even in the "Symposium" of collected comments in the *South Indian Churchman*, no Indian voice is heard but that of the editor, David Chellappa. See also note 5 above.

19. Hill, "The Formative Factors," 62–64.

20. Ibid., 66.

21. D. S. Amalorpavadass, *Towards Indigenization in the Liturgy* (Bangalore: National Biblical Catechetical and Liturgical Centre 1973) 19.

22. Ibid., 23.

23. Cf. E. J. Lott, "Faith and Culture in Interaction: The Alternative CSI Liturgy," in *Reflections* [Festschrift to Rt. Revd. Sundar Clarke, Bishop in Madras], ed. Sathianathan Clarke (Madras: Poompuhar Pathipagam, n.d.) 120–40. This attempts a fairly thorough analysis and evaluation of the alternative liturgy. See also *Worship in an Indian Context*, ed. E. J. Lott (Bangalore: U.T.C. 1986), esp. 1–10, 65–77.

24. In several hundred research theses undertaken at the United Theological College, Bangalore, during the past 45 years, only one is on the CSI liturgy, and that is by a British Methodist, the Reverend Dr. Michael J. Hill.

25. I find it impossible to agree with the Methodist theologian A. Marcus Ward, once my teacher in London, that the CSI liturgy "is markedly *Indian* in character." It *is* more convincing to say, as Ward did, that it "represents a marked advance towards an Indian form of worship" (Ward, *The Pilgrim Church*, 135–36).

Notes to Chapter 4

1. The negative legacy was a plethora of places of worship, especially in the gold fields, and the trauma of the slow but inevitable closure of many such churches in recent years. There are parallels with the early development of American Methodism in its informality and adaptability, but in Australia the patterns of British Methodism were largely transported to new conditions. Wesley made no abridgment of the *Book of Common Prayer* for Australian Methodists, nor did many Australian Methodists know about his American one (1784).

2. The best study of Australian church history is Ian Breward, *A History of the Australian Churches* (St. Leonards, NSW: Allen & Unwin 1993).

3. The 1963 reports had proposed a reformed-episcopal form of church government, with a special link to the [united] Church of South India.

4. The final form was: *The Basis of Union, being the 1971 revision by the Joint Commission on Church Union of the Congregational Union of Australia, the Methodist Church of Australasia, and the Presbyterian Church of Australia* (Melbourne: The Aldersgate Press 1971).

5. Ibid., ¶1.

6. *The Book of Offices, being the Orders of Service authorized for Use in the Methodist Church together with The Order of Morning Prayer* (London: The Methodist Publishing House 1936). This book was the product of British Methodist union in 1932. The *Methodist Hymn-Book* of 1933 carried a supplement authorized by the Australian and New Zealand conferences.

7. James F. White, *Christian Worship in Transition* (Nashville: Abingdon Press 1976) 61–75.

8. Ibid., 102–30.

9. See Raymond George's essay in this volume. From a slightly earlier era, many ministers knew the *Book of Common Worship* (1963) of the Church of South India. Its lectionary was often followed.

10. Some provision (duplicated orders) was made immediately after union for ordinations and inductions of ministers in the Uniting Church, with the expectation that the new Church would be working on more permanent liturgies.

11. I surveyed these booklets in general in "Liturgy in the Uniting Church in Australia," *Studia Liturgica* 15 (1982–83) 214–18.

12. Uniting Church Worship Services, *Holy Communion, Three Orders of Service* (Melbourne: The Joint Board of Christian Education of Australia and New Zealand 1980). This was published both in a small congregational edition and in large print format ("altar size"). Other booklets followed for baptism and related services (1981), marriage (1982), funeral (1984), ordination and induction, and various lay commissionings.

13. Ironically, the prayer which the Anglicans adapted in *An Australian Prayer Book* was written for them by a Uniting Church liturgical scholar, Dr. H. F. Leatherland (a former Congregationalist).

14. "High Church" Congregationalism could certainly be found in England. See such writers as Bernard Lord Manning (*Essays in Orthodox Dissent* [London: The Independent Press 1939]) and Raymond Abba (*Principles of Christian Worship* [New York and London: Oxford University Press 1960]). Abba became Professor of Theology at the Congregational College in Sydney in 1948, and was a minister of the Uniting Church at his death.

15. *Uniting in Worship: People's Book* (Melbourne: Uniting Church Press 1988) and *Uniting in Worship: Leader's Book* (Melbourne: Uniting Church Press 1988).

16. For a detailed discussion of each section, see Robert Gribben, *A Guide to Uniting in Worship* (Melbourne: Uniting Church Press 1990) 43–77. This is also a commentary on all the services in the book.

17. See the wise words of James F. White in his *Sacraments as God's Self Giving* (Nashville: Abingdon Press 1983) 121–24.

18. *The Australian Hymn Book* (Sydney: Collins 1977). Discussions about the production of an ecumenical Australian hymn book were begun in 1968 by representatives of the Anglican, Congregational, Methodist, and Presbyterian Churches, and from these conversations was formed the Australian Hymn Book Committee. In 1973, official approval was granted by the four constituent denominations to proceed with publication of the hymn book. The Liturgy Commission of the Roman Catholic Archdiocese of Sydney, which inquired in 1974 about participation in the project, later approved the publication of *The Australian Hymn Book with Catholic Supplement*.

19. The Uniting Church Commission on Liturgy was influenced by both Anglican (Episcopalian) and Lutheran revisions of the Common Lectionary.

20. The elder in the Uniting Church is a lay leader, as in Presbyterian custom, but with a limited tenure.

21. White, *Sacraments as God's Self Giving*, 128.

22. The Revised Standard Version was judged the best translation at the time; the New Revised Standard Version is now favored, and will probably be used in any subsequent liturgies.

23. For further explanation of the difference between the "warrant" tradition and the "prayer" tradition, see Gribben, *A Guide to Uniting in Worship*, 65. In addition to the principal form of the great thanksgiving, which was specially composed by the Commission on Liturgy for *Uniting in Worship*, eight alternative eucharistic prayers are provided for the Service of the Lord's Day. Each one begins with a rubric indicating whether or not the warrant or prayer tradition is to be followed. Three require the warrant; five include the narrative within the prayer; none of the alternatives provides for a choice between the two options such as is found in the principal service. Most of the prayers have been borrowed from other churches, such as the British Methodist, the United Church of Canada, the United Presbyterian Church in the U.S.A., and the Australian Anglican.

24. See James F. White, *Introduction to Christian Worship*, rev. ed. (Nashville: Abingdon Press 1990) 170:

> In short, the sacraments are older than the written scriptures, which refer to contemporary liturgical practice as well as to a remembered past.
> The church's acts of obedience to Christ, then, are our chief evidence of the foundation of the sacraments rather than words of institution. . . . These acts of the apostles reveal Jesus' intentions as much as any red-letter formulas. This also means that we are not limited to a handful of passages in interpreting Jesus' intentions with regard to acted signs. . . .

25. *Uniting in Worship: Leader's Book*, 78, n. xiv. Similar encouragement is given to providing a decent baptismal font.

26. The Covenant Service in *Uniting in Worship* is more closely connected

with the baptismal covenant than were either Wesley's original or the two official British Methodist versions (1936, 1975).

27. The lines quoted earlier, "By water and the Spirit . . ." then follow, thus completing the paraphrase of Ephesians with verse 8.

28. Mary MacKillop (1842–1909) was a remarkable nun and worker among the poor who was beatified by Pope John Paul II in January 1995, the first Australian to be so recognized by the Roman Catholic Church. Many saints of the Church catholic are recognized in the Uniting Church by the inclusion in the *Leader's Book* of a "Calendar of Other Commemorations" or sanctorale. Use of the calendar is encouraged for times of worship and prayer, fellowship, and study.

Notes to Chapter 5

1. *Uniting in Worship: Leader's Book* (Melbourne: Uniting Church Press 1988) and *Uniting in Worship: People's Book* (Melbourne: Uniting Church Press 1988).

2. Deacons are ordained ministers with a particular focus on service and evangelism, and often work beyond the boundaries of established parishes.

3. *Uniting in Worship: Leader's Book*, 8 and *Uniting in Worship: People's Book*, 8.

4. Robert Gribben, *A Guide to Uniting in Worship* (Melbourne: Uniting Church Press 1990).

5. *The Basis of Union, being the 1971 revision by the Joint Commission on Church Union of the Congregational Union of Australia, The Methodist Church of Australasia, and the Presbyterian Church of Australia* (Melbourne: The Aldersgate Press 1971) 21.

6. Elders in the Uniting Church are lay leaders, elected locally, with a limited tenure.

7. *The Australian Hymn Book* (Sydney: Collins 1977).

8. It has been the policy of the Uniting Church to relocate some of its national Commissions from time to time. After meeting in Adelaide from 1977 to 1991 (and drawing most of its members from the surrounding synod area), the Commission on Liturgy was relocated to Brisbane.

9. *Working Together Nationally* (Melbourne: Joint Board of Christian Education 1990) 24.

Notes to Chapter 6

1. *The Hymnary of The United Church of Canada* (Toronto: United Church Publishing House 1930); *The Book of Common Order of The United Church of Canada* (Toronto: United Church Publishing House 1932; rev. ed. 1950); *Service Book for the use of ministers conducting public worship* (Toronto: Ryerson Press 1969); *Service Book for the use of the people* (Toronto: Ryerson Press 1969); *The Hymn Book of the Anglican Church of Canada and The United Church of Canada* (Toronto: Southam-Murray 1971; repr. 1972); *A Sunday Liturgy for optional use in The United Church of Canada* (The Working Unit on Worship and Liturgy, Division of Mission in Canada 1984); *Songs for a Gospel People: A Supplement to The Hymn Book (1971)* (Winfield, BC: Wood Lake Books 1987); *Voices United: A Sampler for Congregations* (The Hymn and Worship Resource Project 1993).

2. See my *Presbyterian, Methodist and Congregational Worship in Canada Prior to 1925* (Toronto: Evensong Publications 1994).

3. See Bruce Harding's "*The Hymnary*, 1930" in Thomas Harding and Bruce Harding, *Patterns of Worship in The United Church of Canada 1925–1960* (Toronto: Evensong Publications 1995) 27–47.

4. Richard Davidson, "The Book of Common Order and The Book of Common Prayer," *Cap and Gown* [the journal of Wycliffe College, Toronto] (1937) 14.

5. "Notes on Some of the Orders," *Book of Common Order*, v.

6. These are Davidson's phrases: see Richard Davidson, "Common Worship in the Reformed Churches," *Christendom* 4 (1939) 550–54; cf. Arthur G. Reynolds, "The Church: Its Worship" in *The Living Church: A Book in Memory of the Life and Work of Rev. Richard Davidson, M.A., Ph.D., D.D., Principal of Emmanuel College, Toronto*, ed. Harold Vaughan (Toronto: United Church Publishing House 1949) 98–99.

7. Davidson, "The Book of Common Order and The Book of Common Prayer," 13.

8. Davidson believed that the action of the Lord's Supper should follow the four-fold action of Christ: "He took; He gave thanks; He brake; He gave" (cf. Richard Davidson, "The Lord's Supper as the Norm for Common Worship," *Christendom* 5 [1940] 560–68). In the matter of the derivation of the prayers, the opening supplications are from the Liturgy of St. John Chrysostom, an alternative confession is based directly on the Confiteor, both the anamnesis and epiklesis are paraphrases of material in the *Apostolic Constitutions*, the post-communion is a paraphrase of Calvin and an alternative is from the East Syrian Liturgy of Malabar. The Collect for Purity and Gloria in Excelsis are restored to the introductory section, the greeting is restored to the Sursum Corda, the Benedictus qui venit is joined with the Sanctus, and the peace is placed before the reception. Even such a minute detail as the restoration of the traditional Latin punctuation of the preface was not overlooked. See "*The Book of Common Order*, 1932" and "Appendix: Sources of *The Book of Common Order*" in *Patterns of Worship*, 49–73, 123–47.

9. *The Book of Common Prayer with the Additions and Deviations Proposed in 1928* (Oxford: The University Press, n.d.).

10. The United Church produced two further resources in the 1930s, *Songs for Little Children* (Toronto: United Church Publishing House 1937) and *The Canadian Youth Hymnal* (Toronto: United Church Publishing House 1939). The latter was a complete worship resource for the "junior congregation," including responsive readings, prayers, service music, and other liturgical resources.

11. Advent was noted but consisted basically of church school pageants and choir concerts; Lent was a time for midweek prayer services and evangelistic campaigns; Good Friday was typically an ecumenical service with neighboring congregations joining together in worship. "Easter communion" was more often celebrated on Palm Sunday; Pentecost was not generally observed; the fall communion came to be associated with Worldwide Communion Sunday (first in October).

12. *Songs of the Gospel* (Toronto: Gordon V. Thompson 1948).

13. *Observer* (March 15, 1956) 7.

14. In United Church polity elders are lay members of the congregation who, together with the ordained minister(s), have responsibility for the spiritual (as opposed to the temporal) life of the congregation.

The custom of partaking simultaneously was popularized through its use at the Inaugural Service of the United Church of Canada, June 10, 1925. Though there is a variance of opinion as to how and why the practice arose, it appears to have been an attempt to compensate for the loss of the common cup (see *Patterns of Worship*, 12–13).

15. By "liturgical" I mean that it had a set order or flow, recognized as such and purposefully arranged; it involved the worshipers in a specific pattern of familiar responses, both verbal and physical; and it was understood as coming, at least in part, from beyond the local community (it was invested with a sense of tradition).

16. Minutes of the Committee on Church Worship (September 26, 1966) 2, United Church of Canada Archives, Toronto.

17. Minutes (February 28, 1966) 2.

18. Minutes (March 11, 1968) 2–4.

19. Actually three books were planned. The *Service Book for use in Church Courts*, however, was not completed until 1980.

20. "[The] orders emphasize the element of thanksgiving. Stress is laid upon the resurrection and victory of Christ" (*Service Book*, 1).

21. "Dick and Jane" are characters in primary school readers.

22. *Service Book*, Introduction, n.p.

23. *Service Book*, 254. The scheme was originally proposed by A. Allan McArthur (*The Christian Year and Lectionary Reform* [Toronto: Ryerson Press 1958]). McArthur, a minister of the Church of Scotland, had been dissatisfied with the "Romano-Anglican lectionary tradition," his conclusion being that "the traditional Christian Year is a half-year." Rather than beginning in Advent and focusing on the life of Christ, the "Peterhead Lectionary" which McArthur developed (named after Peterhead Old Parish Church of which he was minister) begins on the first Sunday in October with the "Festival of Creation and Harvest Thanksgiving," ordering Genesis 1 as "a most appropriate Harvest lesson." McArthur's work was known in Canada through the St. Andrew's Lectures delivered at Emmanuel College, Toronto and Queen's Theological College, Kingston. See Gerald E. Moffatt, "*The Christian Year and Lectionary Reform* by A. Allan McArthur," *Canadian Journal of Theology* 5 (1959) 208–9.

24. *Service Book*, Introduction, "Worship as Action," and "Worship as Social Action," n.p.

25. *Hymn Book*, The Music, n.p.; cf. also F. R. C. Clarke, "Some Musical Aspects of *The Hymn Book*, 1971" in CanMus Documents 1, *Hymn Tunes in Canada*, ed. John Beckwith, Proceedings of the conference held in Toronto, February 7 and 8, 1986, organized by the Institute for Canadian Music, Faculty of Music, University of Toronto (Toronto 1987) 153–54.

26. Minutes (April 26, 1969) 4.

27. Minutes (April 28, 1969) 2.

28. Patricia Clarke, "Battlefront Report on the New Hymnbook," *Observer* (August 1970) 8.

29. "The New Hymnary," *Observer* (March 15, 1970) 12.

30. F. R. C. Clarke, "Some Musical Aspects of the *Hymn Book*," 150.

31. Ibid., 151. Stanley L. Osborne, editor of the *Hymn Book*, provided over forty harmonizations.

32. Ernest Long, "The Truth About the 'Crisis' in the Church," *Observer* (November 15, 1967) 12–14.

33. "That Joyful Noise," *Observer* (October 15, 1969) 10.

34. Barbara Bagnell, "The Pied Piper of Brantford," *Observer* (June 1976) 23.

35. *The Whole People of God* (Winfield, BC: Wood Lake Books, n.d.).

36. *A Sunday Liturgy*, 3.

37. *A Sunday Liturgy*, 5.

38. Sources of the eucharistic prayers are: The Consultation on Church Union, *Word Bread Cup* (Cincinnati: Forward Movement Publications 1978), with proper prefaces from the *Book of Alternative Services of The Anglican Church in Canada*; Hippolytus' *Apostolic Tradition* (using the 1983 ICEL text); a Canadian Anglican redaction of *Apostolic Constitutions VIII* (*Book of Alternative Services*); a prayer from the American Episcopal *Book of Common Prayer* (considerably revised for the *Book of Alternative Services*); the ecumenical version of a eucharistic prayer of Eastern type (*Word Bread Cup*); a Canadian composition which "makes extensive use of the Jewish tradition, evoking its sense of justice" (*A Sunday Liturgy*, 32); and a "children's prayer" written by Working Unit members.

39. *Songs for a Gospel People*, Foreword, n.p.

40. *Voices United: A Sampler for Congregations*, ii.

41. On several occasions the Methodist General Conference had rejected proposals for reform whereas the 1922 Presbyterian *Book of Common Order* was in the forefront of early twentieth-century liturgical renewal. See *Presbyterian, Methodist and Congregational Worship*, 43–51, 80–82.

42. See *Patterns of Worship*, 71–73. It is significant in this regard that the closest parallels between the *Book of Common Order* and the *Book of Common Prayer* are in the ordination rites.

43. *The New Outlook* (June 6, 1934) 430. Even the editor of the *Observer*, as late as 1950, seemed to be under this misapprehension: "The history of sacerdotalism is not a pretty one. It has led to the conditions against which Jesus protested, against which Luther raised his voice, and from which Wesley led out his Methodists. . . ." ([October 15, 1950] 4).

44. *Observer* (March 15, 1940) 23.

45. Tim Bentley, "Liturgy: Changing traditions," *Observer* (August 1983) 21–27.

46. I am indebted to my wife, the Reverend Louise Mangan Harding, for the application of this phrase to the ecumenical convergence (cf. Kenneth Leech, *Subversive Orthodoxy: Traditional Faith and Radical Commitment* [Toronto: Anglican Book Centre 1992]).

Notes to Chapter 7

1. *The Sunday Service of the Methodists in North America* (London: [Strahan] 1784). Employed for this essay was an edited version with introduction, notes, and commentary by James F. White (Cleveland, OH: OSL Publications 1991). Most of this edition (but not the collects, epistles, gospels, psalms, and hymns) was originally published by *Quarterly Review* (Nashville: The United Methodist Publishing House and the United Methodist Board of Higher Education and Ministry 1984).

The phrase "American Methodist" in this chapter will refer throughout to Methodism in the United States.

2. Ibid., ii.

3. Ibid., iii.

4. *The Doctrines and Discipline of the Methodist Episcopal Church in America*, 8th ed. (Philadelphia: Printed by Parry Hall 1792) 40–41.

5. Ibid., 228–33.

6. For further information on the history of the Sunday Service during the nineteenth century, see William Nash Wade, "A History of Public Worship in the Methodist Episcopal Church and Methodist Episcopal Church, South, from 1784 to 1905" (Ph.D. diss., University of Notre Dame 1981). For changes in the text of the Lord's Supper through 1926, see Nolan B. Harmon, *The Rites and Ritual of Episcopal Methodism* (Nashville: Publishing House of the M. E. Church, South 1926) 75–155.

7. For further information on the observance of the Christian year by Methodists, see Heather Murray Elkins, "'On Borrowed Time': The Christian Year in American Methodism, 1784–1960" (Ph.D. diss., Drew University 1991). Methodist observance of civic holidays is discussed in Leigh Eric Schmidt, "From Arbor Day to the Environmental Sabbath: Nature, Liturgy, and American Protestantism," *Harvard Theological Review* 84 (1991) 299–323.

8. Nashville: Whitmore & Smith (now Abingdon Press) 1938. This hymnal, still in print, remains the musical staple for some church schools—if not for Sunday worship.

9. ¶1385.3–5 and ¶1388, *The Book of Discipline of The United Methodist Church* (Nashville: The United Methodist Publishing House 1968) 437, 439.

10. *The United Methodist Hymnal* (Nashville: The United Methodist Publishing House 1989), and *The United Methodist Book of Worship* (Nashville: The United Methodist Publishing House 1992). For additional information on the process of reform from 1968 to 1988, see *Companion to The Book of Services* (Nashville: Abingdon Press 1988) 9–26; Robert B. Peiffer, "How Contemporary Liturgies Evolve: The Revision of United Methodist Liturgical Texts (1968–1988)" (Ph.D. diss., University of Notre Dame 1992); and Carlton R. Young, *Companion to The United Methodist Hymnal* (Nashville: Abingdon Press 1993) 123–80. Materials of the Commission on Worship before 1972 and the Section on Worship from 1972–1992 are in the United Methodist Archives Center at Drew University, Madison, New Jersey. Additional archival materials relating to *The Sacrament of the Lord's Supper: An Alternate Text 1972* are at Southern Methodist University, Dallas, Texas. For a history on the work of the Book of Worship Committee, see the *Report of The United Methodist Book of Worship Committee to the 1992 General Conference of The United Methodist Church* (Nashville: The United Methodist Publishing House 1992) R1–R50.

11. *The United Methodist Hymnal* (1989), 26–31; and *The United Methodist Book of Worship* (1992), 41–50.

12. *The Sacrament of the Lord's Supper: An Alternate Text 1972* (Nashville: The United Methodist Publishing House 1972); *We Gather Together* (Nashville: The United Methodist Publishing House 1980) 5–11; *The Book of Services* (Nashville: The United Methodist Publishing House 1985) 19–26; *The United Methodist Hymnal* (1989), 6–11; and *The United Methodist Book of Worship* (1992), 33–39.

13. *The Book of Services*, 25. This sentence was taken from *Word Bread Cup* (Princeton: Consultation on Church Union 1978). It had originally been composed, except for the last four words, by Richard Eslinger, a United Methodist member of the COCU Worship Commission.

14. *Word and Table: A Basic Pattern of Sunday Worship for United Methodists* (Nashville: Abingdon Press 1976; rev. ed. 1980); *The Book of Services*, 10–51.

15. *Word and Table* (1980), 12–43; and *Companion to The Book of Services,* 27–70.

16. *At the Lord's Table: A Communion Service Book for Use by the Minister* (Nashville: Abingdon Press 1981) 11; and *Holy Communion: A Service Book for Use by the Minister* (Nashville: Abingdon Press 1987) 10.

17. *Seasons of the Gospel: Resources for the Christian Year* (Nashville: Abingdon Press 1979); *From Ashes to Fire: Services of Worship for the Seasons of Lent and Easter with Introduction and Commentary* (Nashville: Abingdon Press 1979); and Don E. Saliers, *From Hope to Joy: Services of Worship for the Seasons of Advent and Christmas with Introduction and Commentary* (Nashville: Abingdon Press 1984). These books were revised and combined into a single volume: Hoyt L. Hickman, Don E. Saliers, Laurence Hull Stookey, and James F. White, *Handbook of the Christian Year* (Nashville: Abingdon Press 1986).

18. Hoyt L. Hickman, Don E. Saliers, Laurence Hull Stookey, and James F. White, *The New Handbook of the Christian Year* (Nashville: Abingdon Press 1992).

19. For full information on the Revised Common Lectionary and its development, see Consultation on Common Texts, *The Revised Common Lectionary* (Nashville: Abingdon Press 1992).

20. These great thanksgivings were published as a series of leaflets by Discipleship Resources (Nashville): *Advent* (1974); *Christmas* (1974); *Epiphany* (1974); *Lent* (1975); *Maundy Thursday* (1975); *Eastertide* (1975); *Pentecost* (1975); *A People Under God* [Ordinary Time] (1975); *The Communion of Saints* (1975); and *Thanksgiving* (1975). They were first revised and included in *At the Lord's Table* (1981), and then further revised and published in *Handbook of the Christian Year* (1986) and in *Holy Communion* (1987).

21. *Celebremos 1* (Nashville: Discipleship Resources 1979) and *Celebremos 2* (Nashville: Discipleship Resources 1983) from Hispanic heritages; *Songs of Zion* (Nashville: Abingdon Press 1981) from the African American heritage; *Supplement to The Book of Hymns* (Nashville: The United Methodist Publishing House 1982); *Hymns from the Four Winds* (Nashville: Abingdon Press 1983) from Asian American heritages; and *Voices* (Nashville: Discipleship Resources 1991) from Native American heritages.

22. See *Companion to The Book of Services,* 14, 17.

23. The story of the parallel development of the Sunday service in Spanish would require an article in itself. For basic information through 1985, see *Companion to The Book of Services,* 12–18. A Spanish language hymnal and book of worship is being prepared for submission to the 1996 General Conference.

24. *The United Methodist Hymnal,* 876–79; and *The United Methodist Book of Worship,* 568–80.

25. *The United Methodist Hymnal,* 2; and *The United Methodist Book of Worship,* 15.

Notes to Chapter 8

1. Excerpt from an anonymous, undated, and unpublished letter written in response to my essay, "To Be Contemporary or Not to Be: Thoughts on a Liturgical Dilemma," *Circuit Rider* 10 (Dec. 1994–Jan. 1995) 4–6.

2. John Wesley, *The Sunday Service of the Methodists in North America with other Occasional Services* (London: [William Strahan] 1784; repr. Nashville: United Methodist Publishing House 1984; also reprinted as *John Wesley's Prayer Book* [Cleveland, OH: OSL Publications 1991]).

3. James F. White, *Christian Worship in Transition* (Nashville: Abingdon Press 1976) 71–72.

4. Ibid., 78–85.

5. L. Edward Phillips, "Creative Worship: Rules, Patterns and Guidelines," *Quarterly Review* 10 (1990) 9–23; see especially 13–18.

6. James F. White, *Protestant Worship: Traditions in Transition* (Louisville: Westminster/John Knox Press 1989) 160.

7. See the *Methodist Hymnal* (New York: Eaton & Mains 1905), ii. This hymnal was produced jointly by the Methodist Episcopal Church and the Methodist Episcopal Church, South. Eventually these two Churches, along with the Methodist Protestant Church, united in 1939 to form the Methodist Church. This body then, in 1968, joined with the Evangelical United Brethren Church to constitute the United Methodist Church.

8. White, *Protestant Worship*, 163.

9. See in particular the work of Marjorie Procter-Smith (*In Her Own Rite: Constructing Feminist Liturgical Tradition* [Nashville: Abingdon Press 1990]), and Heather Murray Elkins (*Worshiping Women: Re-Forming God's People for Praise* [Nashville: Abingdon Press 1994]).

10. *The United Methodist Book of Worship* (Nashville: The United Methodist Publishing House 1992) 3.

11. ¶439.1a and ¶262.11, *The Book of Discipline of The United Methodist Church, 1992* (Nashville: The United Methodist Publishing House 1992).

12. This report is part of a larger study of the reception process of the *United Methodist Hymnal* conducted in thirteen churches. Under a grant from the Lilly Endowment, I undertook a congregational study of how the new hymnal, with its accent on pluralism and with its reformed services, was actually being received and put into practice. Much of what follows is based on the data of that research, which also included a survey of 135 United Methodist congregations geographically distributed across the United States. The excerpt and the final results of the study are not yet published.

13. Although produced by the denominational press, the *Cokesbury Hymnal*, first published in 1923 and continued through successive editions (e.g., as *The Cokesbury Worship Hymnal*), is not an authorized hymnal of the denomination.

14. This section is adapted from "To Be Contemporary or Not To Be: Thoughts on a Liturgical Dilemma" (see note 1).

Notes to Chapter 9

1. The history of the African Methodist Episcopal Church is recounted in Charles Spencer Smith, *A History of the African Methodist Episcopal Church* (Philadelphia: Book Concern of the A.M.E. Church 1922); Harry V. Richardson, *Dark Salvation: The Story of Methodism as It Developed Among Blacks in America* (Garden City, NY: Anchor-Press/Doubleday 1976); and C. Eric Lincoln and Lawrence H. Mamiya, *The Black Church in the African American Experience* (Durham, NC: Duke University Press 1990).

2. Throughout this chapter, "African Methodist" will refer to those Christians of the African Methodist Episcopal Church.

3. A.M.E. worship and worship in the African American tradition is discussed in such writings as James H. Cone, "Sanctification and Liberation in the Black Religious Tradition with Special Reference to Black Worship," *The A.M.E.*

Church Review 100 (January–March 1985) 18–31; Harold Dean Trulear, "The Lord Will Make A Way Somehow: Black Worship and the Afro-American Story," *Journal of the Interdenominational Theological Center* 13 (Fall 1985) 87–104; Melva Wilson Costen and Darius Leander Swann, eds., "The Black Christian Worship Experience: A Consultation," *The Journal of the Interdenominational Theological Center* 14 (Fall 1986 and Spring 1987); and Melva Wilson Costen, *African American Christian Worship* (Nashville: Abingdon Press 1993).

4. *The Book of Discipline of the African Methodist Episcopal Church, 1976* (Nashville: The A.M.E. Sunday School Union 1976) 11.

5. Daniel A. Payne, *Recollections of Seventy Years* (New York: Arno Press and The New York Times 1968) 253–56.

6. *Discipline*, 12.

7. *The Life Experience and Gospel Labors of the Rt. Rev. Richard Allen* (Nashville: Abingdon Press 1960) 29.

8. Sermon 2, "The Almost Christian," II.1–2, *Works* 1:137–38.

9. Richard Allen, *A Collection of Hymns and Spiritual Songs, from Various Authors* (Philadelphia: Printed by T. L. Plowman 1801; repr. Nashville: A.M.E.C. Sunday School Union 1987).

10. James Cone, *For My People* (Maryknoll, NY: Orbis Books 1984) 150.

11. For a study of A.M.E. worship in Zambia, see Walton R. Johnson, *Worship and Freedom: A Black American Church in Zambia* (New York: Africana Publishing Company for the International African Institute 1977) 75–79.

12. Albert W. Palmer, *The Art of Conducting Public Worship* (New York: Macmillan 1939) 49–52.

13. *The African Methodist Episcopal Church Bicentennial Hymnal* (Nashville: A.M.E. Publishing House 1984).

14. *The African Methodist Episcopal Church Hymnal* (Nashville: A.M.E. Publishing House 1986).

15. *The Book of Worship* (Nashville: A.M.E. Publishing House 1984).

16. Preface, *The Book of Worship*, n.p.

17. *The A.M.E.C. Hymnal*, xiv–xxii; and *The Book of Worship*, 9–22.

Notes to Chapter 10

1. Benjamin Titus Roberts, "Object and Scope of this Magazine," *The Earnest Christian* [henceforth *EC*] 1 (Jan. 1860) 5.

2. In his article "New School Methodism" (first published in July 1857 in *The Northern Independent*), Roberts placed himself at the center of the debate which resulted in the formation of the Free Methodist Church. A classic declensionist account, the article was structured by his articulation of the contrast he saw between "New School" and "Old School" Methodists. The masthead of the denomination's weekly paper, *The Free Methodist* [henceforth *FM*], displayed the biblical quote which came to hold semi-official status as a denominational motto: "Remove not the ancient landmarks which thy fathers have set."

3. *EC* 1 (Jan. 1860) 5. For further discussion of the distinctive nuances of early Free Methodist theological reflection, see Douglas R. Cullum, "What Does it Mean to be a Methodist? An Examination of Denominational Self-Identity in John Wesley, the Methodist Episcopal Church and the Free Methodist Church" (Th.M. thesis, Duke University 1991) 52–63. For an analysis of the practice of Free Methodist worship in relation to the originating issues of the denomination,

see Claude E. Griffith, "Patterns of Free Methodist Worship: Historic Freedoms," (D.Min. diss., Asbury Theological Seminary 1984).

4. [Editorial], "Vital Godliness," *EC* 9 (May 1865) 162.

5. As B. T. Roberts was beginning his ministry, small but significant changes were being made in the *Discipline* of the Methodist Episcopal Church. The MEC's originating conference of 1784 had mandated that all churches "be built plain and decent, but not more expensive than is absolutely unavoidable." The General Conference of 1820 added the phrase, "and with free seats." In the year that Roberts was ordained elder (1852) the rule was softened by the addition of the words: "wherever practicable." See Matthew Simpson, *Cyclopedia of Methodism*, rev. ed. (Philadelphia: Louis H. Everts 1880) 710. The first three numbers of *EC* contained lead editorials by Roberts on "Free Churches."

6. Roberts, "Free Churches," *EC* 1 (Feb. 1860) 38. See also 1 (Jan. 1860) 9, where Roberts contended that "there must not be a mere incidental provision for having the poor hear the gospel; this is the main thing to be looked after."

7. [Editorial], "How to Reach the Masses," *EC* 17 (Apr. 1869) 126.

8. On the issue of pew rents excluding even those of moderate means, see *EC* 1 (Jan. 1860) 9–10; "How to Reach the Masses," 126; and *EC* 28 (Dec. 1874) 189–90, where Roberts revels in the increase of public sentiment against the pew system by quoting from a *New York Tribune* editorial.

9. "How to Reach the Masses," 126.

10. "The Old Landmarks," *EC* 23 (June 1872) 165.

11. Cf. "Pic-nic Religion," *EC* 1 (Nov. 1860) 358 [reprinted in *EC* 3 (May 1862) 177].

12. See T. J. Jackson Lears, "The Religion of Beauty: Catholic Forms and American Consciousness," in *No Place of Grace: Antimodernism and the Transformation of American Culture, 1880–1920* (New York: Pantheon 1981) 183–215.

13. "Vital Godliness," *EC* 9 (May 1865) 160.

14. "Fine Churches," *EC* 13 (Jan. 1867) 25.

15. [Editorial], "Splendid Churches," *EC* 14 (Nov. 1867) 158–59.

16. [Report from General Conference], *EC* 44 (Nov. 1882) 163. On the perception of a church steeple as a symbol of affluence, see "Splendid Churches," *EC* 14 (Nov. 1867) 159: "The money expended upon a steeple would build a comfortable house where hundreds might hear the Gospel preached who are now without the means of grace."

17. See "The Sabbath," *EC* 29 (Apr. 1875) 129–30; and, "The Sabbath," *EC* 49 (May 1885) 156–57.

18. For example, note that the soteriologically ordered table of contents in the *Hymn Book of the Free Methodist Church* (Rochester, NY: B.T. Roberts 1883) includes the Sabbath under the category of "Salvation Provided" along with the Lord's Supper, Baptism, the Bible, the Atonement, the Church, Fellowship, and the Family.

19. H. A. Crouch, "The Sabbath," *EC* 6 (Sept. 1863) 83; and [Editorial], "Sabbath Desecration," *EC* 5 (Apr. 1863) 128; cf. *EC* 8 (Nov. 1864) 163.

20. [Editorial], "Your Money," *EC* 5 (Apr. 1863) 128–29; and [Editorial], "Sinning by Proxy," *EC* 15 (June 1868) 187–88; cf. "Sabbath Railway Travelling," *EC* 53 (Jan. 1887) 11.

21. William Anderson, "The Sabbath," *EC* 13 (Feb. 1867) 61; cf. "Play Things on the Lord's Day," *EC* 3 (Apr. 1862) 99.

22. "No Sabbath," *EC* 46 (Aug. 1883) 51.

23. [Editorial], "The Sabbath," *EC* 31 (June 1876) 203.

24. [Editorial], "Sabbath Desecration," *EC* 5 (Apr. 1863) 127–28.

25. *The Doctrines and Discipline of the Free Methodist Church* (Buffalo: B. T. Roberts, for the Free Methodist Church 1860) 72.

26. *A Digest of Free Methodist Law, or Guide in the Administration of the Discipline of the Free Methodist Church* (Chicago: Free Methodist Publishing House 1901) 68. For a recent examination of these restrictions, see Keith Duane Schwanz, "The 'Wooden Brother': Instrumental Music Restricted in Free Methodist Worship, 1860–1955" (Ph.D. diss., Union Institute 1991).

27. Preface, *The Hymn Book of the Free Methodist Church* (Rochester, NY: B. T. Roberts 1883, 1885) ii.

28. Publisher's Note, *Metrical Tune Book with Hymns and Supplement*, rev. and enl. by Philip Phillips, J. G. Terrill, and T. B. Arnold (Chicago: The Free Methodist Publishing House 1896, 1908) ii. See also the discussion of Leslie R. Marston, *From Age to Age a Living Witness: An Historical Interpretation of Free Methodism's First Century* (Winona Lake, IN: Light and Life Press 1960) 345–48.

29. For example, in 1866 both a form for the examination of parents and the requirement of a parental vow were added. For further analysis, see Marston, *From Age to Age a Living Witness*, 291–92, 340–41.

30. See "St. Charles Camp-Meeting," *EC* 20 (July 1870) 33; "Louisiana Conference," *FM* (Nov. 13, 1889) 4; and *A Digest of Free Methodist Law*, 72.

31. The General Conference of 1886 voted to identify the denomination with the National Holiness Association. For further discussion, see Marston, *From Age to Age a Living Witness*, 291, 339–40, 562.

32. *The Doctrines and Discipline of the Free Methodist Church* (1860) 56.

33. For a more detailed analysis of the development of Free Methodist theological reflection in the twentieth century, see Cullum, "What Does it Mean to be a Methodist," 64–88.

34. J. S. MacGreary, "The Origin and Organization of the Free Methodist Church," *FM* (Aug. 9, 1910) 499.

35. In that same year, Bishop Hogue claimed that the Free Methodist Church was "the first distinctively holiness church organized in the United States," and that holiness or entire sanctification was the real issue in the formation of the denomination. See W. T. Hogue, "The Influence of the Free Methodist Church Beyond the Pale of Its Own Communion," *FM* (Aug. 10, 1910) 508.

36. "Our Church in This Age," *FM* (June 16, 1939) 374–76.

37. For example, see Paul S. Wheelock, "Evangelism in Early Methodism," *FM* (Mar. 5, 1943) 146; William Pearce, "Methodism in Its First Century," *FM* (June 4, 1943) 322; Lyle W. Northrup, "The Wesleyan Church, II: Its Method," *FM* (Feb. 1, 1946) 66; Mary Alice Tenney, "Early Methodism Speaks," *FM* (June 14, 1955) 370; "Pastoral Address," *Light and Life* [henceforth *LL*] (Oct. 1979) 44; and "The Pastoral Address," *LL* (Oct. 1985) 14–18.

38. See the appropriate sections of the *Free Methodist Discipline* for the years 1931–1955. See also the discussion in Marston, *From Age to Age a Living Witness*, 341–45.

39. Preface, *Hymns of the Living Faith* (Winona Lake, IN: Light and Life Press 1951).

40. *Hymns of Faith and Life* (Winona Lake, IN: Light and Life Press 1976; and Marion, IN: The Wesley Press 1976).

41. *Doctrines and Discipline of the Free Methodist Church of North America, 1955* (Winona Lake, IN: The Free Methodist Publishing House 1956) 214; Marston,

From Age to Age a Living Witness, 348–51. In 1985 the paragraph was rewritten so that it emphasized the need for churches to be physically accessible and to consider other long-term needs of the congregation when building.

42. *Doctrines and Discipline of the Free Methodist, 1955*, 40.

43. *Doctrines and Discipline of the Free Methodist Church of North America, 1964* (Winona Lake, IN: The Free Methodist Publishing House 1965) 192.

44. *The Book of Discipline, 1974* (Winona Lake, IN: The Free Methodist Publishing House 1975) 63.

45. Ibid., 67.

46. Ibid., 29.

47. Clyde E. Van Valin, ed., *Pastor's Handbook of the Free Methodist Church*, 2d ed. (Winona Lake, IN: Light and Life Press 1986) 170–71.

48. Paul N. Ellis, "Parents Dedicate, The Church Baptizes," *The Free Methodist Pastor* [henceforth *FMP*] (Summer 1983) 3.

49. For example, see John W. Howell, "Needed: A Liturgy for the Free Methodist Church," *FMP* (Mar. 1979) 1–2; Donald N. Bastian, "Worship in His Presence," *LL* (Sept. 1982) 26; Jeffrey Altman and T. Joe Culumber, "Styles of Worship," *LL* (Nov. 1984) 8; Robert Webber, "Everything But Worship," *LL* (Nov. 1984) 9–10; Donald E. Demaray, "Free Methodist Worship: A Blend of the Best," *LL* (July 1985) 23; John Vlainic, "Worship as Performance," *FMP* (Fall 1986) 6–8; John Paul Clark, "Worship; An Essential Key for Church Growth," *FMP* (Spring 1987) 8–10; and F. Dean Mercer, "The Liturgical Vision of Primitive Methodism," in *In the Church and in Christ Jesus: Essays in Honour of Donald N. Bastian*, ed. Felix W.-L. Sung (Mississauga, Ontario: Light and Life Press Canada 1993) 123–49.

50. "Pastoral Address," *LL* (Oct. 1985) 14–15.

51. These ideas have been gleaned from the newsletter of the Department of Evangelism and Church Growth, entitled *Reaching Out in Love* (Winter 1991–Winter 1995).

52. See news item in *Free Methodist Ministries Update* (July 1994) 2.

53. Clyde E. Van Valin, ed., *Pastor's Handbook of the Free Methodist Church*, 3d ed. (Winona Lake, IN: Light and Life Press 1991) 1.

54. Ibid., 5.

55. "Report of the Study Commission on Doctrine" (The Free Methodist Church of North America, 31st General Conference 1989) 1–17. See also the following essay by Paul W. Livermore which placed the issue of the structure of worship before the Free Methodist Church: "Synaxis and Eucharistia: An Examination of the Structure of Public Worship," in *Kerygma and Praxis: Essays in Honor of Stanley R. Magill*, eds. Wesley Vanderhoof and David Basinger (Rochester, NY: Roberts Wesleyan College 1984) 99–112.

Notes to Chapter 11

1. The title reflects not only Charles Wesley's hymn, "O For a Thousand Tongues to Sing," but also the Korean usage of the number 10,000—a myriad, or all. I would like gratefully to acknowledge the assistance of Dr. Yum Phil Hyung of the Methodist Theological Seminary in Seoul, and Mr. Song Baek Gul, a doctoral candidate at that school, in locating information for this essay. Korean names are written here with the family name first, following Korean custom.

2. A document written in 1886 states, "On Sunday afternoon July 24th in the quiet of his room of his own house with drawn curtains Mr. Appenzeller had

the great joy to Baptize his first Korean convert to Christianity" (Document 184, Appenzeller papers, Union Theological Seminary, New York). Dr. Scranton, also one of the pioneer Methodists, wrote later in 1904: "This was a solemn time with us. We worshipped in secret and in stealth, but we had the first fruits there and the power of the promise, 'Lo, I am with you always, even unto the end of the world'" (quoted in William Elliot Griffis, *A Modern Pioneer in Korea: The Life Story of Henry G. Appenzeller* [New York: Fleming Revell 1912] 209).

3. Henry G. Appenzeller, Monday, October 31, 1887, Diary No. 1, p. 37, Appenzeller papers.

4. On August 31, 1887, Appenzeller wrote in his diary, "It is the general opinion that the Korean Government means to wink at our labor as missionaries" (Diary No. 1, Appenzeller papers). "As missionaries" appears to distinguish evangelistic from educational and medical work, which were not restricted.

5. Appenzeller wrote, "In the p.m. [Christmas day] at two I preached my first sermon in Korean. . . . Text Matthew 1:21 'Thou shalt call his name Jesus,' &c." He added, "I am sure this is the first Methodist sermon ever preached in this country and perhaps the first formal sermon by any Protestant minister" (entry for Sunday, December 25, 1887, Diary No. 1, Appenzeller papers).

6. Ibid.

7. Entry for Sunday, December 25, 1887, Diary No. 1, Appenzeller papers.

8. William Scranton, a medical doctor who had been ordained just prior to his departure for Korea, was also one of the Methodist pioneers. The mention of his prayer having been read suggests that both Appenzeller and Scranton depended upon a written text in the phonetic Korean writing. There is much evidence showing that the learning of Korean was a long, arduous struggle for these early missionaries.

9. I am not certain whether there exists a text of the sermon that was preached on this occasion.

10. We may speculate that Christmas hymns and carols had not yet been translated or that the Korean Christians had not yet learned Christmas hymns. If a Christmas hymn *was* known, it might have been sung as the first hymn in this service.

11. This has been documented in Daniel Davies, *The Life and Thought of Henry Gerhard Appenzeller (1858–1902), Missionary to Korea* (Lewiston, NY: Edwin Mellon Press 1988) 323–24.

12. The Korean phonetic script was invented in 1443 by a group of scholars under the direction of King Sejong. It was intended to make a written form of the Korean language available to ordinary citizens, but the Confucian elite, proud of their literacy in Chinese, considered this "ordinary writing" a crutch for women and discouraged its use. It later became a powerful device for the dissemination of knowledge throughout the population in modern times, and was indispensable in Christian evangelism.

13. The services in the *Doctrines and Discipline* of the Methodist Episcopal Church and Methodist Episcopal Church, South, seem to have been the basic forms which the missionaries used.

14. Henry G. Appenzeller, sermon 138, Appenzeller papers (emphasis in original).

15. Comparisons of these orders of worship makes an interesting study. In the earliest Korean books of *Doctrine and Discipline*, for example, some of the Methodist Episcopal Church, South's elaborations and comments were included in the Korean worship orders that had been translated from the Methodist

Episcopal Church's forms. This can be seen in comparing *The Doctrines and Discipline of the Methodist Episcopal Church, 1908; The Doctrines and Discipline of the Methodist Episcopal Church, South, 1918*; and the related Korean versions of 1910 and 1919.

16. I have compared the Korean text with *The Doctrines and Discipline of the Methodist Episcopal Church, 1928*, and *The Doctrines and Discipline of the Methodist Episcopal Church, South*, for 1926 and 1930.

17. The heading "The Means of Grace for Church Members" is found in *The Doctrines and Discipline of the Korean Methodist Church* [*Kidokyo Chosunkyohoi Kyoli wa Changjong*] (1931) 56–58. This simplification is an interesting replication of the North American reduction of Wesley's Sunday services to a series of rubrics in 1792, which were then used until the mid-nineteenth century, although it seems unlikely that the parallel was intended. It is of interest to notice how John Wesley's listing of the means of grace has been modified, and his distinction dropped between the instituted and prudential means of grace.

18. ¶73, Korean *Doctrines and Discipline* (1931) 57–58. I have translated the text in the exact form given, reflecting some apparent inconsistencies; for example, the adding of "reading" with the New Testament, and the shift from "sacred music" to "special music." Neither variant seems to have significance.

19. Appenzeller and many of the earliest Protestant missionaries were suspicious of the Roman Catholic missionaries' wearing of Korean dress and immersion into Korean culture. One reason was that the Americans were disturbed by the political activities of the French, which they saw as undermining Korean national sovereignty and independence. This led Appenzeller to advocate a frank expression of Americanness in mission work, thus strengthening tendencies toward imposing western Methodist patterns upon Korean church life and worship.

20. During the eighteenth century, Korea had followed the Chinese Neo-Confucian revival, and had carried Confucian social distinctions to rather extreme lengths. Not only were husbands and wives expected to live in separate parts of the home, children were raised separately after early childhood, and when girls were educated, they were not allowed to be in the same schools with boys. Confucianism also reinforced vertical social distinctions, exaggerating tendencies toward authoritarianism in Christian ministry. In addition, the wearing of white mourning garb for long periods as a Confucian expression of filial piety had made Korea into a nation of people dressed in white.

21. These customs are described by Ms. Pauline Kim, former Professor of Christian Education at the Methodist Theological Seminary in Seoul, who is now (in 1995) 96 years of age. The description given here is of her grandmother's baptism.

22. While some Koreans did give thought to the expression of Christian faith in Korean form, most seem to have accepted western forms without question. The association of western ways with progressive social change may have reinforced this attitude.

23. The two principal Methodist sources for investigating worship in Korea today are the *Book of Worship* [*Kidokyo Taehan Kamnihoi Yebaeso*] (Seoul: Korean Methodist Church 1992), and *The Renewal of Worship for Ministry* (Seoul: Methodist Theological Seminary 1991). The former contains a variety of worship services, a lectionary, and many special readings and prayers for the Christian year and special occasions. The latter is a collection of essays related to worship,

including a suggested worship form, historical studies, and theological analyses. So far as I am aware, there are no statistical surveys or studies of worship patterns in Korea. It would be useful if such research could be done, to help identify the extent of certain worship patterns and variations related to such conditions as location and social status.

24. The Korean Methodist Church's 1992 *Book of Worship* gives both a full and shortened order of worship. The shorter form (on pages 14–15) is given as follows:

Prelude

Call to Worship (reading of scripture, or a hymn sung by the choir)

Hymn (standing)

Prayer (the minister leads as appropriate an invocation, a prayer for the day, and the Lord's Prayer)

Reading and Gloria* (standing, read either responsively or together)

Hymn

Scripture Reading

Confession of Faith (standing, reading either the Apostles' Creed or the Declaration of Doctrines [the Korean Creed], responsively or together, followed by sung Gloria*)

Pastoral Prayer

Offering

Offertory Prayer (at the pastor's discretion the offering and offertory prayer may be moved to follow the sermon)

Greetings among the congregation

Anthem (literally, "special music")

Sermon (proclamation of the Word)

Hymn of Commitment (standing)

Benediction

Postlude

*The Korean word here, *songyong*, can mean either a Gloria Patri or a Doxology. The appearance in two places could indicate a combining of different traditions here. Perhaps there is an influence from Presbyterian practice in which the Gloria is placed after the confession of faith as an act of praise.

25. Although the standard form of worship is often retained, including a formal sermon, in services for youth (and even small church school children) some attention has been given to greater flexibility and informality, as exemplified by the use of storytelling, guitars, drama, and visual aids.

26. In the hymnal (*Chansongga*) currently in use, published in 1983, out of 550 hymns (plus eight Amens), sixteen have both words and tunes written by Koreans, while there is one western tune with Korean-composed words. Some of these tunes are quite western in flavor, though others are distinctively Korean.

27. The "Korean Creed" was composed in 1930 at the time when the Korean Methodist Church became autonomous. In Korea it is called the Declaration of Doctrines. At present its origins and composition are not fully known, but it is clear that both Americans and Koreans were involved in its preparation. It has been challenged in Korea in recent years as being too liberal theologically and insufficiently biblical.

28. The older books of *Discipline* instructed that the congregation should stand during the recitation of the creed, but the simplified order of worship in the *Discipline* of 1930 omitted that instruction. Whether this fact accounts for the creed sometimes being recited with the people seated is not clear. The creeds are sometimes recited responsively, a choice allowed in the disciplinary format.

29. This has been a recent development. See the Korean Methodist *Book of Worship*. The lectionary is in the section on the Church year, pages 74–78. This may well be an influence from the United Methodist Church, in view of the large number of references to United Methodist sources in recent Korean writing on worship.

30. In the hymnal there are thirty-three readings from the Psalms, one from Proverbs, seven from Isaiah, and thirty-five from the New Testament.

31. One of the more interesting of these revisions consisted of removing two syllables from the Lord's Prayer. These have no substantial meaning, and reflected an earlier and outdated use of Korean. They have been restored.

32. In Korean Methodist churches elders are qualified before the district conferences, and are installed by the laying on of hands. In Korean Methodism there has been much tension between elders and ordained ministers (who are not called elders as in United Methodism), perhaps because the duties and authority of the elders are not as clearly defined as in Presbyterianism.

Presbyterians are by far the largest Christian group in Korea, and their influence has modified Methodism significantly. Other examples of this influence have been the weakening of the connectional system and the appointive power of the episcopacy. There has thus been a tendency for local pastors to remain in their charges for longer periods of time. Some Methodist pastors, especially those in large churches, now see their appointments as virtually guaranteed for life.

33. This is called *tongsong kido*, or "prayer spoken together." Its origins in Korean Christian worship are obscure. Some have suggested that the practice may be related to shamanism, with its belief in spirits entering persons and speaking through them, and its inducement of ecstatic states. It remains an open question whether Pentecostalism or shamanism is responsible for initiating the custom, but it seems plain that they reinforce one another.

34. I am not sure when or how this Korean oratorical style began, but it seems venerable, and is used in many settings, such as at political rallies and funeral services. It almost certainly predates the introduction of Christian worship into Korean society.

35. Expository preaching and teaching are the rule for the evening services, especially on Wednesday evening, and at the class meetings.

36. The words are a translation of the text by Thomas Ken. This is another place in the hymnal where a new translation was tried, then later rescinded.

37. Birthdays, weddings, graduations, recovery from illness, and other such events are often occasions for thank offerings. It is customary in many churches for a newly employed person to give the first month's salary as a thank offering.

38. The thanksgiving service has come to have a special place in Korean worship, especially as a source of income. This was the time when rural people were most able to bring offerings, so it became a logical focal point for pastoral appeals to support the life and work of the church. The service is not timed to coincide with the Korean autumn moon festival, but usually comes later, in October, which suggests western influence. The thematic content is centered on the harvest and thankfulness for God's gifts, and there is no relating of this thanksgiving to national origins or patriotism. After several weeks of reminders and preparations, the offering is frequently given by the congregation filing forward and placing the envelopes in a basket during the singing of thanksgiving hymns.

39. Although there has been much private relaxing of rigorous standards against alcohol and tobacco use among Protestants, the official position still calls for abstinence, especially among the clergy. As might be expected, such restrictions are not imposed in the Roman Catholic, Anglican, or Lutheran Churches of Korea.

40. This has been an interesting cultural phenomenon. A type of pound cake called *castella*, after a Japanese term presumably acquired from early Portuguese traders there, was for many years the only commonly available form of western-style baked goods in Korea. It was long assumed that this was the most suitable substance to use for bread in the communion service.

41. There are many varieties of both wine and rice cakes in Korea. Rice wine can vary from a milky product with a short life to varieties of flavored wines of high quality. Grape and other types of wine are also now common on the Korean market. Rice cake can be light and crisp, or a sticky product made from glutenous rice. The choice of elements is now a matter of taste and cultural preference, not to mention theological conviction. Some Methodist churches are now using unleavened wafers made specifically for communion. This is very different from the situation, even thirty years ago, when it was difficult to find wine, grape juice, or bread for a communion service. Missionaries and others would sometimes carry back grape-flavored powdered drink mixes for communion use when they returned from the West.

42. While there is a background in the Old Testament and in classic Christian usage for this view of benediction, its introduction here may be evidence of a Christian appropriation of a shamanist belief, wherein spirit power is granted through the physical mediation of a special person. It may also reflect authoritarian tendencies in Korean ministry, where ministers often stress distinctions between laity and clergy.

43. The Korean language has changed greatly during the last century. Not only has Korea opened to the West, but pronounced regional dialects, class-based vertical distinctions, and the older scholarly preoccupation with elegance have been lessened, so that the language has become more uniform, egalitarian, and rapidly changing. An influx of loan words accompanied the Japanese annexation (1910–1945), while the saturation of South Korea by television has further opened the language to international influences and to standardization.

44. Reading and discussing the Bible in English has long been a popular way for students to hone their language skills. Korean translations of some of the more colloquial English translations are understandably well received by young people.

45. Although there has been some debate about the origins of the terms,

hananim appears to derive from the idea of oneness (*hana*), and thus suggest monotheism, while *hanunim* seems to originate from a term for the sky or heaven (*hanul*), and thus connote the Lord of Heaven. This comes close to the meaning of the Chinese *Chonju*, the term Roman Catholics in China chose centuries ago for God, and the one used in the Korean name designating the Roman Catholic Church.

46. *Song* is the usual Korean term for holy. The distinction between *yong*, closer to the more general idea of spirit, and *shin*, more suggestive of god or divine being(s), does not seem to be the basis upon which the use of the term for Holy Spirit has turned. Recent usage seems to favor *songyong* in worship. Though *songshin* is still widely used in theological discussion, it is mainly older people who persist in using it in worship contexts.

47. Aloysius Pieris, a Sri Lankan Jesuit theologian, has discussed these matters incisively in essays found in his *An Asian Theology of Liberation* (Maryknoll, NY: Orbis Books 1988), especially in Chapter 4, "Asia's Non-Semitic Religions and the Mission of Local Churches."

Notes to Chapter 12

1. Theodore R. Doraisamy, *The March of Methodism in Singapore and Malaysia, 1885–1980* (Singapore: Methodist Book Room 1982) 7.

2. Bobby Sng, *In His Good Time: The Story of the Church in Singapore, 1819–1992* (Singapore: Graduates' Christian Fellowship 1993) 89–91.

3. Ibid., 121, 126–27, 145; cf. W. F. Oldham, *Thoburn: Called of God* (New York and Cincinnati: Methodist Book Concern 1918) 136–37.

4. For example, the Malay Chapel of the Presbyterians (1860), the Chinese Gospel Hall of the Brethren (1866), and the Missions Chapel of the Anglicans (1873).

5. Doraisamy, *The March of Methodism*, 16.

6. Sng, *In His Good Time*, 78.

7. Doraisamy, *The March of Methodism*, 63. Bishop Doraisamy was referring to the January and the July 1928 issues of the *Malaysia Message*.

8. As well as Mandarin, the Chinese dialects would include Cantonese, Hokkien, and Hakka. The predominant use of Mandarin as a unifying Chinese language was not found until much later.

9. The first recorded instance of Methodist charismatic experiences was found in the Anglo-Chinese Secondary School.

10. The Seminar on Music Ministries, first hosted by Wesley Methodist Church, and Festival of Praise, hosted by an interdenominational conglomerate of churches including several Methodist churches, are keen on promoting the Praise and Worship format found in Singapore. They feature artists such as Bob Fitts, Tom Brooks, Paul Baloche, Ed Kerr, David Fellingham, and Chris Bowater.

11. The Order of St. Luke, a liturgical order found within the United Methodist Church, was introduced to Singapore in the form of an association. However, this association was dissolved for several reasons. Nevertheless, several persons are still affiliated with the Order on an individual basis.

12. Curriculums from Trinity Theological College and Singapore Bible College, two premier theological institutions in Singapore, reveal that worship and liturgy are required courses for all pursuing theological education at a basic level (M.Div., B.D., B.Th.); however, the courses are basically historical and introduc-

tory in nature. There is no emphasis built into the course on developing liturgy for the local church.

13. To gather information for this essay, a survey was conducted by the author with the assistance of the Rev. Lorna Khoo, then pastor of the Methodist Church of the Incarnation, and Mary Gan, Chairperson of the Council on Worship and Music and a faculty member of Trinity Theological College. Approximately one hundred survey forms were distributed to various leaders of the thirty-seven Methodist churches in Singapore. Responses came from 32 percent of those surveyed. Unfortunately, no results could be obtained from the seven Tamil-speaking churches.

14. See Tom Brooks, ed. *Hosanna! Music, Praise, and Worship* (Mobile, AL.: Integrity Music), vols. 1 (1987), 2 (1988), 3 (1989), 4 (1990), 5 (1991), 6 (1992), 7 (1993); Dave Garatt and Dale Garatt, eds., *Scripture in Songs* (Maryborough, Australia: Scripture in Songs), vol. 1 "Songs of Praise" (1979), vol. 2 "Songs of the Kingdom" (1981, rev. ed. 1983), vol. 3 "Songs of the Nation" (1988); Vineyard Ministries International, *Songs of the Vineyard*, 3 vols. (Anaheim, CA.: Mercy/Vineyard Publishing 1991); and *Songs of Fellowship* (Eastbourne, U.K.: Kingsway Music 1990).

15. *Hymns of Praise* (Singapore: Christian National Evangelism Committee 1978). The original edition of the *Hymnal of Universal Praise* was published in 1936 by the Christian Literature Society in Shanghai. A subsequent edition (1977) was produced by the Chinese Christian Literature Council in Hong Kong. The English edition of this hymnal was published in 1981.

16. Compositions for special occasions include "Let's celebrate His goodness" (Terence Tan of Grace Methodist Church), "Lord bless Singapore" (the Reverend Melvin Huang of Trinity Methodist Church), and the following produced by persons from Wesley Methodist Church: "I will lift you high above" (Hazel Beng); "Give" (Raymond Fong); "Bring Light to the World" (Jusuf Kam); and "The Armour of God" (Alan Samuel).

17. Presently, there are professionals who compose on an occasional basis. These include Bernard Tan (a lecturer at the National University of Singapore), Mary Tan (a lawyer), Samuel Liew (a publisher who has emigrated to the United States), and the author of this essay.

18. This song may have come from either Taiwan or Hong Kong. The composer is unknown.

19. Wesley Methodist Church holds a Wednesday morning communion service primarily for its staff. The Methodist Church of the Incarnation celebrates communion weekly on Thursday evenings.

20. Permission to use this copyrighted music may be obtained by contacting the author at 33 Metropole Drive, Singapore 1545, Republic of Singapore.

Notes to Chapter 13

1. Dr. Thomas Kane, Paulist priest and Weston School of Theology liturgical scholar, has produced an imaginative and entertaining video presentation of African worship, dance, and music. During visits to Ethiopia, Malawi, Kenya, Zaire, Cameroon, and Ghana, he videotaped a variety of Sunday liturgies which employ the rich forms of indigenous African music and dance. Here is a model well worth emulating. The 1992 videotape, subtitled *Video Impressions of the*

Church in Africa, is available from Paulist Press; cf. the appreciative review of R. Kevin Seasoltz in *Worship* 67 (1993) 253–61.

2. Since the mid 1960s, following the promulgation of *Sacrosanctum Concilium* by the Second Vatican Council and the publication of Bolaji Idowu's talks arguing for the indigenization of the Church (*Towards an Indigenous Church* [London: Oxford University Press 1965]), much effort has been devoted to this task. With regard to the African independent or indigenous Christian traditions, the works of Inus Daneel (*Quest for Belonging* [Gweru, Zimbabwe: Mambo Press 1987]) and H. W. Turner (*Religious Innovation in Africa* [London: Oxford University Press 1979]) remain the most thorough and balanced studies available. The works of Aylward Shorter (*African Culture and the Christian Church* [Maryknoll, NY: Orbis Books 1974] and *Toward a Theology of Inculturation* [Maryknoll, NY: Orbis Books 1988]) are representative of the ever-expanding literature related to Africa in the Roman Catholic tradition (cf. Joseph Healey, "Inculturation of Liturgy and Worship in Africa," *Worship* 60 [1986] 412–23 and E. E. Uzukwu, "African Symbols and Christian Liturgical Celebration," *Worship* 62 [1991] 98–112). John Parratt's *A Reader in African Christian Theology* (London: SPCK 1987), in the Theological Education Fund series, includes only two selections related to worship in the African Church, one on initiation, by the Cameroonian priest Marc Ntetem, and the other on healing by the early twentieth-century *Aladura* leader, J. Ade Aina. Concerning non-Methodist Protestant traditions, see Felix N. Nwahanghi, "Contextualization of Christian Liturgy in Igboland: A Pragmatic Approach to African Christian Theology," *African Theological Journal* 20 (1991) 123–35. The recent book of Anglican ecumenical theologian, John Pobee (*Skenosis: Christian Faith in an African Context* [Gweru, Zimbabwe: Mambo Press 1992]), is one of the most profound contributions to date. Based upon an earlier article, one of only two selections by African scholars to appear in *Studia Liturgica* to date, Pobee argues for a *skenosis*, a process of "tabernacling" the soul of the eternal Gospel in the African context (cf. his earlier groundbreaking collection of essays under the title *Religion in a Pluralistic Society* [Leiden: E. J. Brill 1977] and the similar collection of Ram Desai, *Christianity in Africa as Seen by the Africans* [Denver: Allan Swallow 1962]).

3. John Mbiti, *African Religions and Philosophy* (New York: Doubleday 1970) 19.

4. Paul Connerton, *How Societies Remember* (Cambridge and New York: Cambridge University Press 1989) 73–78.

5. Mbiti, *African Religions and Philosophy*, 109, 117, 127.

6. First published in the early 1950s with a revision in 1964 including additional material on *Kiumia Gia Kurugura Kanisa* (service for opening a new church) and *Rwimbo rwa Mugongo* (the national anthem) in its Kiswahili and English versions.

7. Lamin Sanneh, *Translating the Message: The Missionary Impact on Culture* (Maryknoll, NY: Orbis Books 1990) 247.

8. The Meru myths of origin have baffled researchers since they were first well documented by Bernardo Bernardi. Good accounts can be found in Bernardi, *The Mugwe, A Failing Prophet* (London: Oxford University Press 1959) 52–67; Jeffrey A. Fadiman, *When We Began There Were Witchmen: An Oral History from Mt. Kenya* (Berkeley: University of California Press 1993) 19–65; Alfred M. M'imanyara, *The Re-statement of Bantu Origin and Meru History* (Nairobi, Kenya: Longman 1992) 41–44; and D. M. Rimita, *The Njuri-Ncheke of Meru* (Meru, Kenya: Kolbe Press 1988) 7–13.

9. Traditionally among the Meru of Kenya, it is in the religious instruction classes that people were at the same time taught to read and write. Religious instruction classes were, in effect, also literacy classes. Religious instructors were seen and popularly addressed in the community as "teacher" without differentiating whether they were religious or secular teachers. Christianity and the ability to read and write, therefore, were seen as synonymous. All church people were collectively called *Athomi*, literally, "readers."

10. The practice of Africans acquiring European names at the time of baptism was always regarded from the point of view of traditional naming rituals. It is appropriate to observe that many Africans are currently reexamining this practice. Many African Christians are proudly retaining their African names at baptism without the feeling that they are any less Christian in so doing. The practice of acquiring foreign names at baptism is one of the unfortunate legacies of missionary Christianity. Baptism among Methodists in Africa has traditionally been seen in the light of the Gospel injunction to "shed the old nature of sin and corruption and put on the Lord Jesus." It was easy, therefore, for unsuspecting initiates to be stripped of their identity as Africans because of the similarity to their own traditional rites of passage. Concerning other matters related to initiation, see Marc Ntetem, "Initiation, Traditional and Christian," in Parratt, *A Reader in African Christian Theology*, 103–8.

11. Eugene Hillman, *Toward an African Christianity* (New York: Paulist Press 1993) 58. Such practices were common among the Masai also.

12. *Ndimbo cia Kwinira Murungu*, "Ubatithio bwa twana Tunyi" (Baptism of a Child), 118–19.

13. Rodney Needham, "The Left Hand of the Mugwe: An Analytical Note of the Structure of Meru Symbolism," in *Right and Left*, ed. Rodney Needham (Chicago: University of Chicago Press 1973) 114, 119.

14. *Jesu Tawa Pano* is an original composition in Shona by Patrick Matsikenyiri, and should be sung joyfully, accompanied with maracas or other percussive instruments. This is one of over 80 songs which Patrick has composed and which he keeps (in four or more parts) in his head. The transcriber of this song mentioned to Patrick that there seemed to be a clash in the harmony in bar 5, where the tenor sings a major 7th above the bass. To which Patrick laughed and said, "My dear John, if you knew the history of our country, you would know that we have had so many clashes that a little difficulty in the harmony will cause us no problems."

15. The influence of the camp meeting tradition in Zimbabwean United Methodism, similar to that of the East African revival in Kenyan Methodism, has left a strong legacy of "pulpit-centered" worship with little emphasis on the sacramental life of the church. Combined with other factors not dissimilar to those of the American frontier during the early years of Methodism in that context, such as the lack of ordained clergy, transportation difficulties, and the influences of "a-sacramental theological traditions," this influence has militated against the Wesleyan Methodist synthesis of word and sacrament.

16. Quoted in Kwesi A. Dickson, *Theology in Africa* (Maryknoll, NY: Orbis Books 1984) 94.

17. Mercy Oduyoye observes: "On the whole, however, it is the Roman Catholic church, not the Euro-American Protestant churches in Africa, which has taken acculturation seriously" (*Hearing and Knowing* [Maryknoll, NY: Orbis Books 1986] 71).

18. Dickson, *Theology in Africa*, 95.

19. Oduyoye, *Hearing and Knowing*, 72.

20. Zablon Nthamburi, *The African Church at the Crossroads: Strategy for Indigenization* (Nairobi, Kenya: Uzima 1991) especially 55–61.

21. Canaan Banana, *Come and Share: An Introduction to Christian Theology* (Gweru, Zimbabwe: Mambo Press 1991) 75–95.

22. Dickson, *Theology in Africa*, 111.

23. Banana, *Come and Share*, 83. An interesting discussion of tradition and community may be found in Newell S. Booth, Jr., "Tradition and Community in African Religion," *Journal of Religion in Africa* 9 (1978) 81–94.

24. To offer just one example of potential exploration, consider the concept of sacrifice. Justin Ukpong, Nigerian Catholic scholar, has identified no fewer than twenty-seven different types of formal sacrifice among the Ibibio of southeastern Nigeria. So, when the Christian preacher describes the sacrifice of Christ and its relationship to the celebration of eucharist, what is conjured up in the mind of the African? And what depth of insight might African traditional practices offer in the exploration of these themes? See "Sacrificial Worship in Ibibio Traditional Religion," *Journal of Religion in Africa* 13 (1982) 161–88. Also of interest in this regard is J. Omosade Awolalu, "Yoruba Sacrificial Practice," *Journal of Religion in Africa* 5 (1973) 82–93.

Notes to Chapter 14

1. Preface, *The Prayer Book of The Methodist Church* (Peterborough, England: Methodist Publishing House on behalf of the Methodist Church in the Caribbean and the Americas 1992) v.

2. A fuller explanation of the "breakdown" in the standardization of liturgical form is presented in the preface of the 1992 *Prayer Book*.

3. The hymn book used is the *Methodist Hymn-Book* (London: Methodist Conference Office 1933).

4. The first two General Directions read: "(1) The Order of Service has been so designed that PART I may be used as a self-contained unit as well as a Preparatory when either the Sacrament of Holy Baptism or the Sacrament of the Lord's Supper is observed. (2) PART I shall always be used when the Observance of either the Sacrament of Holy Baptism or the Sacrament of the Lord's Supper is observed. Otherwise its use is optional, either in whole or in part, save that the basic pattern and structure are adhered to and that the Introits, Collects, Scripture Readings and the Creed and Intercessions are used at the appointed places in the Order" (*The Prayer Book of The Methodist Church*, 67).

5. Ibid., 68–75.

6. Ibid., 77.

7. These rites are entitled "A Daily Office for the Family," "A Family Office of Preparation for the Lord's Day," and "A Family Office at the Close of the Lord's Day." Ibid., 239–43.

Notes to Chapter 15

1. Text by Sarah Poulton Kalley, the first Protestant woman missionary in Brazil, in *Hinário Evangélico* (São Paulo: Imprensa Metodista 1992) no. 65.

2. Texts by Alfredo H. da Silva and Henry M. Wright in *Hinário Evangélico,* nos. 422 and 399.

3. Source unknown.

4. Extract from the preface of the book of J. J. Ransom, *O Culto Dominical,* in Carl Joseph Hahn, *História do Culto Protestante no Brasil* (São Paulo: Aste 1989) 243–44.

5. Ibid., 244. J. J. Ransom also served as a missionary in Cuba, and there he had a mission to help lay leadership build up the Sunday School and worship.

6. *Cânones da Igreja Metodista do Brasil* (São Paulo: Imprensa Metodista 1950) 148–49.

7. In Pablo D. Sosa, ed., *Todas las Voces: Taller de Música y Liturgia en América Latina* (San José, Costa Rica: Sebila-Clai 1988) 74.

8. Tune written by D. Henriquete Braga in *Hinário Evangélico,* no. 92. Its character as a popular song (*modinha*) is clear: the minor key, the melodic shape, and the phrase endings. In many of these songs, in order to perceive better the style hidden by heavy choral harmonization, it is necessary that the tune be heard to the accompaniment of a guitar.

9. Choruses, generally, are short, repetitive songs which are then added one to the other.

10. Source unknown.

11. Jaci C. Maraschin and Simei Monteiro, *A Canção do Senhor na Terra Brasileira* (São Paulo: Aste 1982).

12. "O Tejo é mais belo que o rio que corre pela minha aldeia. Mas o Tejo não é mais belo que o rio que corre pela minha aldeia porque o Tejo não é o rio que corre pela minha aldeia" (Fernando Pessoa, *Obra Poética* [Rio de Janeiro: Companhia Aguilar Editora 1965] 215).

13. Jaci C. Maraschin, ed., *O Novo Canto da Terra* (São Paulo: Editora do Instituto Anglicano de Estudos Teológicos 1987).

14. Words from the prologue of issue no. 2 of *Cancionero Abierto,* in *La Tradición Protestante en la Teología Latinoamericana—Primer intento: lectura de la tradición metodista,* ed. José Duque (San José, Costa Rica: DEI 1983) 328.

15. Passage adapted for this essay. See Simei Monteiro, *O Cântico da Vida* (São Bernardo do Campo-SP: Aste-Ciências da Religião 1991) 177.

Notes to Chapter 16

1. For the German tradition and "culture" of liturgy and worship, see the magisterial work of Hans-Christoph Schmidt-Lauber and Karl-Heinrich Bieritz, eds., *Handbuch der Liturgik: Liturgiewissenschaft in Theologie und Praxis der Kirche* (Leipzig: Evangelische Verlagsanstalt 1995; Göttingen: Vandenhoeck & Ruprecht, 1995). The book includes an article of James F. White: "Gottesdienst im freikirchlichen und charismatischen Kontext" (pp. 186–94). White gives a short sketch of the Wesleyan roots of worship in the Methodist tradition (pp. 190–91). So my essay may be a kind of German supplement and a small tribute from this country to honor James F. White and his work.

I want to express my thanks to the Reverend Karl Heinz Voigt of Kiel who helped me very much with his advice and by sending me material out of his large collection of Methodist sources.

2. Cf. the articles of Karl Heinz Voigt, Alfred Schütz, and Paul Wüthrich in

Geschichte der Evangelisch-methodistischen Kirche, eds. Karl Steckel and C. Ernst Sommer (Stuttgart: Christliches Verlagshaus 1982) 85–112, 119–31, 149–203.

3. Rev. Dr. John Lyth, in *Der Methodisten Herold* (1872) 92; quoted in Karl Heinz Voigt, "Die Methodistenkirche in Deutschland," in *Geschichte der Evangelisch-methodistischen Kirche,* 86.

4. Letter of Ludwig S. Jacoby, 24 February 1851 (obtained by personal communication with Karl Heinz Voigt).

5. W. W. Orwig, in *Christlicher Botschafter* (1853) 29; quoted in Paul Wüthrich, "Die Evangelische Gemeinschaft im deutschsprachigen Europa," in *Geschichte der Evangelisch-methodistischen Kirche,* 157.

6. There is not much material about our subject from the side of the United Brethren. The hymnbook used in Germany was *Gesangbuch der Ver.[einigten] Brüder in Christo: Eine Auswahl geistlicher Lieder für kirchlichen und häuslichen Gebrauch* (Dayton, OH: W. J. Shuey 1894).

7. In the Evangelical Association there was a common Central Conference in Europe until 1968; the establishment of a special Central Conference of the Methodist Episcopal Church for Germany in 1936 was a very painful experience for the other members of the former Central Conference in Central Europe; cf. Wilhelm Nausner, "Das Werden der Zentralkonferenz von Mittel- und Südeuropa," in *Geschichte der Evangelisch-methodistischen Kirche,* 136–48.

8. This may be seen in many reports from the first days of Methodism in Germany; cf. memoirs of Ahlerd Gerhard Bruns (1833–1925), typescript 1994, Reutlingen Theological Seminary Library. Ludwig S. Jacoby, in his *Handbuch des Methodismus, enthaltend die Geschichte, Lehre, das Kirchenregiment und eigenthümliche Gebräuche, desselben* (Bremen: Verlag von Johann Georg Heyse 1853; 2d ed. 1855), mentions especially the class meetings and love feasts when he deals with the institutions and customs which are peculiar to the Methodists.

9. Cf. the "Pastoraltheologie" of Johannes Schempp, Dean of the Seminary of the Evangelical Association in Reutlingen, in the section "Der Predigtgottesdienst" (typescript [no year], pp. 101ff, Reutlingen Theological Seminary Library). The outline of *Praktische Theologie: Ein Handbuch der Homiletik und Pastoraltheologie vom methodistischen Standpunkt für Prediger und Seelsorger sowie für Mitarbeiter am Reiche Gottes* (Bremen: Verlag des Tractathauses 1879) of Ludwig Nippert, Dean of the Seminary of the Methodist Episcopal Church in Frankfurt, does not even mention the worship service. It may have been of some importance that the Lutheran Church of Württemberg, where Methodism was very strong, had also a very simple pattern of a "Predigtgottesdienst" as its main Sunday service which had its origins in the "Prädikantengottesdienst" in the Free Cities of the late Middle Ages; cf. Eberhard Winkler, "Der Predigtgottesdienst," in *Handbuch der Liturgik,* 248–70.

10. Cf. Ludwig S. Jacoby, *Geschichte des amerikanischen Methodismus und die Ausbreitung desselben unter den Deutschen; seine Missionen, seine Kirchenordnung und gottesdienstlichen Gebräuche, sowie die Lehren des Methodismus überhaupt* (Bremen: Verlag des Tractathauses 1870) 372–89; and Heinrich Mann, "Unsere Ordnung in den öffentlichen Gottesdiensten," *Wächterstimmen* 26 (1896) 17–23.

11. Ludwig S. Jacoby wrote: Methodists are not bound to external forms. In their own congregations they will pray kneeling, but if they attend other churches where people pray standing, they too will stand. ("Solange jedoch ein Leben aus Gott in der Methodistenkirche verbleibt, werden die Methodisten auch auf den Knien ihren Gott und Heiland anbeten, wenn sie auch zu anderen

Zeiten mit eben der Andacht stehend zu Gott beten können, wenn sie sich in der Mitte christlicher Gemeinden befinden, die das stehende Gebet eingeführt haben" [*Geschichte*, 375]). The 1948 liturgy of the Methodist Episcopal Church in Germany gives the instruction to stand during prayer!

12. Part I, Chapter III, Section I.

13. *Liturgie der Bischöflichen Methodistenkirche für die deutschsprechenden Konferenzen des Mitteleuropäischen Sprengels* (Zürich: Christliche Vereinsbuchhandlung 1928; and Bremen: Buchhandlung und Verlag des Traktathauses 1928).

14. *Liturgie der Methodistenkirche: Herausgegeben auf Anordnung der Zentralkonferenz der Methodistenkirche in Deutschland* (Frankfurt am Main: Anker-Verlag 1948).

15. *Christenlieder: Herausgegeben von der Evangelischen Gemeinschaft* (Bern: Christliches Verlagshaus 1952).

16. Evangelische Gemeinschaft in Europa, *Agende* (Stuttgart: Christliches Verlagshaus 1963).

17. Cf. Evangelisch Kirche der Union, *Agende*, Band 1: Die Gemeindegottesdienste (Bielefeld: Luther Verlag 1959) 121–24; the main difference is the omission of the Kyrie eleison.

18. This movement was part of the German Youth Movement of the early 1920s. It encouraged the revival of folk songs, the use of such historic instruments as recorders and lute, and the education of young people in a capella singing. Although not connected with the life of the Church at the beginning, the movement soon became very influential for German sacred music. See W. Blankenburg, "Singbewegung" in *Die Religion in Geschichte und Gegenwart*, 3d ed. (Tübingen: J. C. B. Mohr 1962) 6:45–46.

19. Evangelisch-methodistische Kirche, *Agende* (Stuttgart: Christliches Verlagshaus 1973).

20. Evangelisch-methodistische Kirche, *Agende* (Stuttgart: Christliches Verlagshaus 1991).

21. *Liturgie der Evangelisch-methodistischen Kirche* (Zürich: Verlag CVB Buch & Druck 1981).

22. Christhard Mahrenholz (*Kompendium der Liturgik des Hauptgottesdienstes* [Kassel: Johannes Stauda Verlag 1963]) includes thirteen examples of liturgies for Sunday worship in German Protestant churches, none of which regularly uses a lesson from the Old Testament!

23. Cf. already the letters of Ludwig S. Jacoby to the Board of Mission of the Methodist Episcopal Church from October and November 1855 (*Der Christliche Apologete* [November 15, 1855] 182); and also Wilhelm Körber, "Die Neugestaltung unserer Vierteljahrs-Sonntage" *Wächterstimmen* 64 (1939) 94–98.

24. *Die Lehre und Kirchenordnung der Bischöflichen Methodistenkirche* (Cincinnati: Swarnstedt & Poe 1856) 121.

25. In a letter from April 25, 1851, in *Der Christliche Apologete* (13 [May 22, 1851] 83), Heinrich Nülsen notes that visitors who sought communion were examined by the preacher concerning their state of grace, and especially they were asked whether they abstained from brandy and kept the sabbath. ("Niemand ausser den Gliedern wurde hinzugelassen, es sei denn, er habe sich beim Prediger gemeldet. Vom Prediger werden sie über ihren Gnadenstand befragt und er gibt ihnen alsdann eine passende Ermahnung. Besonders aber werden sie gefragt, ob sie sich des Genusses von Branntwein und der Entheiligung des Sabbats enthalten; nur wenn dieses der Fall ist, können sie zum Heiligen Abendmahl zugelassen werden.")

26. *Ordnung der Verwaltung des Abendmahls des Herrn und der Taufe sowie der Einsegnung der Ehe, Begräbnisfeier und Ordination der Prediger nach dem Gebrauch der Wesleyanischen Methodisten* ([Waiblingen]: Verlag der Wesleyanischen Methodisten-Gemeinschaft 1874).

27. "Eat the bread, which we break, in remembrance that Christ gave His body for thee, and died the bitter death of the cross on Calvary, that thou mayest live forever: feed on Him in thy heart by faith, and be thankful. . . . Drink of this in remembrance that Christ's blood was shed for thee, for the washing away of all thy sins, and the sanctification of thy soul; partake of it in thy heart by faith, and be thankful."

28. *Zions-Harfe: Eine Sammlung von Geistlichen Liedern zum Gemeinschaftlichen Gebrauch* (Winnenden: Verlag der Wesleyanisch-Methodistischen Missionsgesellschaft 1863). The book contains 613 hymns, text only.

29. The second edition, *Zionsharfe: Gesangbuch für die deutschen Wesleyanischen Methodisten* (Cannstatt: Verlag der Wesleyanischen Methodisten-Gemeinschaft 1878 [640 hymns; text with music in harmony for four voices]), has a more explicit outline:

Von Gott (God)

Von Christo (Christ)

Von dem Heiligen Geist (Holy Spirit)

Pfingstlieder (Pentecost Hymns)

Das Wort Gottes (The Word of God)

Die Kirche Christi (The Church of Christ)

Die Gnadenmittel (The Means of Grace)

Von der Heilsordnung (The Order of Salvation)

Von dem christlichen Leben und Wandel (The Christian Life and Walk)

Verschiedene Verhältnisse und Umstände (Various Occasions and Circumstances)

Von den letzten Dingen (The Last Things)

30. *Deutsches Gesangbuch der Bischöflichen Methodisten-Kirche, Eine neue Auswahl geistlicher Lieder für Kirche, Haus und Schule* (Cincinnati: Cranston & Stowe 1865). There was an earlier edition of a German Methodist hymnbook that contained 524 hymns without music: [Wilhelm Nast, ed.], *Sammlung von Geistlichen Liedern für kirchlichen und häuslichen Gottesdienst* (Cincinnati: Swormstedt & Poe 1839; 4th ed. Bremen: J. G. Heyse 1861; 5th ed. Bremen: Verlag des Tractathauses 1864).

31. [W. Nast and H. Liebhardt, eds.,] *Deutsches Gesang- und Melodienbuch der Bischöflichen Methodisten-Kirche* (Cincinnati: Jennings & Pye 1888).

32. *Gesangbuch der Bischöflichen Methodistenkirche für die Gemeinden in Deutschland* (Bremen: Verlag des Traktathauses 1926; 10th ed. Frankfurt: Anker-Verlag 1959). The book comprises 807 hymns with music in harmony. A supplement published in 1956 added twenty hymns.

33. *Gesangbuch für die Evangelische Gemeinschaft* (Reutlingen: Verlag der Evangelischen Gemeinschaft 1873; 9th ed. Stuttgart: Christliches Verlagshaus 1898). No music was provided for the 720 hymns of this collection. The American

edition, *Gesangbuch der Evangelischen Gemeinschaft für öffentlichen und häuslichen Gebrauch* (Cleveland, OH: Verlagshaus der Evangelischen Gemeinschaft 1876), had the same outline with 985 hymns. There were many subsequent editions of this book, and it was revised in 1910.

There was another very popular hymnbook in use within the Evangelical Association: *Geistliche Viole oder Eine kleine Sammlung Geistlicher Lieder zum Gebrauch der Evangelischen Gemeinschaft und heilssuchender Seelen überhaupt* (7th ed. New Berlin, PA: Verlegt von Carl Hammer für die Evangelische Gemeinschaft 1835 [154 hymns]; 12th ed. Cleveland, OH: Hammer 1855 [204 hymns]; also published in Germany: 5th ed. Nürtingen: Selbstverlag der Evangelischen Gemeinschaft 1870 [204 hymns]). The outline of this small hymnbook followed the "way of salvation": from "1. Von der Blindheit und dem elenden Zustand der gefallenen Menschheit" (The blindness and miserable nature of fallen humanity) and "2. Vom Versöhnungs-Werk durch Christus" (Reconciliation through Christ), it went until "26. Vom zukünftigen Gericht" (The Last Judgement). It was used for evangelistic events and formed "a little body of practical divinity" in its own way.

34. *Gesangbuch für die Evangelische Gemeinschaft* (Stuttgart: Christliches Verlagshaus 1931).

35. *Evangelisches Kirchengesangbuch, Ausgabe für die Evangelische Landeskirche in Württemberg* (Stuttgart: Verlagskontor der Evangelischen Gesangbuches 1953).

36. See note 15.

37. *Gesangbuch für die Evangelisch-methodistische Kirche* (Stuttgart: Christliches Verlagshaus 1969; 5th ed. 1991).

38. *leben und loben: Neue Lieder für die Gemeinde* (Stuttgart: Christliches Verlagshaus 1987; 2nd ed. 1989).

39. Fritz Harriefeld, *Gottesdienst in neuer Gestalt*, Beiheft 5 zu "Der Mitarbeiter", Januar 1971 (Stuttgart: Christliches Verlagshaus) 6.

40. The abridged and revised version of the *Agende* of 1991 for the people in the pew with the title "Celebrate and Witness" (*feiern und bekennen: Ordnungen, Gebete, und Bekenntnisse für den Gottesdienst in der Evangelisch-methodistischen Kirche* [Stuttgart: Christliches Verlagshaus 1994]) may be seen as a result of their efforts.

41. Heinz Schäfer, *Der Gottesdienst in der Evangelisch-methodistischen Kirche: Unmassgebliche Überlegungen eines Teilhabers*, Emk heute Heft 58, November 1988 (Stuttgart: Christliches Verlagshaus).

42. See note 37.

43. Dieter Sackmann, "Gottesdienst aus evangelisch-methodistischer Sicht," in *Theologie des Gotteslobs*, eds. Manfred Marquardt, Dieter Sackmann, and David Tripp, Beiträge zur Geschichte der Evangelisch-methodistischen Kirche, Heft 39, (Stuttgart: Christliches Verlagshaus 1991) 24–39; cf. the very important article of David Tripp, "Die Situation des Gottesdienstes in den methodistischen Kirchen," ibid., 39–61.

44. Preface to Hymns and Sacred Poems in *Works* (J) 14:321.

Notes to Chapter 17

1. The original English text is printed in *Baptism, Eucharist and Ministry*, Faith and Order Paper no. 111 (Geneva: W.C.C. 1982). The document was later translated into some forty other languages. A brief record of the relevant parts

of the Lima meeting is found in *Towards Visible Unity: Commission on Faith and Order Lima 1992*, vol. 1 (Minutes and Addresses), Faith and Order Paper no. 112, ed. Michael Kinnamon (Geneva: W.C.C. 1982) 80–87. Having been a member for several years of the "core group" that drafted and revised *Baptism, Eucharist and Ministry*, I chaired the process of final editing at Lima.

2. The responses of the Churches were published in the six volumes of *Churches Respond to BEM: Official Responses to the "Baptism, Eucharist and Ministry" Text*, ed. Max Thurian (Geneva: W.C.C.): 1 (1986), 2 (1986), 3 (1987), 4 (1987), 5 (1988), 6 (1988). A synthesis can be found in *Baptism, Eucharist and Ministry 1982–1990: Report on the Process and Responses*, Faith and Order Paper no. 149 (Geneva: W.C.C. 1990).

3. In what follows, the three sections of *BEM* are abbreviated respectively as *B*, *E*, and *M*.

4. See above, note 2.

5. *Churches Respond*, 2:177–99.

6. *Churches Respond*, 2:200–209 (Central and Southern Europe); 4:167–72 (German Democratic Republic); 4:173–82 (Federal Republic of Germany).

7. *Churches Respond*, 2:210–29.

8. *Churches Respond*, 2:236–44.

9. *Churches Respond*, 2:230–35.

10. *Churches Respond*, 1:78–80 (New Zealand); 4:166 (Benin); 6:131 (Jamaica).

11. *Churches Respond*, 2:69–73 (North India); 2:74–78 (South India).

12. *Churches Respond*, 2:276–86 (Canada); 4:154–65 (Australia).

13. *Churches Respond*, 2:245–54 (Italy); 3:168–82 (Belgium).

14. *Churches Respond*, 3:153.

15. See John C. Bowmer, *The Sacrament of the Lord's Supper in Early Methodism* (London: Dacre Press 1951) 62–81.

16. *Letters* 7:239.

17. *Works* 4:72–84.

18. The text of the *Hymns on the Lord's Supper* can be found in J. Ernest Rattenbury, *The Eucharistic Hymns of John and Charles Wesley* (London: Epworth Press 1948), and in a facsimile reprint of the 1745 edition by the Charles Wesley Society (Madison, NJ 1995). The current British *Hymns and Psalms* (1983) contains the following hymns from the collection: "Come, thou everlasting Spirit"; "Lamb of God, whose dying [bleeding] love"; "God of unexampled grace"; "O thou who this mysterious bread"; "Author of life divine"; "Saviour, and can it be"; "Come, Holy Ghost, thine influence shed"; "Jesu, we thus obey"; "Happy the souls to Jesus join'd"; "Victim divine, thy grace we claim"; "O God of our forefathers, hear"; "See where our great High-Priest"; "God of all-redeeming grace"; "Father, Son, and Holy Ghost, One in Three and Three in One"; "Let him to whom we now belong"; "How happy are thy servants, Lord." The *Australian Hymn Book*, an ecumenical production of 1976 in which the Anglican Church joined with the constituent denominations of the Uniting Church, contains "Come, thou everlasting Spirit"; "God of unexampled grace"; "Author of life divine"; "Come, Holy Ghost, your [thy] influence shed"; "Jesus, we thus obey"; "Let him to whom we now belong"; "How happy are thy servants, Lord."

19. The technical sense of "full membership" in Methodist usage derives from Methodism's "societary" origins within the Church of England. Wesley's Journal shows him occasionally admitting children to holy communion after conversing with them about their spiritual state (see Journal entries for Septem-

ber 5 and 12, 1773 [*Works* 22:387–88, 389] and October 2, 1784 [*Works* 23:333]; and for further instances in other sources, cf. Bowmer, *The Sacrament of the Lord's Supper in Early Methodism*, 120–22).

20. See John C. Bowmer, "A Converting Ordinance and the Open Table," *Proceedings of the Wesley Historical Society* 34 (1963–64) 109–13.

21. Wesley's talk of the Lord's Supper as "a means of conveying to men either preventing, or justifying, or sanctifying grace, according to their several necessities" is again conditioned by the debate with the Moravians, and this context must be taken into account.

22. *Churches Respond*, 3:29.

23. For a period in the 1970s and 1980s United Methodists spoke of Scripture, tradition, reason, and experience as a "quadrilateral" of sources for faith and theology but often with a failure to recognize that these four instances properly operate at different levels and with different functions. See Ted A. Campbell, "The 'Wesleyan Quadrilateral': The Story of a Modern Methodist Myth," *Methodist History* 29 (1990–91) 87–95.

24. For the notion of *anamnesis* as inclusive of "experience anew," see James F. White, "Response to the Berakah Award: Making Changes in United Methodist Euchology," *Worship* 57 (1983) 333–44, in particular 343–44.

Notes to Chapter 18

1. *Works* 19:67 (Journal entry for June 11, 1739). The emphasized words in this text follow Wesley's original edition of the Journal (1742, pp. 55–56), a matter noted by Frank Baker who also suspects this letter was actually dated March 20, 1739. See Frank Baker, *John Wesley and the Church of England* (London: Epworth Press 1970) 63, 360 n.17.

2. The World Methodist Council, currently comprising seventy-one member Churches of the Methodist communion, publishes a newsletter appropriately entitled "World Parish."

3. For a discussion of the structure of the early British Methodist preaching service, see Adrian Burdon, *The Preaching Service—The Glory of the Methodists*, Alcuin/GROW Liturgical Study 17 (Bramcote, Nottingham: Grove Books 1991) 20–23.

4. See David Lowes Watson, *The Early Methodist Class Meeting* (Nashville: Discipleship Resources 1985).

5. "The Caring Church" in *The Hymns and Ballads of Fred Pratt Green* (Carol Stream, IL: Hope Publishing Co. 1982) 17. This hymn is found in several recent Methodist hymnals.

6. For Wesley's theology of worship, see Geoffrey Wainwright, "Worship according to Wesley," *Australian Journal of Liturgy* 3 (1991) 5–20.

7. See Sermon 85, "On Working Out Our Own Salvation," *Works* 3:199–209.

8. See Karen Westerfield Tucker, "Liturgical Expressions of Care for the Poor in the Wesleyan Tradition: A Case Study for the Ecumenical Church," *Worship* 69 (1995) 56–64.

9. See, for example, *Hymns and Psalms* (British Methodist, 1983), *Uniting in Worship* (Uniting Church in Australia, 1988), *The United Methodist Hymnal* (1989), *Agende* (Evangelisch-methodistische Kirche, 1991), and *The United Methodist Book of Worship* (1992).

10. Information provided by the Reverend Ullas Tankler of Parnu, Estonia (interview by author, 27 September 1994, Tallinn, Estonia, meeting of the Executive Committee, World Methodist Council).

11. See the issues developed in Wesley's sermon on "The Duty of Constant Communion" (*Works* 3:428–39).

12. Hymn 415 in the 1780 *Collection of Hymns for the Use of The People Called Methodists* (*Works* 7:589–90).

13. "The Character of a Methodist," §18, *Works* 9:42.

14. From the Love Feast hymn, no. 505 in the 1780 *Collection* (*Works* 7:695).

Notes to Tribute

1. A complete bibliography is given on pp. 347–53 of this volume.

2. White also studied at the Pontifical Liturgical Institute in Rome (Sant' Anselmo), and at Yale University.

3. Forthcoming from Paulist Press.

4. James F. White, *A Brief History of Christian Worship* (Nashville: Abingdon Press 1993) 11.

5. Ibid., 10.

6. Ibid., 11.

7. James F. White, *Christian Worship in Transition* (Nashville: Abingdon Press 1976) 102–30.

8. Ibid., 130.

9. James F. White, "Response to the Berakah Award: Making Changes in United Methodist Euchology," *Worship* 57 (July 1983) 333.

10. Robert B. Peiffer, "How Contemporary Liturgies Evolve: The Revision of United Methodist Liturgical Texts (1968–1988)" (Ph.D. diss., University of Notre Dame 1992). I rely heavily on Peiffer's account in what follows.

11. "Response to the Berakah Award," 333.

12. Ibid., 334.

13. For a full account of the revision process and White's role in it, see Peiffer, "How Contemporary Liturgies Evolve," 1–50.

14. *Christian Century* (September 28, 1977) 842–45.

15. *Circuit Rider* 2 (May 1978) 10–11.

16. *Christian Century* (October 27, 1982) 1074–77.

17. *Christian Century* (January 20, 1982) 82–86.

18. "Our Apostasy in Worship," 842.

19. "Methodist Kitsch," 10.

20. Ibid., 11. Surprisingly, the response to "Kitsch" was quite positive. For letters written in response to the article, see *Circuit Rider* 2 (September 1978) 21.

21. *Sacraments as God's Self Giving: Sacramental Practice and Faith* (Nashville: Abingdon Press 1983) 9.

22. Ibid., 109.

23. Ibid., 113.

24. "Response to the Berakah Award," 335.

25. Ibid., 336.

26. Ibid., 338.

27. Ibid., 344.

28. James F. White, "'Forum': Some Lessons in Liturgical Pedagogy," *Worship* 68 (September 1994) 446.

29. James F. White, *Protestant Worship: Traditions in Transition* (Louisville: Westminster/John Knox Press 1989).

30. "'Forum': Some Lessons in Liturgical Pedagogy," 440.